Historical Justice in International Perspective

This book makes a valuable contribution to recent debates on redress for historical injustices by offering case studies from nine countries on five continents. The contributors examine the problems of material restitution, criminal justice, apologies, recognition, memory, and reconciliation in national contexts as well as in comparative perspective. Among the topics discussed are the claims for reparations for slavery in the United States, West German restitution for the Holocaust, the South African Truth and Reconciliation Commission, the efforts to prosecute the perpetrators of the Khmer Rouge's mass murders in Cambodia, and the struggles of the indigenous people of Australia and New Zealand. The book highlights the diversity of the ways societies have tried to right past wrongs as the demand for historical justice has become universal.

Manfred Berg, the Curt Engelhorn Professor of American History at the University of Heidelberg, is a specialist in the history of the African-American civil rights movement. His book *The Ticket to Freedom: The NAACP and the Struggle for Black Political Integration* was published in 2005. In 2006 he received the David Thelen Award of the Organization of American Historians for the best essay in American history published in a language other than English. Professor Berg has published ten other monographs and edited volumes and roughly forty scholarly articles in both English and German. Before joining the Heidelberg faculty, he taught at the Free University of Berlin and was a research Fellow at the German Historical Institute, Washington, D.C.

Bernd Schaefer specializes in international Cold War history and is a senior scholar with the Woodrow Wilson International Center's Cold War International History Project (CWIHP). Before joining the CWIHP, Dr. Schaefer was a research Fellow at the German Historical Institute in Washington, D.C. He has published extensively on the history of the German Democratic Republic and East Asian communism in the period of détente. He holds a Ph.D. from the University of Halle in Germany (1998) and a Master of Public Administration from the John F. Kennedy School of Government at Harvard University (1991), where he was a John J. McCloy Scholar. His publications include *Staat und katholische Kirche in der GDR, 1945–1989*, an English translation of which is in preparation, and the essay collection *Ostpolitik 1969–1974: European and Global Responses*, edited with Carole Fink.

PUBLICATIONS OF THE GERMAN HISTORICAL INSTITUTE
Washington, D.C.

Edited by Hartmut Berghoff and Christof Mauch
with the assistance of David Lazar

The German Historical Institute is a center for advanced study and research whose purpose is to provide a permanent basis for scholarly cooperation among historians from the Federal Republic of Germany and the United States. The Institute conducts, promotes, and supports research into both American and German political, social, economic, and cultural history; into transatlantic migration, especially in the nineteenth and twentieth centuries; and into the history of international relations, with special emphasis on the roles played by the United States and Germany.

Recent books in the series:

Roger Chickering, Stig Förster, and Bernd Greiner, editors, *A World at Total War: Global Conflict and the Politics of Destruction, 1937–1945*

Kiran Klaus Patel, *Soldiers of Labor: Labor Service in Nazi Germany and New Deal America, 1933–1945*

Michelle Mouton, *From Nurturing the Nation to Purifying the Volk: Weimar and Nazi Family Policy, 1918–1945*

Peter Becker and Richard F. Wetzell, editors, *Criminals and Their Scientists: The History of Criminology in International Perspective*

Jonathan R. Zatlin, *The Currency of Socialism: Money and Political Culture in East Germany*

Andreas W. Daum, *Kennedy in Berlin*

Joachim Radkau, *Nature and Power: A Global History of the Environment*

Nathan Stoltzfus and Henry Friedlander, editors, *Nazi Crimes and the Law*

Carole Fink and Bernd Schaefer, editors, *Ostpolitik, 1969–1974: European and Global Responses*

Historical Justice in International Perspective

HOW SOCIETIES ARE TRYING TO RIGHT THE WRONGS OF THE PAST

Edited by

MANFRED BERG
University of Heidelberg

BERND SCHAEFER
Cold War International History Project

GERMAN HISTORICAL INSTITUTE

Washington, D.C.

and

CAMBRIDGE UNIVERSITY PRESS
Cambridge, New York, Melbourne, Madrid, Cape Town, Singapore, São Paulo, Delhi

Cambridge University Press
32 Avenue of the Americas, New York, NY 10013-2473, USA

www.cambridge.org
Information on this title: www.cambridge.org/9780521876834

© German Historical Institute 2009

This publication is in copyright. Subject to statutory exception
and to the provisions of relevant collective licensing agreements,
no reproduction of any part may take place without the written
permission of Cambridge University Press.

First published 2009

Printed in the United States of America

A catalog record for this publication is available from the British Library.

Library of Congress Cataloging in Publication Data

Historical justice in international perspective : how societies are trying to right the wrongs of the
past / Manfred Berg, Bernd Schaefer.
p. cm. – (Publications of the German Historical Institute)
Includes bibliographical references and index.
ISBN 978-0-521-87683-4 (hardback)
1. Reparations for historical injustices – Case studies.   2. Restorative justice.   3. Human rights –
Moral and ethical aspects.   I. Berg, Manfred, 1959–   II. Schaefer, Bernd.   III. Title.   IV. Series.
JC578.H57   2009
341.6′6–dc22   2008009527

ISBN   978-0-521-87683-4 hardback

Cambridge University Press has no responsibility for the persistence or
accuracy of URLs for external or third-party Internet Web sites referred to in
this publication and does not guarantee that any content on such Web sites is,
or will remain, accurate or appropriate. Information regarding prices, travel
timetables, and other factual information given in this work are correct at
the time of first printing, but Cambridge University Press does not guarantee
the accuracy of such information thereafter.

Contents

Contributors		*page* ix
Preface		xi
	Introduction *Manfred Berg and Bernd Schaefer*	1

PART I. THE POLITICS OF RESTITUTION

1	An Avalanche of History: The "Collapse of the Future" and the Rise of Reparations Politics *John Torpey*	21
2	The Politics of Reparations: Why, When, and How Democratic Governments Get Involved *Angelika von Wahl*	39

PART II. REPARATIONS AND RESTITUTION

3	Historical Continuity and Counterfactual History in the Debate over Reparations for Slavery *Manfred Berg*	69
4	Disputed Victims: The West German Discourse on Restitution for the Victims of Nazism *Constantin Goschler*	93
5	Greenlanders Displaced by the Cold War: Relocation and Compensation *Svend Aage Christensen and Kristian Søby Kristensen*	111

PART III. MEMORY AND RECOGNITION

6 Apologizing for Vichy in Contemporary France 135
   Julie Fette

7 Limited Rehabilitation? Historical Observations on the Legal
   Rehabilitation of Foreign Citizens in Today's Russia 165
   Andreas Hilger

8 Politics, Diplomacy, and Accountability in Cambodia:
   Severely Limiting Personal Jurisdiction in Prosecution of
   Perpetrators of Crimes Against Humanity 187
   Steve Heder

PART IV. RECONCILIATION

9 Settling Histories, Unsettling Pasts: Reconciliation and
   Historical Justice in a Settler Society 217
   Bain Attwood

10 Fitting Aotearoa into New Zealand: Politico-Cultural Change
   in a Modern Bicultural Nation 239
   Richard S. Hill and Brigitte Bönisch-Brednich

11 The Politics of Judging the Past: South Africa's Truth and
   Reconciliation Commission 265
   Bronwyn Leebaw

PART V. CONCLUSION

12 "The Issue That Won't Go Away" 291
   A. James McAdams

Index 307

Contributors

Bain Attwood is a professor in the School of Historical Studies, Monash University, Victoria, Australia.

Manfred Berg is the Curt Engelhorn Professor of American History, University of Heidelberg.

Brigitte Bönisch-Brednich is a professor of anthropology at Victoria University, Wellington, New Zealand.

Svend Aage Christensen is a senior researcher at the Danish Institute for International Studies, Copenhagen.

Julie Fette is an assistant professor of French studies at Rice University, Houston.

Constantin Goschler is a professor of history at the Ruhr University Bochum.

Steve Heder is a lecturer in the Faculty of Law and Social Sciences of the School of Oriental and African Studies, University of London.

Andreas Hilger teaches Russian history at the University of Hamburg.

Richard S. Hill is a professor of New Zealand Studies at the Stout Center for New Zealand Studies, Victoria University, Wellington.

Kristian Søby Kristensen is a doctoral student at the Danish Institute for International Studies.

Bronwyn Leebaw is an assistant professor of political science at the University of California, Riverside.

A. James McAdams is the William M. Scholl Professor of International Affairs and Director of the Nanovic Institute for European Studies at the University of Notre Dame, Indiana.

Bernd Schaefer is a senior scholar with the Cold War International History Project at the Woodrow Wilson International Center for Scholars, Washington, D.C.

John Torpey is a professor of sociology at the City University of New York Graduate Center.

Angelika von Wahl is an associate professor of history at San Francisco State University, California.

Preface

This book grew out of a conference held at the German Historical Institute in Washington, D.C., in March 2003. The editors would like to thank Christof Mauch, the former director of the GHI, and Christian Ostermann, director of the History and Public Policy Program at the Woodrow Wilson International Center for Scholars, for their generous support of this project.

During three exciting days in Washington, twenty-six participants from nine countries and other guests engaged in inspiring discussions of historical justice in theoretical and practical terms and within an international context. We thank all the speakers for their contributions to this meeting. This book includes revised versions of most of the conference papers. We are grateful to all of the contributors for meeting deadlines and their ensuing patience. Also we wish to thank our editor at Cambridge University Press, Frank Smith; the three anonymous reviewers, who read the manuscript and gave us helpful suggestions; and David Lazar, senior editor at the German Historical Institute.

Manfred Berg, Heidelberg
Bernd Schaefer, Washington, D.C.
January 2008

Historical Justice in International Perspective

Introduction

MANFRED BERG AND BERND SCHAEFER

The fall of dictatorships and the growing salience of human rights at the end of the twentieth century have given rise to a broad international debate on how to deal with the injustices and atrocities of the past. Demands for historical justice have been raised all over the world by many different groups, and they cover a wide spectrum of wrongs, ranging from systemic racial or ethnic discrimination to state-sanctioned murder and genocide. Although the mass violence of the twentieth century takes center stage in the politics of the past, there have also been calls for action to address the legacies of slavery in the United States, of Western colonialism, and of the genocidal removal of indigenous peoples. Redress is sought for relatively recent events in which the victims, perpetrators, and beneficiaries of injustices can be identified with a reasonable degree of certainty, while other claims are based on the construction of historical continuities going back several centuries. The material dimensions of historical justice vary from relatively small payments to individuals to demands for a massive redistribution of wealth on a global scale. In addition to material claims, and often as a first step toward this goal, the victims of historical injustices or their descendants fight for the public and symbolic recognition of their suffering.[1]

---

1 Elazar Barkan, *The Guilt of Nations: Restitution and Negotiating Historical Injustices* (New York, 2000), is the first synthesis of the major movements for historical justice; see also John Torpey, ed., *Politics and the Past: On Repairing Historical Injustices* (Lanham, Md., 2003); John Torpey, "'Making Whole What Has Been Smashed': Reflections on Reparations," *Journal of Modern History* 73 (2001): 333–58; John Torpey, *Making Whole What Has Been Smashed: On Reparations Politics* (Cambridge, Mass., 2006). For a systematic inquiry into approaches to historical justice, see Martha Minow, *Between Vengeance and Forgiveness: Facing History after Genocide and Mass Violence* (Boston, 1998). Roy L. Brooks, ed., *When Sorry Isn't Enough: The Controversy over Apologies and Reparations for Human Injustice* (New York, 1999), is a useful documentation of several important cases; for case studies on the politics of the past from Europe, North America, Africa, and Asia, see *Comparativ* (2004) (4/5) and Jürgen Zimmerer, ed., *Schweigen-Erinnern-Bewältigen: Vergangenheitspolitik in globaler Perspektive* (Leipzig, 2005).

The quest for historical justice involves several dimensions.² At the material level, claimants seek the restitution of property and lands or financial compensation for lost property, for the exploitation of their labor, or for their bodily and psychological suffering and injury. In the realm of criminal justice, rectification aims at rehabilitating the victims of persecution and at bringing the perpetrators to justice. As is well known from the attempts to prosecute the perpetrators of crimes against humanity in the wake of the Second World War, the latter is notoriously fraught with intricate legal problems such as retroactive laws, statutes of limitation, the defense of following orders, and the charge of "victor's justice," to list just the most important ones.³ Finally, there is the drive for the recognition of injustice and the restoration of honor and dignity to the victims that often begins with establishing and publicizing a historical record against prevailing patterns of silence and denial. In this vein, truth commissions and expert groups have mushroomed all over the world, even in Switzerland, a nation that has long cherished a self-image of happy insulation from the sordid chapters of history.⁴ Moreover, the politics of recognition extend to official apologies, memorials, and educational programs to integrate the victims into a society's collective memory and, possibly, to help revitalize their cultural identity.⁵

Historical justice may be rendered at the individual, collective, and structural levels.⁶ Individual justice applies to specific victims who receive individualized corrective remedies and to specific perpetrators who are subjected

---

2 For an attempt to develop a nuanced typology of historical justice claims, see Torpey's introduction to *Politics and the Past*, 11–22.
3 For an introduction to the legal difficulties of judging the perpetrators of historical injustices, see Minow, *Between Vengeance and Forgiveness*, 25–51, and Ruti G. Teitel, *Transitional Justice* (New York, 2000), esp. 11–67. For a broad treatment of prosecuting genocide with a special emphasis on the International Criminal Tribunals for the Former Yugoslavia and Rwanda, see William A. Schabas, *Genocide in International Law* (Cambridge, 2000); also see Gerd Hankel and Gerhard Stuby, eds., *Strafgerichte gegen Menschheitsverbrechen. Zum Völkerstrafrecht 50 Jahre nach den Nürnberger Prozessen* (Hamburg, 1995). For reflections on the German experience of dealing with two dictatorships, see Bernhard Schlink, *Vergangenheitsschuld und gegenwärtiges Recht* (Frankfurt am Main, 2002).
4 On the flourishing of truth commissions in the wake of the breakdown of dictatorships, see Priscilla B. Hayner, *Unspeakable Truths: Facing the Challenge of Truth Commissions* (London, 2002), and Robert I. Rotberg and Dennis Thompson, eds., *Truth v. Justice: The Morality of Truth Commissions* (Princeton, 2000). On the South African Truth and Reconciliation Commission, see Chapter 11 by Bronwyn Leebaw in this volume; on the case of Switzerland, see the comprehensive account by Thomas Maissen, *Verweigerte Erinnerung. Nachrichtenlose Vermögen und Schweizer Weltkriegsdebatte 1989–2004* (Zürich, 2005).
5 For an introduction to the politics of memory in the process of historical and transitional justice, see Minow, *Between Vengeance and Forgiveness*, 118–47, and Teitel, *Transitional Justice*, 69–117.
6 This typological distinction is borrowed from Robert W. Gordon, "Undoing Historical Injustice," in Austin Sarat and Thomas R. Kearny, eds., *Justice and Injustice in Law and Legal Theory* (Ann Arbor, 1996), 35–75, esp. 36–9.

to individual retributive sanctions. At the collective level, we deal with groups of victims and perpetrators and with collective forms of liabilities, redress, or amnesties that burden or benefit everyone who is similarly situated. Since historical injustice usually involves the victimization of a significant number of people, collective solutions are seen as more expedient than dealing separately with individual cases. Finally, the structural approach implies that historical injustice must be viewed as both cause and consequence of unjust structures that are deeply embedded in the political, legal, and economic institutions of a society and that continue to shape the present in manifold ways. From this perspective, historical justice can only be achieved by sweeping systemic reforms to eliminate these structures of injustice. In contrast, individual and collective redress does not usually involve demands for a wholesale transformation of society. John Torpey has therefore proposed distinguishing between a "commemorative" type of historical justice aimed at the victims of the past, most prominently of the World War II era, and "transformative" claims for social and political change that are based on the "prolonged disasters of the past." Typically, the latter relates to the legacies of colonialism, slavery, and the marginalization of indigenous peoples.[7] However, the commemorative and transformative approaches may interact in unexpected ways. In the Federal Republic of Germany, for example, many political officials and members of the public regarded *Wiedergutmachung* (literally "making good again") for the Nazis' crimes as a form of commemorative justice that would close the books on that era; those who urged that Germans accept responsibility for the past, by contrast, often saw their efforts as part and parcel of the larger project of transforming West German society.[8]

Since historical justice comprises many different and heterogeneous claims and goals, there is no consensus on an appropriate umbrella concept. In his book *The Guilt of Nations*, Elazar Barkan employs the term "restitution" to cover the "entire spectrum of attempts to rectify historical injustices." But obviously, the legal implications of restitution rather narrowly refer to the actual return of material goods and carry a backward-looking connotation of restoring an earlier state of affairs – a notion that does

---

7 Torpey, "'Making Whole What Has Been Smashed," 337.
8 For a comprehensive account of German *Wiedergutmachung* for the Nazis' crimes, see Karl Döhring et al., *Jahrhundertschuld, Jahrhundertsühne. Reparationen, Wiedergutmachung, Entschädigung für nationalsozialistisches Kriegs- und Verfolgungsunrecht* (Munich, 2001), and Constantin Goschler, *Schuld and Schulden. Die Politik der Wiedergutmachung für NS-Verfolgte seit 1945* (Göttingen, 2005); on the broader concept of coming to terms with the past, see Peter Reichel, *Vergangenheitsbewältigung in Deutschland. Die Auseinandersetzung mit der NS-Diktatur von 1945 bis heute* (Munich, 2001).

not square with Barkan's larger argument that restitution must be a future-oriented process. John Torpey, in contrast, prefers the term "reparation" as the more comprehensive one that also enjoys wider usage.[9] Ironically, the concept of reparations stems from the international law of war and used to refer exclusively to an indemnity that the victor imposed on the vanquished. These were strictly claims among nation-states with very little concern for compensating the victims of war crimes and other atrocities. In fact, in the immediate aftermath of the Second World War, this traditional concept of reparations took precedence over the individual and collective claims by the innumerable victims of the Nazis.[10]

As is not unusual in an emergent field, the conceptualization of historical justice is still in flux, and it will take some time before a widely accepted terminology is established, if ever. What is more important, however, is that the new politics of restitution or reparations is based not on coercion, but on negotiated agreements between the perpetrators and the victims or their respective descendants. Societies increasingly show a willingness to face the painful legacies of their histories and to respond favorably to the demands made on them, even if many of the claimants find the actual results of these efforts wanting. Elazar Barkan has noted that the admission of guilt seems to have become "a new threshold of morality in international politics."[11] To be sure, the willingness to acknowledge responsibility for historical injustices and to make amends is by no means universal. Nevertheless, making an honest effort at coming to terms with the past has undoubtedly become an asset for the international reputation of a nation. While the Federal Republic of Germany is often praised both for the extent to which it has made material compensation for the Holocaust and for undertaking an ongoing process of collective soul-searching about its Nazi past, the Japanese are chided for their continuing denial and amnesia of Japan's aggression and large-scale atrocities in World War II. The fact that both countries are highly integrated into the global economy makes their markedly different attitudes toward coping with a terrible past even more conspicuous.[12] Apparently, economic interests do play a role in the politics of the past as, for example, has been demonstrated

---

9 Barkan, *The Guilt of Nations*, xix; Torpey, *Politics and the Past*, introduction, 3–5.
10 For a comprehensive account of reparations after World War I, see Bruce Kent, *The Spoils of War: The Politics, Economics, and Diplomacy of Reparations, 1918–1932* (New York, 1989); for the Second World War, see Jörg Fisch, *Reparationen nach dem Zweiten Weltkrieg* (Munich, 1992), Goschler, *Schuld und Schulden*, and Chapter 4 of this volume: Constantin Goschler, "Disputed Victims: The West German Discourse on Restitution for the Victims of Nazism."
11 Barkan, *The Guilt of Nations*, xviii.
12 On the comparison between Germany and Japan, see Ian Buruma, *The Wages of Guilt: Memories of War in Germany and Japan* (New York, 1994); Manfred Kittel, *Nach Nürnberg und Tokio: "Vergangenheitsbewältigung" in Japan und Westdeutschland 1945 bis 1968* (Munich, 2004).

by the establishment of the joint government-industry fund to compensate the victims of Nazi forced labor.[13] Nonetheless, they do not account for profound changes in the mental and cultural underpinnings of historical memory and consciousness.

Obviously, military defeat and the domestic overthrow of dictatorships are crucial catalysts in inducing the quest for historical justice. Transitional justice, as the problems of reckoning with the past in the transformation process from dictatorship to democracy have come to be called, has developed into a major field of both research and consulting, including the recent establishment of the nongovernmental International Center for Transitional Justice, based in New York City. Transitional justice deals with issues such as the establishment of truth commissions, judging the perpetrators, lustration of public officials, or the rehabilitation of and compensation for the victims of repression.[14] However, claims for the redress of historical injustices have also been raised in nations that have not experienced a regime change or other radical break with the past. The struggles of the aboriginal peoples of Australia, New Zealand, Canada, and Greenland, for example, fall into this category.[15]

The United States has been confronted with three major demands for historical justice: from Japanese Americans for an apology and compensation for their internment during World War II, from Native Americans for the return of tribal lands and sacred objects, and from African Americans for reparations for slavery and racial discrimination. The Japanese-American campaign for redress was ultimately very successful. Native American efforts have been partly successful in their restitution claims, whereas the call for reparations for slavery has yet to yield tangible results.[16] Of course,

---

13 For American and German accounts of the negotiations leading to the agreement to compensate the surviving forced laborers, see Stuart E. Eizenstat, *Imperfect Justice: Looted Assets, Slave Labor, and the Unfinished Business of World War II* (New York, 2003), and Susanne-Sophia Spiliotis, *Verantwortung und Rechtsfrieden. Die Stiftungsinitiative der deutschen Wirtschaft* (Frankfurt am Main, 2003).
14 For an introduction to the fast-growing literature on transitional justice and a broad documentation of cases, see Neil J. Kritz, ed., *Transitional Justice: How Emerging Democracies Reckon with Former Regimes*, 3 vols. (Washington, D.C., 1995), and A. James McAdams, ed., *Transitional Justice and the Rule of Law in New Democracies* (Notre Dame, Ind., 1997); for a more theory-oriented approach, see Teitel, *Transitional Justice*; on the International Center for Transition Justice, see its 2003/2004 Annual Report (New York, 2004) and its Web site, www.ictj.org; for a comparative study of post-1945 transitions, see Andrew Rigby, *Justice and Reconciliation: After the Violence* (Boulder, 2000); see also Zimmerer, *Schweigen-Erinnern-Bewältigen*.
15 See the chapters in this volume by Bain Attwood (Chapter 9), Richard S. Hill and Brigitte Bönisch-Brednich (Chapter 10), and Svend Aage Christensen and Kristian Søby Kristensen (Chapter 5). On Canada, see Alan Cairns, "Coming to Terms with the Past," in Torpey, *Politics of the Past*, 77–80.
16 On the various cases that affect the United States, see Barkan, *The Guilt of Nations*, 30–45, 169–215, 283–307; Brooks, *When Sorry Isn't Enough*, 157–438; and Manfred Berg, "Vergangenheitspolitik und Restitutionsbewegungen in den USA," *Comparativ* 14, 4/5 (2004): 146–62.

it can be argued that the civil rights reforms of the 1960s represent the equivalent of a regime change, albeit incomplete, in their repudiation of white supremacy and their institutionalization of equal rights and nondiscrimination. But this process of transformation clearly lacked most of the defining characteristics of transitional justice such as trials, truth commissions, the purging of elites, and structural changes in the political system. Nevertheless, the "rights revolution" sparked by the African-American civil rights movement was a major factor in making the idea of redress for the victims of historical injustices a salient feature of American political culture. Historian Roger Daniels has speculated whether the successful campaign of the Japanese-American community may have established a new legal right to the rectification of historical injustices. Beyond the country's shores, American institutions, particularly the federal government and the judiciary, are major international players in cases and controversies pertaining to historical justice. The threat to bring a lawsuit in the United States is often viewed as strong leverage to scare the potential defendants into a costly settlement.[17]

Viewed from a long-term perspective, current American liability law may be understood as the epitome of a secular trend toward what legal historian Lawrence Friedman twenty years ago called "total justice," that is, "a general expectation of justice, and a general expectation of recompense for injuries and loss."[18] This expectation might be most widespread in the United States, but it has gained broad currency throughout the West as the state has increasingly taken on the role of protector against the hazards and risks of modern life. It builds on a rationalistic concept of history according to which suffering, disaster, and misfortune are no longer accepted as fate or as God's punishment for sinful man, but as an intelligible, man-made process of cause and effect. The more the trials and tribulations of human existence were perceived as injustices, the late political philosopher Judith Shklar argued in her book *The Faces of Injustice*, the greater became the need for holding somebody responsible.[19] But once history is conceived as a process subject to causal and moral judgment, it becomes the source of

---

17 Roger Daniels, "Asian Americans: Rights Denied and Attained," in Manfred Berg and Martin H. Geyer, eds., *Two Cultures of Rights: The Quest for Inclusion and Participation in Modern America and Germany* (New York, 2002), 19–32. Ed Fagan, one of America's most controversial class action–suit lawyers, announced plans in 2002 to bring a liability suit in the United States against international corporations for their alleged complicity with the South African apartheid regime. Fagan was later fired by the plaintiffs; the suit has not yet been resolved.
18 Lawrence M. Friedman, *Total Justice* (New York, 1985), 5. For a critique of the hypertrophy of the law and lawyers in American society, see Mary Ann Glendon, *A Nation under Lawyers: How the Crisis in the Legal Profession Is Transforming American Society* (New York, 1994).
19 Judith Shklar, *The Faces of Injustice* (New Haven, 1990), translated into German as *Über Ungerechtigkeit* (Berlin, 1992), esp. 89–136.

political conflict. In the modern world, Elazar Barkan writes, history and its injustices are no longer viewed as past events we can do little about, but as a "crucial field for political struggle."[20]

West Germany's efforts to make amends for the Holocaust, as many observers have noted, have become the paradigm for rectification. The 1952 agreement West Germany concluded with Israel and the Jewish Claims Conference marks "the moment at which the modern notion of restitution for historical injustices was born," according to Barkan.[21] The universalization of the Holocaust provided the victims of many different crimes and injustices with a vocabulary for articulating their claims and grievances. For example, the term "survivor" has been incorporated into historical contexts even where it makes very little sense, like in the case of Chinese immigrants to Canada who were subjected to a discriminatory head tax until the mid-twentieth century. This kind of discourse is often criticized for trivializing the idea of victimization and fueling competition among different groups of victims.[22]

Not surprisingly, the laudable intention not to exclude anybody often leads to a lack of conceptual clarity as to what constitutes a historical injustice calling for rectification. One might consider the following definition by Roy Brooks in the introduction to his valuable anthology *When Sorry Isn't Enough: The Controversy over Apologies and Reparations for Human Injustice*. According to Brooks, human injustice includes

> the violation or suppression of human rights or fundamental freedoms recognized by international law, including but not limited to genocide; slavery; extrajudicial killings; torture and other cruel or degrading treatment; arbitrary detention; rape; the denial of due process of law; forced refugee movements; the denial of universal suffrage; and discrimination, distinction, exclusion, or preference based on race, sex, descent, religion, or other identifying factor with the purpose or effect of impairing the recognition, enjoyment, or exercise, on an equal footing, of human rights and fundamental freedoms in the political, social, economic, cultural, or any other field of public life.[23]

The obvious problem with such a broad definition is that it blurs the line between extraordinary historical crimes and atrocities and the innumerable

---

20 Barkan, *The Guilt of Nations*, x.
21 Barkan, *The Guilt of Nations*, xxiv; Torpey, "'Making Whole What Has Been Smashed,'" 338.
22 For an influential critique of the universalization of the Holocaust, see Peter Novick, *The Holocaust in American Life* (Boston, 1999); for an argument against a Jewish "monopoly" on victimization, see Jean-Michel Chaumont, *La Concurrence des Victimes: Génocide, Identité, Reconnaissance* (Paris, 1997); on the inflationary use of the term "survivor," see Chapter 1 by John Torpey in this volume.
23 Brooks, *When Sorry Isn't Enough*, 7.

ordinary forms of injustice that occur on an almost daily basis in every legal and political order.[24]

As Barkan points out, "the inability to quantify, compare, and rank injustices along an agreed-upon scale" is a major impediment to a theory of historical justice. Nor is there a one-size-fits-all model for restitution.[25] But even if we had such abstract standards, they would not tell us much about the potential success of a particular claim. The chances to obtain material restitution and symbolic recognition may not primarily depend on the magnitude of the injustice, nor on the merit or morality of the claim, but rather on the ability to organize an effective political lobby and to mobilize the support of national and international opinion.[26] Even more fundamental may be the existence of a political culture of rights. The case of recognition of and restitution for the victims of Stalinism, in particular, underscores the importance of the cultural preconditions for righting the wrongs of the past. The scant interest in, and meager results of, the efforts to rehabilitate the dead and living victims of Stalinist terror are due to the unwillingness of both the Russian government and society at large to repudiate deeply entrenched traditions of authoritarianism and nationalism.[27] At the other end of the spectrum we find New Zealand, where the successful demolition of earlier myths about harmonious race relations fostered an official biculturalism that has come a long way in incorporating the indigenous Maori culture into the mainstream.[28]

To be sure, it takes much time and favorable circumstances for a culture of historical justice to develop, and its manifestations are often ambiguous. In the German case, reckoning with the Nazi past and making material restitution to the victims of the Holocaust were accompanied by parallel discourses of German victimization.[29] Julie Fette's account of the apology movement in France during the 1990s stresses, among other factors, the importance of generational change for the French society's new willingness to face the historical record of widespread collaboration with the Nazi occupation under the Vichy regime.[30] Yet with this generational change

---

24 Sarat and Kearny emphasize that injustice is not a phenomenon of extraordinary times: *Justice and Injustice in Law and Legal Theory*, Introduction, 1–17.
25 Barkan, *The Guilt of Nations*, 308–49, esp. 347.
26 See Chapter 2 by Angelika von Wahl in this volume.
27 See Chapter 7 by Andreas Hilger in this volume; also see Steve Heder (Chapter 8) on Cambodia in this volume.
28 See Chapter 10 by Richard S. Hill and Brigitte Bönisch-Brednich in this volume.
29 See Robert Moeller, *War Stories: The Search for a Usable Past in the Federal Republic of Germany* (Berkeley, 2001); see also Chapter 4 by Constantin Goschler in this volume.
30 See Chapter 6 by Julie Fette in this volume.

firmly in place sixty years after the end of the Second World War, Western societies, in particular, have elevated reckoning with the atrocities and injustices of history to the status of a public virtue.

This preoccupation with history has taken a peculiar turn, however, according to some critics. Rather than celebrating achievement and heroism, atrocities and victimization have become the focus of historical consciousness. The catastrophic failure of the utopian projects of the twentieth century, John Torpey argues, has thoroughly discredited the notion of suffering as the inevitable price for a better future that used to be a mainstay of the progressive left. The struggle for justice is no longer defined by visions of the future but by claims for righting the wrongs of the past. At the same time, historical victimhood has become a major factor in the formation of group identity. The Holocaust, Peter Novick suggests, has taken a prominent role in American culture in recent decades because it epitomizes the close linkage between victimhood and the rise of identity politics.[31] Nevertheless, if we are seriously interested in exploring historical injustice and possible ways to ameliorate its consequences, a victim-centered perspective appears inevitable. Of course, this does not mean that claims to victimhood must be accepted at face value. But, as Judith Shklar has reminded us, the powerful have rarely hesitated to offer apologies for past wrongs without doing anything toward offering redress.[32] Calls to let bygones be bygones and to look toward the future certainly have long since been standard rhetorical features in the discourse of denial and evasion.

Advocates of historical justice, of course, strongly contest the charge of being obsessed with the past or promoting narrow group interests. Quite to the contrary, they argue that only by addressing and amending historical injustice will there be a better future for all. The benefits of restitution and recognition are supposed to go far beyond meeting the just claims and material needs of the victims. Historical justice is said to have a therapeutic effect on both the victims and the perpetrators, freeing the former from traumatization and providing an opportunity for purifying atonement for the latter, thus paving the way for true reconciliation and the healing of old wounds.[33] Moreover, historical justice is conducive not only to domestic social peace, according to its proponents, but also to international morality

---

31 Torpey, "'Making Whole What Has Been Smashed,'" 333–4; also see Chapter 1 by John Torpey in this volume and Novick, *The Holocaust in American Life*, 1–15; for a scathing critique of placing emotions of powerlessness and victimhood at the center of identity formation, see Frank Furedi, *Therapy Culture: Cultivating Vulnerability in an Anxious Age* (London, 2003).
32 Shklar, *Über Ungerechtigkeit*, esp. 10–11, 118–36.
33 See, e.g., Roy L. Brooks, *Atonement and Forgiveness: A New Model for Black Reparations* (Berkeley, 2004).

either through the power of persuasion or by sending a stern message to those who persist in perpetrating human rights violations that one day they will be made to pay the price. Restitution, Elazar Barkan hopes, will eventually lead toward a "universe that shares vague liberal political and moral commitments to individual rights as well as to group human rights... a shared political culture, which pays greater attention to history as a formative political force."[34]

While few will disagree with this broader vision, many observers still doubt whether the quest for historical justice can indeed deliver the benefits it promises. Some point to the potentially great costs of making redress or raise the possibility of unintended consequences that are at odds with the high-minded goals put forward by advocates of historical justice. Interestingly, the critics do not focus primarily on the legitimacy and magnitude of financial claims – except of course those who are supposed to pay – but rather on political and cultural issues. Instead of fostering a culture of reconciliation, they contend, moral claims based on the past are often perceived as aggressive accusations projecting attenuated notions of collective guilt and guilt by association.[35] Moreover, if the world is divided into perpetrators and victims and the latter into competing groups, there remains little common ground for developing common visions of the future. The shift from class-based politics of economic redistribution to the politics of recognition based on race and ethnicity, critics on the left fear, has seriously weakened the prospects for social reform that would especially benefit poor minorities.[36]

The skeptics have become particularly critical of what historian Charles Maier, in an influential article published in 1993, called a "surfeit of memory" produced by a self-serving "memory industry." While its proponents see the recovery and recognition of the victims' memories as a necessary and wholesome element of a healing process, its detractors fear that memories of victimization may come to dominate the lives of individuals and the identity of groups, thus perpetuating historical conflicts and grievances instead of resolving them.[37] Moreover, Maier argues that, far from enhancing our understanding of history, the "canonization" of subjective memories threatens to undermine, if not replace, the analytical function and epistemological

---

34 Barkan, *The Guilt of Nations*, x.   35 Gordon, "Undoing Historical Injustice," 67.
36 Torpey, "'Making Whole What Has Been Smashed,'" 351–7; for an influential critique of the divisive effects of multiculturalism, see Todd Gitlin, *The Twilight of Common Dreams: Why America Is Wracked by Culture Wars* (New York, 1995).
37 Charles S. Maier, "A Surfeit of Memory? Reflections on History, Melancholy and Denial," *History and Memory* 5 (1993): 136–52. For a scathing critique of the "Entrepreneurs of Memory," see Chapter 1 by John Torpey in this volume and Rigby, *Justice and Reconciliation*, 2.

standards of historical research. In contrast, historians committed to a multiculturalist perspective vigorously defend memory as necessary to give a voice to the weak and oppressed who are otherwise silenced by the hegemonic objectivist narratives. In his essay on Australia's difficulties in establishing common discursive ground between Aborigines and non-Aboriginal Australians, Bain Attwood insists that memory is the only meaningful way of "sharing histories" across the cultural divide.[38]

There is also disagreement over the question whether the claims for historical justice can ever be satisfied to the point of closure. Obviously, the past cannot be reversed. No amount of compensation could possibly make up for the loss of loved ones, torture, rape, or decades of incarceration. For many victims of wrongs committed or sanctioned by states, the very notion of financial compensation takes on the smell of "blood money" that puts a price tag on their suffering. And indeed, the suspicion that reparations and some degree of symbolic recognition may offer the rich and powerful a golden opportunity to buy themselves respectability and a clean conscience is hardly unwarranted. The consent to compensatory payments is often predicated on the tacit expectation that this will lead to an end not only of further financial demands, but also of public exposure to the blame. The notion that money will affect the moral consequences of a historical injustice, however, almost inevitably turns out to be mistaken. Compensation, legal scholar Gerald Gaus argues, may rectify the misdistribution of resources resulting from an injustice, yet it cannot restore moral equality between the perpetrators of a wrong and their victims. Nor does the admission of guilt and an apology from the aggressor oblige the victim to extend forgiveness and reconciliation.[39]

While restitution and recognition cannot buy forgiveness, let alone forgetting, some find the expectation of partial closure not altogether unreasonable. Charles Maier sees a key function of compensation in restoring a minimum of communication between victims and perpetrators as a

---

38 Maier, "A Surfeit of Memory?" 141–4; for the tension between memory and historical scholarship in different contexts, see, e.g., Konrad H. Jarausch and Martin Sabrow, eds., *Verletztes Gedächtnis. Erinnerungskultur und Zeitgeschichte im Konflikt* (Frankfurt am Main, 2002), and Ira Berlin, "American Slavery in History and Memory and the Search for Social Justice," *Journal of American History* 90 (2004): 1251–68; see, however, Chapter 9 by Bain Attwood in this volume.

39 Brooks, *When Sorry Isn't Enough*, 6; Barkan, *The Guilt of Nations*, 343–4; Gerald F. Gaus, "Does Compensation Restore Equality?" in John Chapman, ed., *Compensatory Justice* (New York, 1991), 45–81, esp. 75. Forgiveness, by its very nature, cannot be a moral imperative for the victims; see Minow, *Between Vengeance and Forgiveness*, 14–21. For an argument for forgiveness as a "civic duty" provided that a sincere apology and adequate reparations have been rendered, see Brooks, *Atonement and Forgiveness*, 163–9; on the meaning and consequences of apologies in social relations, see Nicholas Tavuchis, *Mea Culpa: A Sociology of Apology and Reconciliation* (Stanford, 1991).

precondition for future coexistence. Although this "materialist transformation" may be repulsive to the victims, it serves the purpose "to remove the losses from the realm of the sacred, the never-to-be-forgiven, into the realm of the politically negotiated." This process, without implying moral equality, imposes duties on both parties to the agreement: "Those receiving reparation, in effect, must consent to a degree of closure: not closure on remembering or commemoration, but closure on material claims, assuming that all claims have been met and discussed and agreed on."[40] Others consider closure as an imperative of peace and stability. Peace, Andrew Rigby asserts, is more important than justice; in fact, justice is predicated on peace, and therefore individuals and groups must somehow become capable of accepting loss and moving on so that the cycle of hate and vengeance is not perpetuated.[41] However, for those who take a structural view of historical injustice, all demands for closure are highly suspect and unacceptable as long as the structures of injustice endure, even if they go back to events that happened several generations ago.

Political and legal initiatives to right the wrongs of the past have been and will continue to be highly controversial and at times even bitterly divisive. However, the debates among scholars of historical and transitional justice indicate that there is indeed a fairly broad consensus on the principle of rectification. Skeptics are mostly concerned about the possible dysfunctional and counterproductive effects of a "surfeit" of history and memory. As a rule, they favor material restitution to surviving victims or to persons whose lives have been directly affected by an injustice and are more reluctant to accept claims to reparations that extend over several generations.[42] They also embrace commemoration and recognition of victims as a moral imperative but are suspicious of empty rituals and the professionalization or instrumentalization of memory. On the other hand, there are few advocates of historical justice who advocate an absolute and unconditional right to restitution. Elazar Barkan explicitly rejects claims to unlimited restitution as "fantasy" and insists that "only partial justice is feasible and to attempt a general reversal of the past is utopian." His "neo-Enlightenment" concept of morality stresses the need for negotiated solutions that reconcile local

---

40 Charles Maier, "Overcoming the Past? Narrative and Negotiation, Remembering and Reparation: Issues at the Interface of History and Law," in Torpey, *Politics and the Past*, 295–304, esp. 297–8.
41 Rigby, *Justice and Reconciliation*, 11–12.
42 For a cautious argument in favor of intergenerational justice, see James S. Fishkin, "Justice Between Generations: Compensation, Identity, and Group Membership," in Chapman, *Compensatory Justice*, 85–96; for a limited concept of compensatory justice, see Ellen Frankel Paul, "Set-Asides, Reparations, and Compensatory Justice," in Chapman, *Compensatory Justice*, 97–139.

needs and customs with narrowly defined universal values.[43] Virtually all proponents of restitution emphasize that the righting of past wrongs ought to take competing rights and interests into consideration and must not create new injustices. Any claim to historical justice will have to be weighed on its own merits and due attention be given both to general principles of equity and to the specific context in which justice is to be rendered.

This volume grew out of a conference bringing together an interdisciplinary group of scholars from nine different countries held in March 2003 at the German Historical Institute in Washington, D.C. The book seeks to combine general interpretations of and reflections on the quest for historical justice with a broad array of case studies. Even though many more case studies from all parts of the world would have been desirable, the editors are confident that the arguments, perspectives, and information presented in the following chapters will make a significant contribution to the study of historical justice from an international perspective. The volume opens with two general essays on the salient issue of "politics" in debates on restitution and reparations. They are followed by three groups of national case studies that focus on, respectively, reparations and restitution, memory and recognition, and reconciliation. Issues of memory and recognition are examined with regard to contemporary France, Russia, and Cambodia; attempts at reconciliation are addressed pertaining to the societies of Australia, New Zealand, and postapartheid South Africa. A concluding essay demonstrates why the issue of historical justice "won't go away."

John Torpey defines the widespread contemporary concern with past injustices as an extraordinary shift in progressive ways of thinking about politics. Putative "lessons" of twentieth-century history have encouraged a shift from the labor movement's onetime rallying cry of "Don't mourn, organize" to a sensibility that insists that we must "organize to mourn." Efforts to rectify past wrongs have arisen on the one hand, he contends, as a substitute for expansive visions of an alternative human future and, on the other, as a response to the rise of identity politics.

Angelika von Wahl examines the question of what general factors lead governments to agree to pay reparations. Taking four cases from the World War II era, she demonstrates how political factors influence government involvement and how politically weak lobbies achieve only meager results in terms of reparations, despite the morality of their claims. Ethnically or

---

43 Barkan, *The Guilt of Nations*, 328–30.

racially motivated crimes would stand a better chance of being redressed than human rights abuses pertaining to sexual orientation or gender issues.

Manfred Berg analyzes the historical discourse and theoretical assumptions employed by the participants in the debate over reparations for the descendants of black slaves in the United States. He probes questions of historical continuity and counterfactual analysis that form the conceptual backbone of reparation claims. Although he acknowledges these concepts as legitimate tools of scholarly analysis, Berg considers them questionable sources of moral authority to substantiate material claims. Moreover, the demand for slavery reparations is often brought in the language of an absolute right to infinite corrective justice. This notion is not only illusionary, but it actually impairs the prospects of redistributive social reform on behalf of poor African Americans.

Constantin Goschler deals with the perception of divided "wrongs" within German society from the end of World War II to the present, tracing the tension between the victims of Nazi persecution and German self-victimization. Only with German reunification in the 1990s did claims for compensation of Nazi victims rise to a prominent position in Germany itself, even serving in part as a model for worldwide efforts to redress historical injustices.

Svend Aage Christensen and Kristian Søby Kristensen examine the ongoing dispute over the 1953 relocation of the inhabitants of the hunting settlement of Uummannaq in Greenland due to the expansion of the U.S. Air Force's Thule Air Base. The subject of official investigations, lawsuits, and negotiations between the United States, Denmark, and Greenland, the case of the Greenlanders for adequate reparations, according to the authors, demonstrates the merits of individual versus collective compensation arrangements.

Inquiring into the powerful social force of public apology, Julie Fette analyzes the example of France, where President Jacques Chirac's 1995 official declaration of remorse for the state-sponsored anti-Semitism of the Vichy regime had spurred many groups to step forward to atone for their particular guilt during those years. Fette demonstrates how this process helped French society to transcend its past and how the model of apology may be applied to other historical events, such as the French role during the war in Algeria.

Andreas Hilger focuses on the legal instruments of Russia's efforts to come to terms with the unjust imprisonment of non-Soviet citizens in the wake of World War II. He demonstrates how those efforts are embedded in Russian politics and the inconsistent attitude in Russia today toward the history of the USSR. Hilger emphasizes the disregard of the historical ideologization of Soviet juridical measures. He interprets this as a desire for clinical separation of inseparable parts of history to rebuild a strong Russian state in the present and therefore to create a continuity with former Soviet political priorities.

Steven Heder discusses the evidence of crimes against humanity committed by the Khmer Rouge in Cambodia between 1975 and 1979 and ensuing efforts to bring perpetrators to justice after the fall of that regime. Based on a careful analysis of the dynamics of the Cambodian mass killings, Heder finds fault with the "politically driven" efforts by the United Nations for a trial focusing on the highest echelons of the party leadership according to the "Nuremberg model." This would perpetuate a misconceived "top-down" image of the events and shield from scrutiny "small fish" with still dominant political influence and significant stalling capacity in today's Cambodia.

In his case study on Australia, Bain Attwood considers the ways alternative historical narratives have influenced projects of reconciliation in settler societies. He portrays the problem of historical justice in such societies as being actually much greater than classic cases like Nazi Germany. Colonial pasts are more entrenched, as they involved several generations and problems are thus more intractable. In seeking to redress historical injustices, history's epistemological basis would tend to give rise to singular historical narratives and thus be complicit in the modern state's goal of a unitary nation. By contrast, memory could produce more diverse historical narratives. Therefore, rectification of historical injustices would require nation-states to recognize not only people's different pasts and narratives but also the different visions of citizenship and democracy that these narratives entail.

In contrast, as Richard S. Hill and Brigitte Bönisch-Brednich demonstrate in the case of New Zealand, the negotiation of compensation to Maori for the Crown's past breaches of New Zealand's founding document, the Treaty of Waitangi (1840), has reached an advanced stage. However, they assert that the majority European (*pakeha*) population has yet to realize that this provision of reparations for past wrongs will not suffice. Historical production in New Zealand was heavily involved in the Maori quest for autonomy (*rangatoratanga*) and constituted a major national discourse. There is cause for optimism, as New Zealand has become officially bicultural, in contrast to the assimilationist policies of the past. Biculturalism as an increasing feature of everyday life would provide hope that "Aotearoa" (the Maori name for the country) could take up a significant partnership position within "New Zealand."

Bronwyn Leebaw examines how the concept of restorative justice was adopted by the South African Truth and Reconciliation Commission. She argues that this occurred not only as a way to conceptualize the possibility of healing but also to advance a form of critical historical judgment. Understanding the tensions between those goals is important in assessing future efforts to apply restorative principles to historical justice projects.

In the concluding essay of this book, A. James McAdams reflects on the tension between the temptation to forget about a dreadful past and the promotion of strategies to achieve transitional and historical justice. Rather than looking at the obvious differences between the case studies presented in this volume, he focuses on their commonalities. He does so by exploring a case often seen as too singular to offer useful comparison, postunification Germany. Drawing on Germany's experiences with opening up the files of the East German secret police to its victims, restoring property that had been seized by Soviet and East German authorities, and prosecuting those responsible for shooting deaths at the intra-German border, McAdams has surprisingly good things to say about the performance of German administrative and criminal courts. Nonetheless, the German case holds three broadly applicable lessons that may be disappointing to the proponents of historical justice: (1) the project of transitional justice cannot simply begin with a clean slate but has to build on legal and political precedents; (2) it is impossible to find clear-cut solutions that will satisfy everyone; and (3) it is very likely that the failures and shortcomings of the transition process will resurface in later debates and form the basis of new grievances. All the same, McAdams pleads that the quest for historical justice must be undertaken simply because it is the right thing to do. Leaders who betray the founding ideals of a new democratic successor regime, he hopes, will be held accountable by the citizenry.

It is no coincidence that none of the contributions to this volume attempts to develop a universal model or theory of historical justice. Although general principles of justice, such as equality of respect and treatment, reciprocity, and the rule of the law, form the background of all arguments and case studies, the search for a deductive model from which specific solutions could be derived is not a major concern for most scholars. Obviously, the contexts and discourses of the various cases as well as the needs of the victims are too different to be integrated into a master narrative on how to right the wrongs of the past. But this does not mean that international and historical comparisons are useless. To the contrary, as all well-conceived comparisons do, they may educate us about both the commonalities and the peculiarities of the cases under consideration and help us develop typologies, analytical categories, and, perhaps, moral standards. The purpose of putting the quest for historical justice into an international perspective is not to provoke competition among victims, nor to trivialize experiences of victimization. Rather, by recognizing the many faces of historical injustice, we also recognize that there must be many different paths to historical justice. Unfortunately, as history never was, and never will be, short of injustices and atrocities, this will be an ongoing task.

PART I

The Politics of Restitution

1

An Avalanche of History

The "Collapse of the Future" and the Rise of Reparations Politics

JOHN TORPEY

One need not be committed to a ventriloquist poststructuralism, according to which people act out the discourses that constitute them, to be impressed by the extent to which the idea of "coming to terms with the past" generally, and that of "reparations" in particular, have shaped the political activity of a broad variety of groups around the globe in recent years. This development is the more noteworthy given that the pursuit of "reparations" by these different groups has depended on a sharp reformulation of the meaning of the term. Until World War II, the word "reparations" was mainly used in connection with the damages owed to victors in war; the winners said that the losers had caused the war and demanded to be compensated for their losses. Moreover, the term referred to transactions among *states*; the case of Germany after the Versailles treaty is paradigmatic. Yet the literature of the South African Reparations Movement (SARM), which came into being a little more than two years ago, defines reparations as "a term that refers to what is owed by the wrongdoer to the oppressed to restore the oppressed and dispossessed and [to] return what is rightfully theirs." For SARM and other movements like it, "reparations" is about coming to terms with and making amends for the past misdeeds of states and private enterprises vis-à-vis the groups and individuals (or their descendants) who were once victimized.

This chapter seeks to make sense of the global spread of "reparations politics," by which I mean organized efforts aimed at the acknowledgment of and/or compensation for past wrongdoing; those engaged in reparations politics seek to come to terms with the past in this sense. I argue that the intensified preoccupation with the past is an ambivalent development, representing both an advance in human affairs that "adds to the sum of justice in the world"[1] and an aspect of the decline of the more future-oriented "commonality politics"[2] that had been embodied especially in the socialist and civil rights movements of the twentieth century. The efflorescence of the concern to come to terms with the past reflects a shift in the temporal horizons of politics, especially for "progressives." In contrast to the invocation of the future as the horizon of politics, in which all can be said to be the beneficiaries of our actions now, mining the past for political aims frequently becomes a "competition of victimhoods,"[3] with all the drawbacks of viewing people chiefly as victims rather than as human beings deserving of decent lives.

The past is politically multivocal, so to speak; we can interpret it in a variety of ways, and the ways we do so reflect our contemporary predispositions and concerns. Campaigns oriented to coming to terms with the past span a range of political positions, from mostly past- and in-group-oriented to mostly future- and commonality-oriented. Reparations politics are spearheaded by and rely on the skills of a disparate cadre of what I shall call "entrepreneurs of memory," most of whom are professionals and intellectuals of various kinds who analyze the relationship between the past and the present in terms that reflect their professional and personal backgrounds. Despite their emphasis on the persistent influence of the past on the present, they frequently invoke the future as the horizon of their political aims, insisting that the kinds of talk and action that they wish to spur will have a "cleansing" effect on the traumatized and that their efforts to obtain reparation will serve as a deterrent to future misbehavior. The symbolic work of these entrepreneurs has put the past, politically speaking, where the future once was.

Coming to Terms with the Past

People who have suffered wrongs at the hands of states, businesses, and other corporate entities – and the putative descendants and representatives of those wronged – have in recent years demonstrated a considerable desire to speak out about their experiences, to seek recognition of those experiences

---

1 Marina Warner, "Scene Two: St. Augustine's Confessions," *Open Democracy: Thinking for Our Time*, November 5, 2002, http://www.opendemocracy.net/debates/article.jsp?id=3&debateId=76&articleId=647.
2 The term is Todd Gitlin's; see his *The Twilight of Common Dreams: Why America Is Wracked by Culture Wars* (New York, 1995).
3 Jean-Michel Chaumont, *La concurrence des victimes: genocide, identité, reconnaissance* (Paris, 1997). See also Robert Meister and Catherine Lu, "Debate: Human Rights and the Politics of Victimhood," *Ethics & International Affairs* 16:2 (2002).

from states and wider publics, and to demand compensation for the alleged wrongs. This outpouring of talk and activism concerning past injustices, which has been facilitated by the emergence of the truth commission as an institutional form and of the class-action lawsuit as a way of doing politics,[4] has allowed many people to give voice to their sense of having been wronged and to feelings that have remained bottled up inside them for a long time, perhaps for decades. Those who have spoken out about and sought compensation for what was done to them (or to their forebears) in the past have thereby reversed the pattern typically followed by their forebears, who tended to keep these experiences to themselves.

Many of those who were humiliated and terrorized in the twentieth century — such as survivors of the Holocaust, North Americans of Japanese descent incarcerated during World War II, or the so-called comfort women impressed into sexual slavery by the Japanese army during the war — kept these experiences to themselves in the first years after they endured them. They did so, it has frequently been argued, because they regarded those experiences as shameful or because they wanted to "get along by going along" in the circumstances in which they found themselves after their abasement.

In the meantime, however, the mood has shifted. The stories of those once wronged have been advanced, solicited, and listened to in officially sponsored and unofficial forums around the world that have been designed to bring into the light misdeeds and misfortunes that had previously been shrouded in darkness, or at least had been less attended to than was wished by those who organize these events. For those mistreated, speaking out and demanding recognition for past injustice has meant reaching "the other side of silence."[5]

Explanations of this remarkable public prolixity about past wrongs typically point to the end of the Cold War as inaugurating a relaxation of prior restraints on calling attention to the wrongs in question. Surely the end of the Cold War has had a good deal to do with the flood of talk about prior degradation and abuse. Pressures to suppress awareness of the injustices done on either side of the Iron Curtain fell away as the bipolar division of the world became a thing of the past. Around the same time, and in part for reasons connected to the end of the Cold War rivalry, the collapse of apartheid marked the culmination of an important phase of the larger process of decolonization. As Alan Cairns has noted, the delegitimation of external,

---

4 On the evolution of the class-action lawsuit, see Linda Greenhouse, "Judges Back Rule Changes for Handling Class Actions," *New York Times* national edition, September 25, 2002.
5 To borrow the title of André Brink, *The Other Side of Silence* (London, 2002).

overseas colonialism also led to the delegitimation of its internal variant, whereby nonwhite populations in particular were kept under the thumb of European intruders and their descendants.[6] The norm of antiracism that had come to pervade the post-1945 world led to heightened attention to racial injustice, its sources, and its remedies.[7]

Yet these considerations address only the "supply side" of attention to past injustice, so to speak; there is also a "demand side." There is today a great deal more interest in the narratives of onetime victims than was the case, say, fifty years ago. With all due regard for the differences in gravity and subject matter, one senses that there is at least a superficial connection between the appeal of the theatricalized narration of violence and oppression that occurs in the more formal setting of the truth commission and the popularity (in South Africa as well as in North America, by the way) of such television fare as *The Jerry Springer Show*, where lurid tales of humiliation are the order of the day. Among academics, the widespread interest in "discourse" – inspired by the work of thinkers as diverse as Jürgen Habermas and Michel Foucault and ushering in discursive and linguistic "turns" in the human sciences – has placed talk and text, as opposed to action and behavior, at the center of scholarly attention.

Meanwhile, a burgeoning "trauma industry" thrives on the telling of stories of victimization. Let there be no mistake: those who have been through horrible experiences may very well wish to get these experiences "off their chests." In the past, however, this was more likely to be a private affair, and it was often eschewed in the interest of "putting on a brave face," leaving the past behind, and soldiering on in the face of adversity. In the meantime, the victim has come to be viewed more favorably, and victim status becomes a permanent feature of personal identity. In criticizing the many social services that have arisen to deal with "trauma," Richard Gist, a community psychologist and trauma researcher at the University of Missouri, asks the crucial questions: "Why are we not more fascinated by ... displays of resilience and grace? Why are we only fascinated with frailty?"[8] In particular, the audience for stories of victimization on ethnic

---

6 Alan Cairns, "Coming to Terms with the Past," in John Torpey, ed., *Politics and the Past: On Repairing Historical Injustices* (Lanham, Md., 2003), 63–90.
7 On this point, see Howard Winant, *The World Is a Ghetto: Race and Democracy Since World War II* (New York, 2001).
8 Gist answers his provocative questions by saying that "the trauma industry knows they can make money off of frailty; there are all these psychologists out there turning six figures with their pablum and hubris." I doubt that the problem is only a simple one of greed; it is much more pervasive than that. See Lauren Slater, "Repress Yourself," *New York Times Magazine*, February 23, 2003, 48–53. The quotations from Richard Gist are on p. 51.

or racial grounds has grown dramatically, with little sense that the portrayal of such groups as victims might be harmful in its own way.[9]

Notwithstanding the enlarged market for narratives of past injustice, nothing foreordained the form those narratives would take. As Ian Hacking has noted, however, people talk about the past in terms of "the kinds of knowledge about memory that are current" in a society at a given time.[10] Here we must call attention to the centrality of the Holocaust in contemporary culture, especially in North America. Daniel Levy and Natan Sznaider have shown persuasively that the Holocaust, although its "reception" has varied from place to place, has come to be the chief touchstone of historical consciousness in an incipient cosmopolitan age.[11] While it may be true, as many have claimed,[12] that the Holocaust gets a disproportionate share of the attention given to past injustices, that view misses an important part of the picture. For if the Holocaust has absorbed a large share of the world's awareness of past misery, it has also inspired a massive upsurge of concern for *other* historical injustices. Indeed, the Holocaust template – itself the product of linguistic choices peculiar to particular societies[13] – has provided a whole armamentarium that others have been able to use to highlight experiences that were, or at least could be said to be, "Holocaust-like."

The importance of the Holocaust frame as a device for concentrating the minds of relevant audiences prompts efforts by entrepreneurs of memory to demonstrate the genocidal bona fides of the experiences they wish to highlight. In turn, the characterization of past actions as a "genocide" or a "Holocaust" becomes a crucial element in the framing of the historical events for which recognition or compensation is sought. In addition to the canonical one, therefore, we now have the "American Holocaust" (genocide of the Indians/Native Americans), the "African Holocaust" (slavery/the Middle Passage), the "Herero Holocaust" (the Germans' near-extermination of this group in South-West Africa before World War I), the

---

9 For an analysis of the political vicissitudes of representations of black Americans as "damaged," see Daryl Michael Scott, *Contempt and Pity: Social Policy and the Image of the Damaged Black Psyche, 1880–1996* (Chapel Hill, 1997).
10 Ian Hacking, *Rewriting the Soul: Multiple Personality and the Sciences of Memory* (Princeton, 1995), 94.
11 Daniel Levy and Natan Sznaider, *Erinnerung im globalen Zeitalter: Der Holocaust* (Frankfurt, 2001). See also Dan Diner, *Das Jahrhundert verstehen: Eine universalhistorische Deutung* (Frankfurt, 2000).
12 See, for example, Stéphane Courtois, "Introduction: The Crimes of Communism," in Stéphane Courtois et al., *The Black Book of Communism: Crimes, Terror, Repression*, trans. Jonathan Murphy and Mark Kramer (Cambridge, Mass., 1999), 19.
13 For an intriguing analysis of how the term "Holocaust" came to supersede other terms for the "destruction of the European Jews," see Anna-Vera Sullam Calamani, *I nomi dello sterminio* (Torino, 2001).

"Chinese Holocaust" (the "rape of Nanjing"), the "South African holocaust" (the killing of rebellious Afrikaners by the British during the Boer War/Second War of Independence[14]), and so on. The defenders of the "uniqueness" of the canonical Holocaust presumably must be mortified. Yet the truth is that those who have labored to put the Holocaust at the center of contemporary historical consciousness have performed a major service by supplying a remarkably effective frame with which other entrepreneurs of memory have succeeded in gaining a hearing for wrongs committed in other contexts.[15]

The language pioneered by those commemorating the inferno in Central Europe during World War II or seeking compensation for its victims has thus come to be used by others for similar purposes. Take, for example, the figure of the "survivor." Deployed initially (by the women's movement, if I am not mistaken) as a positive alternative to "victim," the term has nonetheless come to refer to those who strongly identify – or are identified – with previous experiences of victimization. Like the "Holocaust" metaphor itself, the label "survivor" has become widely used to highlight the injustices once suffered by certain groups of people, but it has also undergone considerable inflation in its further application. Thus, for example, activists involved in a campaign for reparations for those would-be Chinese immigrants required to pay a "head tax" before they were permitted to enter Canada have referred to those still alive as "survivors" of the head tax.[16] Having to pay the head tax was a humiliating experience, to be sure, but one wonders whether this is not distorting the term out of all recognizability. Similarly borrowing from the Holocaust lexicon, activists seeking redress for and commemoration of the World War II–era North American Japanese "relocation," "evacuation," and "internment" have stressed that this terminology blunts the edges of the incarceration experience. In actual fact, these activists have insisted, the North American Japanese were not "relocated" at all, but rather were held in "concentration camps."[17] Although this term originated in the early

---

14 See Hennie Barnard, *The Concentration Camps, 1899–1902*, http://www.boer.co.za/boerwar/hellkamp.htm (accessed April 23, 2003).
15 On the question of the "uniqueness" of the Holocaust, see Dan Stone, *Constructing the Holocaust* (London, 2003); A. Dirk Moses, "Conceptual Blockages and Definitional Dilemmas in the Racial Century: Genocide of Indigenous Peoples and the Holocaust," *Patterns of Prejudice* 36:4 (2002): 7–36; Gavriel D. Rosenfeld, "The Politics of Uniqueness: Reflections on the Recent Polemical Turn in Holocaust and Genocide Scholarship," *Holocaust and Genocide Studies* 13 (1999): 28–61; Alan S. Rosenbaum, *Is the Holocaust Unique? Perspectives on Comparative Genocide* (Oxford, 1996).
16 Author's interview with Jonas Ma, Ottawa chapter president, Chinese Canadian National Council, Ottawa, Ontario, December 6, 2002.
17 See Roger Daniels, *Concentration Camps, North America: Japanese in the United States and Canada During World War II* (Malabar, Fla., 1981), and, more recently, the promotional literature of the Japanese

twentieth century in the context of the Boer War, it has of course come to be strongly associated with the Holocaust – heightening the stakes of its usage and the attention to sites where such camps have existed.

Along with the rise of reparations activity and popular awareness related to the Holocaust, the success of the Japanese-American and Japanese-Canadian redress movements in the late 1980s provided an important impetus to other campaigns for coming to terms with the past. Thus, in their campaign for redress, the Herero people of what is now Namibia – some three-quarters of whom were wiped out after they rebelled against their German overlords in 1904 – draw analogies to both the Holocaust and the North American–Japanese cases.[18] The Herero first began their push for reparations soon after the redress settlements were resolved in North America, as the end of the Cold War coincided more or less directly with their independence from South African rule (1990) and thus with the first practical possibility of raising their claims against the Germans. The otherwise obscure Herero thus revealed their political savvy and their awareness of how these other cases might be seen as precedents for their own efforts to come to terms with the past.[19]

"The Collapse of the Future" and the Turn to the Past

Desirable though it is in many respects, the extensive contemporary concern with righting past injustices represents a remarkable transformation in progressive ways of thinking about politics. Indeed, the shift from the millenarian striving for a utopian future to the struggle to "make whole what has been smashed" – even if the latter is seen as the road to the former – constitutes a sea change in thinking about politics. While that change involves, among other things, a greater willingness on the part of the powerful to own up to past misdeeds and to give a hearing to the stories of those who suffered them, it also reflects a major transformation in how we think about past and future. The putative "lessons" of twentieth-century history, which has come to be widely regarded as a thoroughgoing

---

American Citizens League, "A Lesson in American History: The Japanese American Experience," 2002.
18 See Sidney L. Harring, "German Reparations to the Herero Nation: An Assertion of Herero Nationhood in the Path of Namibian Development?" *West Virginia Law Review* (Winter 2002).
19 For some of the legal background, see Jeremy Sarkin, "Holding Multinational Corporations Accountable for Human Rights and Humanitarian Law Violations Committed During Colonialism and Apartheid: An Evaluation of the Prospects of Such Cases in Light of the Herero of Namibia's Genocide Case and South African Apartheid Cases Being Brought in the United States Under the Alien Torts Claims Act," in Eva Brems, ed., *Bedrijven en Mensenrechten* (Maklu, 2003).

catastrophe, have fed a shift from the labor movement's onetime rallying cry of "Don't mourn, organize" to a sensibility that insists that we must organize to mourn. Efforts to rectify past wrongs have thus jostled with, and perhaps to some degree supplanted, expansive visions of an alternative human future of the kind that animated the socialist and civil rights movements of the preceding century. The decline of utopian politics has combined with identity politics to produce "reparations politics."

We have thus been faced in recent years with an avalanche of history – but a history conceived as far different from the heroic, forward-looking tales that have underpinned the idea of progress for more than two centuries. Interestingly, these forward-looking visions were similar in both the national and socialist (not to mention Judeo-Christian) imaginaries: in each case, the past was a story of oppression, but one that prepared the way for a brighter day in the future. Today, what one might call the narrative structure of emancipation appears to have shifted. The hagiographic texts designed to water the roots of national belonging that had characterized history-writing under the sign of Hegel have fallen under suspicion, along with anything else that smacks of a "grand narrative." In their place, we find narratives of rapine, extermination, and plunder, usually across one or another color (or ethno-national) line, with profound consequences that reach well into the present. These critical histories, very often closer than their naively mythopoeic predecessors to the true story of how we got where we are, have helped promote extensive efforts to "repair" what has been damaged en route to the present. Many countries – especially the more developed ones, and especially the more privileged groups within those countries – are thus confronted today with the task of digging themselves out from under the accumulated burdens of their history. All countries can be said to have such histories; in this respect, at least, we are all Germans now.

Yet the rising preoccupation with the past overlaps so directly with the decline of more explicitly future-oriented politics – whether of the nation-state or of socialism – that it is hard to avoid the conclusion that this is more than mere coincidence. Susan Buck-Morss has captured succinctly the broad outlines of the political situation in which we find ourselves: "[T]he mass-democratic myth of industrial modernity – the belief that the industrial reshaping of the world is capable of bringing about the good society by providing material happiness for the masses – has been profoundly challenged by the disintegration of European socialism, the demands of capitalist restructuring, and the most fundamental ecological constraints. In its place, an appeal to differences that splinter the masses into fragments now structures political rhetoric and marketing strategies alike...."[20] Buck-Morss zeros in on the fundamental transformation that has occurred in contemporary political thought: the idea of well-being for the undifferentiated masses has been replaced by the goal of satisfying the wants of minutely nuanced market segments. Mass utopia is out; niche marketing, whether in the consumer or the political realm, is in.

From a sharply different viewpoint, François Furet has maintained that, in the aftermath of the demise of communism, "the idea of *another* society has become almost impossible to conceive of, and no one in the world today is offering any advice on the subject or even trying to formulate a new concept" [emphasis in original].[21] Against the background of this assessment, the intensive and often censorious attention to the past of the last several years may be understood to reflect what one might call the collapse of the future – the decline of the bold, progressive political visions that had been embodied in the socialist and civil rights movements and, indeed, in the project of the nation-state understood as a community of equal citizens.[22] The pursuit of the past during the last decade or two partakes of a larger sense that "the dishes are being cleared" on that epoch of Western culture that can be understood as an allegory of hope and progress.[23] The subjectivism of contemporary intellectual life – its obsession with "identity" and its hostility to "objectivity" – is an important part of this mood. Here it may be worth recalling Goethe's remark that "epochs which are regressive, and in the process of dissolution, are always subjective, whereas the trend in all progressive epochs is objective... Every truly excellent endeavor turns from within toward the world."[24] The fading faith in alternative visions of society and the corresponding rise in subjectivist sensibilities are the soil from which has arisen the upsurge of concern about history, memory, and coming to terms with the past, though of course those pursuing the reckoning with past injustices may well be motivated by the deepest moral concern and may contribute to "the sum of justice in the world."

In our post-utopian context, the reckoning with abominable pasts becomes, for many people, the idiom in which the future is sought; the road to the future has come to run through the catastrophes of the past.

---

20 Susan Buck-Morss, *Dreamworld and Catastrophe: The Passing of Mass Utopia in East and West* (Cambridge, Mass., 2000).
21 François Furet, *The Passing of an Illusion: The Idea of Communism in the Twentieth Century*, trans. Deborah Furet (Chicago, 1999), 502.
22 For a sharp critique of the waning of commitment to the idea of equal citizenship, see Brian Barry, *Culture & Equality* (Cambridge, Mass., 2001).
23 See the discussion in George Steiner, *Grammars of Creation* (New Haven, 2001), 2–11; the quotation is from p. 3.
24 Quoted in Robert Hughes, *The Culture of Complaint: The Fraying of America* (New York, 1993), 10.

Against this background, the stress on coming to terms with the past can be seen as a tactical response to an otherwise recalcitrant political reality – a means to make political progress using a rhetoric about past injustices, and institutions for dealing with them, that have proven successful in other, putatively analogous, cases. We might call this the "involution" of the progressive impulse that has animated much of modern history – the stymieing of what was once regarded as the forward march of progress and its turning inward upon itself, as various groups mobilize to contest the past and to seek compensation for the injustices that were done to them. For each of these groups, such compensation may well constitute a step forward, but this is different from an emancipatory or egalitarian vision to which large, diverse groups are likely to subscribe.

For many people, even those who would unhesitatingly regard themselves as "progressives," the abysmal past has thus extensively replaced the radiant future as the temporal horizon in which to think about politics. This is an extraordinary development. Under normal circumstances, the past returns to us only fleetingly and remains simply part of the stock of ideas from which people draw to make sense of their lives. But it is scarcely the predominant part; for most people, an inclination to dwell on the past is usually a sign that something is amiss. Ordinarily, people maintain a balance among past, present, and future that allows them to move forward in their everyday lives. That balance seems to have been upset in recent years, and a good part of the explanation for this development lies with the symbolic efforts of "entrepreneurs of memory" who have sought to make the past more central to us and to our thinking about politics.

The Entrepreneurs of Memory

Since roughly the end of the Cold War, the distance that normally separates us from the past has been strongly challenged in favor of an insistence that the past is constantly, urgently, present as part of our everyday experience. To some extent, this is simply the culmination of Freud's revolution in modern thought, which emphasized the ways in which the past continued to govern our lives and insisted that coming to terms with the past was essential to human emancipation. Faulkner's widely quoted comment that "the past is not dead; it's not even past" has become one of the signature lines of this sensibility. But merely recognizing the prevalence of talk about the past does not explain why this is occurring now.

In contrast to the disembodied understanding of discourses characteristic of much recent academic analysis, this form of talk has roots in specific social groups. Political scientists emphasize that what they call "political entrepreneurs" play an important part in public life by making an "issue" of things that would not otherwise have become politically salient. Similarly, sociologists speak of the crucial role of certain actors in "framing" social phenomena in such a way that they come to be perceived as "problems."[25] The activities of these kinds of social entrepreneurs involve what Ron Eyerman has called "cognitive praxis," efforts to persuade broader publics to view the world in particular ways that conform to the political aims or vision of the activists in question.[26]

Against this background, an expanding cadre of what one might call "entrepreneurs of memory" has asserted in recent years that our ordinary remove from the past does not and indeed should not exist. As the sociology of knowledge would predict, the entrepreneurs of memory have stimulated the emergence of discourses about the past that are consistent with the professional and personal outlooks of those who articulate them. In itself, of course, there is nothing surprising or nefarious about this tendency; it simply reflects the expanding political importance in modern society of intellectuals and professionals, who play a prominent political role as "opinion leaders."[27] My identification of them is meant merely to identify them as contributors to a trend, rather than to cast doubt on the reality of the troubles they address: the past wrongs to which they wish to call our attention are real enough. The ranks of the entrepreneurs of memory include

- human rights activists concerned with building a better future by putting an end to a so-called culture of impunity in offending states;
- theologians who see history in redemptory terms and who promote a religiously defined conception of "reconciliation" as the remedy for past wrongs;[28]
- therapists who specialize in dealing with the "traumas" of the past and who view history in therapeutic terms governed by the aims of "healing" and "closure";
- attorneys, especially those specializing in class-action suits, who see the past as a series of potentially justiciable offenses;
- historians, who have frequently come to play an important role as consultants and expert witnesses in political and legal efforts to come to terms with the past;[29]

---

25 On these points, see Sidney Tarrow, *Power in Movement: Social Movements and Contentious Politics*, second edition (New York, 1998), and Erving Goffman, *Frame Analysis: An Essay on the Organization of Experience* (Cambridge, Mass., 1974).
26 See Ron Eyerman, *Cultural Trauma: Slavery and the Formation of African American Identity* (New York, 2002).
27 See Alvin Gouldner, *The Future of Intellectuals and the Rise of the New Class* (New York, 1979).
28 For a critical analysis of the role of this sort of discourse in coming to terms with past wrongdoing in South Africa, see Richard A. Wilson, *The Politics of Truth and Reconciliation in South Africa: Legitimizing the Post-Apartheid State* (Cambridge, 2001).
29 On the role of lawyers and historians in the pursuit of reparations for Holocaust-related wrongs, see Ariel Colonomos, "The Holocaust Era Assets and the Globalization of Shame," paper presented at the July 2001 meeting of the International Studies Association, Hong Kong.

- educators with a political "agenda" regarding the presentation of the past to younger people and who see history as redolent with "lessons" for the present;
- and, finally, what one might call – with all due respect – the professionally injured, who are often associated with ethnic organizations and who seek to gain recognition or compensation for those of their kind who have suffered injustices in the past.

By using this last term, I mean no disrespect to those who have been wronged; my purpose is sociological. It is perfectly natural that some of those wronged in the past would adopt this experience as their chief "mission" in life. I derive the category of the professionally injured from Erving Goffman's indispensable discussion of "stigma" and of those who represent groups that share a stigmatizing condition. Goffman usefully reminds us that "representatives are not representative, for representation can hardly come from those who give no attention to their stigma."[30] My point here is that the professionally injured are unrepresentative in precisely the same sense, for they have identified strongly and durably with their onetime victimization, though this need not be and for others is not the case. Some injured persons, though not all, make a profession – one might even say a "calling" – of their past injury. Such persons often do a great deal of work oriented to coming to terms with the past.

In his discussion of the politics of stigma, Goffman goes on to say that the informal community and the organizations that grow up around particular stigmata will define an individual who shares a stigmatized condition "as someone who should take pride in his illness and not seek to get well."[31] Stigmatization, in other words, may be used to produce a sense of self, camaraderie, political purpose. Likewise, the professionally injured seek to encourage such solidarity, and to rally around their flag others who are similarly situated.

Although not even all "survivors" join or participate in the organizations designed to seek amends for the wrongs once done them, it turns out that identification with past injury can even comprise the touchstone of group belonging for the *descendants* of those injured. A group that understands itself as "second-generation survivors" of the Holocaust exemplifies this phenomenon.[32] Presumably such later-generation "survivors" are as doubtfully representative of their group as the professionally injured themselves, even if the claim that inequities currently facing a group are rooted

---

30 Erving Goffman, *Stigma: Notes on the Management of Spoiled Identity* (New York, 1963), 27.
31 Goffman, *Stigma*, 38.
32 Joseph Berger, "'The 'Second Generation' Reflects on the Holocaust," *New York Times* national edition, January 17, 2000.

in past wrongs may be perfectly plausible. Although not all blacks would adhere to a conception of themselves as descendants of slaves,[33] the pursuit of reparations for slavery and legal segregation depends in part on encouraging the notion that today's black Americans are to be understood as the descendants of survivors of those systems. This view is plausible enough, to put it mildly; indeed, if ameliorative policies are to be defended at all, it is necessary that Americans regard blacks above all as the descendants of slaves and not primarily as beneficiaries of the Civil War, the civil rights movement, or affirmative action.[34] The point is that the shared consciousness of past suffering may be deployed to stimulate group self-understanding and political involvement. Like all such notions, the construction of these self-conceptions is not "natural" but the product of political and symbolic effort.

As a result of the activities of the entrepreneurs of memory, we have witnessed the emergence of a "memory industry" that has come to preoccupy large numbers of academics and political activists. A growing catalog of groups and organizations devote themselves to one or another aspect of coming to terms with the past – with "trauma," "memory," "healing," "transitional justice," or "reconciliation." Special lectures, journals, conferences, and nongovernmental organizations addressing these subjects abound; leading foundations pour money into undertakings devoted to examining these issues.

The growing significance of the memory industry is neatly suggested by the changing character of the institutional innovations arising during periods of major social change. In her early 1960s' analysis of "the revolutionary tradition and its lost treasure," Hannah Arendt noted that soviets or councils (*Räte*) "were to make their appearance in every genuine revolution throughout the nineteenth and twentieth centuries." She regarded these "spontaneous organs of the people" as having created "a new public space for freedom which was constituted and organized during the course of the revolution itself," beyond and even against the designs of the nominal leaders of the revolution.[35]

Since the time when Arendt wrote, however, truth commissions – of which more than twenty have been instituted during the last two decades – have come to be the most characteristic institutional novelty associated with

---

33 See the discussion of the idea of reparations in the recent popular movie *Barbershop*, which mostly dismisses the idea as irrelevant.
34 See Dalton Conley, "Calculating Slavery Reparations: Theory, Numbers, and Implications," in John Torpey, ed., *Politics and the Past: On Repairing Historical Injustices* (Lanham, Md., 2003), 117–25.
35 See Hannah Arendt, *On Revolution* (New York, 1965 [1963]), 249.

countries undergoing a "transition" from authoritarianism to (it is hoped) some more democratic form of governance, whether by revolutionary or less dramatic means. Confirming this trend, the Ford Foundation and other philanthropists recently bankrolled the International Center for Transitional Justice, a nongovernmental organization with deep roots in previous efforts at coming to terms with the past.[36] The transition from the spontaneous democracy of the councils, institutions oriented à la Arendt toward the navigation of a common future, to truth commissions, which are devoted to unearthing past injustices, is telling indeed. (The recent rise of the truth commission is especially ironic when set against the background of postmodern doubts about the very possibility of "truth," as Deborah Posel and Graeme Simpson have pointed out.[37])

To be sure, Arendt was deeply concerned about the problem of coming to terms with the past. But her approach to dealing with the past was distinctively forward-looking. In this regard, she differed from her mentor and friend, Karl Jaspers, author of *The Question of German Guilt*.[38] In that seminal text, Jaspers laid out an approach to coming to terms with the past that viewed the perpetrators' embrace of their guilt, and the moral cleansing that he expected would flow from it, as essential to renewing a riven moral order. For Jaspers, the overarching theological conception of reparation involved the restoration of a community in need of healing.

Yet it is not clear that such a community ever existed to be put back together in the first place. In contrast to Jaspers's way of thinking about the past, Arendt was inclined toward a more future-oriented approach that "seeks not to restore an imagined moral order that has been violated but to initiate new relations between members of a polity.... A reconciliatory moment is not construed as a final shared understanding or convergence of world views, but as a disclosure of a world in common from diverse and possibly irreconcilable perspectives."[39] Arendt's approach to coming to terms with the past avoids the fallacious notion that reparations can restore some mythical political *status quo ante* that in fact never existed. Instead, it invokes the achievement of more satisfying relations among citizens in a

---

36 For a profile of the International Center for Transitional Justice and of van Zyl, see Lynda Richardson, "Helping Countries, and People, to Heal," *New York Times*, national edition, November 23, 2001. See also Priscilla Hayner, *Unspeakable Truths: Confronting State Terror and Atrocity* (New York, 2001).
37 Deborah Posel and Graeme Simpson, eds., *Commissioning the Past: Understanding South Africa's Truth and Reconciliation Commission* (Johannesburg, 2002), 1–2.
38 Originally published in German in 1946, an English edition has recently been reissued: Karl Jaspers, *The Question of German Guilt*, with a new introduction by Joseph W. Koterski, S.J. (New York, 2000).
39 Andrew Schaap, "Guilty Subjects and Political Responsibility: Arendt, Jaspers and the Resonance of the 'German Question' in Politics of Reconciliation," *Political Studies* 49 (2001): 762.

future that must be battled out in the public sphere rather than invoked, *ex post facto*, as the supposed restoration of an earlier equilibrium. From Arendt's perspective, it would be impossible to ask "How do we restore communities that have been fractured by racial violence?"[40] There is no "community" to "restore," her writing suggests, only one to create – asymptomatically and ever-anew.

Over time, however, Arendt's political approach to dealing with the past has been trumped by Jaspers's more therapeutic and theological conception, as well as by more legalistic approaches. With respect to the theological side of things, history is frequently discussed today in redemptory tones. This sensibility has been a prominent aspect of the deliberations of the South African Truth and Reconciliation Commission – which, not coincidentally, was headed by two churchmen, Desmond Tutu and Alex Boraine. As Ian Buruma has written, "we deal with history, as with so much in our 'secular' age, in a pseudo-religious manner. The past has become a matter of atonement."[41] The explosion in the use of the notion of "trauma" to describe collective historical events scarcely needs documenting. Tellingly, there is now an International Center for Trauma Studies at New York University offering discussions of "trauma as a human rights issue."[42]

On the legal side, we have witnessed a proliferation of lawsuits designed in one way or another to settle accounts with past injustices – even in the realm of foreign affairs – as well as high-profile efforts to punish state-sponsored wrongdoing, of which the international criminal tribunals for the former Yugoslavia and for Rwanda and the International Criminal Court are the leading examples.[43] More to the point, we have observed a variety of lawsuits pursuing reparations for past injustices in the cases of slavery, apartheid, the Herero genocide, the Chinese "head tax" in Canada, etc. In each of these cases, those seeking reparations for the wrongs done to them and their group frequently say that they are using the legal route as an alternative means to achieving their ends in the face of a recalcitrant political process.[44] That may be a good thing; *Brown v. Board of Education*

---

40 Danny Postel, "The Awful Truth [about Lynching]," *Chronicle of Higher Education*, July 12, 2002. I am grateful to Todd Gitlin for calling this article to my attention.
41 See Ian Buruma, "War Guilt, and the Difference Between Germany and Japan," *New York Times* national edition, December 29, 1998. For a more extended discussion, see Buruma's "The Joys and Perils of Victimhood," *New York Review of Books,* April 8, 1999.
42 See their Web site: http://www.itspnyc.org/index.html.
43 Anne-Marie Slaughter and David Bosco, "Plaintiff's Diplomacy," *Foreign Affairs* (September–October 2000): 102–16.
44 Interview with Paramount Chief of the Hereros Kuaima Riruako, Windhoek, Namibia, January 3, 2003; interview with Jonas Ma, Ottawa chapter president, Chinese Canadian National Council, Ottawa, Ontario, December 6, 2002; Charles Ogletree, co-chair of the Reparations Coordinating

(1954), the landmark Supreme Court decision that declared "separate but equal" facilities unconstitutional, helped to create a climate of opportunity in which the civil rights movement soon flourished. But to the extent that all really successful efforts to repair past injustices involve the legislature and not just the judiciary, the legal route can only be a part of the strategy for coming to terms with the past.[45]

Desirable though these legal initiatives may be in certain respects, we should bear in mind that they may distract from problems more readily addressed today. In addition, the victim-centered conception of justice that animates some of these efforts is problematic. After all, law was designed both to punish wrongdoers and to replace vengeance with due process. Against the background of larger social changes, the theological, therapeutic, and legalistic attitude toward coming to terms with the past presents a challenge both to more immediately civic approaches to attaining a common future and to old-fashioned conceptions of the law as an institution designed to serve the entire society.

My point is not to recommend either nostalgia for bygone enthusiasms or the ahistorical rumination of the cow described in Nietzsche's discussion of the pros and cons of contemplating history: Nietzsche's blissful bovine is untroubled by the remembrance of things past and is thus able, unlike humans, to live vigorously in the present. Rather, the point is simply to recognize that something profound has taken place in our ways of thinking about possible human futures. Nietzsche's trepidation about the debilitating effects of a surfeit of history is entirely apposite to our situation.[46] Furthermore, one needs to assess pragmatically whether calling attention to the past is the most effective way to achieve one's political aims.

Conclusion

Let me conclude with some thoughts concerning the concrete implications of these reflections on the contemporary prominence of reparations politics.

Committee, in a panel discussion of reparations for blacks at Union Chapel, Oak Bluffs, Mass., August 26, 2002; and see Jubilee 2000 South Africa, "Briefing on the Apartheid Debt and Reparations Campaign," n.d., in the author's possession.

45 See Roy Brooks, "Reflections on Reparations," in John Torpey, ed., *Politics and the Past: On Repairing Historical Injustices* (Lanham, Md., 2003), 106.

46 See Friedrich Nietzsche, "On the Uses and Disadvantages of History for Life," in Daniel Breazeale, ed., *Untimely Meditations*, trans. R. J. Hollingdale (New York, 1997), 57–123; see also Charles Maier, "A Surfeit of Memory? Reflections on History, Melancholy, and Denial," *History and Memory* 5:2 (Fall–Winter 1993): 136–52.

A few years back, the sociologist Dalton Conley wrote an op-ed piece in the *New York Times* arguing for reparations for blacks as a means of rectifying the "equity inequity" that resulted from blacks' inability to accumulate property during the centuries of slavery and segregation. He concluded by arguing that, despite the difficulties of sorting out who would pay and who would benefit, and regardless of the form a reparations scheme might ultimately take, it was important for Americans to debate the issue because American society cannot escape the fact that slavery is at the root of the persistent socioeconomic disparities faced by blacks. Letters to the editor raised all the predictable objections: My family arrived here, penniless immigrants, long after slavery was over – do I owe reparations? Who would be the beneficiaries of a reparations plan – and what about the Indians, who were arguably treated worse? Is race the only basis on which we should pay out reparations – why not a plan based on net worth irrespective of race?[47] Because of its connection to Holocaust-related compensation, the term "reparations" typically suggests payments to individuals by governments. At a time when affirmative action is on the ropes politically, does it seem likely that the United States government is going to start issuing checks to individual blacks? To be blunt, the idea is preposterous. Even Barack Obama rejected the idea in a televised debate among candidates for the Democratic presidential nomination sponsored by YouTube.[48]

Given the extreme improbability of the American government mailing checks to blacks for the wrongs visited upon them in the past, what to do? Is this a sensible way to expend one's political energies? The Bush administration and conservative activists have sought in recent years to curb or dismantle government welfare, housing, medical, and old-age insurance programs that disproportionately assist blacks because blacks are disproportionately poor. One wonders what good it does to talk about "reparations" under such circumstances. Particularly in the United States, the cultural self-understanding of which has generally been toward shedding the past and reinventing the self, political arguments rooted in past injustice seem out of tune with national inclinations. It is possible that the discussion about reparations will, as Conley suggests, promote a broader set of reflections on the sources of racial inequality, and this would surely be a good and necessary thing. If it is to do more than that, however – if, in other words, it is to have real policy relevance – it will have to metamorphose

---

47 Dalton Conley, "The Cost of Slavery," *New York Times* national edition, February 15, 2003. The letters appeared on the letters page of the national edition on February 20 and 22, 2003, respectively.
48 July 23, 2007.

into a discussion about what will help the black poor in the United States and help the country at large. It will, in short, have to go beyond the rhetoric of "coming to terms with the past" and speak to a brighter future, rather than simply hammering on the wrongs of the past – real though they were.

2

The Politics of Reparations

Why, When, and How Democratic Governments Get Involved

ANGELIKA VON WAHL

This chapter furthers the comparative study of governmental attempts to provide symbolic and material reparations for human rights abuses.[1] While many states have participated in the infliction of injustice and atrocities – be it during war with neighboring states, the colonization of other countries, or violent acts within their own territories – it seems that relatively few cases of human rights abuse have resulted in reparations. Some states have publicly apologized, paid compensation, or returned lost property, while other states have been able to quite literally "get away with murder." In a time of continued human rights abuse and attendant global restitution claims, it is increasingly important to ask what factors lead governments to make reparations, and, specifically, what kinds of reparations are made, and to whom. This chapter addresses the question of why some claimants are more likely than others to gain access to legal and/or organizational resources and consequently succeed in obtaining some form of reparation.

To understand the politics of reparations as a global phenomenon, I contend that a comparative approach is necessary. The states selected for this study are Germany, Japan, and the United States; the time period is restricted to atrocities committed during World War II. Each state committed human

---

[1] This chapter is based on an ongoing larger research project on the politics of reparations including six case studies. I initially presented a short version of this paper entitled "International Reparations: Why, When and How Democratic Governments Get Involved" at the conference "Historical Justice in International Perspective," March 27–29, 2003, at the German Historical Institute in Washington, D.C. I then presented an expanded version at the Western Political Science Association meetings in March 2005 in Oakland. I thank the conference organizers and participants and the anonymous reviewers for their helpful suggestions. Special thanks go to Richard Buxbaum for his encouragement and to Dieter Rucht and Dieter Gosewinkel for their helpful feedback during my stay at the WZB (Berlin). I'd also like to thank Petra Schäfter, who generously shared her knowledge of transitional justice literature with me, and David Lazar for his editing suggestions.

rights abuses during this time. Although the intentions and actions of the three states were very different, all are recognized to have abused the rights of particular groups,[2] and demands for reparations arose from differing and severe human rights violations. In Germany, the demands for reparations stem primarily from the genocide of the Jews, and more recent claims for reparations have, among others, arisen from the use of slave labor and the incarceration and murder of homosexuals during World War II. In the United States, claims for restitution originate from the internment of Japanese Americans during the war. In Japan, demands for reparations stem mainly from Korean women who served as sexual slaves to the Japanese army during the Pacific War. These human rights violations during World War II against Jews, homosexuals, Japanese Americans, and Korean women are different in scope and extent, but they all constitute severe human rights violations at the same historic time and in states that were either already, or shortly afterward became, stable democracies. Why have these democracies responded so differently to past human rights abuses by their own governments?

Obviously, the extent and nature of the atrocity itself must be taken into account to explain the willingness of governments to recognize and rectify human rights abuses. However, this factor cannot be the only, or even the most important, explanation of how and why some democratic governments apologize or pay reparations. It certainly does not constitute a direct causal link that goes without explanation. Instead, I argue that we have to study the *politics of reparations* to understand government participation.

Regarding the centrality of politics, Samuel Huntington's argument on transitional governments is helpful. In his study of the change from authoritarian to democratic regimes in Latin America, he argues that it is not moral and legal considerations that provide decisive explanations for prosecutions of human rights abuses, but rather politics and "the nature of the democratization process, and . . . the distribution of political power during and after the transition" that play a major role.[3] I argue that the same is true for the politics of reparations: symbolic and material reparations cannot be fully explained by the existence and extent of past human rights abuses; rather they are the outcome of "politics," that is, the distribution of power among competing groups in specific political contexts.

---

2 I am not covering all instances of human rights abuse, but I have chosen to address a few as examples to illustrate a larger point. I am not asserting that the extent and severity of the abuses were similar.
3 Samuel Huntington, *The Third Wave: Democratization in the Late Twentieth Century* (Norman, Okla., 1991), excerpted in: Neil Kritz, ed., *Transitional Justice: How Emerging Democracies Reckon with Former Regimes* (Washington, D.C., 1995), 65–81, here 69.

To explain this process, I focus on the organization of interests and identities of claimants through social mobilization in three democratic states. Political pressure is crucial in receiving governmental recognition and action when it comes to reparations. Governments do not act on the issue of restitution without being prompted, as what is morally and politically right is contested even after the human rights abuses have stopped. This chapter demonstrates that reparations are most likely made when claimants, and their representative organizations, put forward coherent, systematic demands for acknowledgment and redress. This does not mean that other factors, such as changes in international law or public opinion, are not relevant. They are. However, it is the organization of interests and identities of claimants through social movements in specific political context structures that is the driving force behind the political process toward reparations. As a result, survivors of human rights abuses are not equally able to make their experience and demands heard. Thus a patterned hierarchy among former victims emerges.

One pattern that emerges from this analysis shows a possible bifurcation between claims made on the grounds of *ethnicity* and those made on the grounds of *gender and/or sexuality*. It seems from the cases presented here that claims made on grounds of ethnicity are more successful than those made on the basis of sexuality or gender. Although that may be partly due to the chosen cases, the claimants' organizational ability to represent their interests and mobilize supporters, the framing of reparations demands, and the constitution of their identity are also reasons for the differing degrees of success.

While ethnic identity can sometimes be framed in a positive relation to national interests and identities, reparation demands based on gender and/or sexual identity are hampered by the claimants' relative political ineffectiveness, or "otherness." For example, the traditional invisibility of human rights abuses against women is rooted to a large extent in the "naturalization" of inequality between the sexes. Women's subordination *as women* is normalized through the traditional split between private and public spheres, and the associated inequality of civil, political, and economic citizenship.

Related to the subordination of women under patriarchy is the widespread governmental and legal indifference toward violence against women. One effect of this indifference is that the kinds of sexual assault that happen specifically to women during war (e.g., sexual slavery, mass rape, forced sterilization) have been consistently ignored by national governments and the international human rights community.[4] This indifference stems from

---

4 Henry Steiner and Philip Alston, *International Human Rights in Context: Law, Politics and Morals* (Oxford, 2000).

a male-centered definition of what constitutes human rights and mass atrocities.[5] As Catherine MacKinnon argues: "What happens to women [during human rights abuse] is either too particular to be universal or too universal to be particular, meaning either too human to be female or too female to be human."[6] Thus, rape and sexual assault are seen as a specific "women's issue," not as a general human rights issue. Only in the last decade, after the war in Yugoslavia, have feminists increasingly been successful in framing women's rights as human rights.[7]

Historically, homosexual men are also unlikely to be recognized as victims of human rights abuses. In this case, it is not subordination that is normalized, but invisibility. When the existence of homosexuality is acknowledged by governments, it is often criminalized or pathologized. The invisibility and/or governmental criminalization of gays (and lesbians) is likely to have profoundly negative effects on the ability to self-identify as survivors, to frame demands, and to claim reparations. In sum, politics plays a primary role in the struggle over reparations. Merit alone does not turn victims into beneficiaries.

Comparative Reparations Research

The comparative approach to reparations not only leads to interesting questions and hypotheses concerning governmental action, but it also highlights an array of complex methodological concerns, some of which need to be addressed here. What factors lead governments to agree to pay reparations?[8] The surge of reparations payments and apologies and the establishment of truth commissions over the last two decades indicate that these are no longer rare and unique cases of human rights violations and that a shift toward a politics of reparations has occurred. Governments are paying more attention, and paying more compensation, to victims of human rights abuses than ever.

But one first has to address the important issue of comparability of cases. Can reparations that are the outcome of varying human rights abuses, which differ in scope and severity, be compared? Landman acknowledges

---

5 Charlotte Bunch, "Transforming Human Rights from a Feminist Perspective," in Julie Peters and Andrea Wolper, eds., *Women's Rights, Human Rights: International Feminist Perspectives* (New York, 1995), 11–17.
6 Catherine MacKinnon, "Crimes of War, Crimes of Peace," *UCLA Women's Law Journal* 4 (1993): 59–86, here 60.
7 Peters and Wolper, *Women's Rights, Human Rights*.
8 A recent overview of the achievements and agendas of comparative historical research is given in James Mahoney and Dietrich Rueschemeyer, *Comparative Historical Analysis in the Social Sciences* (Cambridge, 2003).

that "it is difficult to judge the relative weight of one type of violation over another, thereby committing some form of moral relativism."[9] For example, there has long been a vigorous debate, especially among historians, about the uniqueness of the Holocaust and whether other genocides can be compared to it.[10] In recent years, comparisons are more common, as scholars have gingerly walked a middle ground between describing unique historic events and making larger comparisons that move beyond an individual case.[11] Three of the four cases I discuss do not all fall under the rubric of "genocide," but other studies have also clustered together some of the four cases I present here.[12] Thus, this chapter draws its conclusions from a variety of examples of governmentally sanctioned human rights abuses. The variety of cases sheds light on different mobilizing capacities of claimants in specific political contexts. My temporal focus here is not on when the atrocities occurred, but on the *period following the end of government-guided crime*.

It is the organization of survivors and the resulting governmental reaction that stands at the center of this chapter. First, what factors lead governments to agree to pay reparations? Stammers, along with Foweraker and Landman, have argued that the struggle for human rights through social mobilization needs to be considered in explaining the degrees to which these countries protect rights.[13] More specifically, I argue in this chapter that social movement theory can be applied productively to reparations research. Claimants' organization, victims' identity, and issue-framing play important roles in government decision making regarding redress.[14] Focusing on the specific

---

9 Todd Landman, "Comparative Politics and Human Rights," *Human Rights Quarterly* 24 (2002): 890–923, here 900.
10 Alex Alvarez, *Governments, Citizens, and Genocide: A Comparative and Interdisciplinary Approach* (Bloomington, 2001); Frank Chalk and Kurt Jonassohn, *The History and Sociology of Genocide: Analyses and Case Studies* (New Haven, 1990); Alan Rosenbaum, ed., *Is the Holocaust Unique? Perspectives on Comparative Genocide* (Boulder, 1996); Yehuda Bauer, "Comparison of Genocides," in: Levon Chorbajian and George Shirinian, eds., *Studies in Contemporary Genocide* (New York, 1999); Ernst Nolte, *Der europäische Bürgerkrieg 1917–1945: Nationalsozialismus und Bolschewismus* (Berlin, 1987). For an excellent critique of the impasse between those who argue for the uniqueness of the Holocaust and those who see this argument as reinforcing hegemonic Eurocentrism, see Dirk Moses, "Conceptual Blockages and Definitional Dilemmas in the 'Racial Century': Genocides of Indigenous Peoples and the Holocaust," *Institute for Jewish Policy Research* 36, 4 (2002): 7–36. See also the *Journal of Genocide Research*.
11 Eric Weitz, *A Century of Genocide: Utopias of Race and Nation* (Princeton, 2003); Norman Naimark, *Fires of Hatred: Ethnic Cleansing in Twentieth-Century Europe* (Cambridge, 2001).
12 John Torpey, ed., *Politics of the Past: On Repairing Historical Injustices* (Lanham, Md., 2003).
13 Neil Stammers, "Social Movements and the Social Construction of Human Rights," *Human Rights Quarterly* 21, 4 (1999): 980–1008; Joe Foweraker and Todd Landman, *Citizenship Rights and Social Movements: A Comparative and Statistical Analysis* (Oxford, 1997).
14 A good introduction to the literature on comparative social movements is provided by Doug McAdam, John McCarthy, and Mayer Zald, eds., *Comparative Perspectives on Social Movements: Political*

issue of reparation payments, Brooks underlines that the organization of redress movements, and the pressure that they are able to apply – that is, through politics – is crucial for when and why reparations are paid.[15] Furthermore, he holds that one element of a successful claim is that the "victims themselves must exhibit unquestioned support for the claims being pressed."[16] Internal cohesion and support within the group then becomes an important issue and reflects aspects of social mobilization. As we will see, some claimants' groups have been united and relatively successful when struggling for symbolic or material reparations; others have been silenced, divided, and dismissed for decades.

The second question that must be addressed is the definition of reparations itself. Since World War II, governments have responded in a variety of ways to human rights abuses – prosecution of perpetrators, public apologies to victims, financial compensation and restitution, the establishment of truth commissions, to name a few – and evidence is mounting that governmental attempts to deal with the past have become a global phenomenon. In Barkan's eyes, the quest for reparations marks the emergence of a new international morality.[17] In contrast to restitution, which is limited to the return of lost property and material items, reparations have a broader meaning. The term "reparation" is also something abstract, as opposed to tangible items, and goes beyond the return of goods and property. According to Roy Brooks, reparations also seek atonement, and so apologies are often part of this process.[18] Also, nonmonetary reparations can come in the form of special services to the victims or their communities, such as medical services, affirmative action, or the creation of educational programs. Reparations may also include attempts to make up for the squandered life choices and opportunities of survivors.

It is important to remember that the term "reparation" originally applied exclusively to the interaction between *states*. After wars ended, the victorious side would extract reparations from the losing side to pay for damages. Sometimes payments went beyond compensation for damages and were designed to penalize. The best-known (and perhaps last) of this kind of extensive reparations is reflected in the Treaty of Versailles after World War I. World War II and the Holocaust experience expanded the reach of

---

Opportunities, Mobilizing Structures, and Cultural Framings (Cambridge, 1996). On framing, see David Snow et al., "Frame Alignment Process, Micromobilization and Movement Participation," *American Sociological Review* 51 (1986): 464–81.

15 Roy L. Brooks, "Reflections on Reparations," in Torpey, ed., *Politics of the Past*, 103–14.
16 Brooks, "Reflections on Reparations," 106.
17 Elazar Barkan, *The Guilt of Nations: Restitution and Negotiating Historical Injustices* (New York, 2000).
18 Brooks, "Reflections on Reparations," 107–8.

reparations beyond the level of nation-states to include subnational groups. Expansion of such human rights discourse was furthered by the spread of international law, the establishment of the United Nations, and the Declaration of Human Rights.[19]

Strengthening human rights through international law, and opening the definition of reparations to include subnational groups, has expanded the number of claimants dramatically.[20] This makes the study of reparations even more urgent. Generally, today's debates about reparations steer attention away from the perpetrators to focus on the suffering of the victims, be they groups or individuals. Simultaneously, the end of the twentieth century was witness to an outpouring of demands for reparations. After all, the twentieth century was a time when millions of people previously silenced found a voice: victories over fascism, the demise of Western colonialism, the ousting of Latin American dictatorships, the fall of communism in Eastern Europe, and the end of South African apartheid have all contributed to this change. It is no coincidence that calls for reparations for serious human rights abuses are currently being raised globally. Nonetheless, former governments and perpetrators often deny or suppress the memory of these issues.

One can convincingly argue that there is "perhaps no more contentious an issue in international human rights today than the question of reparations."[21] Cairns understands this recent development positively as a process of "democratizing the past," while Furedi bemoans the spread of a "therapeutic" approach, which allegedly keeps victims welded to the past.[22] Similarly, Torpey has raised concerns about the cultivation of a "consciousness of victimhood," which, in his opinion, stands in the way of a more universalistic vision for the future.[23] I see little danger of this. Rather, I would argue that any coherent vision for the future cannot be achieved by ignoring legitimate human rights concerns. The claims for apologies and reparations need

---

19 Although the rise of human rights as an internationally recognized field of politics, rights, and law is important, this international framework would *not* be able to explain differences among these three states regarding reparations, since they are all UN members. International human rights law does shed light on the emergence of closer legal observations and a global public opinion that seems to pressure all three states into the same direction, i.e., toward the acknowledgment of past human rights abuses.
20 The penetration of national sovereignty also enabled a disciplinary shift from the exclusive study of reparations as a topic of international law and international relations to comparative politics and sociology.
21 Brooks, "Reflections on Reparations," 103.
22 Alan Cairns, "Coming to Terms with the Past," in Torpey, ed., *Politics of the Past*, 63–90. Frank Furedi, "Therapeutic History and the Politics of Recognition," unpublished paper at the conference "Historical Justice in International Perspective," March 27–29, 2003, German Historical Institute, Washington, D.C.
23 John Torpey (Chapter 1) in this volume; John Torpey, *Making Whole What Has Been Smashed: On Reparations and Politics* (Cambridge, Mass., 2006).

to be understood as a source of dialogue, not a "backward-looking" distraction from progressive social change. The "therapeutic" argument, with its alleged cultivation of victimhood, neglects the majority of actual cases and may undermine just claims for reparation. Barkan argues that while a "general reversal of the past is impossible," antagonistic histories should be fused into "a core of shared history to which both sides can subscribe."[24]

In short, a review of the literature on reparations reveals that the increase in reparations claims since World War II has been interpreted in a variety of ways: some see it as a questionable outcome of identity politics, while others underscore the democratizing impulse and effects of reparations politics. I agree with Minow, in that coming to terms with the past is never easy or painless, yet it is undeniably a positive transitional phenomenon.[25]

The framework introduced here distinguishes among *categorical, individual*, and *collective reparations*. Categorical reparations are minimal since they extend only to an abstract category of victims. If survivors are too intimidated to come forward, even though historical documentation demonstrates that these victims exist, they are not known as individuals or collectives to the public, but only as a category of people. The next level of reparations is constituted by individual restitution, rehabilitation, or apologies to survivors. This implies payments to individual victims and/or letters of apology to specific persons. Some victims are also seen as members of groups who may have lost collective property (churches, libraries, etc.), as well as businesses that belonged to a recognizable community. The community would receive reparations for the destruction of these collectively held entities. Other victims do not have, or are not perceived as having, a "community." They would, at most, benefit only from individual claims. I define the payment of monetary reparations (economic reparations), as well as governmental apologies (symbolic reparations), as a "success" in claims for victims of human rights abuse. In addition, I argue that categorical recognition is not sufficient as a meaningful form of reparation. A combination of apologies and material reparations holds the most promise for the claimants in the cases presented here.

The existing literature offers two main frames for understanding the surge in interest in what Jeffrey Olick and Brenda Coughlin have called the "politics of regret."[26] The first frame focuses on the study of human

---

24 Barkan, *The Guilt of Nations*, 329.
25 Martha Minow, *Between Vengeance and Forgiveness: Facing History after Genocide and Mass Violence* (Boston, 1998).
26 Jeffrey K. Olick and Brenda Coughlin, "The Politics of Regret: Analytical Frames," in Torpey, ed., *Politics of the Past*, 37–62.

rights abuses through the concept of transitional justice. Here the focus is on the transition from one regime type (authoritarian/fascist/communist) to another (democracy). The other frame is a philosophical-jurisprudential discussion of universal human rights in an Enlightenment tradition. When we comparatively assess a government's attempts to right the wrongs of the past, the transitional justice frame is useful, particularly when limited to contextually similar cases.

However, the present study expands the traditional definition of "transition" when comparing Japan, Germany, and the United States, since the term "transition" is usually applied to the transition from authoritarian regime to democracy. Although the United States was a democracy during World War II, certain severe restrictions of civil, political, and social rights of some groups existed, especially regarding African Americans and Japanese Americans. So, while the United States did constitute a democratic regime in a narrow constitutional sense, the actual racial apartheid system of the South and the internment of Japanese Americans during World War II indicate serious democratic shortcomings.

My research focuses on a specific set of comparable states, that is, on advanced capitalist states that have been democracies at least since the end of World War II: Germany, Japan, and the United States. The human rights abuses analyzed here all occurred during World War II. Since then these democratic states have been stable, wealthy, and (theoretically) in an economic position to provide symbolic and material reparations.[27] In addition, democracies are characterized by popular consent, governmental accountability, political participation through voting, free media, and the rights to freely assemble, organize, protest, and sue the government. These shared characteristics mean that the issues of symbolic and material reparations can be brought up by various groups and individual claimants, who may do so without a direct threat of retaliation. The fundamental puzzle then is: Why do states that are situated similarly in terms of their economies – advanced capitalist – and political systems – democracies – respond so differently to a variety of human rights abuses? To begin finding an answer to this question, this chapter compares four cases in which governments have faced demands from survivors of mass violence but have reacted differently to these demands.

---

27 Theo von Boven et al. have noted the importance of the availability of resources. African states pay hardly anything for human rights abuse in comparison to Latin American states: Theo von Boven, "Seminar on the Right to Restitution, Compensation and Rehabilitation for Victims of Gross Violations of Human Rights and Fundamental Freedoms: Summary and Conclusion," in Kritz, ed., *Transitional Justice*, 500–50.

The Federal Republic of Germany and Reparations for the Holocaust

The Nazis began implementing anti-Semitic policies immediately after gaining power in 1933. These policies initially aimed at removing German Jews from their professions, seizing their property, and severely curtailing their political, social, and economic rights. Nazi anti-Semitic policies eventually culminated in the planned extermination and mass slaughter of European Jewry in concentration camps, the so-called Final Solution. What kind of restitution and reparations did Jews receive after Germany's defeat by the Allied powers? What role did the social mobilization of the Jewish community and Jewish survivors play in this process and in the process of framing their claims?

Shortly after the outbreak of World War II, German Jewish refugees, in cooperation with international and American Jewish groups, were already working on the formulation of restitution claims.[28] At the pan-American conference of the Jewish World Congress in Baltimore in 1941, three basic arguments about future restitution were put forward:

- Jewish claims should have priority over all other demands on Germany;
- Non-German European Jews should also have access to redress;
- Jewish demands for restitution should be considered as part of the larger issue of reparations.[29]

It was clear to these Jewish organizations that the question of restitution could not be addressed by law alone and that political action would be crucial. Since the full extent of the Holocaust was not yet publicly known, these early claims seemed premature to many.[30] In addition, Jewish identity had so far been a matter of religious, ethnic, and/or cultural affiliation, and reparations for such groups had never been claimed via international politics. In 1943, the former Viennese lawyer Ernest Munz wrote that the collective attack on European Jews necessitated a collective reaction.[31] The development of these claims was also pushed forward by the Zionist argument for establishment of a Jewish homeland. Zionist George Landauer formulated Jewish claims for reparation as *national* claims. This novel framing of the issue reinforced the demand for a Jewish state before the founding

---

28 Constantin Goschler, *Wiedergutmachung, Westdeutschland und die Verfolgten des Nationalsozialismus (1945–1954)* (Munich, 1992).
29 Goschler, *Wiedergutmachung*, 40.   30 Barkan, *Guilt of Nations*, 4.
31 See Ernest Munz, "Restitution in Postwar Europe," *Contemporary Jewish Record* 6, 4 (August 1943): 373, cited by Goschler, *Wiedergutmachung*, 41.

of Israel. Elazar Barkan argues that "[t]his formulation constructed a fundamental connection between all Jews and Zionist ideology, thereby creating a modern identity that had not existed previously."[32] It was the active connection of a religious/ethnic identity to an emerging national identity that powerfully and effectively advanced Jewish claims for reparations.

Immediately after the war, Jewish organizations tried to get the Allies to force German reparation payments to Jewish victims. Securing such payments did not, however, initially rank high among Allied priorities.[33] For example, as Constantin Goschler shows, American policy makers were concerned primarily with the potential costs and social instability that large-scale immigration of European Jews to the United States might cause,[34] and the U.S. government was reluctant to push for high economic reparations lest they undermine Germany's fiscal recovery. At this time, Jewish activities were at best recognized as pressure from subnational groups, that is, groups that so far had little standing in international politics and law. Hence, it is not surprising that Jewish representatives were not invited to the Paris reparations conference in 1945. Only after intense lobbying did they receive unofficial status as observers; their claims were ignored or marginalized as "special considerations."

Restitution is an established aspect of international law. The Allied military occupation governments in Germany supported restitution and, against the wishes of the provisional German regional governments, quickly enacted legislation to return identifiable property to victims of Nazi persecution. The dominant American occupying forces designated the Jewish Restitution Successor Organization (JRSO) as the legal successor to heirless property. Over the years, Jewish efforts to secure broader forms of reparations intensified, although many survivors did not want to receive "blood money" from the German state. The emerging definition of a Nazi victim embraced persons persecuted because of race, religion, or political beliefs. Non-German victims and groups outside that specific definition were to become the "forgotten victims."

An important turn of events occurred in 1949 when, despite deep ideological disagreement and political fragmentation, twenty-two Jewish groups united in the fight for reparations and formed an organization called the Conference of Jewish Material Claims (later known as the Claims Conference).[35] The founding of the Claims Conference marks the emergence

---

32 Barkan, *Guilt of Nations*, 5.   33 Barkan, *Guilt of Nations*, 6.
34 Constantin Goschler (Chapter 4) in this volume. See also Goschler, *Wiedergutmachung*.
35 Ronald Zweig, *German Reparations and the Jewish World: A History of the Claims Conference* (Boulder, 1987).

of a new Jewish identity in response to the Holocaust and, one could argue, in response to the legal requirements of international negotiations for reparations. This umbrella organization enabled diverse Jewish communities to speak with one voice during their negotiations with the newly established Federal Republic of Germany.

Through agreements signed in 1952, assistance was provided to the newly established state of Israel and to Jewish communities throughout the world. The Federal Republic of Germany agreed to give to Israel DM 3 billion compensation to assist in the integration of uprooted and destitute refugees from Germany and the integration of lands formerly under German rule.[36] The FRG also paid DM 450 million to the Claims Conference. These funds were to be used for the relief, rehabilitation, and resettlement of Jewish victims living outside of Israel.

Following these negotiations, different regulations from the various occupied zones were incorporated in the Federal Restitution Law of 1957 (and its amended version in 1964). The "Restitution Law" limited total payments to Jewish survivors to DM 1.5 billion, along with the provision that all claims were to be satisfied up to at least 50 percent of the damage. Reparations were to go to individual survivors or, when none existed, to the Jewish community and a new Jewish state. The 1964 amendment raised the required damage payments to 100 percent and provided a hardship fund of DM 800 million for those survivors who had not filed their application in time.

By July 1971, the combined total payments from the Federal Law for Compensation of the Victims of National Socialist Persecution (BEG), the Federal Restitution Law (AKG), the Luxembourg Agreement with Israel, and other global agreements amounted to DM 40.91 billion. In 1980, after a number of lobbying attempts from victims' organizations, the federal government agreed to create further hardship funds. In October 1980, DM 400 million were transferred to the Claims Conference, and in 1981, DM 100 million were earmarked for non-Jewish victims of persecution.[37] However, as Pross points out, many claims were stymied by the German bureaucracy and dragged on for years, sometimes decades. Further, claims (such as health damage) from German citizens were more often denied than those from abroad. Of 2,841,621 cases closed in September 1965, 361,010 were

---

36 Kurt Schwerin, "German Compensation for Victims of Nazi Persecution," *Northwestern University Law Review* 67 (1972): 489–520, in Kritz, ed., *Transitional Justice*, vol. 2, 47–60.
37 Christian Pross, *Paying for the Past: The Struggle over Reparations for Surviving Victims of the Nazi Terror* (Baltimore, 1998).

decided in court.[38] Many cases were denied and bureaucratic rules often put up barriers for those who could not prove that they had been persecuted. The current total of reparations today is about DM 115 billion (about $60 billion). The Federal Republic continues to pay monthly pensions to Holocaust survivors around the world.

Interestingly, the West German government moved forward somewhat more slowly on the level of symbolic reparations. German public opinion was undoubtedly hostile toward reparations to Jews in the decade after 1945. Germans saw themselves as victims of the war, especially of the Soviet Union, and were reluctant to pay reparations to the Jewish community or to admit guilt for genocide.[39] Nevertheless, anti-Semitism was thoroughly discredited and lost its support among the public. Shortly after the founding of the Federal Republic of Germany, Chancellor Konrad Adenauer insisted that Germans had a responsibility to make amends for the crimes committed under the Nazis, but he also rejected the notion of German collective guilt. In essence, he said that the Federal Republic was prepared to make payments to Israel or international Jewish organizations to fulfill its responsibilities, not to assuage German guilt. Adenauer and his successors also made numerous formal statements of apology in the Bundestag and internationally commemorated the Holocaust and its Jewish victims. But the debate about the involvement and guilt of the "average" German did not start until the 1960s. As a result of the Auschwitz trials in 1964 and the pervasive social and generational changes associated with 1968, public perception in the Federal Republic shifted toward a more sympathetic view of Nazi victims. Since then, the idea and process of *Vergangenheitsbewältigung*, or "coming to terms with the past," has produced a culture of atonement in Germany.[40]

In this case study, the attainment of symbolic and economic reparations was largely an outcome of the successful organization and mobilization of Jewish interests through diasporic networks and the Jewish Claims Conference, which represented the majority of international Jewish groups. The construction of a new *national* identity – in the form of Israel – which fits into the traditional framework of international state-level negotiations, rendered this mobilization even more effective. Through the founding of Israel, the individual-level identity of Jews in Europe (and elsewhere) expanded

---

38 Pross, *Paying for the Past*, 172.
39 Robert Moeller, "War Stories: The Search for a Usable Past in the Federal Republic of Germany," *American Historical Review* 101 (1996): 1008–48. See also Goschler, "Disputed Victims."
40 Especially when compared to Japan; see Ian Buruma, *The Wages of Guilt: Memories of War in Germany and Japan* (New York, 1994).

from a religious/ethnic identity to include a recognizable national identity. This identity included both men and women, so that the issue of gender – to the limited extent that it was relevant – was subsumed by an ethnic/national identity. The construction of this new identity, and the framing of the issue in national terms, had a tremendous impact on the perception and scope of reparations. The Jewish community became visible and relevant as both an ethnicity/religion and a nation. This shift in status gave reparation claims a stronger political standing.

From the outset, the Claims Conference and the newly established Federal Republic of Germany employed a two-pronged approach to reparations: both individuals and the community (Jewish communities in Germany and Israel) would be recipients of reparations. Not only was it understood that Jewish communities existed and suffered, but a new kind of community – a nation-state – was established and became a recipient as well. Opinions vary on West Germany's efforts at restitution for the Holocaust. Kurt Schwerin, for instance, deems West Germany's record in accepting legal and financial responsibility for the Holocaust "a largely favorable one," especially when compared to the records of Austria and the German Democratic Republic, although the destruction of lives and communities can never be undone. Other observers have been more critical.[41]

The Federal Republic of Germany and Male Homosexuals

The Nazis condemned homosexuals as "socially aberrant," and soon after their takeover they banned all male homosexual and lesbian associations, clubs, and publishing houses. They ransacked Magnus Hirschfeld's progressive Institute for Sexual Science and its medical, psychological, and ethnographical departments. Thousands of volumes from its library were destroyed during a massive book-burning in Berlin. Nazi leader Heinrich Himmler created the Reich Central Office for Combating Homosexuality and Abortion, Special Office II S, a subdepartment of the Gestapo, in 1934.[42] The following year, the antihomosexual Paragraph 175 of the Criminal Code, which had been in force since the founding of the German Empire in 1871, was amended to criminalize "lewd and lascivious" behavior more broadly. The police stepped up raids on homosexual meeting places, seized address books, and created networks of informers. Between

---

41 Schwerin, "German Compensation for Victims of Nazi Persecution," 47; Hubert Kim, "German Reparations; Institutionalized Insufficiency," in Roy L. Brooks, ed., *When Sorry Isn't Enough: The Controversy over Apologies and Reparations for Human Injustice* (New York, 1999), 77–80; Pross, *Paying for the Past*.

42 For more details on nationalism, fascism, and sexuality, see George Mosse, *Nationalism and Sexuality, Respectability and Abnormal Sexuality in Modern Europe* (New York, 1985), chap. 8.

1933 and 1945, an estimated 100,000 men were arrested as homosexuals, and some 37,490 were officially defined as homosexuals to be convicted under Paragraph 175. Most of them served their sentences in regular prisons, but between 10,000 and 15,000 were incarcerated in concentration camps.[43] In the camps, some became victims of medical experiments, sterilization, or castration.[44] Sixty percent of the male homosexuals sent to concentration camps died there. Lesbians were not subject to the same systematic persecution as male homosexuals, who were the focus of Paragraph 175. Nevertheless, some lesbians were probably incarcerated as "asocials" or "prostitutes."[45]

One would expect that the law would have been changed after the war and homosexuals recognized as victims of Nazi persecution, thereby opening the way for some form of restitution. However, under the Allied military governments, some homosexuals were forced to serve out their terms of imprisonment. By 1946, the Allies had decided that Paragraph 175, as amended by the Nazis, could remain on the books. This legal continuity was permitted and enforced even though the Allies did not otherwise allow the retention of laws that had increased in severity under the Nazis. After 1949, the Christian Democratic government of the newly founded Federal Republic of Germany defended the retention of Paragraph 175 and the severe criminalization of homosexual activity and relationships with arguments about the "biological differences of the sexes" and the "natural order of life." Paragraph 175 remained unchanged in the Federal Republic of Germany's criminal code until 1969.

Between 1950 and 1969, in the homophobic climate of West Germany, more than 100,000 investigations were conducted in connection with Paragraph 175, and 59,316 gay men were convicted. Neither homosexual individuals nor the vibrant gay community that had existed when Hitler came

---

43 Ilse Kokula, "Schriftliche Stellungnahme zur Anhörung des Innenausschusses des Deutschen Bundestages am 24. Juni 1987," in Deutscher Bundestag, ed., *Wiedergutmachung und Entschädigung für nationalsozialistisches Unrecht* (Bonn, 1987), 325. The assessment of how many homosexuals died due to Nazi persecution varies dramatically. Reliable estimates range from 5,000 to 15,000: see Rüdiger Lautmann, ed., *Seminar Gesellschaft und Homosexualität* (Frankfurt am Main, 1977). James Steakley gives a self-critical assessment about the inflated numbers – between 200,000 and 300,000 – that were picked up from unsubstantiated press releases and then circulated in the gay and mainstream press in the United States. The American gay movement also picked up the use of the pink triangle as a symbol of the movement and often equated the fate of homosexuals under National Socialism to that of the Jews. James Steakley, "Selbstkritische Gedanken zur Mythologisierung der Homosexuellenverfolgung im Dritten Reich," in Burkhard Jellonek and Rüdiger Lautmann, eds., *Nationalsozialistischer Terror gegen Homosexuelle, Verdrängt und ungesühnt* (Paderborn, 2002), 55–68.
44 Deutscher Bundestag, 14. Wahlperiode, Drucksache 14/2619, *Unrechtserklärung der nationalsozialistischen Paragraphen 175 and 175a Nr. 4 Reichsstrafgesetzbuch sowie Rehabilitierung und Entschädigung für die schwulen und lesbischen Opfer des NS-Regimes*, 27.01.2000, 1–8.
45 Claudia Schoppmann, *Nationalsozialistische Sexualpolitik und weibliche Homosexualität* (Pfaffenweiler, 1991).

to power was recognized as having been "persecuted" in the legal sense during the Nazi era.[46] Because of this lack of recognition and continued criminalization, homosexuals were not included in the aforementioned BEG. In this threatening political and social climate, the great majority of homosexuals who were entitled to compensation under the 1957 Federal Restitution Law (Allgemeines Kriegsfolgengesetz, or AKG) avoided the risk of further persecution and did not seek compensation. By December 31, 1959, the general deadline for compensation claims, only fourteen gay men had dared to disclose their pasts and their sexual orientation in petitioning the government for reparations.[47] The invisibility and criminalization of homosexuality in postwar West Germany contributed to the inability of homosexual survivors of Nazi persecution to claim victim status and organize effectively. These are the main reasons why some scholars address the potential claimants as the "forgotten victims" and argue the existence of a "hidden holocaust."[48]

When the Social Democratic–Free Democratic coalition government took office in 1969, Paragraph 175 was revised. It was revised again in 1973 to decriminalize homosexual acts between men over the age of eighteen. This reform was not, however, accompanied by any sort of apology or reparations initiative to the homosexual victims of Nazi persecution. Only four gay men in Germany currently receive regular payments from the Federal Restitution Law Hardship Fund, and sixteen survivors received a onetime payment of DM 5,000. No homosexuals receive payments from the more generous fund established by the BEG for victims of the National Socialist regime.

Why did gay men fare so badly in the Federal Republic despite willingness of the state to pay restitution for the Nazis' other human rights abuses? I argue that the invisibility of the victims and the absence of any corresponding social pressure and network explain much of the disparity between the experiences of homosexuals and other victim groups. The Allied occupation authorities did nothing to support homosexuals' claims, and the new republic was able to get away with continued use of the identical law the

---

[46] As an example, see Rainer Hoffschildt, "'Nach der Befreiung wieder in Haft,' Der bündische Widerstandskämpfer Paul Hahn," in Joachim Müller and Andreas Sternweiler, eds., *Homosexuelle Männer im KZ Sachsehausen* (Berlin, 2000), 354–8. See also Susanne zur Nieden, "... als Opfer des Faschismus' nicht tragbar.' Ausgrenzung verfolgter Homosexueller in Berlin 1945–1949," in KZ-Gedenkstätte Neuengamme, ed., *Verfolgung Homosexueller im Nationalsozialismus: Beiträge zur Geschichte der nationalsozialistischen Verfolgung in Norddeutschland,* vol. 5 (Bremen, 1999), 93–103.

[47] *Antrag auf Unrechtserklärung der nationalsozialistischen Paragraphen 175 und 175a Nr. 4 Reichsstrafgesetzbuch sowie Rehabilitierung und Entschädigung für die schwulen und lesbischen Opfer des NS-Regimes, Deutscher Bundestag,* 14/2619, 27.01.2000, 1–7.

[48] Günter Grau, ed., *Hidden Holocaust? Gay and Lesbian Persecution in Germany 1933–45* (Chicago, 1995).

Nazis had used to criminalize homosexuality. Understandably, most gay men were afraid to speak up as individuals. Only in the late 1960s and early 1970s, when a modern gay social movement emerged in West Germany (as in other Western states), did the continued silencing, criminalization, and prosecution of gay citizens finally come under widespread criticism.

The dominant legal position from the postwar years into the 1980s was that gay men, although targeted for persecution by the Nazis, had been imprisoned or sent to concentration camps to maintain "order" and "security."[49] Gay victims of National Socialism certainly did not enjoy political support in either West or East Germany. Under these circumstances, the development of a common and cohesive identity was hampered because their own maintenance of invisibility functioned to protect homosexuals from continued state repression. This made social and political organizing and positive framing of the demands difficult, thus limiting public claims for reparations in fundamental ways.

In 1985, homosexuals were openly named for the first time as victims of National Socialism by West German President Richard von Weizsäcker in a famous speech commemorating the fortieth anniversary of the end of World War II. An official apology from then-Chancellor Helmut Kohl was not, however, forthcoming. In 1994, and again in 1996, Kohl's conservative government put forward a position that the incarceration of gay men had not been a typical Nazi injustice or "*rechtsstaatswidrig*" (contrary to the rule of law). However, Paragraph 175 was at last abolished on June 11, 1994. When the Social Democrats and Greens formed a more progressive government in 1996, important changes followed. On December 7, 2000, the Bundestag officially apologized to the homosexual victims of the Nazi regime and annulled their convictions.[50] The Bundestag also apologized for the fact that until 1969 the laws of the Federal Republic of Germany supported the continued harassment and criminalization of homosexuals.

Despite this progress, the men who were imprisoned under the Nazis on account of their sexuality have not received financial compensation as victims of Nazi persecution. This is due to the legal assessment that prosecution of homosexuals was legal under criminal law. Also, the eradication of

---

49 Hans Giessler, "Die Grundsatzbestimmungen des Entschädigungsrechts," in Bundesminister der Finanzen in Zusammenarbeit mit Walter Schwarz, eds., *Das Bundesentschädigungsgesetz, Teil 1*, Die Wiedergutmachung nationalsozialistischen Unrechts durch die Bundesrepublik Deutschland, Bd. 4 (Munich, 1981), 1–116; see specifically 13–14.
50 A debate over other forms of symbolic reparations, such as memorials commemorating the persecution of homosexuals, has been ongoing since the 1980s. An excellent introduction and overview of this debate can be found in: Heinrich-Böll Stiftung, ed., *Der homosexuellen NS-Opfer gedenken* (Berlintung, 1999).

gay and lesbian publishing houses, stores, restaurants, and infrastructure, as well as the destruction of all content of the Institute for Sexual Science, has not been addressed in terms of compensation, because the existence of a gay "community" prior to 1933 is still not acknowledged. The state's refusal to see the gay community as a "real" community has limited the claims of victims to an individual level, a level where these claims have been – despite a handful of payments – overwhelmingly unsuccessful.

Japan and the Sexual Slavery of "Comfort Women"

The importance of politics as an explanation for the extent, timing, and content of reparations becomes very clear in the case of sexual slavery in territories under Japanese rule during World War II. Here it is especially significant that initial claims were brought forward by neither individuals nor a community – the result is that victims have existed to a large extent only as an abstract category of people. Despite a number of early publications on the issue of the "sexual comfort facilities" – that is, military brothels – and the women survivors forced to work in them, it was not until the early 1990s that a handful of women were willing to come forward and publicly discuss their wartime servitude.[51] Without identifiable survivors, the formulation of common claims and the organization of a social movement were considerably delayed. In addition, the process of redress ran up against legal and political hurdles. A male-centered definition of human rights, the dynamics of sexism, and the use of international agreements against female survivors are all factors explaining why the Japanese government has rejected claims for reparations and calls for an apology. However, as Margaret Stetz argues, the supporters of the "comfort women" have been tremendously successful in the "court of public opinion."[52]

During World War II, the Japanese army ran an extensive system of military brothels in Japan's colonies and occupied territories. The exact number of women coerced into sexual labor, or sexual slavery, is not known. Estimates range from 50,000 to 400,000, and recent studies suggest the latter figure is more likely.[53] It is estimated that 80 percent of the women were

---

51 See the early literature on the issue listed in Barkan, *Guilt of Nations*, 51–3, and George Hicks, "The Comfort Women Redress Movement," in Brooks, ed., *When Sorry Isn't Enough*, 113–25.
52 Margaret Stetz, "Representing 'Comfort Women': Activism Through Law and Art," *Iris* 45 (Fall 2002): 26. Stetz also sees overlap between the cases of recent legal and political victories of Holocaust survivors, specifically the slave laborers employed by German firms, and the applicability of such cases to the sexual slavery of women.
53 Chunghee Soh, "Human Rights and the 'Comfort Women,'" *Peace Review* 12, 1 (2000): 123–9. These numbers exclude the brothels in China because China has not reported most of them. In

Korean, and although not all were forcibly drafted (Korean collaboration existed), most were. Only about a third of the comfort women are believed to have survived.[54]

After its defeat, Japan neither apologized nor provided material reparations to the surviving comfort women. The fact that the Japanese government was directly complicit in a system of forced sexual slavery was generally denied by the government and ignored by the public, although the existence of the military brothels had been documented in a number of publications.[55] As late as December 2003, it was still regarded as news that the Japanese military ran sex-slave brothels.[56]

It took more than a generation for individual former sex slaves to break the silence and rouse public interest. In 1988, around the time of the Seoul Olympic games, Asian women's groups brought the issue to international attention. There were many individuals and organizations behind this activism, including Professor Yun Chong-ok and the South Korean Church Women's Alliance. The issue of reparations was framed within the rhetorical and organizational context of the movement opposing "sex tourism" in Asia. In 1990, the Korean Comfort Women Problem Resolution Council was formed. Subsequently, women's organizations in both South Korea and Japan demanded that the two governments investigate the issue and compensate victims. That same year, the issue of the forced recruitment of comfort women during the war was brought forward in the Japanese political arena by a Socialist senator in the Japanese Diet, Motooka Shoji.

One year later, Korean survivors filed a class-action suit against the Japanese government. Suits filed by Filipino and Chinese women followed in 1993 and 1995. Like the Japanese government, Japanese courts have refused to recognize Japan's legal responsibility for this human rights violation. The only exception occurred in 1998, when a court ruled in favor of three survivors. That ruling was, however, overturned on appeal in March 2001, on the grounds that "no constitutional violations occurred."[57]

In an attempt to answer demands for compensation and respond to growing international pressure, Japan set up the privately funded Asian Women's Fund (AWF) in 1995. Payments to surviving sexual slaves from this fund were accompanied by a personal letter of apology from Prime Minister

---

Shanghai alone, there were 90 sex-slave brothels, with about 500 women at each location; see the report in *San Francisco Chronicle*, December 7, 2003.
54 Soh, "Human Rights and the 'Comfort Women,'" 124.
55 See the literature cited in Barkan, *Guilt of Nations*, 51–3, and George Hicks, "The Comfort Women Redress Movement," in Brooks, ed., *When Sorry Isn't Enough*, 113–25.
56 *San Francisco Chronicle*, December 7, 2003, A 19, Connie Kang.
57 "Japan: Wartime Brothel Case," in "World Briefing," *New York Times*, March 30, 2001.

Miyazawa Kiichi. The fund, dependent entirely on private donations, was intended rather generally "to address contemporary issues regarding the honor and dignity of women."[58] It was not a government-financed effort, nor did it acknowledge past atrocities. Because of these conspicuous omissions, the creation of the fund did not imply admission of guilt by the Japanese government or constitute a formal apology. The comfort women's movement, human rights activists, and Korean nationalists have understood both the extremely vague language and the private nature of the fund as Japan's evasion of legal responsibility and lack of true atonement. As a result of the controversy, only eighty women, most of them Filipina, have received compensation.

It is noteworthy that some women's movement leaders, as well as the governments of South Korea, Taiwan, and Indonesia, have taken the position that claimants should not accept any payments from Japan. To nationalists in these states, national pride stands in the way of compensation to individuals, as Soh convincingly argues.[59] The nationalist position in formerly occupied states prevents recognizing the wishes of the majority of claimants and interrupts the compensation process for those individual women who wish to receive these funds.

Considering the extent of the human rights abuse of this case, one has to wonder why the issue first emerged in the 1990s rather than during the immediate postwar period, when between 17,000 and 65,000 of the comfort women were still alive. Furthermore, one has to ask why the women themselves articulated demands and organized for redress as late as the 1980s and early 1990s (i.e., nearly two generations after the actual human rights abuse occurred). I would argue that the main obstacle to organized demands from survivors has to do with the invisibility of rape as a human rights abuse, the lack of social bonds among the victims, and the related difficulty of creating a sense of shared identity among the claimants. In a traditional patriarchal society, shame is often attached to the victims, not the perpetrators, of rape. To identify with a group of rape victims means association with disgrace, dishonor, and guilt. In addition, the majority of these sex slaves were not Japanese citizens, so their claims could be easily ignored in domestic Japanese politics.

However, the claimants were also ignored at the international level. While international laws and regulations on restitution and reparations apply to states and, since Nuremberg, to individuals for "crimes against humanity,"

---

58 You-me Park, "Comforting the Nation: 'Comfort Women,' the Politics of Apology and the Workings of Gender," *Interventions* 2, 2 (2000): 199–211.
59 Soh, "Human Rights and the 'Comfort Women.'"

mass rape was not seen as an international crime, but rather as a side-effect of war. Only after the wars that accompanied the disintegration of Yugoslavia in the 1990s has mass rape become a crime against humanity under international law. Ignoring the treatment of comfort women as a form of mass rape, South Korea accepted a lump sum as reparation in 1965. For the Japanese government, the matter has been closed since.

While one would assume it is generally easier to demand reparations after a rights-abusing regime loses a war, as the victors may dictate some of the new rules, this does not seem to have been the case with Japan, or at least not to the same extent as with Germany. Thus, the organization of victims is crucial to understanding why, how, and when democratic governments apologize and pay reparations. Claimants have to overcome considerable hurdles of social judgment and psychological/social isolation, and they are faced with the political, organizational, and financial difficulties of building an international social network or movement.

The process of dealing with the past has been severely hampered in Japan by what Ian Buruma has described as "historical amnesia."[60] Much like the Germans immediately after the war, the Japanese have primarily thought of themselves as victims. Of central importance to this perception in Japan are the American atomic attacks on Hiroshima and Nagasaki. The key difference is that most Germans soon stopped thinking of themselves as victims, but the Japanese have largely retained this perspective. The perception of victimization by the United States still crowds out the horrors of Nanking and the comfort women. South Korean nationalists point to Korean suffering under Japanese colonial rule and deny Korean collaboration in providing comfort women for the Japanese military brothels. They stand in the way of the Korean women who are willing to accept private donations from Japan, calling them "traitors."[61] As an alternative to the private payments from Japan, the South Korean government has started to pay small sums of money to female citizens who have officially registered as comfort women. The wishes of isolated individual claimants, however, took a backseat to national politicking.

The United States and the Internment of Japanese Americans

Imperial Japan's attack on Pearl Harbor in 1941 triggered the entry of the United States into World War II and, in turn, the roundup and incarceration

---

60 Buruma, *The Wages of Guilt*.
61 Sarah Soh, "Gender, Class, Nation: Korean Comfort Women," paper presented at San Francisco State University, March 9, 2005.

of Japanese Americans. Shortly after the attack, President Franklin Roosevelt issued Executive Order 9066, directing the removal of all persons of Japanese ancestry from "military areas," which were broadly defined as the coastal Western states. Some 120,000 Japanese Americans, two-thirds of whom were American citizens by birth, were forcibly removed from their homes in California, Oregon, and Washington and moved inland to internment camps.[62] The FBI and Office of Naval Intelligence argued that all persons of Japanese ancestry posed special dangers of espionage and sabotage and had to be removed and incarcerated in remote areas where they could not aid the enemy.[63] While the United States was constitutionally a democracy at this time, the country's entry into war brought about the curtailment of civil and political rights of minorities perceived as "enemy aliens."

Before their removal to internment camps, Japanese-American families tried to quickly sell their houses, businesses, and other property. Unsurprisingly, they typically received much less than actual value for their property, and many families were economically ruined. These Japanese Americans also suffered psychologically – their self-esteem was shattered, and their families were torn apart.[64] Mitchell Maki argues that "exclusion and incarceration were blatant violations of human rights, civil rights and the spirit of the Constitution."[65] In 1949, it was estimated that internees suffered property and income losses totaling between $77 million and $400 million.[66] After the war, the U.S. government agreed to minor compensation, paying about ten cents for every dollar in property lost. Between 1949 and 1950, only 232 of 26,000 claims filed were adjudicated.

After the war, the internment was publicly addressed by neither the victims nor the American government. However, one generation after the internment, the Japanese American Citizens League (JACL), the leading lobbying organization for Japanese Americans, began to draw attention to this forgotten chapter of American history.[67] The campaign for redress began

---

62 Leslie T. Hatamiya, *Righting a Wrong: Japanese Americans and the Passage of the Civil Liberties Act of 1988* (Stanford, 1993).
63 The places where Japanese Americans were moved were called "relocation centers" or "internment camps" by the government; some scholars call them "concentration camps." In the following section, I use the term "internment camp," even though the centers were surrounded by barbed wire, watch towers, and armed guards. However, they were not death camps, as the term "concentration camp" implies.
64 Mitchell T. Maki et al., *Achieving the Impossible Dream: How Japanese Americans Obtained Redress* (Urbana, 1999).
65 Maki, *Achieving the Impossible Dream*, 45.
66 Wendy L. Ng, *Japanese American Internment During World War II: A History and Reference Guide* (Westport, 2002). 100.
67 William Hohri, *Repairing America: An Account of the Movement for Japanese American Redress* (Pullman, 1984).

in 1970 and slowly gathered support among the Japanese-American community. In 1970, the JACL called for a convention to establish the National Committee on Redress, where the committee argued for a $25,000 reparation payment per person. Two years later, President Gerald Ford made the first formal apology for the internment in a bicentennial-year executive order, and he officially revoked Executive Order 9066. However, not all Japanese Americans supported this increased attention to the wartime violation of their civil liberties, and many feared a backlash of increased anti-Japanese sentiment at a time when Japanese economic success was widely perceived as a threat to many American industries.

The turning point for the Japanese-American redress movement came in 1978, when the JACL issued a statement that drew a parallel between the experience of Japanese Americans during the war and the Nazis' genocide of European Jews. The association between the Holocaust and Japanese-American internment made the internment seem less a precautionary measure and more a case of injustice and general human rights abuse.[68] In 1981, the Commission on Wartime Relocation and Internment of Civilians, established by Congress to review past policies and to recommend remedies, held twenty days of Senate hearings. The Senate hearings are credited with bringing widespread attention to the American internment policy. In addition, legal action was taken in 1987 in a class-action suit filed by the more vocal National Council for Japanese American Redress, which demanded $27 billion on behalf of 120,000 victims. The suit was rejected on procedural grounds, but the public mood had shifted, and the previous internment was increasingly perceived as illegal. It is important for the outcome of social mobilization that members of the affected group were by this time serving in the U.S. Congress: Senators Daniel Inouye and Spark Matsunaga and Congressmen Norman Mineta and Robert Matsui – the latter two had been evacuated and interned as children. Having committed allies and supporters in the political elite gives social movements access to power and can tip the balance in their favor. As Leslie Hatamiya observes for this case, "it is not far-fetched to say that redress would not have succeeded, or at least not when it did, without their leadership."[69]

Gradually, the public came to see restitution as doing justice to Japanese Americans as American citizens. Political opposition to reparations by veterans groups waned. In 1988, President Ronald Reagan signed the Civil Liberties Act, which provided for individual redress payments of $20,000 to each individual, and recipients also received a letter of apology from

---

68 Barkan, *Guilt of Nations*, 35.   69 Hatamyia, *Righting a Wrong*, 110.

Reagan's successor, President George H. W. Bush. In all, 82,219 people received the full sum.[70] Although the payments were less than what it had initially sought, the JACL welcomed the compensation, as the official acknowledgment of injustice done to Japanese Americans was more important than the specific sum of the payments.[71]

The case of interned Japanese Americans illustrates several things. First, democracies are not immune to severe human rights violations; human rights can be undermined in all governmental systems. Second, even in established democracies it takes time for survivors to identify themselves as victims and to organize on the basis of that identity and their shared experience. It also takes time for democratic governments to revoke unjust laws and regulations. Third, this case again illustrates that ethnic identity can come to be understood as a *national* cause that may support the claims of victims. Interestingly, the Japanese-American case is one of political *inclusion*, because they finally came to be perceived as *American* citizens who were treated unjustly. Their cause became a general rallying point for fairness with the help of elected elite advocates, indicating how the initially supported removal and internment of this population has been totally reframed over time. Once the issue was framed in terms of fairness for Americans and the public had accepted Japanese Americans as fellow Americans, opposition waned. Strong community support for reparations and favorable political factors, such as successful framing through the comparison to the Holocaust and support in Congress, brought about the success of the Japanese-American redress campaign.

Comparing Governmental Responses to Reparations Claims

This chapter demonstrates, first, that the international comparison of governmental responses to reparations claims can produce politically and theoretically relevant hypotheses, and, second, that social movement theories can be productively applied to the analysis of reparations. I have focused on a variety of carefully chosen cases with contextually relevant similarities to ask why three democratic nations have responded so differently to reparation claims. My finding indicates that we are witnessing the "politics of reparations," driven to a large extent by political opportunities and social mobilization.

---

70 Maki, *Achieving the Impossible Dream*, 225.
71 Roger Daniels, "Japanese Relocation and Redress in North America: A Comparative View," *The Pacific Historian* (1991), reprinted in Charles McClain, ed., *The Mass Internment of Japanese Americans and the Quest for Legal Redress* (New York, 1994), vol. 3, 376–87, quotation on 386.

The cases presented here also suggest a notable bifurcation between reparation claims based on ethnicity/nationality and claims based on gender/sexuality. The comparison of these cases shows that if claims based on ethnic identity can be framed in terms of the assumed characteristics of the dominant national identity or attached to a project of nation-building, they are likely to be more successful.[72] Importantly, claims based on ethnicity can be recognized as "community" claims, while that is unlikely on account of gender or sexuality.[73] If the findings of this project were to be corroborated by additional cases in the future, the result for scholarship on reparations and redress would be significant.

Human rights abuses against women are less visible than those against ethnic minorities or political groups and often do not fit into male-defined categories of violence. Rape is a common and individual-level occurrence that is socially normalized.[74] Institutionally organized rape is hard to prove, as the continued denials of the Japanese government and recent cases in the Balkans, Sudan, and Congo show. The guilt and shame attached to rape so silenced the former comfort women that they were initially known only as a category of victims, not as individuals who had endured violent sexual abuse. And as Simone de Beauvoir has shown, women do not form a common identity based on their gender *as women* but understand themselves as members of the different religious, ethnic, and social groups to which they belong.[75] Identification with these other categories keeps women separated from each other, even if they suffer the same gender-based atrocities and have similar interests in protecting themselves or seeking reparations as women. Women do not form communities in the same way ethnic groups do, and hence they do not receive community-level reparations.

The unequal treatment of two different victim groups in Germany reflects two facts. First, "there has never been an all-comprising identity of Nazi victims," and as a result different groups have been treated differently.[76] Thus, the diversity and categorization of victims by the Nazis showed its

---

72 "Success" is defined here as timely acknowledgment of the injustice they suffered and governmental willingness to undertake material and symbolic reparations.

73 Not all ethnic groups can frame their claims in national terms, as the example of the Sinti and Roma shows. An independent nation-state of Sinti and Roma is not an option, nor have these minorities been fully accepted and integrated into the states in which they live. It follows that those ethnic groups who cannot reframe their experience and who rely on resources or elite support to link up their concerns to the larger national community, will probably be much less successful in their claims.

74 One of the earliest and most influential analyses of rape as an integral part of patriarchal culture is Susan Brownmiller, *Against Our Will: Men, Women, and Rape* (New York, 1975).

75 Simone de Beauvoir, *The Second Sex* (New York, 1952).

76 Goschler, "Disputed Victims."

dark legacy for decades afterwards. Second, the German examples also support the argument that the victims' identity and social mobilization play important roles in symbolic and material reparations. The case of the German homosexual men illustrates that victims were unable to make claims under a democratic system because of invisibility and/or continued criminalization – this is not true for German Jews. In addition, when no victim collectivity exists, the former regimes may, even if they lose the war, "get away with murder."

Although it seems an obvious point to make, it is still worth noting that in the conflict over reparations, publicly recognized, better organized, more broadly financed, and internationally supported movements and networks for redress are more successful at pressuring governments than are groups of survivors who cannot safely address their suffering within their societal or political environment. The Korean case also illuminates how justified demands for reparations can be hijacked by nationalist sentiments and become functionalized by influential opponents of redress. The ability of perpetrators to get away with murder sheds light on the weakness of demands that are meritorious but politically ineffective.

The designation of these groups as "forgotten victims" is a misnomer. The claims of women and homosexuals were not "forgotten"; rather, they were pushed aside and silenced by governments. Victims of former regimes are not encouraged to come forward so that others remember what happened to them; in fact, in some cases they are actively discouraged from doing so.

It is worthwhile to note how the ethnic/national framing of the reparations issue has profoundly differed in two of the cases presented here: Japanese Americans have experienced *incorporation* into the larger society of the nation-state and have received reparations as American citizens who were treated unjustly. In the case of genocide against German and European Jewry, ethnic identity has played out very differently, with many of the survivors becoming part of a new nation-state, Israel. In this case, a profound *separation* between perpetrators and victims has taken place. This separation was hastened by the scope and severity of the mass murder and the consequential strengthening of Zionism after World War II. In contrast, the United States has been able to successfully integrate the victims of human rights abuses it committed. Germany, on the other hand, has lost this cause due to the gravity and extent of the atrocities, as well as the desire and opportunity of survivors and other supporters to form a new nation. It would be worthwhile to investigate how incorporation versus separation affects the symbolic acknowledgment of past atrocities, material reparations, and the national identity of claimants and perpetrators.

Table 2.1

Frame	Symbolic Reparations	Economic Reparations
Categorical	Homosexuals (1985)	
Individual	German Jews (1952)	German and non-German Jews
	Japanese Americans (1972)	(1952 until today)
	Comfort women (1990)	Japanese Americans (1988)
	Homosexuals (2000)	
Community	German Jewish communities (ongoing)	German Jewish communities (ongoing)
	Israel (1952)	Israel (1952)

Two of the countries in this case study were among the losers of World War II, the other was among the victors. The two defeated regimes were supplanted by new democratic systems. Importantly – and counterintuitively – one cannot simply conclude that a defeated state will be more inclined to make amends to victims of human rights abuse. As shown by the Japan and Germany cases, victory or loss (i.e., the question of regime change) seems to have much less of an impact on the extent and timing of reparations for individuals and communities than the social mobilization of claimants and the framing of issues.

My findings are summarized in Table 2.1, which distinguishes between symbolic reparations (e.g., governmental apologies), economic reparations (e.g., restitution, pensions), and claimant type (categorical, individual, community).

Issues of identity, framing, and resources for mobilization loom large in explanations of why some groups receive reparations shortly after the rights violation occurred and others only long after, if ever. In the cases presented here, the form of reparation found most often exists at the intersection of *symbolic* reparations and *individual* claimants. That cases are crowded together in this quadrant indicate that in democracies victims are usually able to move from an abstract category of people to the level of individual claimant. However, it also reminds us that for a variety of reasons governments will attempt to resist perceiving claimants as parts of communities, and as a result they may construct or sustain a hierarchy among survivors.

PART II

Reparations and Restitution

3

Historical Continuity and Counterfactual History in the Debate over Reparations for Slavery

MANFRED BERG

The breakdown of dictatorships and the growing respect for human rights at the end of the twentieth century have given rise to a broad international debate on how to deal with historical injustices. All over the world societies have shown a new willingness to face the painful legacies of their pasts and to address the suffering of victims through material compensation and symbolic recognition. In his book *The Guilt of Nations: Restitution and Negotiating Historical Injustices*, Elazar Barkan has noted that in the post–Cold War era the admission of guilt seems to have become "a new threshold of morality in international politics." Although the mass violence of the twentieth century takes center stage in restitution politics, demands for historical justice also include reparations for the enslavement of millions of Africans and the legacies of Western colonialism.[1]

It is therefore no coincidence that the issue of reparations for 250 years of racial slavery has resurfaced in the United States. This demand, to be sure, is an old one that can be traced back as far as the antebellum abolitionists. Indeed, at the end of the Civil War, the emancipated slaves were given reason to believe that they would receive at least some compensation for their many years of unremunerated toil when Union General William T. Sherman issued his famous Special Field Order No. 15 of January 1865.

---

[1] Elazar Barkan, *The Guilt of Nations: Restitution and Negotiating Historical Injustices* (New York, 2000), xviii; also see John Torpey, ed., *Politics and the Past: On Repairing Historical Injustices* (Lanham, Md., 2003); John Torpey, "'Making Whole What Has Been Smashed': Reflections on Reparations," *Journal of Modern History* 73 (2001): 333–58. For a systematic inquiry into differing approaches to historical justice, see Martha Minow, *Between Vengeance and Forgiveness: Facing History after Genocide and Mass Violence* (Boston, 1998). Roy L. Brooks, ed., *When Sorry Isn't Enough: The Controversy over Apologies and Reparations for Human Injustice* (New York, 1999), is a useful documentation of various important cases.

In this decree, Sherman set apart a large tract of abandoned lands along the coasts of South Carolina, Georgia, and Florida for the settlement of liberated slaves and allotted a plot of forty acres to each family. Later he also provided for the loan of mules and horses to the settlers. By June 1865, about 40,000 blacks had taken advantage of Sherman's order and occupied a total of 400,000 acres. However, a few months later, President Andrew Johnson, seeking reconciliation with the defeated South, ordered the restoration of the lands to their former owners. When many of the freedmen resisted eviction, the U.S. Army forcibly removed them.[2]

Many historians consider the failure to enact a land reform in favor of the freedmen as the crucial tragedy of Reconstruction. Unable to establish economic independence, the vast majority of freedmen were forced into a system of sharecropping and tenancy that came close to a new form of bondage. Once the former slaveholders thus regained power, the civil and political rights guaranteed the freedmen by the new constitutional amendments were rendered a dead letter. It is true that small landownership would hardly have created a solid economic base for blacks in the post-Reconstruction South. Nevertheless, the freedmen firmly believed in their right to the land they had worked as slaves, and they were deeply imbued with the American ideal of the self-reliant yeoman farmer. Hence, for generations of African Americans, the famous phrase "forty acres and a mule" became an expression of their disappointed hopes and a rallying cry for historical justice among their descendants to this day.[3]

In the late 1960s, activists of the Black Power movement renewed the quest for historical justice, demanding "reparations due us as people who have been exploited and degraded, brutalized, killed and persecuted." Two decades later, their cause gained new momentum when Congress issued an apology for the internment of Japanese Americans during World War II and paid roughly $1.6 billion in indemnification to the survivors or the immediate heirs of the internees. The most important impulse for the recent reparation debate, however, came from the campaign to compensate the surviving forced laborers of the Nazi regime. That the U.S. media usually referred to them as "slave laborers" offered a welcome discursive link to the issue of black reparations. Moreover, reparation activists have been inspired by the successful strategy of the "German slave labor" lawyers

---

2 See "Special Field Order No. 15," in Brooks, *When Sorry Isn't Enough*, 365–6; Claude F. Oubre, *Forty Acres and a Mule: The Freedmen's Bureau and Black Land Ownership* (Baton Rouge, 1978), 18–20, 46–71; Eric Foner, *Reconstruction: America's Unfinished Revolution* (New York, 1988), 70–2.
3 On the failure of land reform and black attitudes toward landownership, see Foner, *Reconstruction*, 102–10, 153–70; Oubre, *Forty Acres and a Mule*, 181–98, passim.

who threatened German companies with protracted billion-dollar lawsuits in order to obtain a large settlement. For many Germans, it may come as a surprise to learn that leading African-American reparation advocates have frequently hailed Germany's compensation of Nazi victims as a model.[4]

In March 2002, Ed Fagan, one of America's best-known and most controversial class-action lawyers, filed suit on behalf of several black plaintiffs against the insurance company Aetna and seven other U.S. corporations. Two years earlier, Aetna, whose history goes back to the antebellum period, had publicly apologized for having profited from slavery by insuring the lives of slaves as property. Fagan announced litigation against up to one hundred firms, involving claims for damages "in the trillions of dollars." This would hopefully make "the defendants see the wisdom of acceding to what are reasonable demands." At the same time, a group of reparation activists and African-American intellectuals, including legal scholar Charles Ogletree and black studies professor Cornel West, teamed up with high-powered class-action lawyers to prepare a lawsuit against the U.S. government. Its antebellum predecessors, they charge, had been responsible for enforcing the laws of slavery and thus participated in "a crime against humanity" for which the present government should be held liable.[5]

Most legal experts, however, are rather skeptical as to the merits and prospects of such lawsuits. The doctrine of governmental sovereign immunity, the statute of limitations, standing in court, and privity between plaintiffs and defendants are but the most important legal barriers that the reparation claimants face. As a matter of fact, several lawsuits brought by the descendants of former slaves in the early 1990s were dismissed in federal court for exactly these reasons. In late 2000, *Harper's Magazine* asked four of the most experienced and successful class-action lawyers in America to ponder possible strategies for reparation litigation. Remarkably, even these seasoned and sympathetic practitioners found it hard to devise a convincing legal theory to circumvent the statute of limitations. After all, as one of

---

4 See the famous "Black Manifesto" of 1968 by James Forman, in Boris I. Bittker, *The Case for Black Reparations* (New York, 1973), 167–75, quote on 168. On the apology to the Japanese-American internees, see Barkan, *The Guilt of Nations*, 30–45; for praise of German *Wiedergutmachung* by reparation advocates, see Bittker, *The Case for Black Reparations*, 177–91; Randall Robinson, *The Debt: What America Owes to Blacks* (New York, 2000), 204, 221–4; Roy L. Brooks, *Atonement and Forgiveness: A New Model for Black Reparations* (Berkeley, 2004), xv.

5 Kevin Canfield, "Lawsuit Puts a Price on Slavery: Complaint to Name Aetna and Other U.S. Companies," *Hartford Courant*, March 26, 2002, http://new.blackvoices.com/news/bv-slavery 020326.story (July 2, 2002); Deborah King, "Recent Lawsuits Just the Beginning of Larger Legal Effort to Seek Reparations for Slavery," Associated Press, April 4, 2002, http://www.homestead.com/ wysinger/reparations.html (July 2, 2002). See the plaintiffs' brief in *Farmer-Paellmann v. FleetBoston, Aetna Inc., CSX*, in Raymond A. Winbush, ed., *Should America Pay? Slavery and the Raging Debate on Reparations* (New York, 2003), 348–60.

them conceded, a strong liability suit first and foremost requires two things: "living victims and a quantifiable economic case." Still, with U.S. liability law and juries becoming ever more unpredictable, the future prospects of reparations suits cannot be dismissed completely. As in the "German slave cases," the defendant companies might prefer to settle.[6]

Even if reparation advocates insist on the legal merits of their cause, most of them will admit that the battle in the court of public opinion is probably more important. Reparations, many supporters insist, are not meant to be divisive, but are all about the recognition of past wrongs and racial healing today. In his recent book *Atonement and Forgiveness: A New Model for Black Reparations*, Roy Brooks cloaks reparations in an inclusive, consensus-oriented, even patriotic message that tries to place racial reconciliation at the center of the debate. According to his formula, atonement by the U.S. government as the legal entity accountable for slavery and Jim Crow requires a sincere apology plus reparations to transform the apology into a "meaningful, material reality." In turn, blacks would then have to extend forgiveness as a "civic obligation... to participate in a process of reconciliation." Today's white population, unconnected to slavery, "should be *grateful* rather than *apologetic*... [and] collectively acknowledge slavery's contribution to our society and to their privileged position within that society." The slaves should be memorialized as "heroic men, women, and children [who] were denied freedom so that all Americans might live in the freest and most prosperous nation humankind has ever known."[7]

There is little evidence, however, that such good intentions strike a sympathetic chord among the broader public. Instead of facilitating a dialogue on race relations in America, the reparation debate has become a contentious battleground in the American culture wars. Militant reparation activists revel in juggling with astronomical sums and boast of making their cause the centerpiece of a new revolutionary black mass movement, while their conservative opponents denounce them as a cabal of greedy

---

6 See Barkan, *The Guilt of Nations*, 290; "Forum: Making the Case for Racial Reparations," *Harper's Magazine*, November 2000, 37–51, 42. On the limitations of the "German slave cases" as precedent, see Anthony Sebok, "The Brooklyn Slavery Class Action: More Than Just a Political Gambit," http://writ.corporate.findlaw.com/sebok/20020409.html (July 2, 2002). For an overview of reparation litigation since 1995, see Baba Hanibal Afrika et al., "Current Legal Status of Reparations, Strategies of the National Black United Front, the Mississippi Model, What's Next in the Reparations Movement," in Winbush, *Should America Pay?* 363–83, 364–8.

7 For a detailed elaboration of his atonement model, see Brooks, *Atonement and Forgiveness*, 141–79, quotes 155, 168, 154 (italics in the original), 142; for apology and reparations as a conciliatory measure, see the 1997 resolution by U.S. Representative Tony P. Hall (D-OH), reprinted in Brooks, *When Sorry Isn't Enough*, 350–1.

lawyers, tenured radicals, and un-American fanatics. Most mainstream liberals will acknowledge the historical burden of slavery and segregation but dismiss the demand for reparations as an empty gesture that diverts attention away from the substantial social reform that poor African Americans really need. By offending white middle-class voters and fueling an already growing movement of white nationalism, political scientist Carol Swain argues, the demands for reparations may even be "positively harmful in terms of improving race relations and garnering support for policies to help the truly distressed."[8]

Can historians play a useful role in a debate that has been characterized by impassioned polemics? Obviously, the issue of reparations relates to the politics of memory rather than the history of slavery. As historian Ira Berlin has oberved, the history and memory of slavery are often at loggerheads. "The memory of slavery," he writes, "is immediate, emotive, and highly selective.... For those who draw on the remembered past, the study of slavery is not something that can be viewed dispassionately, questioned, inspected, and debated. Their truth is not one among many." While Berlin acknowledges that memory connects history with the lives and concerns of ordinary people, he warns against creating "myths with footnotes" and calls for "testing memory against history's truth and infusing history into memory's passions."[9]

To be sure, there is much need for setting the empirical record straight in the reparations debate, since the arguments made by both sides are often based on seriously flawed history. Many reparation activists, for example, grossly inflate the mortality on the slave ships to an alleged 25 million victims, which, they claim, dwarfs the Nazi genocide of the Jews of Europe. Virtually all historians of the transatlantic slave trade agree, however, that the total volume of the trade ranged from 10 million to 13 million between 1500 and the late nineteenth century and that roughly 2 million Africans died during the infamous "middle passage" from Africa to the Americas. Reparation critics, on the other hand, tend to warm up outdated notions of

---

8 For the militant protagonists of the reparation movement, see Clarence J. Munford, *Race and Reparations: A Black Perspective for the Twenty-First Century* (Trenton, 1996); Salim Abdul-Khaliq, *Slavery: Its Horrors, Why We Should Get Reparations and What White People Owe Africans in America* (Chicago, 1995). Winbush, *Should America Pay?*, includes both radical and moderate (and a few opposing) voices; an attack on the reparation movement has recently been waged by the conservative author and editor David Horowitz, *Uncivil Wars: The Controversy over Reparations for Slavery* (San Francisco, 2002); see also Carol Swain, *The New White Nationalism in America: Its Challenge to Integration* (New York, 2002), 179–81.

9 Ira Berlin, "American Slavery in History and Memory and the Search for Social Justice," *Journal of American History* 90 (2003–4): 1251–68, quotations 1265, 1266, 1268.

North American slavery as a benevolent and paternalistic system in which slaves had "rights" and enjoyed the protection of the laws.[10]

In addition to setting the historical record straight, and perhaps even more importantly, historians are called on to analyze the historical discourse and theoretical assumptions employed in the debates over restitution. In this regard, the demand for reparations for slavery is one of the most challenging cases because it makes a bold and far-reaching argument for intergenerational historical justice. Obviously, all slaves and slaveholders are dead and gone and cannot be compensated nor made to pay. Rather, the descendants of the victims are seeking reparations from the descendants of the perpetrators on a group rights basis. An inquiry into the logic of this case promises, I believe, an improved understanding of the fundamentals and limits of material restitution and indemnification for past injustices.

Two conceptual cornerstones of intergenerational justice are of particular concern to historians. First, the notion that claims for repairing historical injustices should transcend generational boundaries implies that these injustices continue to cause serious harm to people in the present. The analysis of causal sequences and historical continuity remains one of the most important tasks of historical scholarship. Second, intergenerational justice is predicated on the construction of "counterfactual, possible people – the people who would have existed had an injustice not occurred," as legal scholar James Fishkin puts it. Counterfactual history is often dismissed as purely speculative, but, as Max Weber demonstrated in his methodological writings, all causal judgments by historians are necessarily based on the implicit or explicit construction of counterfactuals. Constructing alternative historical sequences helps us to comprehend the causal factors that determined the actual course of history.[11]

---

10 See Robinson, *The Debt*, 9, 33, passim; Munford, *Race and Reparations*, 3, 421, passim. For standard accounts of the transatlantic slave trade, see Philip D. Curtin, *The Atlantic Slave Trade: A Census* (Madison, 1969); Herbert S. Klein, *The Atlantic Slave Trade* (Cambridge, 1999); Joseph Inikori, *Forced Migration: The Impact of the Export Slave Trade on African Societies* (London, 1981); James Rawley, *The Transatlantic Slave Trade: A History* (New York, 1981); Hugh Thomas, *The Slave Trade: The Story of the Atlantic Slave Trade, 1440–1870* (New York, 1997). For a concise discussion of the limits of the Holocaust analogy, see Seymour Drescher, "The Atlantic Slave Trade and the Holocaust: A Comparative Analysis," in Seymour Drescher, ed., *From Slavery to Freedom: Comparative Studies in the Rise and Fall of Atlantic Slavery* (New York, 1999), 312–38. Horowitz's book is replete with this paternalistic image: see *Uncivil Wars*, 81–2, 113–14, passim. For a nuanced discussion of the paternalism paradigm, see Peter Kolchin, *American Slavery 1619–1877* (New York, 1993), 93–132; for a convincing argument that the alleged "rights" of slaves served to protect their masters' property interests, see Andrew Fede, *People Without Rights: An Interpretation of the Fundamentals of the Law of Slavery in the U.S. South* (New York, 1992).

11 For causation and continuity as key components of a meritorious claim for historical justice, see Brooks, *When Sorry Isn't Enough*, introduction, 7–8; James S. Fishkin, "Justice Between Generations: Compensation, Identity, and Group Membership," in John W. Chapman, ed., *Compensatory*

In the case of reparations for slavery, the problems of causation, continuity, and counterfactual history can be stated as follows: How are African Americans today affected by the legacy of slavery? In what position would African Americans be today if slavery had never existed in the New World or, alternatively, if adequate compensation had been rendered immediately after emancipation? The answers to these questions determine the answers to the more practical aspects of the debate: Who, if anyone, is liable for the damage caused by slavery and who, if anyone, is entitled to reparations and in what form?

Of course, the construction of historical continuity and counterfactuals may be considered as a mere rhetorical device to confer historical legitimacy on a presentist political agenda. It is certainly true, as John Torpey writes, that for many proponents of reparation movements "the road to the future runs through the prolonged disasters of the past." However, for these claims to gain broad public acceptance, morally suggestive rhetoric and shrewd political tactics are not enough. In cases of intergenerational justice without living victims, propositions of causality and continuity also have to be based on persuasive conceptual arguments and empirical evidence.[12]

In order to evaluate the reparation controversy, it is also necessary to clarify how material historical justice can be achieved. Following a categorization by legal theorist Robert Gordon, I suggest the following typological framework. But whereas Gordon focuses on agency and structures as the causes of historical injustice, my classification relates to the differing scope of claims to restitution, their political acceptance, and the counterfactual reasoning implicit in each type.[13]

> *Individual justice*: The victims of historical injustices or their immediate heirs present concrete claims against the perpetrators or beneficiaries of such injustices. Justice is done either by material restitution or by financial compensation for property losses or the exploitation of the victims' labor, respectively. Such claims are based on counterfactual assumptions about unbroken life histories

---

Justice (New York, 1991), 85–96, 85; on the need for and problems of counterfactual constructions in reparatory justice, see also Jeremy Waldron, "Superseding Historic Injustice," *Ethics* 103 (1992): 4–28, 7–14; Max Weber, "Adäquate Verursachung und objektive Möglichkeit in der historischen Kausalbetrachtung," in Johannes Winckelmann, ed., *Max Weber: Gesammelte Aufsätze zur Wissenschaftslehre* (Tübingen, 1988), 266–90, 266; for a recent restatement of Weber's concept of causal analysis, see Fritz Ringer, "Max Weber on Causal Analysis, Interpretation and Comparison," *History and Theory* 41 (2002): 163–78.

12 Torpey, "'Making Whole What Has Been Smashed,'"337, 351–7, comments critically on "identity politics run wild." For a defense of causal analysis as a key task of historians as opposed to a preponderance of memory discourse, see Charles S. Maier, "A Surfeit of Memory? Reflections on History, Melancholy and Denial," *History and Memory* 5 (1993):136–52, esp. 141–3.

13 Robert W. Gordon, "Undoing Historical Injustice," in Austin Sarat and Thomas R. Kearny, eds., *Justice and Injustice in Law and Legal Theory* (Ann Arbor, 1996), 35–75, 36–9.

and the binding force of a legal order that protects private property and individual liberty. As a general rule, this kind of limited counterfactual reasoning meets with a high level of acceptance since it is part of the "normal" liability law in democratic-capitalist societies. For example, the postunification restitution of property seized or confiscated by the former German Democratic Republic was largely predicated on these principles.[14]

Collective justice: The claims are brought by the representatives of a distinct group whose members have been collectively victimized. The addressees are legal entities that are held responsible and liable for the historical injustice perpetrated against this group. Rectification may be enacted by international treaty, national legislation, voluntary agreement, or court rulings and typically entails financial payments that can be distributed among the group members or earmarked for communal purposes. Since complete restitution for large collective injustices is impossible, counterfactual assumptions play a much smaller role than in the quest for individual justice. Politically speaking, collective justice is most acceptable if the compensation goes directly to the actual victims or if there is at least a close relationship between the life histories of the recipients and the historical injustice. As a 1990 special report by the United Nations Commission on Human Rights on the right to restitution states, "Reparation may be claimed by the direct victims and, where appropriate, the immediate family, dependents or other persons having a special relationship to the direct victims." German *Wiedergutmachung* for the Nazi crimes is certainly the most important case of collective justice.[15]

Structural justice: This type of justice is not predicated on individual or collective agency but on the proposition that the victim status of a particular group is deeply embedded in a continuous history of oppression and discrimination that has supposedly shaped both the institutions and the cultural values of the broader society. The claims for the rectification of structural injustices are brought against society at large and the state in particular and ultimately aim at sweeping social and political reforms to break the ongoing historical cycle of victimization. They employ strong causal hypotheses about the lasting impact of past injustices and complex counterfactual reasoning about alternative paths of development. To be politically acceptable, they require conclusive evidence

---

14 The legal fiction in this case was that the West German Basic Law and its guarantee of private property were also valid for the GDR, even if it could not be enforced; see Birgit Strobl, "Die Rückgabe von Vermögen in der ehemaligen DDR" (diss. Freie Universität Berlin, 1992), 98–105.

15 See Theo van Boven, "Study Concerning the Right to Restitution, Compensation and Rehabilitation for Victims of Gross Violations of Human Rights and Fundamental Freedoms," in Neil J. Kritz, ed., *Transitional Justice: How Emerging Democracies Reckon with Former Regimes*, 3 vols. (Washington, D.C., 1995), vol. I, 505–50, 548; on *Wiedergutmachung* for the Nazi crimes, see Karl Döhring et al., *Jahrhundertschuld, Jahrhundertsühne. Reparationen, Wiedergutmachung, Entschädigung für nationalsozialistisches Kriegs- und Verfolgungsunrecht* (München, 2001); Constantin Goschler and Jürgen Lillteicher, eds., *"Arisierung" und Restitution. Die Rückerstattung jüdischen Eigentums in Deutschland und Österreich* (Göttingen, 2002); Constantin Goschler, *Wiedergutmachung: Westdeutschland und die Verfolgten des Nationalsozialismus (1945–1954)* (München, 1992); and Chapter 4 by Constantin Goschler in this volume.

that the legacies of a historical injustice continue to determine the social position of the victims or their descendants. The spokespersons for the victims of colonialism, racism, and slavery typically shape their arguments along these lines.[16]

It goes without saying that these three types cannot be neatly separated from each other when it comes to actual cases. Nor are they mutually exclusive. On the contrary, in the distinct historical situation of regime change from dictatorship to democracy, the search for transitional justice will typically include elements of individual, collective, and structural redress plus a broad array of retributive and symbolic measures, including trials, purges, apologies, and truth commissions. Transitional justice, however, primarily focuses on recent victims and perpetrators and not on relatively distant historical events.[17]

I shall now discuss the controversy over reparations for slavery along these lines: On which concepts of historical continuity or discontinuity do the protagonists build their arguments? What is their counterfactual frame of reference? Which modes of material redress do they favor?

The proponents of reparations for slavery usually espouse an activist concept of history according to which former victims transform themselves into forceful agents. They may not be able to alter the past, but they can at least change some of its consequences and thus determine their own future. In striking contrast to this optimistic vision, however, stands a deterministic analysis of the historical roots and ramifications of slavery that carries the concept of historical continuity to its extreme. In this view, slavery and racism are the primordial forces that have shaped American history and culture since the beginning of European settlement. Clarence Munford, one of the most radical reparation advocates, seriously asserts that racism and a "genocidal instinct" are encoded in the "DNA of white civilization." From this perspective, the legacy of slavery appears to be all-encompassing: racism past and present explains all social disparities between black and white Americans. Political scientist and reparation activist Ronald Walters puts the argument unequivocally: "There is a straight line from slavery to the socio-economic and psychological conditions of African-Americans today."[18]

16 Torpey, "'Making Whole What Has Been Smashed,'" 337.
17 For an introduction to the fast-growing literature on transitional justice and a broad documentation of cases, see Kritz, ed., *Transitional Justice*; A. James McAdams, ed., *Transitional Justice and the Rule of Law in New Democracies* (Notre Dame, Ind., 1997); Ruti G. Teitel, *Transitional Justice* (New York, 2000); Priscilla B. Hayner, *Unspeakable Truths: Facing the Challenge of Truth Commissions* (London, 2002).
18 Munford, *Race and Reparations*, 3. Since the author respectfully refers to the so-called melanin deprivation theory, which argues that the lack of melanin produces an innate aggressiveness in whites, his language is evidently not just metaphorical, see 7–8; Walters quoted in King, "Recent Lawsuits."

Notably, this historical continuity is often constructed in the language of pathology as, for example, in Roy Brooks's proposition that "today's blacks have inherited from their slave ancestors a social virus that diminishes their power, wealth, and privileges." Others take the pathological consequences of slavery quite literally by asserting a "posttraumatic slave syndrome." According to this theory, "African Americans sustained traumatic psychological and emotional injury as a direct result of slavery and continue to be injured by traumas caused by the larger society's policies of inequality, racism, and oppression." This traumatization directly translates into a "persistent slave health deficit," including significantly lower life expectancy, higher mortality, and the prevalence of serious diseases among the black population in the United States, a deficit that amounts to nothing short of "genocide."[19]

Although the civil rights movement of the twentieth century won "a few human rights and political advances," reparation activists contend that the history of oppression continues more or less unabated and manifests itself in numerous social indicators, such as significantly lower income and higher poverty rates among African Americans, a grossly disproportionate number of incarcerated blacks, and the decline of the black family. "What can you say to the black man on death row?" asks Randall Robinson, author of the influential book *The Debt: What America Owes to Blacks*, "the black mother alone, bitter, overburdened and spent? Who tells them that their fate washed ashore at Jamestown with twenty slaves in 1619?" The traditional civil rights agenda, the reparation proponents argue, has spent its force and no longer provides an answer to the plight of black Americans.[20]

Rather than being content with limited civil rights and affirmative action, the reparation movement demands a massive redistribution of wealth to make amends for centuries of exploitation. It does not matter that the vast majority of present-day white Americans are not descendants of slaveholders. The obligation to indemnify blacks does not depend on individual or collective guilt and responsibility; it emanates from the structural racism of American society at large from which all whites benefit in one way or another. Just as Europeans are said to be rich because they exploited the wealth of Africa, sociologists Joe Feagin and Eileen O'Brien maintain, the

---

19 Brooks, *Atonement and Forgiveness*, 96; Jewel Crawford et al., "Reparations and Health Care for African Americans: Repairing the Damage from the Legacy of Slavery," in Winbush, *Should America Pay?* 251–81, 267–72, 267–8, 281.
20 Johnita Scott Obadele, "Reparations: Linking Our Past, Present, and Future" (quote) www.ncobra.com/nBusiness/ncobranews/newsdocuments/infoncobra.html (April 23, 2001); Robinson, *The Debt*, 216–17. On the exhaustion of the traditional civil rights agenda, see also Robert Westley, "Many Billions Gone: Is It Time to Reconsider the Case for Black Reparations?" *Boston College Law* Review 40 (1998): 429–76, esp. 429–30.

wealth of white Americans has been built on the continued exploitation of blacks. "For many generations now," they conclude, "white children have inherited ill-gotten gains from the anti-black actions of whites before them. Recognition of this inheritance of privilege is key to understanding arguments for reparations, and key to bringing about reconciliation between blacks and whites."[21]

To assess the extent of the "unjust enrichment" that whites reaped from slavery, the supporters of reparations assume hypothetical equality of opportunity between the races throughout American history as their counterfactual frame of reference. Methodologically, these calculations can be based on either a historical or an ahistorical approach. The former attempts to compute the actual profits that white society has accumulated over time from slavery and racial discrimination. For example, economists build their estimates on the fictitious wages that were denied to slaves or they use the prices of slaves and the slaveholders' rate of return on their human investment as the baselines for compounding the debt owed to black America. One simple, if incredibly expensive, historical proposal calls for paying each descendant of a slave the current equivalent of forty acres and a mule, which is said to amount to $200,000. Such estimates easily add up to fantastical sums, but they have obvious disadvantages. The historical data are difficult to establish, the economic variables such as interest rates and adjustment for inflation are highly conjectural, and they project counterfactual scenarios that are intelligible only to a small band of cliometricians.[22]

The ahistorical approach avoids these difficulties by assuming that black and white Americans would enjoy roughly the same level of wealth and prosperity if equality of opportunity had prevailed throughout American history. Perhaps the most attractive and popular formula has been devised by legal scholar Boris I. Bittker, who proposes taking the gap in the per capita income between blacks and whites and multiplying this amount by the number of African Americans. The product gives us the necessary annual income transfer to the African-American community that should be paid

---

21 Joe Feagin and Eileen O'Brien, "The Long-Overdue Reparations for African Americans," in Brooks, *When Sorry Isn't Enough*, 417–21, 420. Feagin's view on the continuation of both intentional and structural racism in the post–civil rights era are further developed in Joe R. Feagin, *White Racism: The Basics* (New York, 1995). For the classical statement of the underdevelopment thesis, see Walter Rodney, *How Europe Underdeveloped Africa* (London, 1972).
22 I borrow the terminology from Andrew Valls, "The Libertarian Case for Affirmative Action," *Social Theory and Practice* 25 (1999): 299–323, 311–14. The most comprehensive attempt along the lines of the historical method is represented in the various contributions to Richard F. America, ed., *The Wealth of Races: The Present Value of Benefits from Past Injustices* (New York, 1990); see esp. the introduction by William Darity, "Forty Acres and a Mule: Placing a Price Tag on Oppression," 3–13. On the proposal to pay the current value of forty acres and a mule, see Barkan, *The Guilt of Nations*, 288–9. If all 35 million blacks in America are considered the descendants of slaves, implementing this proposal would cost the fantastic sum of $7 trillion.

as reparations until the income gap is approximately closed. According to the latest figures from the Census Bureau, which set the black population at 35.5 million and the black-white income difference at $9,174, the Bittker formula would currently require transfer payments of roughly $321 billion per year.[23]

The ahistorical approach is certainly less mind-boggling than the historical one, but it entails problems of its own. On closer examination, it becomes clear that it is grounded in a circular argument. It presupposes that all material disparities between present-day black and white Americans are caused by the legacy of slavery and discrimination and at the same time takes the factual evidence for these disparities as proof for the continuing and overriding impact of history. Moreover, its rationale implies that every group with a per capita income below the white average and a credible history of discrimination in America may be considered putative victims of historical injustice entitled to reparations. For example, if we substitute class for race, we may argue that all poor Americans are the historical victims of capitalism, which has consistently denied them equality of opportunity. While many reparation activists will eagerly agree to this proposition, it is doubtful whether issues of social justice can and should be reduced to issues of historical justice.[24]

The notions as to how reparations should be paid vary considerably. Perhaps we may neglect exotic demands such as a separate state for African Americans or government-financed "repatriation" to Africa, even if they have a long and venerable history in black intellectual discourse. For the most part, the term "reparations" implies the payment of huge amounts of money. Demands oscillate between surprisingly moderate sums, such as the $2 billion reparations fund suggested by the National Coalition of Blacks for Reparations in America (N'COBRA) to be supplied by tax-deductible $10 donations by taxpayers, and gigantic claims of up to $16 trillion. While the obsession with throwing around provocative figures undercuts the appeal of the reparation movement among the broader public, activists insist that

---

23 Bittker, *The Case for Black Reparations*, 131–2. Bittker sees his formula as a conservative approach that does not account for the accumulated disparities in wealth. For an argument that the baseline of redistribution should not be the income gap but rather the gap in accumulated wealth between the races (net worth), see Dalton Conley, "Calculating Slavery Reparations: Theory, Numbers, and Implications," in Torpey, *Politics and the Past*, 117–25.

24 Munford, e.g., sees reparations as an attack on capitalism: his "Reparations: Strategic Considerations for Black Americans," in Brooks, *When Sorry Isn't Enough*, 422–6. The redistributive purpose of reparations, however, need not be framed by a Marxist approach. Valls, "The Libertarian Case for Affirmative Action," makes the argument that libertarianism also requires that the distribution of wealth and power must not be based on past injustices and violations of rights; see in particular 300–3.

these sums could be paid for by cuts in the military budget, postponing interest payments on the national debt, and an income tax hike for the wealthy.[25]

The distribution and use of the reparation money, should it ever be forthcoming, raise two key questions. Are all African Americans, regardless of their individual social positions, entitled to reparations by virtue of descent, or should the beneficiaries be limited to the needy? After all, according to recent census information, roughly one-quarter of all black Americans live below the official poverty level – twice the national average and three times the rate for non-Hispanic whites. While the reparation movement emphatically insists that all blacks are victims of slavery and racism and are therefore entitled to historical justice, "handouts" are not considered a good idea. Obviously, individual payments would raise some very inconvenient issues, including the need to determine who is black. Even a sympathetic author like Bittker warned against reviving the old Jim Crow system of racial classification, even if it is with a benevolent intent. In the same vein, paying reparations to fabulously rich professional athletes or entertainers is hardly a popular idea. Hence, most reparation supporters agree that the funds should go to a legitimate African-American organization to serve as a trustee and should be used to finance social projects, education, and loans to small businesses. In order to make the historical and moral debt of white America unmistakably clear, however, they insist that "reparation needs to be called by its proper name" and that the black community must have unconditional control over the money.[26]

To emphasize the rehabilitative character of reparations, its advocates have increasingly focused their demands on education. Because the continuing harm of slavery is supposedly most obvious in the educational and human capital deficits of the black population, Roy Brooks calls for an atonement trust fund to finance the education of all black children up to the age of twenty-five. And Molefi Kete Asante demands "free public and private education to all descendants of enslaved Africans for the next 123 years, half the time Africans worked in this country for free." Along the same lines,

---

25 On "repatriation," see Robert Johnson, Jr., "Repatriation as Reparations for Slavery and Jim-Crowism," in Brooks, *When Sorry Isn't Enough*, 427–34. There is no evidence whatsoever that "the deteriorating living conditions of the African American masses" (432) have advanced interest in emigration to Africa; Johnita Scott Obadele, "Reparations: Linking Our Past, Present, and Future" (fn. 17); Munford, *Race and Reparations*, 428–9, 432–3; most estimates by pro-reparations economists amount to about $1.5 trillion, see Darity, "Forty Acres and a Mule," 11.
26 Bittker, *The Case for Black Reparations*, 93–9. On rich black celebrities, see "Forum: Making the Case for Racial Reparations," 43; Johnita Scott Obadele, "Reparations: Linking Our Past, Present, and Future"; Munford, *Race and Reparations*, 435.

the proponents of a "persistent slave health deficit" conclude that "remedial actions must first and foremost provide for free health care for prevention, screening, diagnosis, and treatment of all physical and mental disorders as well as providing for holistic wellness and preventive care." Given that the soaring costs of education and health care are arguably the most pressing financial concerns of ordinary Americans of all races, the proposals of free health care and education for blacks as atonement and compensation for slavery and racism are political bombshells that no mainstream politician will touch.[27]

In comparison, the controversial affirmative action programs designed to eradicate the legacies of the past by creating equality of opportunity in employment and higher education appear rather moderate. As a matter of fact, the history of slavery and discrimination was a major consideration when these programs were first proposed during the height of the civil rights movement. In his famous 1965 speech at Howard University, President Lyndon B. Johnson declared that "the scars of centuries" could not simply be wiped away by telling blacks that now they were "free to compete with all the others." America, he continued, needed "equality not just as a right and theory, but equality as a fact and as a result." Yet most Americans have viewed affirmative action as a transitional measure at best and object to its permanent establishment as violating the American ideal of a color-blind meritocracy. Remarkably enough, the archconservative commentator Charles Krauthammer has long supported a onetime reparation payment to African Americans in exchange for a complete repeal of affirmative action and an end to further demands for ameliorative policies based on race. Reparation supporters suspect that this proposal is mere tokenism aimed at letting white America off the hook. At least it serves as a reminder that reparations, should they ever be paid, could easily be construed as a final settlement that gives American society the right not to be bothered with slavery and racism anymore.[28]

---

27 Brooks, *Atonement and Forgiveness*, 36–97, 159–63; Molefi Kete Asante, "The African American Warrant for Reparations: The Crime of European Enslavement of Africans and Its Consequences," in Winbush, *Should America Pay?* 3–13, 12–13; Crawford, "Reparations and Health Care for African Americans," 276.
28 See Johnson's speech, "To Fulfill These Rights," in George E. Curry, ed., *The Affirmative Action Debate* (Reading, 1996), 16–24, 17–18; Charles Krauthammer, "Reparations for Black Americans," *Time*, December 31, 1991, 18; "Forum: Making the Case for Racial Reparations," 45–6. On affirmative action as a low-cost alternative to reparations, see Valls, "The Libertarian Case for Affirmative Action," 314–18; Stanley H. Masters, "The Social Debt to Blacks: A Case for Affirmative Action," in *America: The Wealth of Races*, 179–89. For an argument against affirmative action as an instrument of compensatory justice, see Ellen Frankel Paul, "Set-Asides, Reparations, and Compensatory Justice," in Chapman, *Compensatory Justice*, 97–139, 104–22.

Since the demand for reparations has mostly been on the margins of respectable political discourse, the antireparation argument largely consists of op-ed commentary with a penchant for ridicule on the one hand and a few critical references in the scholarly literature dealing with restitution issues on the other. The recent book by the conservative author and editor David Horowitz, *Uncivil Wars: The Controversy over Reparations for Slavery*, for example, does not offer a systematic and historically sound argument. Instead, most of the book is a self-congratulatory account of how in early 2001 the author tried to place an antireparation advertisement in college newspapers and then became the target of censorship and intimidation by campus radicals. Horowitz's "Ten Reasons Why Reparations for Slavery Is a Bad Idea – and Racist Too" is a hodgepodge of some serious and valid points, a good deal of historical mythology, and a rather condescending call for African Americans to be grateful to "the Nation That Gave Them Freedom." Still, his arguments are heeded by many reparation detractors and represent a useful summary of the popular antireparation discourse.[29]

While some critics argue that the claim for reparations has no legal basis because slavery was not even against the law prior to 1865, very few will publicly deny that it was a human injustice of truly horrendous proportions. However, they fervently contest the historical continuities alleged by their antagonists and the concomitant moral indictments that Horowitz denounces as a "hostile assault on America and its history." In part, the antireparation argument dwells on a quite fatalistic concept of history, according to which injustice and suffering are simply universal aspects of the human condition that sooner or later are visited on all nations and individuals. In this vein, the Civil War, with its 600,000 dead and its vast destruction of wealth, including the wealth of the Southern slaveholders, is understood as atonement of a kind for the sins of slavery. Viewed from this perspective, the 350,000 fallen Union soldiers paid the ultimate reparations by giving their lives for the emancipation of the slaves. Needless to say, this interpretation represents a highly selective reading of both Northern war aims and the motivation of Union soldiers to fight.[30]

---

29 Horowitz, *Uncivil Wars*, esp. 12–16. Horowitz's attacks on the tenured radicals and un-Americans of the left betray the typical fervor of the apostate.

30 Horowitz, *Uncivil Wars*, 119–20 (Civil War), 134 (quote); most historians of the Civil War agree that the overriding war aim of Lincoln and the North was to preserve the Union and that emancipation grew out of political and military necessities. Moreover, dedicated abolitionists were a small, if by no means insignificant, minority among the Union soldiers. See, e.g., the accounts by the leading expert on the subject, James M. McPherson, *What They Fought For, 1861–1865* (Baton Rouge, 1994), and *For Cause and Comrades: Why Men Fought in the Civil War* (Oxford, 1997).

Much more typical, however, is a discourse of historical progress that sees slavery and racism as regrettable aberrations from the dominant course of American history, which is supposedly aimed at redeeming the promise of universal liberty and equality. To its credit, the reparation critics contend, America has purged itself of its racist legacies. The adoption of comprehensive civil rights legislation in the 1960s, it is said, represents nothing less than an active and unambiguous apology for past racial discrimination. Whatever residual racism is left in American society today is viewed as a phenomenon on the lunatic fringe that is socially ostracized and checked by the law. The remaining socioeconomic disparities between black and white Americans are either interpreted as a fast-shrinking historical gap or attributed to specific "pathologies" of the so-called black underclass. Some conservative critics of the welfare state even want to credit welfare payments to blacks as a trillion-dollar equivalent of reparations.[31]

Virtually all reparation opponents strongly object to the concept of historical justice over several generations and to the notion of a broad liability of society for wrongs that were committed in a distant past. For the proponents of an individualistic theory of victimization and rectification, justice "requires identifiable victims ... [not] victims long dead, nor counterfactual victims." Since present-day Americans do not bear any responsibility for slavery, the reparation movement is dismissed as a scheme by self-styled victims who demand money for harms they did not suffer from people who did not perpetrate them. From this perspective, the demand for reparations presents a special injustice to postbellum immigrants and their descendants. "The two great waves of American immigration," Horowitz states, "occurred after 1880 and then after 1960. What logic would require Vietnamese boat people, ... Jews, Mexicans, Greeks, or Polish, Hungarian, Cambodian and Korean victims of Communism, to pay reparations to American blacks?" And by what logic other than hypocrisy and political correctness, he continues, are the descendants of African rulers and traders exempted from the demand for historical justice? After all, African leaders sold millions of black slaves to the Europeans at handsome profits and

---

31 Bernard H. Siegan, "The United States Has Already Apologized for Racial Discrimination," in Brooks, *When Sorry Isn't Enough*, 413–16. For a broad-based optimistic account of black progress, see Stephan Thernstrom and Abigail Thernstrom, *America in Black and White: One Nation Indivisible* (New York, 1997). For the argument that racism has become marginal and discrimination often represents a "rational" response to the pathologies of the ghetto, see Dinesh D'Souza, *The End of Racism: Principles for a Multiracial Society* (New York, 1995). Horowitz, *Uncivil Wars*, claims that welfare payments since the 1960s add up to $1.3 trillion (124); for a similar argument as part of the conservative denunciation of the war on poverty, see Myron Magnet, *The Dream and the Nightmare: The Sixties' Legacy to the Underclass* (New York, 1993), 133.

strongly protested the abolition of the transatlantic slave trade in the early nineteenth century.[32]

Reparation critics are also inclined to dismiss counterfactual history as pointless "metaphysical speculation." Still, they argue that the appropriate counterfactual framework for assessing the consequences of an alternative history without Atlantic slavery would be the condition of West Africans today. From this perspective, black Americans might seem to be in an enviable position. As legal theorist Ellen Frankel Paul argues," If not for the slave trade, most of the descendants of the slaves would now be living in Africa under regimes known neither for their respect for human rights, indeed for human life, nor for the economic well-being of their citizens. The typical denizens of one of these states... would envy the condition of the black teenage mother on welfare in one of this country's worst inner cities." The freedom and prosperity that blacks are now enjoying in the United States, one is tempted to infer, should make them retrospectively grateful for the abduction and enslavement of their ancestors. As a normative standard, the comparison with Africa is, of course, highly gratuitous. The history of Africans in America must be held against the universal promise of liberty, equality, and pursuit of happiness on which the United States prides itself.[33]

Nevertheless, the skeptics conclude that even though most black people were undeniably excluded from the American dream for more than three hundred years, the historical moment to compensate the real victims of slavery was unfortunately missed and cannot be brought back. Like other minorities who have suffered discrimination in America – notably Asian Americans – African Americans should free themselves from the spell of the past and take advantage of the opportunities that the postracist American society has to offer. In the end, reparations for slavery would do nobody any good. They would only reinforce the stereotype that blacks cannot compete in a free market and would benefit a small group of rapacious lawyers and "racial hustlers... who empower themselves by dispensing a warm drug, a surrender of the will to the feelings of victimization." At last, all taxpayers and consumers, including African Americans, would have to fund the bill for a past wrong for which they neither feel nor bear any responsibility.[34]

---

32 Paul, "Set-Asides, Reparations, and Compensatory Justice," 115; Debra Saunders, "No Justice in Reparations," www.townhall.com/columnists/debrasaunders/printsds20020331 (July 20, 2002); Horowitz, *Uncivil Wars*, 13, 131–2.
33 Paul, "Set-Asides, Reparations, and Compensatory Justice," 119. For a similar comparison between the living conditions of blacks in Africa and in the United States, see Horowitz, *Uncivil Wars*, 129–30.
34 See Marti Sapp Linder, "Slavery Reparations Lawsuits: All Races Will Get the Shaft," *The Progressive Conservative*, April 12, 2002, www.geocities.com/way_leroy/PCVol4Is39RacesShaft.html. (July 2,

It is probably safe to predict that in the political arena the opponents of reparations will prevail. As the supporters themselves concede, the ultimate success of their cause "would require a revolutionary transformation of American society." Presently, this is not a very likely scenario, to put it mildly, but perhaps Clarence Munford is right that "history is patient and bows to determination." Perhaps the reparation movement, like the civil rights movement of the 1960s, will grow into a mass movement that is capable of forcing its agenda on a reluctant nation. Optimists cite polls according to which up to 80 percent of black Americans agree that the federal government should both apologize to them and compensate them for slavery. N'COBRA confidently asserts that "reparations is the most unifying issue that our race has." Whether many blacks consider reparations as a realistic prospect worth fighting for or as "a morally just but totally hopeless cause" is a very different matter, however. The 88 percent rejection rate among whites, on the other hand, must be taken very seriously because it plainly expresses their unwillingness to pay. It is no coincidence that even President Bill Clinton, whom many African Americans viewed as genuinely receptive to their rights and interests, consistently refused to issue a formal apology for slavery, lest it be construed as an admission of legal liability.[35]

Obviously, the scant support for reparations among white Americans says nothing about the moral or factual justification of the claim itself. Indeed, the widespread refusal to make amends for slavery and Jim Crow might be regarded as additional proof of America's structural racism. Still, it seems to me that this is a too facile and convenient explanation. As Robert Gordon suggests, structuralist group claims for intergenerational justice tend to "rely on such attenuated notions of blame and causation as to subvert their moral plausibility and thus undermine possibilities of political fraternity." By way of conclusion, I will attempt to specify the analytical and empirical weaknesses of the pro-reparation argument from a historian's perspective.[36]

Far-reaching causal hypotheses and counterfactual thought experiments are legitimate, indeed necessary, heuristic tools of historical scholarship in

---

2002); Horowitz, *Uncivil Wars*, 14; Armstrong Williams, "Presumed Victims," in Winbush, *Should America Pay?* 165–71, 168.

35 Darity, "Forty Acres and a Mule: Placing a Price Tag on Oppression," 12 (quote); Feagin and O'Brien, "The Long-Overdue Reparations for African Americans," 421; Munford, "Reparations: Strategic Considerations for Black Americans," 425. For opinion polls on black and white attitudes toward reparations, see Feagin and O'Brien, "The Growing Movement for Reparations," in Brooks, *When Sorry Isn't Enough*, 341–3; Johnita Scott Obadele, "Reparations: Linking Our Past, Present, and Future"; Winbush, *Should America Pay?* introduction, xxi; Jack E. White, "Don't Waste Your Breath: The Fight for Slave Reparations Is a Morally Just But Totally Hopeless Cause," *Time*, April 2, 2001, 63.

36 Gordon, "Undoing Historical Injustice," 69.

explaining historical developments, but as a source of moral and normative authority to substantiate material claims they are highly questionable. Just as the historian as an expert witness in court cannot substitute for the judge charged with applying the law, historiographical concepts of causation, continuity, and counterfactuals cannot be directly translated into legal or political claims for restitution or reparations.[37]

The same applies to ahistorical constructions of justice in a world of perfect equality of rights, holdings, and opportunity. For example, Andrew Valls, building on Robert Nozick's libertarian theory of rectification, argues that the distribution of wealth in the present must not rest on past violations of rights, but he does not indicate how far back in history we must go to achieve equity. Since it is very difficult, perhaps impossible, to distinguish between justly and unjustly acquired wealth, why not wipe the historical slate clean and redistribute all wealth on a basis of absolute equality so everybody is in the same starting position for a truly fair competition? In a similar vein, James Fishkin holds that reparations for African Americans can be justified on the grounds that in a hypothetical "alternative nonracist world" they would be nonexistent as a group in America. If a particular group was originally created by a historical injustice, Fishkin argues, this would be the benchmark for a group right to compensation. But which ethnic groups would exist in a nonracist world? Are victim groups forever defined by the historical injustice they suffered? Is there a universal right to live in a nonracist world from which retroactive legal claims can be derived? The construction of counterfactual history and ideal worlds certainly is an instructive intellectual exercise, but it offers little practicable guidance in balancing the conflicting rights, interests, and values of the real world.[38]

On the contrary, it seems as if large historical and philosophical constructions are particularly conducive to uncompromising demands and political grandstanding. Perhaps the powerful semantics of slavery makes it irresistible for reparation activists to lock themselves in a rhetorical cage. If slavery was "a human rights crime without parallel in the modern world," then the sentence must fit the crime. Unlike the civil rights movement,

---

[37] For the indefinite relationship between counterfactual assumptions and normative conclusions, see Waldron, "Superseding Historic Injustice," 10–11; for a clear-cut separation between these two roles, see Norbert Frei et al., eds., *Geschichte vor Gericht: Historiker, Richter und die Suche nach Gerechtigkeit* (Munich, 2000), esp. the essays by Dirk van Laak, Raphael Gross, and Michael Stolleis.

[38] See Valls, "The Libertarian Case for Affirmative Action," 300–3; Fishkin, "Justice Between Generations," 93–4. For a critique of models of original equality, esp. those of Rawls and Habermas, and a plea for acknowledging particularistic interests and subjective values as the basis for a fair and pragmatic balancing of interests and rights, see Rainer Werner Trapp, "Politisches Handeln im wohlverstandenen Allgemeininteresse," in H.-J. Koch et al., eds., *Theorien der Gerechtigkeit* (Stuttgart, 1994), 54–78.

which fought for a future-oriented concept of social reform, the reparation movement insists that the future of American society is dependent on a large-scale reversal of the past. "No justice, no peace," as Molefi Asante proclaims. By constructing a transhistorical community of destiny between present-day African Americans and their enslaved ancestors, the reparation advocates try to suggest the possibility of restorative justice that reaches far back into history. But redistributive justice can only apply to the present and the future. It must be legitimized through the democratic process, and it must take into account considerations of equity, fairness, legal peace, and reconciliation. Historical justice is but one aspect of a broader concept of social justice.[39]

This is not to say that there is no more room to address the manifold historical injustices blacks have suffered in the United States. There is no need to detail here the gruesome history of racial violence perpetrated against African Americans during the twentieth century, including pogrom-like mob riots, lynchings, racially motivated murders, and innumerable acts of brutality against civil rights activists. It is clear that only a minuscule fraction of this horrendous history can ever be subjected to legal or political review. But the $2 million compensation that the Florida legislature awarded in 1994 to the survivors of the 1923 Rosewood massacre shows that the efforts to do so are not entirely futile. In particular, cases of racist violence that relate to specific events and identifiable victims of the post–World War Two period and that involve the negligence or collusion of local, state, or federal authorities present fewer legal problems and meet with much more political support than the general claim for reparations.[40]

From the perspective of the reparation movement, such individualized compensation would be insufficient at best, since it does not acknowledge that all African Americans were and still are victims of racism. But to what extent does such a deterministic view of historical continuity really explain the past and present of African Americans? For starters, it must be noted

---

39 Robinson, *The Debt*, 216; Asante, "The African American Warrant for Reparations," 5. The mythical community of destiny is often coined in Afrocentric terms; see Robinson, *The Debt*, 13–28; Munford, *Race and Reparations*, 3–25. For an emphatic plea of restitution as a negotiated process, see Barkan, *The Guilt of Nations*, 308–49. For a perspective that stresses reconciliation as the ultimate goal of transitional justice, see Andrew Rigby, *Justice and Reconciliation: After the Violence* (Boulder, 2001). For a concise introduction to the fundamentals of social justice, see Peter Koller, "Soziale Güter und soziale Gerechtigkeit," in Koch et al., *Theorien der Gerechtigkeit*, 79–104.

40 The literature on racial violence in the United States is enormous. See the (incomplete) overview of events by Michael Newton and Judy Ann Newton, *Racial and Religious Violence in America: A Chronology* (New York, 1991). On the Rosewood case, see Barkan, *The Guilt of Nations*, 297–9; Kenneth B. Nunn, "Rosewood," in Brooks, *When Sorry Isn't Enough*, 435–7. For the preference of post–World War II cases, see "Forum: Making the Case for Racial Reparations," 42.

that this fatalism stands in striking contrast to modern historical scholarship. For the past forty years or so, historians have demonstrated that blacks were able to develop a remarkable communal life and an astounding degree of personal dignity and agency even under the successive yokes of slavery and Jim Crow. If slavery and segregation had had an all-powerful crippling effect on black consciousness and aspirations, it is quite inconceivable how the civil rights movement could have become the most important social movement in all of American history.[41]

The radical champions of reparations, however, have revived the victimization discourse and carried it to new heights. Ironically, when in 1965 Daniel P. Moynihan, with the best of liberal intentions, blamed the disruption of black family life in America on the lingering effects of slavery, he was almost crucified by black and other radicals for allegedly disseminating distorted racist images of black life. Nowadays, reparation advocates essentially say the same things as Moynihan: "The effects of slavery are still with us, we all know that: single parents, black men wandering off from their families, a tradition of not going to school, distrust of the future. This is not black culture. It's slave culture." In fact, the dramatic disintegration of the black family is a modern phenomenon that sharply accelerated between the early 1960s and mid-1990s: in that period, the proportion of black children living with two parents dropped from two-thirds to one-third and the rate of out-of-wedlock births rose from 22 percent to 70 percent. The legacy of slavery for African-American family life cannot be reduced to a linear and unbroken chain of causation. Recently, the resurgence of the image of black Americans as permanently damaged victims of history has drawn sharp criticism from authors of divergent ideological persuasions who argue that, even if employed to justify liberal and inclusive social policies, these images have done more harm than good.[42]

---

41 For a competent introduction that also denotes the limits of "slave autonomy" and the pitfalls of romanticizing the slave community, see Kolchin, *American Slavery*, 133–68. On black life during the heyday of segregation, see Leon Litwack, *Trouble in Mind: Black Southerners in the Age of Jim Crow* (New York, 1998).

42 For the text and the reaction to the Moynihan Report, see Lee Rainwater and William L. Yancey, eds., *The Moynihan Report and the Politics of Controversy* (Cambridge, Mass., 1967). For a recent restatement of the thesis that the black family crisis goes back to patterns forged under slavery, see Orlando Patterson, *Rituals of Blood: Consequences of Slavery in Two American Centuries* (Washington, D.C., 1998), 25–53. Patterson, however, does not construe his argument as an apology for irresponsible behavior. Quotation from black lawyer Dennis C. Sweet, "Forum: Making the Case for Racial Reparations," 39. On the statistics, see Thernstrom and Thernstrom, *America in Black and White*, 237–41. For a recent critique of the focus on "victimology" among the black community by a black conservative, see, e.g., John McWhorter, *Losing the Race: Self-Sabotage in Black America* (New York, 2000). For a longer historical perspective, see Daryl Michael Scott, *Contempt and Pity: Social Policy and the Image of the Damaged Black Psyche 1880–1996* (Chapel Hill, 1997).

The key evidence for the continuity thesis, of course, is the desperate situation of the so-called black underclass, which lives in a nightmarish world of poverty, drugs, violent crime, and social disintegration. For example, Jacqueline Jones, a well-respected social historian, concludes her history of American underclasses with a remarkably fatalistic and ahistorical judgment: "Thus does a society conceived in slavery perpetuate itself, and postindustrial America remains colonial Virginia writ large." Such a pessimistic outlook is simply unable to explain why the poverty rate among African Americans fell from a staggering 87 percent in 1940 to less than 25 percent according to the 2000 census. Nor can it explain the emergence of a viable black middle class or the growing political clout of African Americans. Not surprisingly, the proponents of structural racism tend to dismiss black progress as either a myth or the marginal benefit an opportunistic black leadership reaps from endearing itself to the white elites.[43]

The United States, to be sure, is not the color-blind meritocracy that neo-conservative panegyrists like Horowitz claim it to be. Racism continues to be an all-too-frequent experience for African Americans, and their average socioeconomic position is still far from being on a par with that of whites. But it is equally misleading to let the ghetto define the image of black America. In his emphatic plea against the "overracialization of Afro-American life," sociologist Orlando Patterson contends that "the real Afro-Americans are diverse, surprisingly happy, and very American." This may or may not be the case. In my view, however, there is little convincing evidence that the lives of 35 million black Americans are still dominated by the legacies of slavery and segregation to an extent that qualifies them for collective victimhood.[44]

Where does this leave the claim for reparations? Asserting an absolute right to the rectification of a historical injustice for all members of a victim group, regardless of concrete life histories and the social position of individuals, comes close to asserting a right that history must retroactively

---

43 Jacqueline Jones, *The Dispossessed: America's Underclasses from the Civil War to the Present* (New York, 1992), 292; see also her *American Work: Four Centuries of Black and White Labor* (New York, 1998) for an expanded argument of continuity. On the decline of poverty among black Americans, see Thernstrom and Thernstrom, *America in Black and White*, 232–7. For a highly critical view of black leadership, see Manning Marable, *Black Leadership* (New York, 1998); Robert C. Smith, *We Have No Leaders: African Americans in the Post–Civil Rights Era* (Albany, 1996). I have discussed the various positions in the controversies over the black underclass elsewhere; see Manfred Berg, "Struktureller Rassismus oder pathologisches Sozialverhalten? Die Debatte über die Black Underclass in den USA," in Winfried Fluck and Welf Werner, eds., *Wie viel Ungleichheit verträgt die Demokratie? Armut und Reichtum in den USA* (Frankfurt, 2003), 47–70.

44 Orlando Patterson, *The Ordeal of Integration: Progress and Resentment in America's "Racial" Crisis* (Washington, D.C., 1997), 4, 171–203; for a similar conclusion, see Thernstrom and Thernstrom, *America in Black and White*, 533.

be brought in line with the principles of justice and equity. And indeed, American legal culture in general and liability law in particular have come a long way in developing an all-encompassing concept of "total justice," as historian Lawrence Friedman called it almost twenty years ago, that is to say, "a general expectation of justice, and a general expectation of recompense for injuries and loss."[45] This is a highly ambiguous and controversial notion, to say the least. While some defend it as a noble humanitarian vision to protect the weak and powerless, others reject it as a gateway for the frivolous abuse of the judicial system and for the tyranny of moralism. To be sure, in a culture that values rights and justice, all claims for rectification at least deserve a fair hearing. But whenever far-reaching demands for justice are based on history, historians are called on to subject them to critical scrutiny, employing the empirical knowledge and analytical tools of their discipline.

45 Lawrence M. Friedman, *Total Justice* (New York, 1985), 5, 43–52.

4

Disputed Victims

The West German Discourse on Restitution for the Victims of Nazism

CONSTANTIN GOSCHLER

Over the last few years, restitution for victims of historical injustice has become increasingly important on both the political and historical agendas. However, there are conflicting assessments of this trend. Elazar Barkan, who adheres to a cultural concept of restitution, points to the potential power of restitution to settle deep-rooted conflicts between nations and ethnic groups. Restitution, from this viewpoint, may be described as a means of reinventing the past and, consequently, altering identities by fusing "polarized antagonistic histories into a core of shared history to which both sides can subscribe and from which each will benefit."[1] Others, like John Torpey, are more concerned about the cultivation of victimhood, which in Torpey's opinion goes hand in hand with the new politics of restitution. Whereas Barkan sees settling disturbing issues of the past as a means of gaining a better future, Torpey considers the current trend toward restitution a symptom of a now-prevalent catastrophic view of twentieth-century history. In Torpey's view, universalistic ideas of a better future are increasingly being replaced by particularist attempts on the part of various ethnic groups to utilize their historical suffering as a political weapon to improve their situation.[2]

This chapter is based on a comprehensive study by the author, *Schuld und Schulden. Die Politik der Wiedergutmachung für NS-Verfolgte seit 1945* (Göttingen, 2005). See also Goschler, "German Compensation to Jewish Nazi Victims after 1945," in Jeffry M. Diefendorf, ed., *Lessons and Legacies VI: New Currents in Holocaust Research* (Evanston, Ill., 2004), 373–412.

1 Elazar Barkan, *The Guilt of Nations: Restitution and Negotiating International Justice* (Baltimore, 2001), 329. See also Elazar Barkan and Alexander Karner, eds., *Taking Wrongs Seriously: Apologies and Reconciliation* (Stanford, 2006).
2 John Torpey, "'Making Whole What Has Been Smashed': Reflections on Reparations," *Journal of Modern History* 73 (2001): 333–58; Torpey, "Introduction: Politics and the Past" in Torpey, ed., *Politics*

The question at hand, then, is whether the current politics of restitution is a symptom of a negative utopia arising from the loss of universalistic ideals or an attempt to revive Enlightenment ideals in the postmodern, globalized world. One problem with this debate, however, is its inherent presentism, given its focus on developments that date from only the 1990s. As an alternative, I propose to recontextualize historical examples of restitution. West German restitution to the victims of the Nazis' crimes is an especially useful case because it took shape over more than fifty years. Furthermore, it has frequently been used as a point of reference in recent discussions of claims to restitution for wrongs ranging from slavery and the consequences of colonialism to a variety of war crimes. This is also part of the more general trend of using the case of West Germany as a model of a successful transition from dictatorship to democracy run by the United States – a trend that was especially strong in the early days of operation "Iraqi Freedom," when some called not only for a "Debaathization" process on the lines of denazification but also for an Iraqi Adenauer. Such attempts to use an almost mythical picture of the past for present-day political purposes, another aspect of the aforementioned presentism, also need to be confronted with sober historical analysis. Hence, the point of departure of the following discussion will not be the success or failure of German restitution, but the question how compensation for Nazi victims could come about at all.

This chapter focuses on the main variations in the public restitution discourse in Germany from 1945 to the present, which have been marked by a triple competition. First, from the very beginning, restitution for Nazi victims has collided with war reparations, which are a well-established element of international law. The German term *Wiedergutmachung* (literally "making good again") has been frequently used in the sense of (war) reparations. This understanding was also preceded by the German translation of the Treaty of Versailles. The attempt to distinguish between the German victims of Nazi offenses and the foreign victims of the war constituted a main controversy in the realm of restitution for Nazi crimes after 1945. It found its expression in the so-called principle of territoriality (*Territorialitätsprinzip*), which became one of the cornerstones of West German indemnification legislation. This principle maintained that only those who had been in some personal relation to the territory of the German Reich were entitled to compensation. German restitution for the Nazis' victims defended a traditional concept of the sovereign modern nation-state – while Nazi rule in Europe had done

and the Past: On Repairing Historical Injustices (Lanham, Md., 2003), 1–34; Torpey, *Making Whole What Has Been Smashed: On Reparations Politics* (Cambridge, Mass., 2006).

much to erode this principle, thus heavily contributing to what Charles Maier recently described as the crisis of territoriality.³ Hence, we shall inquire into the question of how changes with respect to the boundary between Nazi victims and foreign victims of the war came about: Which wrongs were considered Nazi crimes, and which wrongs were considered mere consequences of "ordinary" German warfare?

Second, support for restitution to the Nazis' victims has always been in competition with the widely held view among Germans that the German people were themselves victims of World War II, a view that has gained only limited official recognition. In this view, victims of Nazi crimes were not considered part of the German people; thus, the idea of a purified German *Volksgemeinschaft* (national community) survived beyond 1945. Discussion of German restitution to the Nazis' victims must therefore consider not only how Nazi persecution has been defined, which has been influenced by changing views of the nature of the Nazi regime, but also the consequences of "separate suffering" – that is, of the competition among the different groups who experienced adversity as a result of Nazi rule. Therefore, I will ask which forms of suffering were addressed in Germany after 1945 through restitution and how that was related to widespread feeling among the German public that they themselves were victims of historical wrongs resulting from the war.

Third, there has always been a competition among the groups targeted for persecution under the Nazis.⁴ Some groups of the Nazis' victims may have tried to use restitution for the purpose of building a group identity, but there has never been a common identity encompassing all the groups who suffered Nazi persecution. This is due primarily to the diversity – ethnic, religious, national, and social – of the Nazis' victims. Their only point in common was Nazi persecution, which had established many distinctions among victims. That also clearly limits the possibility of developing a common narrative of the past, even among victims. The construction of a "Memorial to the Murdered Jews of Europe" in Berlin, for instance, prompted calls from other victim groups, notably Roma and Sinti, for similar recognition. In speaking of the victims of Nazis, consequently, one must always be aware of the highly volatile nature of this category, which is the result of both political and legal considerations and processes of individual and collective identity construction. We will therefore have to ask how far competition among

---

3 Charles Maier, "Consigning the Twentieth Century to History: Alternative Narratives for the Modern Era," *American Historical Review* 105 (2000): 807–31.
4 See esp. Jean-Michel Chaumont, *La concurrence des victimes. Génocide, identité, reconnaissance* (Paris, 1997).

groups of victims contributed to the processes of inclusion and exclusion that marked the restitution discourse from the outset.

Germany Under Occupation: Restitution and Reparations

It was by no means self-evident at the end of the war that the Nazis' victims would receive restitution. Restitution was possible only once it was understood that Nazi persecution could not be addressed within existing moral and legal frameworks. Due to the omnipresence of the Holocaust discourse today, it is hard to understand that this could have been different during or after the war. But both before and after 1945, the consequences of Nazi persecution were widely considered only one, and probably not even the most important, of many pressing problems. Nor were the Nazis' victims the only claimants demanding compensation. The reparation claims put forward by many of the nations overrun by the Wehrmacht – particularly in Eastern Europe – figured most prominently among the competing claims. In 1945, the war, not the Holocaust, stood at the center of the master narrative of recent historical wrongs.

A basic understanding of who would be considered a victim of Nazism had already emerged during the war. In brief, this definition embraced persons who had been persecuted for reasons of race, religion, or political beliefs. However, except for the Jewish Agency for Palestine and the World Jewish Congress, no one at that point was considering non-German victims of Nazi persecution possible claimants of restitution. Both German opponents of Nazism and the United States government considered only onetime German nationals or stateless persons as being entitled to future restitution. Non-German victims – including victims of the Holocaust – were viewed within the context of the problem of war reparations.[5] The reason German and stateless victims were entitled to restitution was that they would not be entitled to reparations under traditional international law. In the long run, however, the expectation that foreign victims, who would be indirectly entitled to war reparations, would end up better off than German or stateless victims proved false. West Germany established a comprehensive system of restitution for Germans who suffered material losses as a result of Nazi persecution or the war, but it evaded most of its reparations obligations and thus also the claims of foreign victims of Nazism. The 1953 London Debt Agreement was especially important in this regard: it blocked the claims of millions of victims, namely, the foreigners forced

---

5 For more detail, see Goschler, *Schuld and Schulden*.

into service as laborers in the German war industry.[6] As a result, there was constant pressure on the West German government from the 1950s on to open German restitution to non-German nationals. Yet it was only in the decades to come that the distinction between (internal) restitution for Nazi victims and (external) reparations for war damages gradually weakened.[7]

In the immediate postwar period, there were two distinct calls for restitution to victims of Nazism. The first came from the Western Allies, especially the United States. They were motivated above all by the pressing social welfare problem that impoverished victims posed, both in occupied Germany and in the countries where hundreds of thousands of German and Austrian emigrants had sought refuge before the war. Forced emigration and, thereby, the export of social problems was seen as a new weapon employed by dictatorial regimes of the twentieth century. Restitution was therefore seen as a means of deterring other dictators from using that weapon in the future. In calling for restitution, the Western Allies were by no means interested in creating an enduring group identity for victims of Nazism: their aim was the integration of the victims in German society or the societies where they had found refuge. Restitution was far removed from identity politics at that time.

The United States in particular was also under pressure to do something about the property of German Jews that had been expropriated, stolen, or sold under duress during the Nazi era. This was a matter of both interest and principle. On the one hand, former German nationals who had escaped to the United States were calling for restitution for their losses. On the other hand, U.S. occupation policy sought to reestablish the liberal concept of property and the certainty of property rights, which had been undermined by the large-scale expropriation of Jews' property during the Third Reich. By contrast, restitution did not figure prominently in the Soviet zone, where property rights were established according to socialist principles step by step after 1945.

Both motives – social stability and stability of property rights – also stood behind German initiatives for restitution. But because there was no German

---

6 See esp. Ulrich Herbert, "Nicht entschädigungsfähig? Die Wiedergutmachungsansprüche der Ausländer," in Ludolf Herbst and Constantin Goschler, eds., *Wiedergutmachung in der Bundesrepublik Deutschland* (Munich, 1989), 273–302; Jörg Fisch, *Reparationen nach dem Zweiten Weltkrieg* (Munich, 1992), 117–22; Cornelius Pawlita, *"Wiedergutmachung" als Rechtsfrage? Die politische und juristische Auseinandersetzung um Entschädigung für die Opfer nationalsozialistischer Verfolgung (1945 bis 1990)* (Frankfurt am Main, 1993), 238–55; Goschler, *Schuld und Schulden*, 248–53.
7 For more detail, see Hans Günter Hockerts, Claudia Moisel, and Tobias Winstel, eds., *Grenzen der Wiedergutmachung. Die Entschädigung für NS-Verfolgte in West- und Osteuropa 1945–2000* (Göttingen, 2006).

political body above the level of the states (*Länder*), those initiatives were much more limited in scope than the restitution programs the Allies envisioned. Another factor played an important part in circumscribing German restitution efforts: the politicians vying for office and influence in western Germany's fledgling democracy were acutely afraid of being accused by their voters of acquiescing to another Versailles-style settlement by accepting financial obligations imposed from outside. And since German public opinion was not in favor of restitution, democracy proved to be of little help with respect to claims of the Nazis' victims. In their efforts to avoid assuming responsibility for restitution laws that they sometimes considered too far-reaching, German politicians occasionally preferred that the Allies enact the laws. That was, for example, the case with property restitution.[8]

The 1950s: Restitution for Victims and Integration of *Volksgenossen*

In contrast to the immediate postwar period, when the public sphere in Germany was heavily restricted by the occupying Allied powers, the years following the establishment of the Federal Republic in 1949 saw the emergence of a German public discourse on restitution. The Nazi persecution of the Jews became a central focus of that discourse; conversely, the victims of political persecution, who had stood at the center of the restitution debate in the immediate postwar years, moved into the background. This change was due in large measure to the Cold War: increasing political tensions led to a split in the Vereinigung der Verfolgten des Naziregimes (Association of Persecutees of the Nazi Regime), which for a short time had represented all Germans who had suffered at the hands of the Nazis. (Foreigners had never been represented within this organization.) Consequently, victims did not speak with one voice in the 1950s – or, in fact, for many years. Jewish victims could, however, rely on influential representative organizations. In 1951, twenty-three Jewish organizations from all over the world established the Conference of Material Claims against Germany, and in the following decades the Claims Conference became an important political player in the area of restitution – even if, strictly speaking, it was not an organization *of*, but rather *for*, Jewish victims of Nazism. One of the Claims Conference's major achievements was that it could present itself as the sole representative of Jewish claimants even when there were serious disagreements among Jewish claimants, especially between German and non-German Jews.

---

8 See Goschler, *Schuld and Schulden*, 100–21; Jürgen Lillteicher, *Raub, Recht und Restitution. Die Rückerstattung jüdischen Eigentums in der frühen Bundesrepublik* (Göttingen, 2007).

For a long time, Jewish victims were in competition less with other victim groups than with German victims of the war. The plight of expellees, prisoners of war, and other victims of the war touched the hearts of the West German public much more strongly than did the suffering the Nazis' victims had experienced.[9] Simply put, most Germans saw themselves as victims of the war, whereas those who had been excluded from the *Volksgemeinschaft* during the Nazi era in effect remained excluded from the mainstream of West German society after the war. There was even less empathy toward the Nazis' foreign victims. In any event, though, the majority of surviving victims, including onetime German nationals, no longer lived in Germany after 1945, and those who did were more often regarded as witnesses to a haunting past than as fellow citizens deserving of support.

Although the Federal Indemnification Law (Bundesentschädigungsgesetz) for victims of Nazism, enacted in 1953, did not receive much public attention, two other facets of the restitution issue were intensely debated: the Luxembourg Treaty (1952) and the enforcement of the restitution laws enacted by the Western Allies between 1947 and 1949. Because of its high symbolic value, the Luxembourg Treaty between the Federal Republic, Israel, and the Claims Conference has often been equated with West German restitution policy as a whole.[10] Konrad Adenauer, the first chancellor of the Federal Republic, had pressed agreement against opposition on the part of most of the public and even within his governing coalition. A frequent argument against the treaty was that it would jeopardize the traditional friendship between the Germans and Arabs. In countering opposition to the treaty, Adenauer used a combination of moral and pragmatic arguments, which makes it hard to distinguish between his personal convictions and political tactics. He seemed, though, to think it important to point to the allegedly strong interest of the United States in a positive outcome as well as to the allegedly strong position of "world Jewry" – an expression that Nahum Goldmann, the first president of the Claims Conference, also frequently used in his talks with the Germans – to

---

9 Robert G. Moeller, *War Stories: The Search for a Usable Past in the Federal Republic of Germany* (Berkeley, 2001); Moeller, "Deutsche Opfer, Opfer der Deutschen. Kriegsgefangene, Vertriebene, NS-Verfolgte: Opferausgleich als Identitätspolitik," in Klaus Naumann, ed., *Nachkrieg in Deutschland* (Hamburg, 2001), 29–58; Constantin Goschler, "Versöhnung und Viktimisierung. Der deutsche Opferdiskurs und die Vertriebenen," *Zeitschrift für Geschichtswissenschaft* 53 (2005): 873–84.

10 The high estimation of the Luxembourg agreements is also reflected in the intensity of scholarly work on this topic. See esp. Nana Sagi, *German Reparations: A History of the Negotiations* (New York, 1986); Lily G. Feldman, *The Special Relationship between West Germany and Israel* (Boston, 1984); Ronald W. Zweig, *German Reparations and the Jewish World: A History of the Claims Conference*, 2nd ed. (London, 2001); Goschler, *Wiedergutmachung*, 257–85; Yeshayahu A. Jelinek, *Zwischen Moral und Realpolitik. Eine Dokumentensammlung* (Gerlingen, 1997); Niels Hansen, *Aus dem Schatten der Katastrophe. Die deutsch-israelischen Beziehungen in der Ära Konrad Adenauer und David Ben Gurion. Ein dokumentierter Bericht* (Düsseldorf, 2002).

convince his governing coalition. It was only with backing from the opposition Social Democrats that Adenauer was able to secure Bundestag ratification of the agreement.

There was even greater resistance to the restitution of Jewish property under the terms of the occupation-era laws.[11] The explanation for that is simple: whereas the costs of individual and global settlements were borne by taxpayers collectively, perhaps as many as 100,000 West Germans would be individually affected by the restitution of identifiable property to former Jewish owners. The number of people who might have to turn property over to previous owners was sometimes put as high as 300,000 – probably inaccurately – in public discussion.[12] Opinion polls also showed that West Germans favored state-run compensation payments more heavily than individual restitution of Jewish property, which was widely considered an injustice against Germans. One may draw the conclusion that, at least in the 1950s, West Germans generally did not see the Nazi-era "aryanization" and expropriation of Jewish property as unfair; rather, those actions were still widely viewed as a kind of restitution to the German people, who had allegedly been exploited by the Jews during the international economic crisis of the 1930s. The Allies thus had a difficult time ensuring the restitution of property to Jews in the late 1940s and the 1950s in the face of deep-rooted resentment on the part of many Germans.

A glimpse at West German popular culture in the 1950s attests to the intense interest in the fate of German victims of the war and limited interest in the Nazis' victims. While in 1946 Wolfgang Staudte's *Die Mörder sind unter uns* ("The Murders Are Among Us") had addressed the issue of German responsibility for the atrocities of the Nazi era, during the 1950s, by contrast, POWs were the subject of touching movies like the famous *Der Arzt von Stalingrad* ("The Doctor from Stalingrad"), and expellees found their way into the notorious *Heimatfilme*. The Nazis' victims, by contrast, were only rarely depicted in films of that genre. When Jewish victims showed up in West German films of the 1950s, they were usually presented as embodiments of a generous, universal humanism, as, for example, in the play *Anne Frank* and the movie *Der Teufel spielte Balalaika* ("The Devil Played the Balalaika," released abroad under the English title *Destination Death*).[13]

---

11 See Constantin Goschler and Jürgen Lillteicher, eds., *"Arisierung" und Restitution. Die Auseinandersetzung um die Rückerstattung des jüdischen Eigentums in Deutschland und Österreich nach 1945 und 1990* (Göttingen, 2002).
12 Walter Schwarz, *Rückerstattung nach den Gesetzen der Alliierten Mächte* (Munich, 1974), 368.
13 See Moeller, *War Stories*, 123–70.

What did restitution to the Nazis' victims mean for efforts to come to terms with the Nazi past in the Federal Republic during the 1950s? Perhaps ironically, restitution played an important part in providing justification for the social integration of groups of individuals incriminated by their participation in the Nazi regime. Leaving their own views aside, West German politicians of every stripe had to keep in mind that sweeping political purges would be extremely unpopular. Some measure of restitution was thus considered necessary if the integration of those compromised by the past was to be made acceptable. At the very least, the minority of West Germans in favor of restitution as a matter of principle could use the issue of integration for leverage.

The West German government's position on restitution in the first decade of the Federal Republic's existence could be described as a policy of quid pro quo. Each time a measure was enacted on behalf of the Nazis' victims, the West German public demanded action of behalf not only of incriminated groups such as the owners of expropriated Jewish property but also for "victims of the war" in the widest sense of the term. Those demands were sometimes successful. The simplest explanation of why the government acceded to such demands is that "victims of the war" were an important voter group and the Nazis' victims were not. Restitution measures for the Nazis' victims could, therefore, serve as a fig leaf for the integration of groups tainted by their pasts. The best example is the Nazi-era civil servants who lost their jobs after 1945. In 1952, a law providing compensation to civil servants who had lost their jobs in 1933 was enacted but only in exchange for a law that provided far-reaching compensation for Nazi-era civil servants who had been dismissed after 1945.[14] This suggests that there was a sense of justice that recognized that the claims of civil servants dismissed by the Nazis could not be ignored while former Nazi civil servants received benefits.

To sum up, the issue of reparations, initially pressed by the Western Allies, became largely a German concern during the 1950s – the still-existing Allied controls notwithstanding. Reparation to the Nazis' victims was in large part linked to questions of integration – the integration of incriminated groups within West German society and, in turn, the Federal Republic's integration in the Western alliance. In the end, a delicate balance between benefits for the Nazis' victims and benefits for the German victims of the war was established that provided a foundation for both social stability at home and acceptance abroad, at least within the West.

---

14 See Goschler, *Wiedergutmachung*, 234–41; Norbert Frei, *Adenauer's Germany and the Nazi Past: The Politics of Amnesty and Integration* (New York, 2002), chap. 3, "The Rehabilitation and Pensioning of the '131ers,'" 41–66.

The 1960s: Clear-Cut Break with the Past

It has often been noted that the broad reluctance among West Germans to deal with Nazi crimes began to change at the end of the 1950s. This was in part a reaction to several spectacular criminal cases involving accused Nazi perpetrators. The prosecution of members of SS *Einsatzgruppen* (death squads) in Ulm in 1958, the Eichmann trial in Jerusalem in 1961, and the Auschwitz trial in Frankfurt in 1964 drew public attention to the mass killings in Central and Eastern Europe and thereby destroyed the mental block many Germans had developed in response to the Nuremberg trials. In considering the discussion of restitution during the 1960s, however, we encounter a seeming paradox. At the same time the West German public was becoming ever more aware of the Holocaust, it was also increasingly eager for a clear-cut, final legislative response to the issue of restitution. In 1965, the Bundestag passed a final version of the Federal Indemnification Law, which remains in effect today; to indicate that the law was intended to be the last word on the issue, the term *Schlussgesetz* – "final law" – was added to its title. That same year, Chancellor Ludwig Erhard gave voice to a widespread desire among West Germans when he announced "the end of the post-war era" in his inaugural speech before the Bundestag.[15]

It would be simple to explain the desire to bar further revisions to the indemnification legislation as an expression of the desire to suppress all memory of the Nazis' crimes. As previously noted, the growing support for a final settlement on restitution to the Nazis' victims in the 1960s went hand in hand with growing public awareness of the mass murder carried out under the Nazis. One explanation for this seeming paradox might be that these two trends reinforced one another, as both were linked to the desire on the part of most Germans to dissociate themselves from a terrible past. The more that became known about the Nazis' crimes, the more Germans wished that they would not be forever associated with this horrible aspect of their history. The Federal Republic provided for restitution to the Nazis' victims in the expectation that doing so would help close the book on the Third Reich, but not all the victims, particularly the Jews, were ready to accept that line of reasoning.

This divergence in perspectives can be illustrated by the West German government's response to Nahum Goldmann's request for a final symbolic gesture of restitution in 1964. Goldmann suggested that Bonn help finance

---

15 Ludwig Erhard, in Proceedings of the Deutsche Bundestag, 4. Meeting, Nov. 10, 1965, Stenographische Berichte, vol. 60, 17.

the establishment of a museum in Israel devoted to the memory of the destroyed Jewish communities of Central and Eastern Europe. In an internal memorandum, a high-ranking official in the Federal Finance Ministry argued strongly against this project:

> Experience shows that such museums do not constitute monuments for the German will for restitution, however, they reinforce the memory to National Socialist persecution. Of course, all the terrible events should not be forgotten. But as experience shows, such institutions work as permanent sources of a malicious anti-German propaganda.[16]

Three years earlier, President Heinrich Lübke had publicly expressed his hope "that the Jews will not leave the goodwill present in our contribution to restitution unanswered."[17] By the early 1960s, after ten years of restitution payments, West Germans increasingly expected that at least the material issues arising from the Nazi past would eventually be settled once and for all. That expectation was closely tied to the hope that such compensation would be understood as part of an effort to atone for Nazi crimes. Whereas the representatives of Jewish organizations looked on restitution as an open-ended process, the West German conception of restitution rested on the assumption that the process would eventually be completed and brought to a close.

The 1970s and 1980s: Civil Society and "Forgotten Victims"

Although many West Germans – members of the public and of the political class alike – considered the subject of restitution closed after the mid-1960s, the issue was soon reopened as a result of both generational and political change. In his capacity first as foreign minister in the Christian Democratic–Social Democratic "grand coalition" and then as leader of the Social Democratic–Liberal coalition, Willy Brandt sought a new understanding with the nations of Eastern Europe; the result was the so-called *Neue Ostpolitik* Bonn pursued during Brandt's chancellorship. One consequence of *Ostpolitk* was that West Germany was confronted with millions of victims of the Nazis living behind the Iron Curtain who had yet to receive any sort of restitution. These countries could claim that they had been excluded from West German restitution efforts on account of the Cold War, while eleven Western European countries had received payments to aid the victims of Nazism living there. The Brandt government was very

---

16 Féaux de la Croix to Federal Minister of Finance, January 30, 1964, Bundesarchiv Koblenz, B 126/109454.
17 See quotations in Jeffrey Herf, *Divided Memory: The Nazi Past in the Two Germanys* (Cambridge, Mass., 1997), 332.

much afraid that reopening the restitution issue would also open the door to claims that it thought could jeopardize the country's economic and political stability – as well as the social reforms that stood atop its domestic agenda.

Consequently, the Brandt government avoided formal recognition of East European restitution claims and, at the same time, provided "indirect restitution" to Poland and Yugoslavia in the form of economic aid and low-interest credits. West German public opinion, however, did not buy such subtle distinctions: newspapers attacked "restitution for Tito bandits," and in the Bundestag the claims of Polish victims were counterbalanced by the claims of German expellees. Eastern Europe was vividly portrayed in this public debate as a slaughterhouse where countless Germans perished in the immediate postwar period, but there was little mention of what had happened in those countries under German occupation.[18]

West German public opinion on the question of restitution began to change only in the late 1970s, and the change became truly marked in the course of the 1980s.[19] The middle-of-the road weekly *Die Zeit* can stand as an example. During the debate on the final version of the Federal Indemnification Law, *Die Zeit* had asked critically for how long and how much the Germans should pay restitution, thereby indicating that it, too, was in favor of a final settlement.[20] In 1986, however, *Die Zeit* both echoed and reinforced a growing mood when it vigorously criticized the shortcomings of West German restitution policy.[21] The year before, Chancellor Helmut Kohl and President Ronald Reagan had come under heavy criticism when they in effect equated the suffering of the Nazis' victims and German war victims by their combined visits to the Bergen-Belsen concentration camp memorial and the Bitburg military cemetery, where members of the Waffen-SS were interred along with other military personnel. The strong public protests against the Bitburg visit were a clear signal that times had changed, or at least that cultural hegemony had shifted. The delicate balance between the victims of Nazism and German victims of the war that had once prevailed was no longer possible.

18 For more detail, see Goschler, *Schuld and Schulden*, 309–22.
19 On the developments of the West German attitude to the Nazi past, see esp. Herf, *Divided Memory*; Helmut Dubiel, *Niemand ist frei von der Geschichte. Die nationalsozialistische Herrschaft in den Debatten des deutschen Bundestages* (Munich, 1999); Peter Reichel, *Vergangenheitsbewältigung in Deutschland. Die Auseinandersetzung mit der NS-Diktatur von 1945 bis heute* (Munich, 2001); Helmut König, *Die Zukunft der Vergangenheit. Der Nationalsozialismus im politischen Bewußtsein der Bundesrepublik* (Frankfurt am Main, 2003).
20 Ernst Ehrmann, "Wiedergutmachung," *Die Zeit*, March 3, 1964.
21 Dörte von Westernhagen, "Wiedergutgemacht?" *Die Zeit*, October 10, 1984.

How did this change come about? One explanation might be generational change: the change in attitude was, so to speak, part of the aftermath of the student revolt of 1968. Another important factor may have been the sense of contentment that prevailed in the Federal Republic during the 1980s. That decade was a period of broad prosperity in the Federal Republic, and that encouraged many West Germans to think that paying restitution to victims who had thus far been excluded would not be an unbearable burden. Furthermore, calling for restitution to the "forgotten victims" became a way to criticize the government of Helmut Kohl, which had promoted a more conservative historical-political climate since coming to power in 1982. At the same time, though, the new West German restitution discourse was also marked by an element of inwardness: many projects aimed at solutions at a local level and were, given the enormous dimensions of the problem, inadequate in many respects. West German civil society could hardly provide a satisfactory response to the state-run Nazi persecution of millions of people during the Second World War. Finally, another important aspect of these projects was that they moved away from the predominance of the Nazis' Jewish victims within the restitution discourse. One might ask how far this was motivated by a desire to evade the sometimes almost unbearable moral pressure exerted by the existence of Jewish Nazi victims by pointing to other groups who had largely been excluded from the restitution discourse and from material restitution.

The 1980s saw the fight for the "forgotten victims": Gypsies, homosexuals, Wehrmacht deserters, victims of compulsory sterilization, and foreign forced laborers. The battle to provide restitution to these victims was very much inspired by recent changes in social values – and, conversely, it was also invoked for the purpose of trying to change West German values. The groups recognized as "forgotten victims" in the 1980s had in fact not been forgotten during the 1950s but rather were deliberately excluded. The call for improvement in the situation of minorities during the 1980s was bolstered by morally loaded references to the persecution they suffered in the Nazi era. In this way, the Federal Republic participated in the shift from universalistic ideologies – embodied in the role of the "fighter" – to the discourse of identity – embodied in the role of the "victim" – that took place in all Western societies.[22] The transformation of the West German

---

22 Pieter Lagrou, "Frankreich," in Volkhard Knigge and Norbert Frei, eds., *Verbrechen erinnern. Die Auseinandersetzung mit Holocaust und Völkermord* (Munich, 2002), 163–75, here 174.

restitution discourse thus reflected the rise of the politics of victimization, which has increasingly marked Western political culture in recent decades.

Germany United: Globalization and the Universalization of Restitution

While restitution discourse reflected internal West German political divisions and debates on values during the 1980s, German reunification placed restitution in an international framework once again in the 1990s. The Nazis' victims were not, of course, at the top of the agenda during the political process that led to German reunification. Nevertheless, without reunification – and, more broadly, without the end of the Cold War – the restitution issue would not have been reopened. As a result, the main focus of the restitution discourse shifted from the mostly non-Jewish "forgotten victims" back to Jewish victims and victims, both Jewish and gentile, in the former Eastern bloc countries.

In the first years after German unification, the restitution debate focused on the problem of applying West German policies in the former German Democratic Republic. East Germany had chosen a different path from West Germany in dealing with the Nazis' victims. It looked on its own existence as a form of restitution because, as East German officials regularly asserted, the establishment of a socialist state had truly eradicated the roots of fascism. East Germany established a comprehensive system of social privileges that benefited mostly communists who had resisted the Nazis. Although Jews and members of other persecuted groups were eligible, since 1965 this system of benefits distinguished between "fighters" *against* and "victims" *of* fascism, and the latter were held in lower regard and received lower material benefits. Since privileges for those who had suffered at the hands of the Nazis were limited to citizens of the GDR, they benefited only a comparatively small number of victims – some 10,000 East Germans – as opposed to the more than 1 million individuals around the world who received some form of compensation from the Federal Republic. In short, restitution in the GDR meant, first and foremost, considerable privileges for communist resistance fighters, who received attentive care because, as representatives of an antifascist tradition, they provided the governing Socialist Unity Party with important political capital. Very little expropriated or stolen property was returned to Jews in the GDR. That was due in large measure to the changes in property rights that came with the creation of a socialist economy. It probably also had something to do with the desire to avoid bothering onetime "little Nazis,"[23] who, much as in the Federal Republic, had generously been offered integration into the new East German social order during the 1950s.

As a result of pressure from Jewish organizations, West German policies on property restitution were adopted in the new eastern states of the Federal Republic. Restoring expropriated property to Jews contributed, however, to the cultural clash between eastern and western Germans. Some easterners felt they were being stripped of their property by a coalition of West German bureaucrats and Jewish organizations, thereby showing a lack of sensitivity to the historical injustice associated with "aryanized" property.[24] More than fifty years after the war, after the revolutions in property rights, it was often hard for East Germans affected by restitution claims to accept that their inherited property was no longer theirs. The situation was probably exacerbated by the eagerness of West German bureaucrats to promote the restitution process to show that they had learned a lesson from the criticism of the West German restitution policies of the 1950s. East Germans felt that this demonstration on the part of the West Germans was coming at their expense. Such views did not play a significant role in German public discourse; rather, they were articulated in the private sphere. But they may have contributed to a widespread feeling of victimization among easterners, many of whom were hard hit by the economic consequences of unification. The impact of restitution of expropriated Jewish property should not be overstated, however; the issue was overshadowed by the debate on restitution of property nationalized in 1949 with the establishment of the GDR, which encompassed vastly more property. That may be part of the reason why restitution of Jewish property after 1990 did not provoke public unrest on the same scale as it had in West Germany after 1945.

The year 1996 marked yet another turning point in restitution discourse. Civil suits against Swiss banks brought before courts in the United States opened the way for the globalization of restitution to the Nazis' victims. More than ever, restitution became dependent on the ability to exert political pressure by organizing publicity. Of course, restitution policy had always been influenced by the capacity of the different groups of victims to draw public attention to the issue and to influence public opinion. But since the 1990s, the restitution discourse is no longer a matter of the German, North

---

23 See Christoph Hölscher, *NS-Verfolgte im "antifaschistischen" Staat. Vereinnahmung und Ausgrenzung in der ostdeutschen Wiedergutmachung* (Berlin, 2002), 103 f; Goschler, *Schuld und Schulden*, 361–7.

24 See, in more detail, Jan Philipp Spannuth, *Rückerstattung Ost. Der Umgang der DDR mit dem "arisierten" Eigentum der Juden und die Rückerstattung im wiedervereinigten Deutschland* (Essen, 2007).

American, and Israeli public spheres; it has, rather, in effect been globalized. And one consequence of this development is that Germany is no longer the exclusive target of restitution claims. Many countries in Europe and even beyond have come under scrutiny for their wartime conduct vis-à-vis the Nazis' Jewish victims. In all, twenty-three countries established historical commissions to examine their actions during the Nazi era. The globalization of restitution discourse thus went hand in hand with a universalization of restitution as a response to historical wrongs.[25]

During this time, Germany was under pressure to pay compensation to foreigners who had been forced into service as laborers in Germany's wartime munitions industry. For more than four decades, the exploitation they had suffered was not seen as a form of Nazi persecution but rather as an aspect of "ordinary" warfare, which excluded them from restitution by putting them into the framework of reparations. The division between victims of the Nazis and victims of German warfare implies a distinction between Nazi rule and an untainted German state and Wehrmacht. Since the 1980s, that distinction has struck more and more Germans as unviable. But the government of the Federal Republic has always insisted on this distinction because otherwise the issue of war reparations might be reopened – which might, in turn, bring tremendous financial consequences.

Primarily in response to international pressure, the German government and business community established the Foundation "Remembrance, Responsibility, and Future" (Stiftung "Erinnerung, Verantwortung und Zukunft") in 2000 to settle the issues of compensation for foreign forced laborers and, secondarily, of stolen Jewish property.[26] That was the last German attempt to date to bring the restitution debate to a much-desired close. It is possible that this settlement has contributed to the view now prevailing in the Federal Republic that Germany has made sufficient recompense for its wrongdoing in the past. And if West Germany had long considered it necessary to act as the good ally in order to give reassurance that it had put the Nazi past behind it,[27] German foreign policy today is no longer constrained by such considerations. To be sure, Nazi crimes and, in particular,

---

25 See Martin Dean, Constantin Goschler, and Philipp Ther, eds., *Robbery and Restitution: The Conflict over Jewish Property in Europe* (Oxford, 2007).
26 See Matthias Arning, *Späte Abrechnung. Über Zwangsarbeiter, Schlussstriche und Berliner Verständigungen* (Frankfurt am Main, 2001); John Authers and Richard Wolffe, *The Victim's Fortune: Inside the Epic Battle over the Debts of the Holocaust* (New York, 2002); Stuart E. Eizenstat, *Imperfect Justice: Looted Assets, Slave Labor, and the Unfinished Business of World War II* (New York, 2003); Susanne-Sophia Spiliotis, *Verantwortung und Rechtsfrieden. Die Stiftungsinitiative der deutschen Wirtschaft* (Frankfurt am Main, 2003); Goschler, *Schuld und Schulden*, 450–75.
27 See Herf, *Divided Memory*, 299.

the Holocaust have been firmly incorporated in the negative nationalism that is part of the Federal Republic's political foundations.[28] Nonetheless, we are currently witnessing a tremendous increase in interest in German victims of the war, especially in the realm of public discourse and popular culture. With enormous success, novels and television documentaries have drawn attention to the Germans who fell victim to Soviet submarine attacks or British and U.S. air raids.[29]

What effect might the extension and universalization of restitution have in Germany? My tentative answer is twofold. First, the universalization of the principle of restitution will probably encourage efforts to include victims of German warfare. There have been such efforts over the decades, but they have not had much success. The most recent was the restitution claim put forward – unsuccessfully – by relatives of the inhabitants of a Greek village who had been murdered en masse by the German military in a retaliatory action during World War II. Such claims still run up against the well-established legal distinction between "legitimate" and "illegitimate" wrongs. The former is related to the concept of the modern sovereign state and to the modern concept of war. The latter, on the other hand, is related to the idea of the persecution of minorities, which in the past decade has increasingly come to include attacks on ethnic identity. The actions of the Nazi regime did much, however, to blur the distinction between these two types of wrongs.

Second, the universalization of restitution will probably bolster efforts to secure compensation for German – or Austrian – victims of wartime or postwar injustices. This is not merely a theoretical possibility. When German expellees from Silesia recently put forward their claims to lost property once again, it was clear that they had learned a lesson from the international restitution discourse. Instead of pinning its hopes on political assistance from the German government, the expellees' organization now uses a different language from in the past. It is not only pressing for a "serious apology" from the Polish government, but it has also threatened to file class-action suits in U.S. courts.[30] And on the same day that this chapter was completed, German newspapers reported that the Preußische Treuhand GmbH & Co., which explicitly likens itself to the Jewish Claims Conference, had announced

---

28 See Reinhard Koselleck, "Formen und Traditionen des negativen Gedächtnisses," in Knigge and Frei, eds., *Verbrechen erinnern*, 21–32; Volkhard Knigge, "Statt eines Nachworts: Abschied der Erinnerung. Anmerkungen zum notwendigen Wandel der Gedenkkultur in Deutschland," in Knigge and Frei, eds., *Verbrechen erinnern*, 423–40.
29 See esp. W. G. Sebald, *Luftkrieg und Literatur* (Frankfurt am Main, 2001); Günther Grass, *Im Krebsgang* (Göttingen, 2002); Jörg Friedrich, *Der Brand. Deutschland im Bombenkrieg 1940–1945* (Berlin, 2002).
30 See "Schlesier fordern Entschuldigung," *Frankfurter Allgemeine Zeitung*, July 14, 2003.

its intention to persuade Poland to return the former property of German expellees; this announcement caused considerable public unrest in Poland.[31] The "undeserving victims," as Elazar Barkan has dubbed such groups, have pressed their claims for restitution since the end of the war, but those claims were always rejected because the implicit likening of German victims of the war to the Nazis' victims has been regarded, rightly, as frivolous. The ongoing extension and universalization of the principle of restitution might complicate the picture, however.[32] We will increasingly be forced to discuss the question of whether it is possible to put different cases of historical wrongs on equal footing – and if not, why. The case of German restitution to the Nazis' victims might offer an important lesson in the discussion of redressing historical wrongs – even if it turns out to be a different and more complicated lesson than one might have initially expected.

31 See "Entrüstung in Polen über die 'Preußische Treuhand,'" *Frankfurter Allgemeine Zeitung*, October 6, 2003.
32 Cf. Barkan, *The Guilt of Nations*.

5

Greenlanders Displaced by the Cold War

Relocation and Compensation

SVEND AAGE CHRISTENSEN AND KRISTIAN SØBY KRISTENSEN

The intensifying conflict between the Soviet Union and the United States following the end of the Second World War gave new geostrategic importance to the high Arctic region. During the summer of 1951, accordingly, the United States began construction of an Air Force base at Thule in northwestern Greenland. A small settlement of Inughuit[1] hunters lived near the base at Uummannaq, and it quickly became evident that the base was having an adverse effect on hunting opportunities in the area. At the same time, the Air Force wanted to expand the base. The coexistence of the base and the community at Uummannaq soon became increasingly difficult. Danish colonial authorities therefore decided in 1953 to force the residents of Uummannaq to relocate. On very short notice, the residents were moved to a new settlement to the north.

The forced relocation of the residents of Uummannaq was handled quietly by the Danish authorities at the time. The Thule Air Base has played an important part in the triangular relations between the United States, Denmark, and an increasingly autonomous Greenland (formerly a Danish colony, Greenland was incorporated into the Kingdom of Denmark in 1953 and was granted home rule in 1979). Since the mid-1980s, the Uummannaq relocation has been the subject of intense political controversy, official investigations and lawsuits, and governmental negotiations. The issue has been on and off the domestic political agenda within Denmark and

---

1 Inughuit (Great People) is the name the indigenous population of Thule call themselves. This denotes them as a population distinct from the broader indigenous people of Greenland known as Inuit. Whether the Inughuit form a distinct indigenous people in a legal sense is a matter of discussion. See Steen Wulff, "The Legal Bases for the Inughuit Claim to Their Homelands," *International Journal on Minority and Group Rights* 11 (2005): 63–91 and note 36. This issue is, of course, a central matter in deciding where exactly the Inughuit have a right to return. We use the term merely to distinguish the community of Thule from the larger indigenous population of Greenland.

has sometimes put a severe strain on relations between Copenhagen and the Greenland Home Rule Government. Several different compensation schemes have been developed and implemented in part, but that has not brought a decisive resolution to the issue. As one Greenlandic politician has observed, it has been impossible so far to "kill an old ghost from the colonial past" once and for all.[2] No solution proposed to date has proven capable of making right the wrongs of the past in the eyes of all actors involved.

This chapter tells the story of the relocation of the Uummannaq community and examines the Danish government's attempts to address the issue of the relocation. The issue is a complicated one. It touches on both international and domestic politics, and it encompasses questions of security and defense policy as well as of legality and justice. The first section of this chapter sketches the historical background, and the second discusses the relocation. To make clear the political importance of the relocation, we then briefly outline the history of Greenland and Thule Air Base during the Cold War, before turning to the political debates and legal proceedings that began in the 1980s and are still going on today.

The American Military in Greenland

The American military presence in Greenland dates back to the Second World War. Following the German occupation of Denmark, all communication with the colony was effectively severed, and the United States took over responsibility for providing Greenland's inhabitants with necessary supplies. As the United States became directly involved in the war, the need for an American military presence in Greenland became apparent. Greenland became an important transfer point for the transport of men and equipment to Europe during the war, and the United States built a series of military bases and meteorological stations there, mainly on the southern part of the island.[3]

In 1951, Denmark, which had aligned itself with the West by joining the NATO alliance, and the United States signed an agreement that codified American base rights in Greenland and reaffirmed Danish sovereignty.[4]

---

2 Member of the Greenlandic Home Rule Parliament Augusta Salling, quoted in *Jyllands-Posten*, November 15, 2002.
3 Clive Archer, "The United States Defence Areas in Greenland," *Cooperation and Conflict* 23 (1988): 123–5. Legally, the foundation for the establishment of these bases was shaky, to say the least. The Danish delegation in Washington – acting entirely on its own initiative – signed an agreement in 1941 providing the United States unlimited rights to establish military bases on the island.
4 "Agreement Between the Government of the United States of America and the Government of the Kingdom of Denmark, Pursuant to the North Atlantic Treaty, Concerning the Defense of Greenland,"

Still in force today, the 1951 Defense Agreement entitles the United States, without compensation to Denmark, "within agreed defense areas and the air spaces and waters adjacent thereto," to fit the areas for military use (Article II). The agreement also stipulates that "United States aircraft may fly over and land in any territory in Greenland, including the territorial waters thereof, without restriction except as mutually agreed upon" (Article V).

It was clear in the 1950s that the American bases in southern Greenland would play an important role in the event of new hostilities in Europe, as they had during World War II. It was also clear that northern Greenland had acquired a new strategic importance. From northern Greenland, the Soviet heartland was within range of American bombers. The American military thus considered bases in northern Greenland a necessity.

On July 9, 1951, 120 American ships carrying 12,000 men arrived at Thule to build what was to become Thule Air Base. During the 1950s, the base was a very important staging point for nuclear bombers in the U.S. Air Force's new polar strategy. It also served as a base for fighter interceptor aircraft, reconnaissance flights, air rescue operations, and air transport. From 1957 to 1960, Thule was a primary strategic operating base of the Eighth Air Force and Strategic Air Command (SAC). In 1960, the base was transferred from SAC to Air Defense Command (ADC), and it then served mainly as part of the early warning system against ballistic missiles and as a satellite tracking station.[5]

In 1953, American officials decided the newly established Thule Air Base needed to be expanded. Antiaircraft artillery, they determined, had to be moved further from the main base. "In order for [antiaircraft] guns effectively to accomplish their mission," a brochure issued by the U.S. Army maintained, "it is necessary that they be so sited as to be able to engage hostile aircraft during their bomb run and prior to reaching the bomb release

---

April 27, 1951; text reprinted in *Grønland under den kolde krig. Dansk og amerikansk sikkerhedspolitik 1945–68*, Bilag, vol. 2 (Copenhagen, 1997), 144–53. On jurisdiction in foreign relations, Act 577 (November 29, 1978) of the Greenland Home Rule Act states:

(1) The central authorities of the Realm shall have jurisdiction in questions affecting the foreign relations of the Realm.
(2) Measures under consideration by the home rule authorities which would be of substantial importance for the foreign relations of the Realm, including participation by the Realm in international cooperation, shall be discussed with the central authorities before any decision is taken.

Text available online at: http://dk.nanoq.gl/TEMA.asp?page=tema&objno=31837.

5 *Grønland under den kolde krig. Dansk og amerikansk sikkerhedspolitik 1945–68*, vol. 1 (Copenhagen, 1997), 221f., 306–8.

line. As altitudes and aircraft speeds increase this bomb release line moves further away from the target area. The guns must move with it."[6] With the expansion of the base came the relocation of Uummannaq's residents, which was to be one of the most controversial aspects of the American military presence in Greenland.

Thule Air Base played a variety of roles as American military strategy and hardware changed over the course of the Cold War. The end of the Cold War has not diminished Thule's military importance, as American plans for a missile defense system attest. There is thus little chance the U.S. military will want to give the base up in the foreseeable future. Consequently, the existence of the base continues to influence attempts to resolve the problems that originated in the base's expansion in 1953.

Displacement

The proximity of the Uummannaq settlement to the Thule defense area had from the outset been a source of concern to the Danish government's Greenland Department, which had considered relocating the settlement in 1951.[7] In general, the government's policy in Greenland was to shield the residents from contact with outsiders in order to safeguard their traditional lifestyle. In keeping with the paternalistic thinking of the times, the Greenland Department sought to tightly control the modernization of Greenlandic society and to protect the Inuit from what it deemed unmanageable outside influences.[8]

That held true in the case of the American military presence. One of the few concessions the Danish government won in the 1951 agreement was a clause limiting contact between American military personnel and the local population. According to Article VI of the agreement, "Due respect will be given by the Government of the United States of America and by United States nationals in Greenland to all the laws, regulations and customs pertaining to the local population and the internal administration of Greenland, and every effort will be made to avoid any contact between United States personnel and the local population which the Danish authorities do not consider desirable for the conduct of operations under this

---

6 "Antiaircraft Artillery: Thule AB, Greenland. Data Brochure," CINCNE, October 22, 1952. NARA, RG 349, entry 86, box 13, folder: Army 1956. Reproduced in *Grønland under den kolde krig*, vol. 2, 171–97.
7 For instance, Letter by Governor (landshøvding) P. H. Lundsteen to Permanent Secretary Eske Brun, May 24, 1951, quoted in Jens Brøsted and Mads Fægteborg, "Invasionen af Thule og befolkningens fordrivelse," *Tidsskriftet Grønland*, no. 7 (1995), 315.
8 *Grønland under den kolde krig*, vol. 1, 257.

Agreement."⁹ The best-case scenario would obviously have been to restrict the construction of U.S. bases to uninhabited areas, but that was not always possible. Thule, for instance, was better situated for a base than other locations along the northwest coast: most notably, it has a natural harbor that remains ice-free for a comparatively long period each year. The possibility of relocating the Uummannaq settlement was apparently considered as early as 1950, but no decision was taken at that time. The position of the Greenland Department was clear, however. In a memo to the Danish Ministry of Foreign Affairs, the department permanent secretary wrote in 1951, "It is necessary . . . that the iron-curtain between the Americans and the civilian population in Greenland be maintained more vigorously now than ever."[10]

When the question of positions for antiaircraft artillery surfaced "as a matter of utmost urgency" in 1952, the original Danish concerns were reawakened and events began to happen quickly.[11] On the American side, officials believed that "any U.S. control over the movement and activities of the Danish citizens, such as would be necessary to the security of the proposed gun battery position, would be distasteful to the Danish government."[12] They thus turned the initiative over to the Danish authorities. In early May 1953, the representatives of the colonial administration in Thule – a government inspector and a local clergyman – were hastily summoned to Copenhagen. It was thereupon decided that the residents of the Uummannaq settlement would be relocated to Qaanaak, some 160 kilometers to the north. The Danish government issued a statement on May 11 announcing that the Greenland Department and the Hunters' Council of Thule had agreed on the relocation due to diminished hunting possibilities in the area as a consequence of the activities at the air base, and that the relocation had indeed been requested by the "Eskimos."[13]

That version of events, as the Danish Eastern High Court determined in 1999, was not entirely accurate. Although the opening of the Thule Air Base had apparently diminished the game in the area, none of the members of the Hunter's Council had expressed a desire to move the settlement in the

---

9 "Agreement between the Government of the United States of America and the Government of the Kingdom of Denmark, pursuant to the North Atlantic Treaty, concerning the defense of Greenland," in *Grønland under den kolde krig*, vol. 2, 144–53.
10 Permanent Secretary Eske Brun, quoted in *Grønland under den kolde krig*, vol. 1, 257, translation by the authors.
11 Letter, Office of the Secretary, Department of the Air Force, to Sec/State, October 31, 1952. NARA. DS 711.56359A/10–3152. Reproduced in *Grønland under den kolde krig*, vol. 2, 198.
12 Memorandum from James H. Douglas, Department of the Air Force, to SecDef, April 3, 1953. NARA. RG 330. Correspondence Control Section, Decimal File, entry 200B, folder 092.2, November–December 1953. Reproduced in *Grønland under den kolde krig*, vol. 2, 199.
13 Ritzaus Bureau, May 11, 1953. *Grønland under den kolde krig*, vol. 1, 189–90.

spring of 1953.[14] The decision was taken solely by the colonial authorities in the Danish Greenland Department. That point was confirmed in a ruling by the Danish Supreme Court in November 2003.

The forced relocation of Uummannaq's residents took place in late May 1953. The residents had been given only four days' notice. Their new houses in Qaanaaq were not yet finished and would not be ready until September. In the meantime, the relocated Inughuit had to make do with tents in the very harsh arctic climate. The approximately one hundred people who were relocated from Thule constituted one-third of the Inughuit population in the district. Another two hundred who lived a comfortable distance from the base were not forced to move.

The issue of the relocation from Thule was effectively closed for the next thirty years. The Danish press had no reason to doubt the accuracy of the account of the events given in the Danish government's press statement. The Greenlanders themselves, isolated and still holding to their traditional way of life, did not have the means to put the issue back on the political agenda at that time. By default, they had to accept the relocation decision. Moreover, the Danish and American authorities did not want to draw any more attention than necessary to American military activities in Greenland or their impact on the indigenous population.

Greenland in Danish Security Policy

To understand the relocation of the Inughuit from Thule and why it continues to be a matter of contention between Denmark and Greenland, it is necessary to recognize the importance of the American military presence in Greenland to Danish security policy during the Cold War and since. In the aftermath of the German occupation during the Second World War, it seemed obvious to Danish decision makers that the traditional policy of neutrality was no longer a viable strategy for guaranteeing the country's security. An alliance with strong partners was needed. After a short Nordic intermezzo, Danish leaders decided that NATO membership and the American security guarantee that came with it would be the preferable option for Denmark.

From the beginning of the Cold War, Greenland was an important foreign policy issue in Copenhagen. Allowing American military bases in Greenland was a significant contribution to NATO, and it was one of the factors guaranteeing close Danish-American cooperation in security policy.

---

14 Brøsted and Fægteborg, "Invasionen af Thule," 310–20.

Greenland thus provided Denmark with a major strategic and political advantage. The island was useful to Denmark when it joined the NATO alliance and would prove its value to Denmark repeatedly throughout the Cold War. Greenland, scholars agree, gave Denmark an important political bargaining chip.[15] Playing the "Greenland card" was one of the means by which Denmark could try to keep allied criticism within bounds on occasions when Denmark was inclined not to follow the general line of NATO policy.[16] At the same time, the American military presence in Greenland was not unproblematic for Copenhagen. As a frontline state in the Cold War, Denmark did not want to antagonize or provoke the Soviet Union with an overtly confrontational foreign policy.[17] Domestically, too, the U.S. presence in Greenland could be a source of tension. Many Danes were ambivalent about NATO membership, and there was often debate about what some saw as NATO's excessively bellicose polices.[18]

Successive Danish governments somehow had to balance the advantages and disadvantages of the American bases in Greenland. The way the relocation of the Inughuit was handled in 1953 can be seen as an attempt to find a balance between accommodating the Americans and not antagonizing the Danish public. Politically, it would have been very inconvenient to the Danish government if the Danish public learned that the relocation had been prompted in large part by the Americans' wish to enlarge the defense area. The relocation thus had to be framed as a voluntary act on the part of the Uummannaq community.[19]

Copenhagen faced a similar balancing act when the United States sought to deploy nuclear weapons in Greenland. In 1957, Prime Minister Hans Christian Hansen secretly gave the green light to U.S. deployment of nuclear weapons in the defense areas in Greenland. This decision was contrary to Denmark's official nuclear policy; publicly, the government said there were no nuclear weapons on Danish territory.[20] The prime minister had played the "Greenland card" without the knowledge or consent of either the Danish parliament or the Greenlanders. Nuclear bombs were stored

---

15 Clive Archer, "Greenland, US Bases and Missile Defense: New Two-Level Negotiations?" *Cooperation and Conflict* 38, 2 (2003): 133; *Grønland under den kolde krig*, vol 1, 273–75; Poul Villaume, *Allieret med forbehold. Danmark. NATO og den kolde krig. Et studie i dansk sikkerhedspolitik 1949–1961* (Copenhagen, 1995), 390; Nikolaj Petersen, "Negotiating the 1951 Greenland Defense Agreement: Theoretical and Empirical Aspects," *Scandinavian Political Studies* 21, 1 (1998): 2.
16 The most cited example is the continuously lower than NATO average Danish defense spending. See, for example, Archer, "New Two-Level Negotiations," 133.
17 *Grønland under den kolde krig*, vol. 1, 291–9.
18 Villaume, *Allieret med forbehold*.
19 *Grønland under den kolde krig*, vol 1, 191–3.
20 *Grønland under den kolde krig*, vol 1, 277–302.

at Thule for a period of only about eight months in 1958. Beginning in 1961, though, Greenland's air space was continuously patrolled by nuclear-armed American B-52 bombers as part of the Airborne Alert program. The "double policy" of allowing American nuclear deployment while denying it publicly lasted until 1968.[21] A B-52 on an Airborne Alert mission crashed on the ice near Thule Air Base, provoking a debate in Denmark about what was actually going on at the American defense areas in Greenland. The Danish government subsequently pledged that nuclear weapons would not be stationed at Thule and that Greenlandic airspace would no longer be patrolled by nuclear-armed aircraft.[22]

Using Greenland to ensure close relations with the United States during the Cold War, in short, meant that the Danish government had to accede to American military requests in Greenland, even if those requests were not always in accord with Danish policy or Denmark's democratic principles. That was certainly the case with both the relocation of the Inughuit and the double policy on nuclear weapons. In both instances, the Danish government relied on secrecy to resolve the dilemma posed by trying to comply with American wishes while not antagonizing the Soviet Union or the opposition parties at home. Secrecy worked well in the short term, but disclosure of the secret decisions of the Cold War era in the 1980s and 1990s created political complications, not least on account of the changes in Greenland's status vis-à-vis Denmark.

The Development of Home Rule in Greenland

As the relocation of the Uummannaq Inughuit community was under way in late May 1953, Danish voters went to the polls and approved an amendment to the country's constitution. Among its provisions, the amendment changed Greenland's status from colony to constituent part of the Kingdom of Denmark.

The change in Greenland's status also marked a change in Denmark's dealings with the Inuit in general. While Greenland was still a colony, the Inuit, isolated from the outside world, had lived according to their traditional ways. Once the island became a part of Denmark, Danish authorities made a great effort to modernize Greenlandic society – to confer the material

---

21 *Greenland During the Cold War: Danish and American Security Policy 1945–68. Summary* (Copenhagen, 1997), 26. Hans Mouritzen, "Thule and Theory: Democracy vs. Elitism in Danish Foreign Policy," in Bertel Heurlin and Hans Mouritzen, eds., *Danish Foreign Policy Yearbook 1998* (Copenhagen, 1998), 81.
22 *Grønland under den kolde krig*, vol 1, 277–302.

benefits of the modern Danish welfare state on Greenland's inhabitants. Danish government policy, in other words, shifted from trying to protect the Inuit from external influences to trying to accelerate their integration and assimilation within the Danish welfare state.[23]

Due in part to the government's modernization policy, Greenland's residents became more politically aware over time and came increasingly to favor greater self-determination. The push for self-determination resulted in the 1979 Home Rule Act, which placed responsibility for many areas of policy in the hands of Greenlandic authorities. One of the few important areas where authority continued to rest solely in Copenhagen was foreign policy. Nonetheless, an understanding developed whereby Copenhagen recognized that the Home Rule Government had a legitimate claim to a say on foreign policy issues bearing on the island. A generally cooperative relationship between Greenlandic and Danish authorities developed step by step, and Greenlandic politicians came to participate in the formulation and implementation of, in formal terms, Danish foreign policy.[24] This cooperation has been limited, however, to "soft" areas of foreign policy; security policy, by contrast, has been a source of considerable disagreement.

The relocation of the Inughuit from Thule and the responses to the disclosure of the actual circumstances of the relocation cannot, consequently, be viewed in isolation. Discussion of the events of 1953 must take the relations between the Danish government and the Greeland home rule authorities as well as the more general debate on the morality of Denmark's Cold War policies into account. Indeed, 1953 has been like a ghost haunting Danish-Greenlandic relations.

The Relocation Becomes a Political Issue

In 1985, Jens Brøsted and Mads Fægteborg published the first account of the relocation of the Inughuit from Uummannaq that challenged the Danish government's version of events and, by pointing to possibly unlawful actions on the part of the government, put the 1953 relocation back on the political agenda.[25] It was clearly in the interest of Greenland's recently established Home Rule Government to reopen the issue of the relocation. Taking on the Danish government, the Greenlandic authorities argued

---

23 *Grønland under den kolde krig*, vol 1. This is actually a fundamental change in Danish policies toward Greenland. Before World War II, Greenland was totally closed territory, and access was only given on a case-by-case basis by the Danish administration.
24 Permanent Secretary of State for Foreign Affairs, Friis Arne Petersen, "Rigsfællesskabet og det internationale arbejde for oprindelige folk," *Udenrigs* 2 (2001): 75–83.
25 Jens Brøsted and Mads Fægteborg, *Thule – fangerfolk og militæranlæg* (Copenhagen, 1985).

that Danish security policy had collided with the rights and interests of the Greenlanders. Greenland's role in American strategy was also on the political agenda in the mid-1980s on account of its possible role in President Ronald Reagan's Strategic Defensive Initiative, the "Star Wars" program.[26] The 1953 relocation and the Danish government's subsequent handling of the issue provided Greenlanders with a strong argument for a larger say on security policy. Active Greenlandic participation in formulating policy, they contended, would be the only way to avoid a repetition of the events of 1953.[27]

The relocation thus posed two issues that needed to be resolved. There was, first, the question of rectifying the wrong done to the Inughuit by the Danish state. We first consider the legal questions raised by the relocation and the attempts to resolve them in the courts. We then turn to the political importance of the relocation in the relations between Greenland and Denmark.

Lawsuits and Compensation

The Inughuit relocated from Uummannaq received compensation in the broadest, most direct sense in the form of new houses as well as supplies and household goods from the government-run store at Thule. As the permanent secretary of the Greenland Department noted in an internal memorandum at the time, "when in reality you force people from their homes, you necessarily have to be generous with the terms you offer them at the new location."[28] About half of the cost of the relocation was paid by the Americans.

The former residents of Uummannaq made their first attempt to secure additional compensation and acknowledgment of the wrong done to them in 1960. The Hunters' Council petitioned the Greenland Department for financial compensation on the grounds that the loss of hunting rights and the concentration of the population in the northern part of the district had caused economic hardship for many of the inhabitants. It is impossible to determine what came of the petition. The Hunter's Council never received a

---

26 Archer, "The United States Defense Areas," 138–43.
27 For instance, Hans Pavia Rovsing, member of the Greenlandic Home Rule Parliament: "We can no longer dismiss the problem only because defense matters [. . .] are under the jurisdiction of the Danish government"; quoted in Archer, "The United States Defense Areas," 138–43.
28 Note to the Danish Prime Minister by Permanent Secretary Eske Brun June 11, 1953, quoted in the "Danish Supreme Court Ruling in Case 489/1999 and 490/1999," *Ugeskrift for Retsvæsen*, 2004, 13, 425, translated by the authors.

response from the Greenland Department, and the Greenland Department's file on the matter was thought to have been lost.[29]

Nothing happened on the question of the relocation for the next twenty-five years. Only with the publication of Brøsted and Fægteborg's book and subsequent efforts of the Greenlandic authorities did the relocation become a public issue in Denmark. The first result was that the Danish government decided in 1987 to establish a commission to investigate the official account of the relocation and to determine whether, as Brøsted and Fægteborg contended, Danish authorities committed illegal acts in connection with the relocation. In 1994, the commission announced its findings: the Danish colonial administration in Greenland, it reported, had committed no unlawful actions.[30]

The commission's report did not satisfy the Greenland Home Rule Government. In a 1995 letter to the Danish prime minister, the Home Rule Government sharply criticized the commission's work. The commission, it contended, did not understand Inughuit culture and the nature of the relationship between the Inughuit and the Danish colonial administration in the 1950s; consequently, the commission had utterly misinterpreted the testimony of the Inughuit witnesses. The Home Rule Government argued further that the commission had neglected several important aspects of the matter, in particular questions of international law.[31]

In 1996, the organization Hingitaq 53, with 610 individual Inughuit co-plaintiffs, was created with the purpose of filing a lawsuit against the Danish state. The suit raised four questions that the court had to decide: Had the plaintiffs been wronged in the 1953 relocation? Did they have the right to return to the Thule area? Had Thule Air Base been built illegally, and if so, should it be closed to make way for the returnees? And, finally, were the plaintiffs entitled to financial compensation?[32]

---

29 "Danish Supreme Court Ruling in Case 489/1999 and 490/1999," *Ugeskrift for Retsvæsen*, 2004, 14, 597. The file was apparently later found in its correct location in the archives by Jens Brøsted, "Thules forsvundne erstatningssag," *Ugeskrift for Retsvæsen*, 2000, 49, 621–34. Brøsted argues that the file was actually hidden from the commission of 1987 by members of the Danish government administration.
30 Undersøgelsesudvalget af 4. juni 1987, "Beretning om undersøgelse af de nærmere omstændigheder i forbindelse med flytningen af Thulebefolkningen i 1953 fra det nuværende forsvarsområde til Qaanaaq" (Copenhagen, 1994), 5–21.
31 Letter to the Danish Prime Minister by the Greenland Home Rule Government, quoted in Danish in "Supreme Court Ruling in Case 489/1999 and 490/1999," *Ugeskrift for Retsvæsen*, 2004, 14, 512–16.
32 Jørgen Dragsdahl, "The Danish Dilemma," *Bulletin of the Atomic Scientists*, September/October, 2001, 45–50; DeNeen L. Brown, "Trail of Frozen Tears: The Cold War Is Over, But to Native Greenlanders Displaced by It, There's Still No Peace," *Washington Post Foreign Service*, October 22, 2002.

The Eastern High Court of Denmark ruled on the suit in 1999. The court found that the Danish government had indeed violated the rights of the Inughuit. It noted that members of the Uummannaq community had not made any sort of request to leave the Thule area and that the decision to relocate the community had been taken exclusively by the Danish authorities. On May 25, 1953, according to the court's reconstruction of events, a meeting had taken place "during which the inspector had informed the people present about the relocation and that it had to take place in a few days' time. Then the people were promised merchandise and new houses would be available as compensation." The fact that the Uummannaq residents did not make formal legal objection to the relocation, the court maintained, did not mean that they had made the move from Uummannaq to Qaanaaq voluntarily; as the court noted, the Inughuit are not a people to challenge authority. The court further emphasized that there was evidence that the Danish authorities knew long in advance of the American plans; there was thus "nothing to prevent the authorities from giving the people fair notice to prepare themselves and to carry out the relocation." The authorities, the court added, could also have done more to facilitate the move to the new village.[33]

Although the court found that the residents of Uummannaq had been wronged, it rejected the solution the plaintiffs sought, the right to return to Thule. The court saw "no evidence to prove that Thule Air Base was illegally established." If the Inughuit rights were restored in full, the Danish government would "be obliged to demand the base be dismantled," the court explained, and the plaintiffs did not have legal grounds to "succeed in their claim in that respect."[34] Accordingly, since the base had not been constructed illegally, the Inughuit had no legal right to return. The expropriation of the land per se was legal, in the court's view, even though the Danish administration had not followed the legal procedures and principles regarding expropriations in force at the time.

The court awarded the Thule community collectively 500,000 kroner (then U.S. $73,000) in damages for the loss of hunting and fishing rights. Furthermore, each of the surviving sixty-three plaintiffs directly affected by the relocation was awarded individual compensation of 25,000 kroner or 15,000 kroner, depending on his or her age at the time of the relocation. All together, according to the junior counsel to the treasury, the compensation amounted to 1,765,000 kroner ($259,000).

33 Eastern High Court, *Pressemeddelelse*, August 20, 1999. Sag nr. B-3426–1996.
34 Dragsdahl, "The Danish Dilemma," 48.

This settlement could be viewed as both a victory and a defeat for the Greenlanders. On the one hand, the suit brought forth the first unequivocal acknowledgment that the Danish state had acted illegally and had seriously infringed on their rights. The Eastern High Court's ruling on the suit prompted a formal apology from the Danish government. Then–Prime Minister Poul Nyrup Rasmussen said:

> Nobody, today, can be held responsible for former generations' actions, close to fifty years ago. But in the spirit of the Danish Realm and with respect for Greenland and the Thule population, the Government will, on behalf of the Danish State, convey an apology – utoqqaterpugut – to Inughuit, the population of Thule, and to all of Greenland for the manner in which the decision about the relocation was reached and carried out in 1953.[35]

Furthermore, the court's recognition of the indigenous people of the Thule district as a "population," as defined in a 1989 international convention, was considered at least a partial victory. Article 16.3 of the convention, which was negotiated through the UN International Labor Organization and ratified by Denmark, states: "Whenever possible, these people shall have the right to return to their traditional lands, as soon as the grounds for relocation cease to exist."[36] On the other hand, the court's ruling on several issues of the case went against the plaintiffs. Because the establishment of the base was deemed not to have been illegal, the land was not returned to the plaintiffs. Furthermore, although the Inughuit were recognized as a distinct population, they were not granted the legal "right to return" as a separate *indigenous* population, distinct from the larger Inuit population with special collective rights.

Hingitaq 53 was not satisfied with the Eastern High Court's ruling. Its attorney argued that the court had not ordered adequate compensation for either the hardship the plaintiffs had endured as a result of the relocation or their loss of hunting rights. In 1999, Hingitaq 53 decided to appeal the ruling. The suit thus landed in the Danish Supreme Court.

The Danish judicial system's final word on the 1953 relocation came in November 2003 with a unanimous ruling by the Supreme Court. The court upheld the view of the Eastern High Court that the government's expropriation of land for the expansion of Thule Air Base in the 1950s was legal, as was the establishment of the base. The court also rejected the plaintiffs' original demand for 235 million kroner in compensation, and it found no

---

35 Brown, "Trail of Frozen Tears."
36 Dragsdahl, "The Danish Dilemma," 48. It should be noted, though, that the ILO has refused to recognize the Thule population as an "indigenous people," i.e., as a "people" different from the population of Greenland as a whole.

reason to increase the compensation the Eastern High Court had awarded. Finally, it ruled that the Thule community should not be considered a separate indigenous population apart from the Inuit as a whole.[37]

When the Supreme Court announced its ruling, Christian Harlang, the lawyer representing the Inughuit, said he would recommend to Hingitaq 53 that the issue be presented to the European Court of Human Rights in Strasbourg.[38] That was indeed the course of action chosen by Hingitaq 53. The argument Harlang put forward in his petition to the European court was more or less the same as that which he presented before the Danish courts: the plaintiffs should be recognized as a distinct indigenous population, allowed to return to Thule, and given additional compensation. Going a step further, he also argued that the Danish state denied certain of the Inughuit their basic human rights after the relocation. The Inughuit did not have judicial recourse to challenge the decisions of the Danish administration in the years following 1953, for instance, and Danish politicians had sought to discourage the Inughuit from taking legal action concerning the relocation. Harlang's petition also cites the lost and found files dealing with the 1960 compensation claim as an instance of the denial of the Inughuits' human rights.[39] The European Court of Human Rights (ECHR) dismissed the case on January 12, 2006, arguing that the actual relocation took place before jurisdiction of the court was established in Danish law. The ECHR could thus not rule on the relocation as such. As for the subsequent handling of the case in the Danish legal system and eventual human rights violations in that process, the court found it in accordance with established legal norms and thus found no reason to pursue the matter further.[40]

The decision of the European Court of Human Rights notwithstanding, it is clear from the court proceedings in Denmark that perceptions of the relocation have changed fundamentally since 1953. But even if the wrong done to the inhabitants of Thule has been formally acknowledged, the relocated community and their fellow Greenlanders did not think that they had

---

37 Danish Supreme Court, *Pressemeddelelse, Højesteret stadfæster landsrettens dom i Thulesagen*, November 28, 2003, online at http://www.hoejesteret.dk.
38 Jan Olsen, "Greenlanders Lose Battle over Airbase," November 29, 2003, online at http://news.independent.co.uk/europe/story.jsp?story=468271 and http://home.btclick.com/caab/2003-11-29Greenlanders.htm.
39 Christian Harlang, "Application to the European Court of Human Rights," submitted May 28, 2004, online at: http://www.harlang-adv.dk/ch/thule/application280504.PDF.
40 For the ruling of the court, see "First Section Decision as to the Admissibility of Application no. 18584/04 by Hingitaq 53 against Denmark, The European Court of Human Rights (First Section), Sitting on 12 January 2006," online at http://cmiskp.echr.coe.int/tkp197/view.asp?action=html&documentId=791882&portal=hbkm&source=externalbydocnumber&table=F69A27FD8FB86142BF01C1166DEA398649.

been done justice by the court rulings. The judicial process has, however, been only one part of the attempt to rectify the wrongs of 1953. On numerous occasions, Danish governments have tried to close the case politically through agreements with the Greenland Home Rule Government, which has often skillfully used the issue to its own advantage.

The Political Significance of the Relocation

Politically, the relocation has been an embarrassment, both at home and abroad, to the Danish government. The dispute over the 1953 relocation does not fit Danes' self-perception or the image they would like to present – the image of Denmark as a genuinely democratic and morally aware state that respects the rights of its former colonial subjects.[41] Officials in Copenhagen have, accordingly, proposed a number of deals to Greenlandic authorities in the hope of resolving the issue once and for all. Greenlandic politicians, on the other hand, are well aware of the political value of this embarrassing past.[42]

Negotiations were already taking place in 1985 between the Danish minister for Greenland and the municipal authorities in Qaanaaq about a political agreement that would, among other things, improve the infrastructure, limit the base area, and provide job opportunities for the indigenous population on the base, as a form of compensation for "the mistakes of the past." At the same time, the minister made it clear that he wanted to "look ahead" with this agreement, and there was no mention of either direct compensation or an official inquiry into the legality of the relocation. The implication was that the political agreement should settle the issue.[43] It did not, however. Even though the Danish government delivered on some of the items of the agreement,[44] the Greenlanders continued to press their call for an investigation into the events of 1953.

---

41 For further aspects in general about a distinct Danish liberal moralistic foreign policy profile, see, for example, Christine Ingebritsen, "Norm Entrepreneurs: Scandinavia's Role in World Politics," *Cooperation and Conflict* 37, 1 (2002): 11–23; Lene Hansen, "Sustaining Sovereignty: The Danish Approach to Europe," in Lene Hansen and Ole Wæver, eds., *European Integration and National Identity: The Challenge of the Nordic States* (London, 2002); Peter Lawler, "Scandinavian Exceptionalism and European Union," *Journal of Common Market Studies* 35, 4 (1997): 565–94.
42 On the use of the past by indigenous people in general, see Ronald Niezen, "Recognizing Indigenism: Canadian Unity and the International Movement of Indigenous Peoples," *Comparative Studies in Society and History* 42, 1 (2000).
43 Record of meeting between Minister for Greenland Tom Høyem and representatives of Qaanaaq municipality, November 18. 1985, reproduced in "Danish Supreme Court Ruling in Case 489/1999 and 490/1999," *Ugeskrift for Retsvæsen*, 2004, 14, 482–3.
44 Most notably, eliminating Art. VI of the 1951 Defense Agreement, allowing contact between the defense areas and the Greenlandic population, thus providing work opportunities.

In 1995, after the commission appointed in 1987 had delivered its report – a report the Greenlanders found unsatisfactory – the Danish government and the Greenland Home Rule Government again held political negotiations. The recent disclosure of Denmark's double policy on nuclear weapons drew considerable public attention to Greenland's experience of the Cold War and greatly increased the salience of the unresolved issue of the 1953 relocation. The result was yet another compensation scheme, this time involving air traffic infrastructure in Qaanaaaq. The Danish government agreed in 1997 to pay 47 million kroner toward the construction of an airport at Qaanaaq.[45] It was once again clear that the Danish government was hoping to close the book on the relocation. According to the agreement, "The parties agree . . . that a satisfactory solution has been found on all questions of the Thule case."[46] Speaking before the Danish parliament, then–Prime Minister Poul Nyrup Rasmussen claimed, "We agree on a political solution, and we agree on looking ahead. We thus also agree that no more questions remain between us in the Thule case."[47] Rasmussen nonetheless had to concede that the agreement had no bearing on the compensation suit then in the courts. Nor did the agreement prevent the Greenland Home Rule Government from joining as a signatory to the lawsuit against the Danish state in 1999.

The airport opened in September 2001. In the end, the Danish government and the Greenland Home Rule Government each contributed approximately 60 million kroner to its construction. The deal has been characterized as a political horse trade between the two sides. There had been no attempt to assess the airport's economic viability before it was constructed, and its contribution to the local economy thus far has been meager, to say the least. After five years of operation, the airport was serving roughly sixty passengers per month. A roundtrip ticket from Nuuk to Qaanaaq cost nearly 20,000 kroner ($3,000) in 2006. The head of the local administration in Qaanaaq has been quoted as saying that it is grotesque to have a 120 million kroner airport that local residents cannot afford to use.[48] Clearly, good intentions do not necessarily lead to wise decisions.

Greenlandic authorities have used the political leverage provided by the 1953 relocation for far more than just economic advantage. Indeed, the

---

45 Press announcement by the Danish Prime Minister's Office, January 31, 1997, online at http://www.borgerraadet.gl/NyhedsBreve/NB1997/nb1–1997.htm.
46 Press announcement by the Danish Prime Minister's Office, January 31, 1997, online at http://www.borgerraadet.gl/NyhedsBreve/NB1997/nb1–1997.htm.
47 Danish Prime Minister Poul Nyrup Rasmussen in the Danish Parliament, February 5, 1997, quoted in "Danish Supreme Court Ruling in Case 489/1999 and 490/1999," *Ugeskrift for Retsvæsen* 2004, 14, 517.
48 According to the Statistical Bureau of Greenland, the average income in Qaanaaq municipality in 2002 was approximately 115,000 kroner, online at http://www.statgreen.gl/dk/publ/indkom/04–1indk4.pdf.

relocation and the continued presence of Thule Air Base have given the Home Rule Government an important say in, legally speaking, Danish foreign policy. As the Inughuit compensation suit was making its way through the court system, it was becoming increasingly clear to everyone in Greenland and Denmark that the United States would likely want to incorporate Thule Air Base in its controversial missile defense project. By 1999, it was widely expected that Thule would figure in the Americans' plans, and with the election of George W. Bush to the presidency most Danes and Greenlanders assumed it was only a matter of time before the issue would have to be addressed.[49] In December 2002, the Danish government received a formal request from the U.S. government for permission to upgrade the radar at Thule to enable it to provide tracking information for the missile defense system.[50] Even before Washington submitted this request, it was clear that Greenland's Home Rule Government would have to be included in the decision-making process, even though it had no constitutional role in foreign policy. As a direct consequence of the history of Thule – including the relocation – any Danish decision not endorsed by the Home Rule Government would lack both moral and political legitimacy.[51]

The first meeting to discuss the American request took place on December 18, 2002, in Washington, and representatives of the Greenland Home Rule Government participated. The Greenlanders categorically demanded that the 1951 Defense Agreement between Denmark and the United States be renegotiated as a precondition for any deal on missile defense. As the new Greenlandic premier Hans Enoksen said in his New Year's speech two weeks later, "It is also an indispensable requirement on our part that the 1951 Defense Agreement is updated. In this connection it would be logical to normalize the relationship between the United States and Greenland so as to ensure that Greenland will be treated on an equal footing with other friends and allies."[52] Greenland's stance on the missile defense negotiations was clear: the Home Rule Government wanted to increase its influence on

---

49 President William J. Clinton, "Statement Announcing the President's Signature of the National Missile Defense Act of 1999," White House Press Release, July 1999, online at http://www.clw.org/coalition/whnmd072399.htm. On the early Danish debate, see, for instance, Frede P. Jensen, "Danmark skal ikke støtte stjernekrigsprojekt," *Politiken*, January 19, 2001, kultur og debat 4, underscoring the need to incorporate the Greenlanders on any decision.

50 Danish Ministry of Foreign Affairs, *Missilforsvar og Thule-radaren. Redegørelse fra regeringen* (Copenhagen, 2003), 4. See also "Letter from Colin Powell to Per Stig Møller," December 17, 2002, online at http://www.um.dk/upload/sikkerhed/thule_brev.pdf.

51 For an elaboration of the use of the past by Greenlandic politicians, see Kristian Søby Kristensen, "Greenland, Denmark and the Debate on Missile Defense: A Window of Opportunity for Increased Autonomy," *DIIS Working Paper* 14/2004, online at www.diis.dk.

52 Greenland Home Rule, New Year's Speech by Premier [2003]. The demand was backed by a large majority in the Home Rule Parliament, online at http://dk.nanoq.gl/nyhed.asp?page=nyhed&objno=43115.

security policy decisions of importance for Greenland and thus increase the scope of Greenland's autonomy from the central authorities in Copenhagen. The missile defense issue had provided an opportunity for achieving that objective.

The Greenlandic claims per se are less interesting than the means by which they have been pursued: it is the past wrongdoings of Danish governments that provide the core of the Greenlanders' argument for increased autonomy. Throughout the long-running debate on missile defense in Denmark and Greenland, Greenlanders have made reference to the past in making the case for expanded autonomy. "It is widely known, that in 1953 [the] people [of Thule] were moved, in 1957 nuclear weapons were deposited, in 1968 an airplane crashed if not on them then around them and polluted the area," Lars Emil Johansen, a Greenlandic member of the Danish parliament, noted during a 2003 parliamentary debate. "So it is these people that face the risk." And as it is already known that they faced the risk without being asked, Lars Emil Johansen can forcefully ask, "Do they have something to say in this?"[53]

Denmark, Greenland, and the United States came to an agreement on the missile defense project in late May 2004, and in many ways the agreement can be seen as a victory for the Greenlanders.[54] Most importantly from their perspective, the 1951 Defense Agreement was amended to acknowledge Greenland as an independent actor with certain rights in regard to the defense areas. That amendment gives the Greenlanders the "equal footing" they had long sought.[55]

One can argue that Denmark's Cold War–era "Greenland card" has been supplanted by the "colonial past card" the Home Rule Government now plays in its negotiations with Copenhagen. That card has been played irrespective of the Greenlanders' pursuit of their claims through legal action. In September 2002, for example, negotiators from Denmark, the United States, and Greenland announced they had reached an agreement removing

---

53 Lars Emil Johansen, debate in the Danish parliament, April 29, 2003. For further examples of this line of argument, see Kristensen, "Greenland, Denmark and the Debate on Missile Defense," 12–19.
54 On the negotiations between Denmark, Greenland, and the United States on missile defense, see Kristian Søby Kristensen, "Negotiating Base Rights for Missile Defence: The Case of Thule Air Base in Greenland," in Bertel Heurlin and Sten Rynning, eds., *Missile Defence: International, Regional and National Implications* (London, 2005).
55 *Agreement Between the Government of the United States of America and the Government of the Kingdom of Denmark, Including the Home Rule Government of Greenland, to Amend and Supplement the Agreement of 27 April 1951 Pursuant to the North Atlantic Treaty between the Government of the United States of America and the Government of the Kingdom of Denmark Concerning the Defense of Greenland (Defense Agreement) Including Relevant Subsequent Agreements Related Thereto*: see especially Article IV of the agreement, online at http://www.um.dk/NR/rdonlyres/EF0F61CB-500B-491A-9465-C9E95B6BA0B4/0/ModerniseringafForsvarsaftalenaf1951.DOC.

the Dundas peninsula from the Thule defense area. The Inughuit had been relocated from Dundas, and now the peninsula was to be returned to them in full.[56] The then-leader of the Greenland Home Rule Government, Jonathan Motzfeldt, welcomed the agreement, saying, "We will now have access to the area from which the Thule population was moved in 1953. It is a day of joy for the Home Rule Government and a victory for Greenland."[57] But the Home Rule Government clearly did not regard the issue as settled and continued to use it for political leverage in the missile defense debate. Although the Home Rule Government was a signatory to Hingitaq 53's suit against the Danish government, it had no trouble coming to agreement with Denmark in June 2003 on terms for negotiations with the Americans on the upgrade of the radar installation at Thule. The Greenland Home Rule Government came under criticism among ordinary Greenlanders for reaching that agreement while the suit before the Supreme Court was still pending.[58]

These two issues show that the Home Rule Government and Hingitaq 53 do not necessarily see eye to eye on the issue of Thule Air Base. The continued existence of the base is in fact important to the Home Rule Government. Just as the base provided Denmark with a useful tool in its relations with the United States during the early days of the Cold War, it is now *the* foreign policy tool for Greenland's government. The government has used the base successfully in its efforts to gain wider autonomy from Denmark, and because of the continued strategic importance of the base, Washington has been careful to maintain good relations with Greenland.[59]

Thule Air Base is also important economically to Greenland. One-eighth of the total direct tax revenue in Greenland is derived from the staff of Danish Arctic Contractors at the base. Since 1987, the U.S. government has paid $250,000 annually for the use of dumps. The money goes to the Thule Foundation, but the annual fee is not adjusted for inflation and is now

---

56 *Memorandum of Understanding Between the Government of the United States of America and the Government of the Kingdom of Denmark (Including the Home Rule Government of Greenland) Concerning the Dundas Area*, February 20, 2003, Articles I, II, and IV.
57 Greenland Home Rule, Dundas back to Greenland (2002), online at http://dk.nanoq.gl/nyhed.asp?page=nyhed&objno=36747.
58 In regard to the Dundas agreement, Aqqaluk Lynge, president of the Inuit Circumpolar Conference, said that the location constituted only 5 percent of the area that the indigenous people of Thule want to have returned or be compensated for, and that the agreement should not have been signed before the ruling of the Supreme Court; see Brown, "Trail of Frozen Tears." The same criticism was raised on the missile defense deals.
59 The value attributed to Greenland by the United States was symbolically shown when Secretary of State Colin Powell traveled to Greenland to sign the final missile defense deal. Further, in the actual negotiations, the United States – at least from its own point of view – went to great lengths to secure an agreement satisfying all parties.

effectively worth only a fraction of its original value. The Americans also pay for a vocational school for twenty-five students at the base. Greenland benefits from cargo traffic to the base handled by Air Greenland and the shipping company Royal Arctic Line, both of which are partly owned by the Home Rule Government. The deal on the missile defense system promises further economic advantages to Greenland.[60]

The Home Rule Government, in sum, derives substantial political and economic advantages from the presence of Thule Air Base and has no interest in closing the base. Moreover, even if closing the base were on its agenda, the missile defense agreements it signed with Denmark and the United States would make it impossible to do so. However, that does not preclude the continued use of the 1953 relocation and other Danish colonial-era mistakes in political dealings with Denmark. The past continues to be a powerful political tool in discussions of Greenland's status within the Kingdom of Denmark.

Conclusion

The story of the relocation of the Inughuit shows how hard it is to right the wrongs of the past. It took decades for Denmark to acknowledge the misconduct of the colonial authorities. The Greenland Home Rule Government, by contrast, has put the past at the center of political discourse. Both of these trends have served to prolong the search for a settlement.

The next question is what the future will bring. With the completion of the negotiations on the use of Thule Air Base for the American missile defense project, the Greenland Home Rule Government secured a role in security policy. Its policy so far has been to get what it can out of the American military presence, and it is likely to remain committed to the continued existence of the base. This suggests that the base will be a less salient issue in coming years than it was before the deal on missile defense.

Prime Minister Anders Fogh Rasmussen recently set up a joint Danish-Greenlandic commission to review the legal framework of the Home Rule system. This provides the Greenland Home Rule Government with yet another opportunity to use the past in negotiating with the Danish state. One reason the strategy of invoking the past has worked well for the Home Rule Government is that the Danish government has been more interested

---

60 The agreement is available online at http://www.um.dk/NR/rdonlyres/45B44E9B-8BF9-4D66-9112-9E314CCAB9E2/0/Oekonomisktekniskerklaering.doc.

in a political solution to the issue – that is, in making deals with the Home Rule Government – than in addressing the wishes of the local Inughuit.

That leads to the question of how the wrongs of the past can actually be righted. Certainly, the Danish government has not been very successful in its efforts to do so. It took a major step in 1999, when it finally made a formal apology; the symbolic importance of this gesture should not be underestimated. The political agreements on compensation, by contrast, have not worked very well. The airport at Qaanaaq could serve as an illustration of how not to proceed.

Compensation entails two questions: Who is to receive compensation, and how are they to be compensated? Any plan for compensation should be implemented in close cooperation with the people affected by the 1953 relocation. Compensation could take the form of payments to individuals or economic aid for the community. All Arctic economies are fragile, and the restrictions on fur exports were a hard blow to Greenland's economy.[61] Support for new business ventures would be one way to help make up for that loss. Another possible compensation option would be to increase support for higher education in Greenland and to give young Inuit more opportunities to study abroad.

One thing is certain: a final resolution of the issue that satisfies *all* parties involved would be very welcome. Healing the still-open wound of 1953 is, of course, immensely important to the people affected. A final resolution would also have important implications for political relations between Denmark and its increasingly independent former colony. Closing the wound of 1953 might put the old colonial ghost to rest once and for all.

---

61 See, for example, Lisa Mastny, "Coming to Terms with the Arctic," *World Watch*, January/February 2000, 24–36.

PART III

Memory and Recognition

6

Apologizing for Vichy in Contemporary France

JULIE FETTE

In societies coming to terms with historical injustices, public apology has emerged as a powerful force. This was particularly true of France in the 1990s, where the state served as a catalyst for a multifaceted apology trend within civil society for the persecution of Jews in France during the Second World War. Following President Jacques Chirac's official apology in 1995 for the Vichy regime's anti-Semitic policies, various civil groups stepped forward to address their specific wartime pasts. This French wave of repentance, together with a multitude of international acknowledgments for past wrongdoing, demonstrates that apology is decidedly in *"l'esprit du temps."*[1]

Scholars have suggested several reasons for the emergence of apology on a global scale at the end of the twentieth century: the challenge against "racial hierarchies that sustained empires" and the collapse of communist dictatorships;[2] a new international focus on morality;[3] a revised understanding of universal human rights, state sovereignty, and international law;[4] a willingness of state actors to show feelings of caring and regret and to view apology not as a weakness but as a manifestation of strength;[5] the globalization of memory in the post–Cold War era;[6] and the decline of the nation-state

---

This chapter draws on two other studies by the author: "The Apology Moment: Vichy Memories in 1990s France" in *Taking Wrongs Seriously: Apologies and Reconciliation*, edited by Elazar Barkan and Alexander Karn (Stanford, 2006); and "Apology and the Past in Contemporary France," *French Politics, Culture & Society* 26 (2008). The author is grateful to Stanford University Press and Berghahn Books for permission to use previously published material here.

1 Philippe Moreau Defarges, *Repentance et réconciliation* (Paris, 1999), 9.
2 Alan Cairns, "Coming to Terms with the Past," in John Torpey, ed., *Politics and the Past: On Repairing Historical Injustices* (Lanham, Md., 2003), 66.
3 Elazar Barkan, *The Guilt of Nations: Restituting and Negotiating Historical Injustices* (New York, 2000).
4 Mark Gibney and Erik Roxstrom, "The Status of State Apologies," *Human Rights Quarterly* 23 (2001), 923–6; Mireille Delmas-Marty, cited in Dominique Dhombres, "De la difficulté de vivre ensemble," *Le Monde* (December 12, 1998).
5 Nicolaus Mills, "The New Culture of Apology," *Dissent* 48.4 (Fall 2001), 113–16.
6 Claire Andrieu, cited in Philippe Bernard, "Réparer les crimes du passé," *Le Monde*, April 10, 2002.

and of *raison d'état*, as well as increased demand for recognition by past victims.[7] According to Jeffrey K. Olick and Brenda Coughlin, two sociologists studying the phenomenon, apology is rooted in the very structure of modernity, with its freedoms and individualism, but also its networks of relations, which impose guilt for choices of action or inaction.[8] "The time of repentance is that of another perception of history," writes Philippe Moreau Defarges, a French political scientist: one that will no longer be written by the winners, the powerful, and the authorities of states, but by previously ignored, dominated, and excluded peoples.[9] In addition to these transnational factors, particular developments in France prepared the ground for the emergence of public apologies in the 1990s. The expansive historiography of the Vichy era and mediatized trials of Vichy bureaucrats established the responsibilities of the state and certain segments of French society for the passage of racial laws and the deportation of Jews.

The extent of Vichy collaboration in the Holocaust has been fully documented for several decades. The consensus today is to view the Vichy regime as fully complicit in the legal, social, and eventually physical separation of Jews from the French national community. Renée Poznanski, among many others, offered a vivid description of the gradual identification, exclusion, spoliation, internment, and deportation of Jews in wartime French society.[10] Although three-quarters of the Jewish population in France survived the war experience, 76,000 were deported, of whom 2,500 returned. But before this history became known in the 1970s, several myths dominated French thinking: the Gaullist "resistancialist" myth that France was a nation of resisters; the "parenthesis theory" of the exceptionality of the Vichy regime in French history; and the argument that French anti-Semitic policies and actions were imposed by the Nazi occupiers.[11] These myths finally broke down during a new era of memory work that began in the 1970s and ran through the end of the century, an era that historian Henry Rousso has called a time of "obsession" with French guilt.[12] As a years-long series of fiftieth anniversary commemorations of World War Two events ran its course in the early 1990s, multiple questions about the past continued to be

---

7 Michael Cunningham, "Saying Sorry: The Politics of Apology," *The Political Quarterly* 70, 3 (July–September 1999), 292; Philippe Moreau Defarges, *Repentance et réconciliation*, 18–23, 27–30.
8 Jeffrey K. Olick and Brenda Coughlin, "The Politics of Regret: Analytical Frames," in John Torpey, ed., *Politics and the Past: On Repairing Historical Injustices*, 46–7.
9 Philippe Moreau Defarges, "Le temps de la repentance," *Cahiers français: La mémoire, entre histoire et politique* (July–August 2001), 44, 46–7.
10 Renée Poznanski, *Etre juif en France pendant la Seconde Guerre mondiale* (Paris, 1994).
11 Henry Rousso, *Le Syndrome de Vichy: de 1944 à nos jours* (Paris, 1987).
12 Eric Conan and Henry Rousso, *Vichy: An Ever-Present Past* (Hanover, 1998).

raised by filmmakers, television producers, novelists, historians, journalists, and memoirists. Amid this surge, the remembrance of Jewish deportation took center stage in public debate.[13]

This end-of-the-century emergence of Holocaust memory in France arose in the shadow of several high-profile court cases trying wartime actors accused of crimes against humanity. This legal context weighed heavily on the apology trend. After Klaus Barbie, the Gestapo chief of Lyon, was tried in France in 1987 and the efforts to bring to justice Vichy police chief René Bousquet and his aide Jean Leguay were aborted by their deaths, two Frenchmen were finally brought to trial and found guilty for crimes against humanity: Paul Touvier, former chief of intelligence of the *milice* in Lyon, and Maurice Papon, secretary general of the Gironde prefecture during the war. Papon's trial in 1997–8 for his role in the deportation of 1,690 Jews from Bordeaux was significant in that the defendant was not a zealous *milicien* but a public servant. As a result, his case came to symbolize a trial not of an individual but of the French state as a whole and its administrative role in the Holocaust.

In addition to the growing memorialization of Vichy and the legal context of the 1990s, scandals about the legacy of Vichy emerged constantly, followed by public demands for reckoning. Pierre Péan's 1994 biography of President François Mitterrand revealed sensational information about the socialist's flirtation with an extreme right league while he was a law student in the 1930s, his decoration by Vichy authorities in 1943, and his postwar friendship with the accused René Bousquet.[14] Revelations that the city of Paris still possessed Jewish property that had been "aryanized" during the occupation[15] and that French national museums still held thousands of works of art that had been stolen from Jews in France during the war[16] led state authorities to review their records and make restitutions. In addition, a "Jewish card file" created by the Paris police during the war was found in the archives: such a discovery of French fingerprints on anti-Semitic policies shocked public opinion and led to the creation of a historical commission and to facilitated access to wartime records.

These developments paved the way for apology to become a key tool in a national healing process, an integral element in the tripartite strategy of apology, court trials, and reparations to address the Vichy past in 1990s

---

13 Olivier Lalieu, "L'Invention du 'devoir de mémoire,'" *Vingtième siècle* 69 (January–March 2001), 83–94.
14 Pierre Péan, *Une jeunesse française: François Mitterrand, 1934–1947* (Paris, 1994).
15 See Brigitte Vital-Durand, *Domaine privé* (Paris, 1996).
16 See Hector Feliciano, *The Lost Museum* (New York, 1997).

France. This chapter focuses specifically on the dynamics of apology, marked by the expansion of the practice of atonement into the public sphere. Indeed, one of the unique characteristics of the French case is the transfer of apology from the official level into civil society. Triggered by Chirac's official apology, professional groups, the Catholic Church, and various state institutions subsequently offered apologies, recognitions, or acknowledgments for their particular roles in fostering wartime anti-Semitism. The apology trend in contemporary France responded to a social demand: rather than an obsession or a narrow communitarianist movement, apology satisfied a widespread desire of French society to face the past.

State Apology: A Radical Departure from the Past

When Jacques Chirac was elected to the presidency in May 1995, he marked his arrival in office with several brash moves to distinguish himself from his predecessor.[17] In addition to resuming nuclear test blasts in Mururoa and slashing the budget to qualify for the euro, Chirac became the first French president to acknowledge French responsibility in the Holocaust. On July 16, 1995, the fifty-third anniversary of the Vélodrome d'Hiver tragedy – when French authorities rounded up 13,000 Jews in this former bicycle stadium in Paris, interned them in concentration camps, and supervised their deportation – Chirac officially recognized the French state's role in the Holocaust.

Chirac's statement of recognition radically departed from the prevailing official attitudes toward the Vichy past. Chirac admitted French guilt and took responsibility for its "collective fault": "France, land of the Enlightenment and of Human Rights, land of hospitality and asylum, France, on that day, committed the irreparable." Chirac alluded to a sentiment of debt to Jewish victims, without specifying whether it was moral or material: "We have an immutable debt toward those left unprotected by France." He concluded with a warning against future injustice and a hope for an open, tolerant France: "Let us know how to learn the lessons of history. Let us refuse to be passive observers or accomplices of the unacceptable."[18] Although Chirac did not offer any reparation to Jews, his proclamation that France was accountable for the crimes of Vichy allowed for that eventuality.[19]

---

17 Sylvie Kauffmann, "Le bulldozer Chirac étonne les Américains," *Le Monde* (August 11, 1995).
18 "Pour la première fois, un président français reconnaît la responsabilité de la France dans la déportation et l'extermination de juifs pendant la seconde guerre mondiale," *Agence France Presse* (July 16, 1995); database online, available from LexisNexis.
19 Félix Chiocca, "Une juste réparation morale," *Témoignage Chrétien*, July 21, 1995.

Having thus officially and unambiguously taken responsibility for Vichy crimes, Chirac was nonetheless careful in his declaration to emphasize that the French deviation from human rights had been influenced by the context of defeat and occupation: "Yes, the criminal folly of the occupant was seconded by the French, by the French State." Further, Chirac specifically distinguished another France, a France that "had never been at Vichy... [but was] alive and thriving in London," a France that "saved three-quarters of the Jewish population." Several observers noted that such emphases in fact diluted the impact of Chirac's apology and perpetuated the conceptual distancing between Vichy and the Republic in an ambivalent and even insidious manner.[20] Henry Rousso, on the other hand, congratulated Chirac's careful rendering of the historical complexities of the period.[21]

Generational change in leadership partially explains the shift in paradigm that allowed for this French state apology in 1995 for the crimes of the Vichy regime. Mitterrand's compromised personal history prevented him from leading the nation to come to terms with the past. In the last few years of his presidency, Mitterrand repeatedly refused to apologize for Vichy despite mounting pressure from intellectual circles and Jewish groups.[22] Mitterrand conceded in 1993 to make July 16 a national day of commemoration for racist and anti-Semitic persecutions, but he reaffirmed in 1994, "I will not apologize in the name of France. The Republic has nothing to do with that. I believe that France is not responsible."[23] Paradoxically, it took an heir of Gaullism to finally shatter the myth of Vichy's historical parenthesis. Only seven years old at the beginning of the Second World War, Chirac was free to apologize without risking his personal career. As historian Raoul Girardet has asserted more generally, Chirac could only benefit from taking a moral stand against others' failings.[24] Nonetheless, juxtaposed against Mitterrand's refusals and reactive half-gestures, Chirac's precise inventory of French responsibilities, full apology, and call to avoid

---

20 Peter Carrier, "'National Reconciliation?' Mitterrand, Chirac and the Commemorations of Vichy 1992–95," *National Identities* 2, 2 (2000), 135–6, 139–40; Alain-Gérard Slama, "Le nostra culpa du Président," *Le Point* (July 22, 1995).
21 Henry Rousso, "Sortir du dilemme: Pétain, est-ce la France?" *Le Débat* 89 (March–April 1996), 198–204. In 2005, Christine Albanel, who was responsible for drafting Chirac's 1995 official apology, related that the president had wished to be even more frank than was the case in the final text of the apology and that he had not anticipated the amazing reaction his discourse generated. In Béatrice Gurrey, "En 1995, la reconnaissance des 'fautes commises par l'Etat'," *Le Monde*, January 26, 2005.
22 For a full account, see chapter 1 in Conan and Rousso, *Vichy: An Ever-Present Past*.
23 Quoted in Jean Baptiste de Montvalon, "M. Chirac reconnaît la faute collective commise envers les juifs," *Le Monde*, July 18, 1995.
24 Raoul Girardet, "Repentances sélectives," *Le Figaro*, October 29, 1997.

injustice in the future satisfied the majority of the French public.[25] A public opinion poll conducted a few days after the ceremony at the Vélodrome d'Hiver revealed that 72 percent of the French approved of Chirac's declaration, indicating that the reception of apology went well beyond satisfaction of Jewish claims.[26]

As apology constitutes an "acknowledgment of the human dignity and moral worth of victims," Chirac's speech engendered a positive response from French Jews.[27] All major Jewish leaders – including Joseph Sitruk, the chief rabbi of France; Henri Hajdenberg, president of the Representative Council of Jewish Institutions in France (CRIF); Serge Klarsfeld, president of the Association of Daughters and Sons of Deportees; and Robert Badinter, former minister of justice under Mitterrand – saluted Chirac's declaration.[28] Among Jewish intellectuals, Alain Finkielkraut and Blandine Kriegel commended the initiative,[29] but Claude Lanzmann raised questions about the artificiality of apology. For the director of *Shoah*, official recognition voided remembrance of its true content. He reminisced that before July 16 was designated a national holiday, "the ceremonies at Vél' d'Hiv' had warmth: people who gathered there fervently shared a very strong memory, like a shared secret. Now there are dignitaries sitting on government-issue chairs reading ministerial speeches. It is what Flaubert in *Madame Bovary* called 'the mechanical genuflection of hurried parishioners.'"[30]

Political reaction to the official apology revealed that a consensual vision of the Vichy past had not yet been achieved. Rather, the Manichaean divide between True France and Vichy France was forcefully reiterated in the political arena. Old guards of Gaullists and Mitterrandists shared a concern about describing precisely "who" was guilty. Some of Chirac's fellow party members, sensitive to defending the Gaullist heritage, rejected his apology outright. Philippe Séguin refused to link the Vichy state with the French nation and rejected an admission of collective guilt; Pierre Mazeaud argued that the French republic had continued to exist in exile in London under de

---

25 "Le président du CRIF salue le discours que l'on n'attendait plus," *Le Monde*, July 18, 1995. Offering an alternative view, Nathalie Heinich argues that the two presidents' approaches to the Vichy past are not as different as they appear, for they both emphasize guilt over responsibility, in "Face à Vichy: responsabilité ou culpabilité?" in Thomas Ferenczi, ed., *De quoi sommes-nous responsables?* (Paris, 1997), 232–46.
26 Maurice Szafran, "Vichy et les juifs: Chirac a raison," *L'Evénement du jeudi*, July 27, 1995; "M. Badinter approuve la prise de position de M. Chirac sur Vichy," *Le Monde*, July 28, 1995.
27 Trudy Govier and Wilhelm Verwoerd, "The Promise and Pitfalls of Apology," *Journal of Social Philosophy* 33, 1 (Spring 2002), 69.
28 Félix Chiocca, "Une juste réparation morale."
29 Blandine Kriegel, "Pardon et crime d'état," *L'Histoire* 193 (November 1995).
30 Claude Lanzmann, "Parler pour les morts," *Le Monde des débats* (May 2000).

Gaulle; and Jacques Baumel complained that Chirac's apology diminished the legacy of the resistance.[31] In the Mitterrandist camp, Jack Lang, Claude Bartolone, and Louis Mexandeau similarly insisted that the only guilty party was the Vichy regime and not the French republic.[32] Yet Lionel Jospin, socialist leader in the post-Mitterrand era, strongly seconded Chirac's apology,[33] as did other socialists such as Jacques Attali, Robert Badinter, and Michel Rocard,[34] as well as the head of the French Communist Party, Robert Hue.[35] On the extreme right, National Front leader Jean-Marie Le Pen vehemently rejected any notion of French collective responsibility and claimed that Chirac's declaration dirtied the honor of the nation.[36] Le Pen further accused Chirac of using the apology to pay an electoral debt to French Jews.[37] The variety of strong political responses to Chirac's declaration, Nathan Bracher argued convincingly, attested to "stubborn ideological contentiousness and... persistent efforts to make the memory of the past subservient to present political agendas."[38] The divisiveness of the political arena, therefore, contrasted with the overwhelmingly positive reception of Chirac's apology among the wider public, as revealed in opinion polls.

Despite the polarization of political reactions, Chirac's state apology and the Papon trial together symbolized a climate of change. The causal link between apology and judicial reckoning was stressed in many instances. Laurent Greilsamer of *Le Monde* viewed the court ruling that had finally allowed the Papon trial to occur after decades of legal wrangling as a radical shift: "France no longer has the same regard for its history since Jacques Chirac publicly recognized its immutable debt towards Jewish deportees from France. The long parenthesis of the Gaullist mythology, which overestimated resistance France to better hide collaborationist France, is over.

---

31 Patrick Jarreau, "Vichy: Lionel Jospin en juge de paix," *Le Monde*, October 23, 1997.
32 Jean-Baptiste de Montvalon, "La controverse provoquée par François Mitterrand s'estompe dans les rangs du Parti socialiste," *Le Monde*, October 8, 1997; Pascal Virot, "Déportation: les propos de Chirac sèment la discorde au sein du PS," *Libération*, July 20, 1995; "Les propos de M. Chirac sur Vichy divisent le Parti socialiste," *Le Monde*, July 19, 1995.
33 "Vichy: Jospin approuve Chirac," *Les Echos*, July 26, 1995; "M. Jospin approuve la position de M. Chirac sur Vichy," *Le Monde*, July 26, 1995; *Le Monde*, October 8, 1997.
34 "Jacques Attali crédite Jacques Chirac d'une image de dynamisme et d'action," *Le Monde*, August 18, 1995; Michel Rocard, "Les mots justes de Jacques Chirac," *Le Monde*, July 19, 1995; Robert Badinter, "L'Etat criminel," *Le Nouvel observateur*, August 2, 1995.
35 *L'Humanité* (July 24, 1995); "Etat Français: Robert Hue se déclare sans hésitation d'accord avec l'essentiel des propos tenus par Jacques Chirac," *Le Monde*, July 26, 1995.
36 Christiane Chombeau, "M. Le Pen accuse M. Chirac de salir la nation," *Le Monde*, July 20, 1995.
37 "Polémique," *Les Echos*, July 18, 1995.
38 Nathan Bracher, "La Mémoire vive et convulsive: The Papon Trial and France's Passion for History," *The French Review* 73, 2 (December 1999), 323.

Officially."[39] Yet at the same time, Chirac's apology reduced the stakes of the Papon case. The trial was no longer the exclusive means of coming to terms with the Vichy past, since apology and reparation constituted new forms of redress.[40] Papon's lawyer was quick to utilize this evolution for the benefit of his client by arguing that apology should substitute for judicial process and Papon should not have to stand trial.[41] These debates posited two views. On the one hand, the official state apology constituted a final resolution of the past. On the other hand, Chirac's apology could be seen as just a beginning, a point of departure leading from state recognition of official complicity in the Holocaust to a more extensive examination of responsibility on the part of particular sectors of French civil society.

Apology's Civil Turn: Professional Recognition of Responsibility

In April 1997, former Minister of Justice Robert Badinter published a book documenting the French legal profession's role in the Holocaust. It told the story of how the French law bars carried out Vichy's exclusionary legislation establishing a 2 percent quota on Jewish lawyers. French lawyers evaluated the personal, professional, and military credentials of their Jewish colleagues and decided whom to ban from law practice. Badinter summarized the complacency of the legal community toward Jews: "Throughout it all, in the countryside as well as in Paris, not at any moment... was a single protest made against the exclusion of Jews from the Bar... not a single declaration of principles formulated, not a single gesture of solidarity offered to fellow colleagues who would be thus eliminated."[42] Lawyers' precipitous, active response to Vichy's exclusionary legislation can be explained by the widespread belief of professional overcrowding that permeated the law profession in the twenty years prior to the war. Among other factors,

---

39 Laurent Greilsamer, "Un arrêt historique," *Le Monde*, September 20, 1996. See also Dominique Vernier, "Papon, un accusé combatif et plein d'assurance," *Le Monde*, April 1, 1998.

40 Chirac's apology has led to reparations. The Matteoli Mission documented hundreds of thousands of instances of Jewish spoliation in France during the war, offered compensation of 1 billion francs to orphans of Jewish deportees, and created a memory foundation with 1.4 billion francs to provide assistance to Holocaust victims and heirs in need. French insurance companies and financial institutions restituted an additional $22.5 million as part of an agreement signed between France and the United States, one of the legal bases for which was Chirac's 1995 declaration of responsibility. See *Embassy of France in the US – Matteoli Commission*, http://www.info-france-usa.org/news/statmnts/2000/jewish.asp accessed February 14, 2003.

41 "L'Etat de santé de Maurice Papon pèsera sur la suite du procès," *Le Monde*, October 11, 1997.

42 Robert Badinter, *Un antisémitisme ordinaire, Vichy et les avocats juifs (1940–1944)* (Paris, 1997), 190. See also Josyane Savigneau, "La douleur de Robert Badinter; soumission ou complaisance?" *Le Monde des Livres*, April 25, 1997.

the anti-Semitic quota was seen by many lawyers as a felicitous chance to reduce competition.[43]

A mere few weeks after Badinter's publication, the Paris bar issued a resolution recognizing the injustices committed toward Jewish and foreign lawyers during the war. Mentioning the historical evidence presented in Badinter's book, the Paris Bar Council admitted that contrary to its mission, its members helped implement the laws of 1940 and 1941 excluding Jews and foreigners from practice. The recognition concluded, "Conscious of its responsibilities to the history of the bar, the Council bows its head to those who had been victims." At the same time, the Paris bar signaled to the press that it would open its archives.[44] Although the apology was not representative of the entire French legal profession, the Paris bar is by far the most prestigious and important bar in France, and its actions had affected more Jewish lawyers than had any other during the war.[45]

The facts in Badinter's book were not entirely new; scholars had begun to examine the wartime moral collapse of the French legal profession a few years earlier.[46] But lawyers paid attention to this publication because of Badinter's reputation and public role. A former president of the elite Constitutional Council and a prominent member of the Paris bar, he had earned his fame by abolishing the death penalty in France in 1981 as minister of justice under Mitterrand. In addition to Badinter's influence, other factors explain why the law profession was the first civil group to face its Vichy past and take responsibility for its predecessors' actions in the wake of Chirac's collective apology. Looming on the legal horizon was the trial of Maurice Papon, which would raise new questions about the links between justice and history. Since institutions often apologize "in order to restore an institutional reputation ... or to defuse a volatile situation,"[47] the lawyers' initiative was likely motivated in part by a desire to face the past on their own terms before being dragged into it by the media covering

---

43 Julie Fette, "Xenophobia and Exclusion in the Professions in Interwar France," Ph.D. diss., New York University, 2001.

44 "France-justice-juifs," *Agence France Presse*, May 13, 1997, database online, available from Lexis-Nexis; "Occupation: le barreau de Paris bat sa coulpe," *Les Echos*, May 14, 1997; "Antisémitisme: le conseil de l'ordre du barreau de Paris ... " *Le Monde*, May 15, 1997.

45 A few months later, in the midst of the Papon trial, a former president of the Bordeaux law bar asked for forgiveness for the five wartime victims of his bar and urged his colleagues to do the same. Dominique Simonnot, "'Moi si je vole, je vais au gnouf tout de suite'," *Libération*, October 14, 1997. While the 1997 apology may have thus had resonance beyond Paris, no other bar seconded the gesture.

46 See Richard Weisberg, *Vichy Law and the Holocaust in France* (New York, 1996); *Juger sous Vichy* (Paris, 1994); *Le Droit antisémite de Vichy* (Paris, 1996).

47 Robert R. Weyeneth, "The Power of Apology and the Process of Historical Reconciliation," *The Public Historian* 23, 3 (Summer 2001), 22.

the Papon trial. But pragmatism alone did not prompt the legal profession to become the first civil group to acknowledge its specific responsibility in Vichy anti-Semitism. Lawyers' recognition of past faltering in their mission to serve the rights of man and protect the oppressed was matched by a more activist role in contemporary moral legal issues. In early 1997, for example, the Paris Bar Council intervened several times in parliamentary debates over immigration to demand the removal of measures that infringed on the rights of foreigners guaranteed by the constitution.[48] The law bar declaration of 1997 can therefore be analyzed as "an act of discourse that modifies a situation."[49] It signified a broad evolution of the law bar away from its conservative past toward an identity more steeped in the post-1989 human rights culture.

Catholic Repentance for Passivity

Bishops representing the French Catholic Church offered an apology to the Jewish community in a solemn commemoration at the site of the former Drancy camp outside Paris on September 30, 1997, a week before the opening of the Papon trial. A "declaration of repentance" was pronounced by Bishop Olivier de Berranger of Saint-Denis, the diocese where the Drancy camp had existed, and was signed by all bishops whose diocese had housed an internment camp controlled by Vichy. With no media pomp, words held center stage at the ceremony, which was followed by separate religious observations by bishops and rabbis.[50]

For what did the Catholic Church repent? Whereas the French state and the law bar apologized for their active participation in the Holocaust, the French episcopate apologized for not having raised its voice against persecution, for its silence and passivity. The Catholic Church made no protest against the promulgation of the anti-Semitic Statute on the Jews. Silence was the French church's response to discriminatory legislation and mounting social exclusions. Only after the very public roundups in the southern zone of France in the late summer of 1942 did any church official publicly denounce the treatment of Jews. Although a handful of bishop-resistants emerged in the late years of the war, only six of seventy-six bishops ever spoke out against Vichy's anti-Semitism.[51] Numerous factors had prompted

---

48 "Avocats," *Les Annonces de la Seine* 19 (March 10, 1997).
49 Olivier Abel, "Le pardon ou comment revenir au monde ordinaire," *Esprit* (August–September 2000), 76.
50 Marie-Françoise Masson and Bernard Gorce, "'Maintenant, nous pouvons nous embrasser,'" *La Croix*, October 2, 1997.
51 Patrick Henry, "The French Catholic Church's Apology," *The French Review* 72, 6 (May 1999), 1102.

the Catholic Church's embrace of Vichy's "National Revolution": most broadly, the return to conservative religious values and the restoration of the church's prestige (concretized by the reestablishment of religious teaching in public schools and the restitution of church property appropriated since 1905).[52] The bishops' apology in 1997 directly criticized their church's loyalty to the Vichy regime: "In their majority, the spiritual authorities, entangled in a loyalism and docility going well beyond traditional obedience to established powers, remained stuck in an attitude of conformism, prudence and abstention."[53]

It is useful to consider in detail the bishops' speech-act because it set the benchmark for a candid apology that exceeded Chirac's declaration. It specifically acknowledged the church's silence in the face of anti-Semitism: "In February 1941, 40,000 Jews were interned in French camps, while... the church hierarchy was concerned about protecting its own faithful and maintaining its institutions.... Facing the breadth of the drama and the extraordinary character of the crime, too many pastors of the church, by their silence, offended the church itself and its mission." An explicit connection was made between past and present clergy members: "It is our church, and we must recognize that ecclesiastical interests interpreted in an excessively restrictive manner came before the commandments of the conscience and we must ask ourselves why." Furthermore, the bishops linked the church's failure during Vichy with centuries of Catholic anti-Judaism: "On this soil flourished the venomous plant of hatred for the Jews." The declaration concluded: "This failing of the church of France and its responsibility toward the Jewish people are part of our history. We confess this sin. We beg forgiveness of God and ask the Jewish people to hear these words of repentance."

Not unexpectedly, the bishops' declaration was heavily imbued with religious language. A cynical view points to the stiff, literary, and almost medieval evocation of the word "repentance," as one writer suggested that the church had chosen it carefully in order to distance the wartime acts from the present church.[54] Yet the bishops' apology used the terms "sin" and "repentance" as concepts that apply to both individuals and institutions. The significance of the declaration therefore resides in its condemnation of

---

52 Robert O. Paxton, *Vichy France: Old Guard and New Order, 1940–1944* (New York, 1972), 148–53. See also Etienne Fouilloux, *Les chrétiens français entre crise et libération, 1937–1947* (Paris, 1997).
53 The integral text was reprinted in *La Croix* (October 2, 1997) and *Témoignage chrétien*, October 3, 1997). *Le Monde* had published a draft of the text on October 1, which differed significantly from the final version. Jean Duchesne, "Letter from Paris," *First Things* 80 (February 1998), 12–14.
54 Pierre Georges, "Repentance," *Le Monde*, October 1, 1997.

the church as an institution and of its leaders as a group, creating the conditions for a thorough "examination of its collective conscience."[55]

The French Catholic Church's apology can best be understood in the context of three distinct evolutions. First, the church repentance reflected the new contours of memories of Vichy in French society. Second, it can be viewed in the perspective of transnational Catholic calls for repentance. The French declaration was a response to the Vatican's signal for national churches to reconcile with communities that had suffered from Catholic intolerance. The Polish and German episcopates had already set an example for the French church, and Swiss bishops followed in the year 2000.[56] Third, the apology testified to a transition toward greater social activism on the part of the French church in the 1990s. Like the legal profession, the church had begun to criticize harsh policies toward immigrants, and it drew up a document about immigration for Catholic parishioners entitled "A Call to Live Together."[57] This progressive stance was reflected in the French church's commitment to apply the lessons of Vichy to contemporary human rights abuses. One framer of the church apology noted the precedent set by public repentance: "If we repent for what happened under Vichy, it is also in order to think, for example, about what is currently happening in Algeria, in East Africa, about everything that, in the West, can lead to denials of the conscience. The church must speak out. No matter what the situation."[58]

The church apology was symbolically validated by its formal acceptance by the French Jewish community. Henri Hajdenberg, for instance, responded to the bishops at the Drancy ceremony: "Your request for forgiveness... cannot but be heard by victim survivors and their children."[59]

---

55 Henri Tincq, "L'épiscopat français va demander pardon à la communauté juive," *Le Monde*, September 22, 1997.
56 Ironically, the Vatican's own acknowledgment, filled with ambiguity and euphemism, was a disappointment to Jews and many others when it was finally issued in March 1998. Zeev Sternhell, "Une occasion manquée," *Le Monde*, March 21, 1998. See also Henri Tincq, "Le silence persistant du Vatican sur la Shoah," *Le Monde*, October 2, 1997; François Bédarida, "Des controverses à la repentance," *Le Monde*, September 30, 1997.
57 Henri Tincq, "L'épiscopat souhaite un changement d'orientation de la politique d'immigration," *Le Monde*, November 11, 1997.
58 Olivier de Berranger, bishop of Saint-Denis, quoted in Jean-Paul Monferran, "Déportation des juifs sous Vichy: l'épiscopat français se repent," *L'Humanité* (September 30, 1997). Several years later, the church reasserted its resolution. On the occasion of the sixtieth anniversary of the liberation of Auschwitz in January 2005, the French Council of Christian Churches (CECEF, an assembly of Catholic, Protestant, and Orthodox churches) issued a declaration affirming its commitment to fight anti-Semitism: "Christian memory and Church repentance cannot erase what people have inflicted on the Jewish people. [...] We ask all churches never to stop their denunciation of all forms of anti-Semitism. [...] We must remain vigilant." In "Eglises en France: 'Non, à tout prix,'" *Le Monde*, January 26, 2005.
59 "Votre déclaration marquera son temps," *La Croix*, October 2, 1997, and quoted in Anne-Emmanuelle Kervella, "Une aussi longue attente," *Réforme*, October 16, 1997.

Jean Kahn, president of the Central Consistory of France, welcomed the apology despite its tardiness and its limited number of signatories.[60] For his part, former chief rabbi René-Emmanuel Sirat found it theologically impossible to grant forgiveness on behalf of the victims: "Pardon cannot be given by those who were not offended.... The request for forgiveness is pronounced, but there is no response. We are simply witnesses of this act."[61]

General public opinion was also favorable to the bishops' repentance. In a poll taken a few days afterward, 45 percent of the French approved of the declaration, while 41 percent declared themselves indifferent and 9 percent disapproved.[62] With one year's distance from the event, 68 percent of the French polled said the bishops were right to apologize and 24 percent disapproved.[63] How to account for this clarifying of sentiment more distinctly into the "for" and "against" camps, apart from the typical polling pitfalls? To an optimistic observer, the growth in approval for the church's repentance suggests that the passage of time allows apologies to breathe into their full potential for reconciliation, whereas the increase in disapproval may reflect mere annoyance with the close attention paid to the Vichy past in France during the 1990s. In any case, the high approval ratings demonstrate that apology was not just an affair between victims and perpetrators but that it impacted the whole of French society.

Among practicing Catholics, a minority in French society, the response to the church's apology was divided.[64] Whereas the Catholic press was unanimously supportive of the repentance,[65] some parishioners expressed hostility in their correspondence with the clergy.[66] Common criticisms postulated that the church's apology overshadowed Catholics' rescue efforts during the occupation[67] and that the church would be weakened by focusing

---

60 "Déclaration de repentance des évêques; un acte 'positif' mais 'tardif,'" *Agence France Presse*, September 29, 1997, database online, available from LexisNexis.
61 Quoted in Claude-François Jullien, "Nous nous retrouverons tous à Jérusalem," *Le Nouvel observateur*, October 2, 1997.
62 "Le repentir de l'Eglise catholique laisse de nombreux Français indifférents," *Agence France Presse*, October 8, 1997, database online, available from LexisNexis.
63 Henri Tincq, "L'acte de 'repentance' des évêques largement approuvé," *Le Monde*, November 27, 1998.
64 Jean Duchesne, "Letter from Paris," *First Things* 80 (February 1998), 12–14.
65 Henri Tincq, "La presse confessionnelle unanime après la repentance de Drancy," *Le Monde*, October 4, 1997.
66 Elie Maréchal, "Mgr. de Berranger: 'L'Eglise doit se purifier,'" *Le Figaro*, November 6, 1997; "La déclaration de repentance de l'Eglise suscite des incompréhensions," *Le Monde*, November 6, 1997.
67 Albert Chambon, "Le 'silence de l'Eglise,'" *Le Figaro*, October 16, 1997; Henri Tincq, "Pour Henri Hajdenberg, la repentance de l'Eglise est un acte capital," *Le Monde*, October 1, 1997; "Les évêques de France se moquent du monde!" *Minute*, October 1, 1997; Henri Tincq, "La presse confessionnelle unanime après la repentance de Drancy," *Le Monde*, October 4, 1997.

on its mistakes.[68] By contrast, a writer for *La Croix* insisted, "The image of the church will emerge from this event reinforced."[69]

Against the view that institutions apologizing for wartime wrongs had purposefully waited for protagonists to die off so as to distance themselves from their past,[70] church historian Etienne Fouilloux observed, "Even though the church could have spoken out fifty years ago, it is not so late either: the university, the magistrature, the medical order ... also have something to say along the lines of what the church pronounces today. The state did so, recently and with difficulty. The church's gesture is part of a movement of general recognition that I esteem important for Jews and that I hope will take on even greater scope."[71] Fouilloux was not the only one to call for other civil groups to follow the church's lead.[72] Henri Hajdenberg publicly hoped that similar engagements would be taken by professionals and by state organs such as the police, the Councilors of State (who put into technical application the Statute of the Jews and other exclusionary legislation), magistrates (who interpreted the statute), and professors (who taught the statute in their law courses).[73] Novelist and member of the Académie Française Bertrand Poirot-Delpech also called on state organs, in particular the university (which had implemented the Vichy dictate of a 3 percent quota on Jewish students), to imitate the church's apology.[74]

Police Embrace the Ritual of Apology

Immediately following the French Catholic Church's declaration of repentance, a police officers' union stepped forward to apologize for the active collaboration of the French police in the rounding up and deporting of Jews during the war. The ritual of public apology in France was by now well established. First, the National Union of Uniformed Police (SNPT) issued a press release recognizing the guilt of its predecessors under Vichy and expressing its "eternal regret." Second, an apology was offered in an

---

68 Abbé René Laurentin, "L'autoaccusation de l'Eglise," *Le Figaro*, October 3, 1997; Claude-François Jullien, "Une très discrète 'repentance,'" *Le Nouvel observateur*, October 23, 1997.
69 Michel Kubler, "Entre repentance et espérance," *La Croix*, November 4, 1997.
70 Annie Delorme, "Demandes de pardon," *Réforme*, October 30, 1997; Christian Terras, "L'Eglise et les juifs, le repentir ambigu," *L'Evénement du jeudi*, October 2, 1997.
71 Quoted in Jean-Paul Monferran, "Déportation des juifs sous Vichy: l'épiscopat français se repent," *L'Humanité*, September 30, 1997.
72 Gobry, Pascal, "Le devoir de responsabilité des fonctionnaires," *Le Monde*, October 14, 1997; Daniel Psenny, "Les pages noires du patronat," *Le Monde*, October 27, 1997.
73 "Réaction d'Henri Hajdenberg à l'annonce d'une déclaration de repentance sur les silences de l'Eglise pendant la période de Vichy," *Le Monde*, July 12, 1997; Henri Tincq, "Pour Henri Hajdenberg, la repentance de l'Eglise est un acte capital," *Le Monde*, October 1, 1997.
74 Bertrand Poirot-Delpech, "Mea culpa," *Le Monde*, October 1, 1997.

organized ceremony with representatives of the Jewish community at the memorial of the Unknown Jewish Martyr in Paris. Third, the speech-act contained specific acknowledgment that 4,500 Parisian policemen participated in the Vélodrome d'Hiver roundup and that throughout the war the French police force served as a zealous executor of state policies of internment and deportation. Finally, the police union requested pardon from French Jews for the actions of their predecessors "in the name of the republican policemen that we represent, so that never again will men let themselves commit such acts of barbarity."[75]

The apology was limited, however, by lack of representativity: the SNPT was a small union representing only a minority of Parisian police officers. Its apology was also diminished by the strong dissent it provoked within the larger police corps. Another police union, the SGP-CUP (Syndicat général de la police–Centrale unitaire de la police), whose membership counted the majority of Parisian uniformed police officers, characterized the SNPT gesture as "incoherent": "It is stupid and borderline dangerous to equate collaborators with resistants and traitors with patriots by assuming a collective responsibility of the 'police institution.'"[76]

The SNPT's apology was therefore not an example of a widespread outpouring of remorse. Nevertheless, the verbal and ceremonial recognition of guilt was significant for two reasons. First, as the SNPT noted, the role of police personnel in the persecution of Jews in Vichy France was direct and physical, in contrast to Maurice Papon's bureaucratic paper-pushing. The union's apology thus constituted a straightforward acknowledgment of the strong-arm actions most commonly associated with the Holocaust in the public mind. Second, as an organ of the state, police were theoretically "covered" by the official apology offered by Chirac, yet the SNPT nonetheless chose to embrace the ritual therapy of apology.

Turning the Unread Page in Medicine

The French medical profession joined in civil society's embrace of apology. At an annual meeting on October 11, 1997, the Order of Doctors issued a declaration of regret for discrimination against Jewish doctors during the Vichy period. Protectionist and xenophobic sentiment had culminated during the war in a hasty adoption of anti-Semitic and antiforeigner regulations. Like lawyers, it was doctors themselves, through their professional

---

75 Philippe Bernard, "Un important syndicat policier demande pardon au 'peuple juif,'" *Le Monde*, October 8, 1997.
76 "Vichy," *Le Monde*, October 9, 1997.

order, who put into practice the 2 percent quota on their Jewish colleagues. In a "symbolic request for forgiveness in the name of the medical community" extended to Jewish doctors, the president of the order, Bernard Glorion, admitted, "Colleagues became guilty, voluntarily or not . . . [and] had to participate in this sad and shameful operation of discrimination and exclusion. . . . We can only regret and repudiate with gravity and humility." The order's pronouncement concluded, "It is up to us today in the name of the medical community to remind all those who succeed us that our duty, their duty, will be never to yield to the temptation of exclusion and never to accept, even by our silence, any discrimination or rejection of any group."[77] The apology was complemented by an effort at transparency: the order agreed to open its archives to the public, something historians had requested for years.[78] At stake was the release of internal records that would elucidate denunciation and exclusion practices within the medical corps. It was reputed that sacks filled with thousands of letters from French doctors denouncing colleagues as Jews, foreigners, and charlatans were found after the war and subsequently burned in an effort to rebuild the nation. The surviving records of the order had never been made public.

The order's apology contained several weaknesses. Ambiguous references to doctors who "voluntarily or not" "had to participate" in anti-Semitic actions constituted a significant recoil from responsibility. The "duty to remember" invoked by the order only called for remembrance of the "admirable and anonymous behavior of doctors who, risking their lives, obeyed their duty and assisted the sick and often their fellow colleagues" and not of excluded Jewish doctors. The apology was further undermined by an artificial distancing between past and present: the declaration asserted that the Order of Doctors was refounded after the Liberation and was therefore a completely distinct institution from the wartime order. The tainted origins of the order – created by the Vichy regime after decades of medical lobbying (partly to exclude unwanted social categories from the profession) – had been a source of illegitimacy for the postwar medical profession. But in fact, many of the same doctors who had participated in discriminatory policies and collaborative activities during the war persisted in order leadership roles after the war. Only with institutional cleansing performed through memory work, apology, and mourning, Minister of Health Bernard Kouchner provocatively argued, could the order reclaim its dignity.[79]

---

77 Bruno Keller, "Le Pr Glorion: 'Un sentiment de regret, un souci de vérité, un devoir de mémoire,'" *Le Quotidien du médecin*, October 14, 1997.
78 Philippe Roy, "Vichy: après la repentance, l'ouverture des archives," *Le Quotidien du médecin*, October 15, 1997.
79 Cited in Annette Lévy-Willard, "L'examen de conscience de l'ordre des médecins," *Libération*, October 11, 1997.

Apologizing for Vichy in Contemporary France 151

The most serious problem with this apology was that the Order of Doctors – whether conceived as an institution, an ensemble of individuals, or their designated leaders – did not support it. The president of the order had issued the apology on his own initiative, and the members of the organization had neither discussed nor approved it.[80] The order's monthly journal made no mention of the apology in the months that preceded or followed it,[81] and no sign of it appeared on the institution's Web site.[82] Nor did local order leaders cooperate with the national directive to open archives.[83] The vice-president of the Gironde departmental order council proclaimed, "It's very late, too late. We should have opened the drawers in the 1950s. To do so today is to attack the memory of those who had taken on responsibilities and whom we are incapable of judging outside of the context of the period." According to the president of the Northern departmental order council, there was nothing of interest in the archives.[84] The Order of Doctors's apology can thus be categorized as one "undercut by subsequent denials from others within it."[85] Indeed, physicians' letters to the editors of medical journals provided evidence of acerbic dissent. One doctor, for instance, had "had enough of these mediatized-epileptic tremors over the Second World War. I was not there. I did not do anything. So leave me alone.... Collective responsibility does not exist."[86] The claim that some doctors assisted Jews figured prominently among the reactions to the apology:[87] "What would all the big names in French medicine who fought against the invader and who constantly risked their lives to save Jewish lives think of this 'repentance'?"[88]

Nonetheless, positive reaction to the apology surfaced within the French medical profession as well. Despite disappointment over the hedged language of the declaration, Jewish doctors expressed overall satisfaction.[89] Several medical journals followed up on the apology by investigating the history of the profession under Vichy.[90] A grim view of the order's past emerged

80 Jean-Yves Nau, "Le président de l'ordre des médecins fait acte de 'repentance,'" *Le Monde*, October 12, 1997; H.R., "Le mea culpa de l'Ordre," *Impact médecin hebdo*, October 17, 1997.
81 Search undertaken for the *Bulletin de l'Ordre des médecins* from September 1997 to January 1998.
82 See *Conseil National de l'Ordre des Médecins*, http://www.conseil-national.medecin.fr, accessed February 14, 2003.
83 Philippe Roy, "Vichy: l'Ordre des médecins entre en repentance," *Le Quotidien du médecin*, October 10, 1997.
84 Roy, "Vichy: après la repentance."
85 Trudy Govier and Wilhelm Verwoerd, "The Promise and Pitfalls of Apology," *Journal of Social Philosophy* 33, 1 (Spring 2002), 76.
86 "Le Quotidien des lecteurs," *Le Quotidien du médecin*, October 20, 1997.
87 Roy, "Vichy: après la repentance, l'ouverture des archives."
88 "Le Quotidien des lecteurs," *Le Quotidien du médecin*, October 23, 1997.
89 Philippe Roy, "L'Ordre sous Vichy: le Pr Kahn critique les conseils départementaux," *Le Quotidien du médecin*, October 13, 1997.
90 For example, see the dossier "Les médecins de Vichy," *Impact médecin hebdo*, October 10, 1997.

from these inquiries: "Zealous and obedient creature of Pétain . . . the Order was subservient to the regime. The departmental medical council leaders were the perfect implementers of the exclusionary laws."[91] For some, the apology came as a long-awaited reckoning: "Fifty-seven years! We had to wait fifty-seven years for the Order to beg forgiveness."[92] Some doctors sought to link the apology to contemporary French debates about immigration and public memory. The Committee of Foreign-Diploma Doctors, for instance, drew a comparison between wartime exclusion and current discrimination against foreign doctors.[93] Others in the medical profession expressed hope that a similar process of acknowledgment would be undertaken for acts of torture committed during the Algerian War.[94]

Since its Vichy origins, the Order of Doctors has had a conservative reputation both for its role in sociopolitical affairs (its fight against the legalization of abortion) and for its internal governance (its favoring of colleagues over patients in medical disputes). But it has nonetheless evolved in recent years toward more open and democratic ways, especially under the presidency of Glorion.[95] His recognition of medical anti-Semitism during Vichy can be viewed as part of this evolution. Ultimately, however, the apology proved to be abortive. Although it stimulated discussion of the order's past, the declaration was ambivalent and unrepresentative, and it conveyed the impression that it was reluctantly given. Conflicts were buried anew with no final sense of reconciliation.[96] One doctor's frustration summed it up: "This individual and timid 'repentance' is not enough. . . . The Order wants us to 'turn the page' that no one has read yet."[97]

State Institutions Acknowledge Their Pasts

One of the most prestigious state institutions was swept up in the wave of repentance for Vichy injustices. The Conseil d'Etat (Council of State) is the highest administrative court in France. It is consulted for interpretation of legislative texts and is responsible for elaborating laws into applicable decrees. At issue during this moment of apology was the use of the French legal positivist tradition to legitimize wartime exclusionary laws. In

---

91 "Pétain impose ses lois," *Impact médecin hebdo*, October 10, 1997.
92 Roy, "Vichy: l'Ordre des médecins entre en repentance."
93 Keller, "Le Pr Glorion: 'Un sentiment de regret, un souci de vérité, un devoir de mémoire.'"
94 "Le Quotidien des lecteurs," *Le Quotidien du médecin*, October 20, 1997.
95 Paul Benkimoun, "L'homme qui a fait bouger l'ordre des médecins," *Le Monde*, July 11, 2001.
96 See Mark Gibney and Erik Roxstrom, "The Status of State Apologies," *Human Rights Quarterly* 23 (2001), 929–34.
97 "Le Quotidien des lecteurs," *Le Quotidien du médecin*, October 20, 1997.

a seminal article, legal scholar Danièle Lochak has argued that the French judiciary during Vichy interpreted anti-Semitic law under the rationale of neutralism. Accordingly, French jurists' resolute commitment to objectivity blinded them to the ethical and human consequences of discriminatory legislation. Their elaboration of legal doctrine and jurisprudence also served to normalize anti-Semitic law as a legitimate discipline with its own set of legal experts.[98]

This critical view of the French judiciary during the war made its way into the leadership of the Council of State in 1997. During a colloquium on the Council of State and regime change in French history – one element of the celebration of the Council's second centenary – a member of the Council of State recognized the institution's legal conformism under Vichy and admitted that its councilors had interpreted anti-Semitic and xenophobic laws in a rigidly Cartesian manner. Occasionally, they had also demonstrated an unmistakably discriminatory bent in their opinions.[99] Indeed, one French legal scholar has documented that most Council of State members during Vichy never tried to impede or stall the application of anti-Semitic law and in fact widely approved its content.[100] In its defense, however, the Council of State also argued in 1997 that its jurisprudence tended to be more liberal after 1942 and that its margin of maneuver under Vichy authorities was particularly narrow. As was true of some of the other institutions examined herein, internal reactions among members of the Council of State were split over the acknowledgment of the Council's Vichy record. Some members deemed it courageous and honest and suggested that the institution could in fact have done better to counter anti-Semitism, whereas others expressed outright anger.[101]

The declaration was not quite an apology. Had it been voted by the members of the Council of State and issued by its president (it was delivered by the president of the finance section, Jean Massot), it would have constituted a more representative and authoritative recognition of responsibility.

---

98 Danièle Lochak, "La doctrine sous Vichy ou les mésaventures du positivisme," in CURAPP, *Les usages sociaux du droit* (Paris, 1989), 252–85; Danièle Lochak, "Ecrire, se taire... Réflexions sur l'attitude de la doctrine française," in *Le Droit antisémite de Vichy*, 433–62. Against Lochak, Michel Troper argued that, on the contrary, it was because the French judiciary lost touch with its positivist heritage during Vichy that it supported legal exclusion. See M. Troper, "La doctrine et le positivisme (à propos d'un article de Danièle Lochak)," in *Les usages sociaux du droit*, 286–92.
99 Jean Massot, "Le Conseil d'Etat et le régime de Vichy," *La Revue administrative*, numéro spécial (1998), 28–45. For a lightly edited version of the same text, see Massot, "Le Conseil d'Etat et le régime de Vichy," *Vingtième siècle* 58 (April–June 1998), 83–99.
100 Jean Marcou, "Le Conseil d'Etat: juge administratif sous Vichy," *Juger sous Vichy*, 92.
101 P.-H. D., "1940–1944: les accommodements du Conseil d'Etat," *Le Figaro*, November 17, 1997; Rafaële Rivais, "Le Conseil d'Etat reconnaît ne pas avoir lutté contre Vichy," *Le Monde*, November 16–17, 1997.

Different in nature from the more repentant tone of other civil groups' declarations, this gesture nonetheless represented a breakthrough for the French judicial system in general. Because the Council of State is one of the *grand corps* of the French state, it was in theory, like the police, encompassed within Chirac's official 1995 apology for Vichy. Rather than considering the Council of State exempt from historical reckoning, however, Massot stressed the influence of Chirac's apology on the institution's desire to come to terms with its own past.

The Council of State's revisiting of its history was also perceptible in its involvement in the Papon trial. Following Papon's condemnation for crimes against humanity, the Council of State determined that the French state was obliged to pay half of Papon's legal fees owed to victims since the "acts and actions of the French government, which did not directly result from the constraints of the occupier, allowed for and facilitated, independently of the personal actions of Maurice Papon, operations that constituted the prelude to deportation."[102] By rendering the Fifth Republic financially accountable for actions of the wartime administration, this ruling gave legal teeth to Chirac's symbolic recognition that the Vichy regime was not a parenthesis in French history.

The Council of State was the last state organ to engage in declarative recognition of its Vichy past. However, performative apology was not the only avenue for state or civil institutions to address their respective histories. At the end of the decade, the creation of historical commissions to research institutional activities during Vichy coincided with the apology trend. For instance, the Ministry of Youth and Sports established a historical commission in 1997 to examine its role in propaganda and collaboration.[103] Similarly, and in response to lawsuits alleging complicity in crimes against humanity, the French national railroad company, SNCF, initiated a research colloquium in 2000 to examine its involvement in the deportation process.[104] SNCF's leadership has, however, adamantly refused to apologize despite one plaintiff's dogged pursuit for verbal recognition

---

102 Communiqué de presse: "Le Conseil d'Etat statuant au contentieux, sur le rapport de la 1ère sous-section de la Section du contentieux, No. 238689, Séance du 5 avril 2002," available online at www.conseil-etat.fr; "L'Etat français responsable des déportations sous l'Occupation," *Libération*, July 9, 2002; J.-M. Dy, "Le Conseil d'Etat oblige l'Etat à payer la moitié du montant des condamnations civiles prononcées contre Maurice Papon," *Le Monde*, April 13, 2002.

103 Benoît Hopquin, "Le sport français s'interroge sur son attitude sous Vichy," *Le Monde*, December 11, 1998.

104 Clara Dupont-Monod, "La SNCF rattrapée par les fantômes d'Auschwitz," *Marianne*, August 23–9, 1999, 26–9; Philippe Boggio, "La juste distance," *Marianne*, August 23–9, 1999, 28; "La SNCF poursuivie pour complicité dans l'Holocauste," *Le Monde*, June 15, 2001; Emmanuelle Réju, "La SNCF fait son devoir de mémoire," *La Croix*, June 21, 2000.

of responsibility.[105] For its part, the magistrature had already organized an investigative colloquium in 1993 entitled "To Judge under Vichy."[106] The momentum for inquiry has not waned at the start of the twenty-first century: straddling civil service and intellectual corps, ethnographers also assembled a colloquium on their Vichy past in 2003.[107] Like trials, institutional historical commissions brought academics and apologizers into a close relationship that has been criticized by proponents of maintaining a scholarly distance from current events. The rise of the "historian-expert" in the 1990s dismayed many members of the historical profession who resented the transformation of scholarship into narrow expertise put to use in trials and commissions.[108] Despite this controversy over intellectuals' role, the apology trend both benefited from and elicited new scholarly inquiry.

Extending the Apology Model

The French wave of apology for World War Two injustices ended with the acknowledgment of the Council of State. Public satiation served to brake the phenomenon. While several of the apologies had received minimal publicity, those offered by Chirac and the Catholic Church attracted saturation-level press coverage. One observer bemoaned, "I repent, we repent... It is currently the most common verb in the French language. The churches, the doctors and the police parade and contrive. We are now waiting for the postmen, the train conductors and the truck drivers to join the great self-flagellating movement.... Me too I ask for forgiveness. Forgiveness for not wanting to repent."[109] After the first few mediatized acknowledgments of responsibility, apologies became perceived by some as empty words and routinized display. As one French political scientist put it, "Repentance is not a miracle remedy. It is also fundamentally 'impure,' inseparable from power struggles, weighted with ulterior motives and calculations.... In the end, everything gets old; what was originally a solemn gesture becomes mechanical over time."[110]

Thus, several arguments against public apologies had become commonplace in France by the end of 1997: it is impossible to apologize for the actions of predecessors; institutions cannot be guilty; individuals cannot

---

105 Airelle Niepce, "La SNCF poursuivie dans la déportation des juifs," *Libération*, March 20, 2003.
106 *Juger sous Vichy* (Paris, 1994).
107 Nicolas Weill, "Mémoire de Vichy: le mea culpa des ethnographes," *Le Monde*, May 7, 2003.
108 See, among others, Gérard Noiriel, *Sur la "crise" de l'histoire* (Paris, 1996).
109 Luc Beyer de Ryke, "Refus de repentance," *Réforme*, November 13, 1997.
110 Philippe Moreau Defarges, "Repentance, la rédemption et le calcul," *Débat* 112 (2000), 133–4.

apologize for a collectivity.[111] The argument that "apologies have their place, but they cannot be substitutes for action,"[112] was expressed scathingly by a philosophy professor who labeled repentance a gratuitous "rip-off" serving as a screen against truth and reparations, especially in the case of colonialism.[113] Others denounced the inconsistency of the apology trend: Why were apologies only being offered for certain injustices? Such criticism led to a phenomenon of "victim competition" and to the politicization of apology as an ideological gesture.[114] This occurred when, in response to the publication of *The Black Book of Communism*,[115] the political right opposed the focus on Vichy with a competing narrative of communist criminality. The far-right National Front went so far as to demand from French communists an apology for Stalin's crimes.[116] The overwhelming focus on Vichy alone bothered several intellectuals. Historian Raoul Girardet warned against "selective repentance,"[117] whereas writer François Maspéro urged the French to pay attention also to current events for which they might have to apologize in 2040.[118]

The social demand for apology did in fact reach beyond the Vichy question into other episodes of the French past. At the centenary of Emile Zola's "*J'accuse*" in January 1998, the Catholic journal *La Croix* apologized for the treatment of Jews in its pages during the Dreyfus Affair.[119] The 150th anniversary of the abolition of slavery in France that same month also prompted calls for a state apology, although a proposal for reparations was unable to garner support among parliamentarians.[120] In February 1998,

111 See, François Maspéro, "Tous coupables?" *Le Monde*, December 11, 1997; Pierre Bourget, "Au guichet de la repentance," *Le Monde*, October 23, 1997.
112 Robert R. Weyeneth, "The Power of Apology and the Process of Historical Reconciliation," *The Public Historian* 23, 3 (Summer 2001), 25–9.
113 Jean-Jacques Delfour, "L'Arnaque des repentances," *Raison présente* 133 (2000), 63–8.
114 See Jean-Michel Chaumont, *La concurrence des victimes: génocide, identité, reconnaissance* (Paris, 1997).
115 Stéphane Courtois et al., *Le Livre noir du communisme: crimes, terreur et répression* (Paris, 1997).
116 Christiane Chombeau, "Un meeting catholique traditionaliste dénonce les crimes du communisme," *Le Monde* (November 11, 1997); Lucien Kieffer, "Les mêmes instincts," *Le Monde*, December 15, 1997; Pascal Virot, "Ouverture du XXXe congrès du PCF," *Libération*, March 23, 2000.
117 Raoul Girardet, "Repentances sélectives," *Le Figaro*, October 29, 1997.
118 François Maspéro, "Tous coupables?" *Le Monde*, December 11, 1997. See also Max Milner, "De quoi oublierons-nous de nous souvenir?" *Le Monde*, November 22, 1997.
119 "La République célèbre le 'J'accuse,'" *La Tribune*, January 12, 1998; Alain Salles, "La repentance de *La Croix* et l'affaire Dreyfus," *Le Monde*, January 13, 1998; Pierre Georges, "Ici et maintenant," *Le Monde*, January 16, 1998; Daniel Schneidermann, "Au revoir, M. Zola," *Le Monde*, January 19, 1998.
120 Philippe-Jean Catinchi, "Penser l'abolition; Réponse à la mondialisation," *Le Monde*, April 24, 1998; "La dette de l'esclavage," *Le Monde*, April 27, 1998; Jean-Louis Saux, "Une proposition de loi qualifie l'esclavage de crime contre l'humanité," *Le Monde*, February 19, 1999; Louis Sala-Molins, "Esclavage: une mémoire à peu de frais," *Le Monde*, February 23, 1999; Amadou Lamine Sall, "Pardonner sans jamais oublier," *Courrier international*, March 18, 1999.

the treatment of indigenous populations came to the forefront of the apology agenda when New Caledonia demanded repentance for French brutality during the conquest of the island in 1853.[121] Although these requests mostly remained unmet, their presence indicated that apology had become deeply rooted in French public discourse. Concomitantly with this French phenomenon, the demand for a wide range of apologies for historical injustices increased significantly on the world stage as the millennium approached.

From Vichy to Algeria

For French society, the cresting wave of apology shifted direction in the late 1990s to gather in its wake the Algerian question as the next historical object of reckoning. To use a more grounded metaphor, apologizing for Vichy had paved the way – linguistically, socially, and politically – for a French engagement with its colonial past. Like Vichy, the Algerian War was "characterized by domestic strife, a tarnishing of the French image of guardian of human rights, and a decisive decline in French power."[122] Often the two histories intersected, for instance, when revelations about Papon's role as Paris police prefect in the 1961 massacre of Algerians surfaced during his trial as a Vichy bureaucrat for the deportation of Jews. Memory of the Algerian War emerged more forcefully after public preoccupation with memories of Vichy had subsided in France. Of course, debates over French actions in Algeria were far from new in the 1990s; they had begun during the war itself.[123] And historians have long since exposed the "massive and widespread" practice of torture perpetrated by the French military and approved by the highest echelons of political authority during the war.[124] But the memory of the Algerian War, and the torture issue in particular, took an apologetic turn only after a language of repentance had been established by the debates over Vichy. Questions asked about Vichy were then applied to Algeria.

While the Vichy apology movement served as a model for a deeper memorial reckoning with the Algerian War, other causes also explain the

---

121 Jean-Louis Saux, "Le document confidentiel sur le contentieux colonial," *Le Monde*, February 25, 1998.
122 Henry Rousso, "La guerre d'Algérie et la culture de la mémoire," *Le Monde*, April 4, 2002. See also Rousso, "La guerre d'Algérie, la mémoire et Vichy," *L'Histoire* 266 (June 2002), 28–9; and William B. Cohen, "The Algerian War and French Memory," *Contemporary European History* 9.3 (2000), 489–500.
123 See the works of Benjamin Stora on the historiography and memory of the Algerian War.
124 Christian Delacampagne, "Torturante Mémoire," *French Politics, Culture and Society* 19.3 (Fall 2001), 98.

recentering of Algeria in the French conscience at the end of the twentieth century. As a new generation of political leaders arose and key actors in the war disappeared, more parties stood to gain from a denunciation of past wrongdoing. The growing historiography also elucidated the details and complexity of the Franco-Algerian war, providing the groundwork for a more honest memory of the past. At the same time, revelations about the war ignited several scandals in French society in the 1990s, demonstrating that *known* history had not yet completed its transformation into *understood* history embedded in the collective French consciousness. Heightened public "receptivity" culminating late in the year 2000 with a series of attention-getting exposés of wartime incidents, argued historian William Cohen, "laid the foundation" for a future public apology for French acts of torture committed in Algeria.[125] The most provocative of these scandals was the publication of retired general Paul Aussaresses's memoirs justifying the use of torture and summary executions by French troops in Algeria during the war.[126]

A number of signs testify to an increased social demand for reconciliation with the Franco-Algerian past. Now shared by much of mainstream public opinion, the demand for transparency and for acknowledgment of French wrongdoing first emerged within intellectual circles and among victim groups. Scholars have stepped up research on the Algerian War and its memory and have urged political leaders to make redress.[127] Referring directly to Chirac's apology for Vichy anti-Semitism as a model, a dozen prominent French intellectuals publicly petitioned the president and prime minister to acknowledge and condemn past French practices of torture in Algeria.[128] And the *harkis* – Algerians who fought on the side of France but whom France later abandoned – have increasingly vocalized their claims for recognition.

In response to this demand from below, French authorities have taken steps toward reconciliation. In June 1999, the Parliament declared the Algerian conflict a "war," officially ending a state denial that had never held sway among French public opinion. Following some material reparations made to *harkis* in the late 1990s, the date September 25, 2001, was designated a national day of commemoration of the *harkis*, and in 2005 the French Parliament passed a law increasing indemnities for *harkis* and their

125 William B. Cohen, "The Sudden Memory of Torture: The Algerian War in French Discourse, 2000–2001," *French Politics, Culture and Society* 19, 3 (Fall 2001), 85–8, 91.
126 Paul Aussaresses, *Services spéciaux Algérie, 1955–1957* (Paris, 2001).
127 Alain Joxe, "Repentons-nous sur l'Algérie et parlons vrai," *Le Monde*, November 11, 1997; Cohen, "The Algerian War and French Memory."
128 Published in *L'Humanité* on October 31, 2000.

descendants and expressing French "recognition" of *harkis*, although the law did not satisfy leftist parliamentarians' push to employ the term "responsibility" for the French abandonment of *harkis* after the war.[129] The murderous attacks on Algerians in Paris on October 17, 1961, were also publicly commemorated in 2001 by the erection of a plaque near the Pont St. Michel. No national politicians attended this ceremony, but the socialist mayor of Paris, Bertrand Delanoë, lent an official presence to an annual commemoration that had for years remained occult.[130] In another quasi-official manifestation of French readiness to confront the Algerian past, French Ambassador to Algeria Hubert Colin de Verdière recognized in early 2005 the French "massacre" of tens of thousands of Algerians in Sétif, a small city in eastern Algeria, in May 1945, in response to the Armistice Day Algerian rebellion that had killed 109 French persons. The ambassador's characterization of the French repression as an "inexcusable tragedy" led Algerian groups to amplify their demands for a full official apology from France for the war.[131] And in reaction to the Aussaresses scandal, Prime Minister Lionel Jospin authorized the opening of national archives pertaining to the war years in order to facilitate historical inquiry.[132] But philosopher and social critic Christian Delacampagne argued that since the facts of French injustices have already been well documented by historians, Jospin's gesture was meant to distract attention away from the calls for apology.[133]

An official public apology for French acts, including torture, committed during the Algerian War still remains wanting as this book goes to press. Whereas the state initiated the apology wave for Vichy anti-Semitism that trickled down into civil society, those same civil groups that made amends for their particular Vichy pasts seem to be waiting for a similar cue from the state in regard to Algeria. Neither the military establishment nor the corporatist groups that actively or passively enabled colonial injustices to

---

[129] Sylvia Zappi, "Une journée d'hommage unique reconnaît officiellement le drame des harkis," *Le Monde*, September 24, 2001; Sylvia Zappi, "M. Chirac exprime 'la reconnaissance de la nation' aux combattants harkis," *Le Monde*, September 26, 2001; Philippe Bernard, "Le projet de loi sur les 'Français rapatriés' déçoit les harkis," *Le Monde*, February 9, 2005; "La France adopte une loi exprimante sa 'reconnaissance' aux harkis," *Le Monde*, February 11, 2005.

[130] "'A la mémoire des algériens...'; 17 octobre 1961," *Libération*, October 18, 2001; Jean Jacques Bozonnet and Christine Garin, "Les controverses politiques sur la guerre d'Algérie marquent la commémoration du 17 octobre 1961," *Le Monde*, October 19, 2001; Brigitte Jelen, "17 octobre 1961–17 octobre 2001: Une commémoration ambiguë," *French Politics, Culture and Society* 20, 1 (Spring 2002), 30–43.

[131] Florence Beaugé, "Paris reconnaît que le massacre de Sétif en 1945 était 'inexcusable,'" *Le Monde*, March 9, 2005.

[132] "Guerre d'Algérie: Lionel Jospin se dit hostile à une repentance générale," *Les Echos*, May 17, 2001.

[133] Delacampagne, "Torturante Mémoire," 98.

occur – lawyers and judicial bodies enacting discriminatory legislation, doctors dealing with injured victims of repression, Catholic missionaries, law enforcement and security forces – have preempted the state in an apologetic gesture regarding Algeria.

Why does French leadership still appear unready to admit injustices, recognize victim groups, and reconcile with the nation's Algerian past through the path of a formal apology, as it did for the anti-Semitism of the Vichy period? In addition to the usual explanations for resistance to a public historical apology – ideological posturing, electoral politicking, fear of reparations and court trials – an important obstacle to full public acknowledgment involves the French military.[134] First, amnesty and the statute of limitations for crimes committed during the war constitute two blockages to legal redress, thus dampening significantly a juridical climate of reconciliation that could foster apology.[135] Second, President Chirac himself served as a young lieutenant in Algeria during the war,[136] a fact that, analogous to Mitterrand's resistance to accountability for Vichy, could explain much of Chirac's reluctance to repeat his bold Vichy apology. One might conjecture that the inauguration in Paris in December 2002 of a national memorial of the Algerian War and of the Moroccan and Tunisian conflicts, in honor of the more than 22,000 "soldiers who died for France in North Africa almost a half-century ago,"[137] was meant to placate French veterans before political leaders could apologize in their name. Chirac's historic presidential visit to Algeria a few months later in March 2003 indeed encouraged hopes for a French apology to its ex-colony but only produced a "declaration of friendship" between the two countries. The question remains: How can France apologize for acts of torture without addressing its overall pursuit of the war to retain Algeria, as well as its entire colonial enterprise?

However, a French apology to victims in Algeria does not seem to be far off, in part because of the normalization of apology and its perceived benefits as a means of mourning the past and ameliorating the future. The state in this case may need to catch up with public opinion: 56 percent of French surveyed in 2001 were in favor of an official apology.[138] There is growing consensus that an apology would improve Franco-Algerian relations and

---

134 Cohen, "The Sudden Memory of Torture," 88–91; Delacampagne, "Torturante Mémoire," 100.
135 See Raphaëlle Branche, "Désirs de vérité, volontés d'oublis: la torture pendant la guerre d'Algérie," *Cahiers français: La mémoire, entre histoire et politique* (July–August 2001), 68–74.
136 Raphaëlle Bacque and Florence Beauge, "Chirac l'Algérien," *Le Monde*, March 1, 2003.
137 "Chirac inaugure le mémorial de la guerre d'Algérie à Paris," *Agence France Presse*, December 5, 2002, database online, available from LexisNexis.
138 "Plus de la moitié des Français pour la repentance," *Agence France Presse*, May 9, 2001, database online, available from LexisNexis.

enhance the integration of Maghrebi immigrants and their descendants in contemporary French society.[139] An apology would thus help to reshape the identities of weak and vulnerable population groups by publicly recognizing that "the culture of the victim group is not now, and never was, morally inferior to that of the offender group."[140] France facing its Algerian past, albeit slowly and with difficulty, signifies a new and huge market for apology in a postcolonial world.

Apology: Between Past and Future

Apology is in vogue, noted an American journalist in Paris in the late 1990s, "but nowhere, perhaps, is the process more fraught or obsessive than in France's contemplation of its treatment of the Jews during World War II."[141] Whether obsessive or not, the apology trend reversed the terms of French public memory. Less than a year before Chirac's declaration, few could imagine the possibility of a radical departure from postwar myths. Tony Judt, for instance, argued in 1994 that the "absurd sophism" of denying the Republic's responsibility for the acts of Vichy would prevent France from ever coming to terms with its past.[142] For Judt, reincorporating Vichy into the mainstream course of French history seemed like a daunting prospect precisely because in France, "modern identity is indissolubly linked to the idea of the universal Republic." However, triggered by Chirac's formal statement, apologies for Vichy ultimately served to stimulate a public reexamination of a buried past. Moreover, apology in France has affirmed a historical continuity and a symbolic generational link between "them" (the actors of 1940–5) and "us" (French society today).

Apology has also fostered the integration of Jewish memory into the French national historical narrative. The Shoah is no longer external to the classic dichotomy between resistance and collaboration but rather is part and parcel of the French wartime history. The focus of apologies on the

---

139 Alain Joxe, "Repentons-nous sur l'Algérie et parlons vrai," *Le Monde*, November 11, 1997; Jean Baptiste de Montvalon, "Alain Madelin célèbre la France pluriculturelle et plurielle et appelle à la repentance," *Le Monde*, November 11, 2000; Mohamed Haddouche and André Wormser, "Justice pour les harkis, en Algérie et en France!" *Le Monde*, June 17, 2000; "Plus de la moitié des Français pour la repentance"; Nacira Guenif-Souilamas, "En finir avec l'impensé colonial," *Libération*, January 24, 2002.
140 Kathleen Gill, "The Moral Functions of an Apology," *Philosophical Forum* 31 (Spring 2000), 23. On the power differential between perpetrator and victim groups, see also J. Harvey, "The Emerging Practice of Institutional Apologies," *The International Journal of Applied Philosophy* 9, 2 (1995), 57–65.
141 Roger Cohen, "France Confronts Its Jews, and Itself," *New York Times*, October 19, 1997.
142 Tony Judt, "Entre le tabou et l'obsession," *Le Monde*, September 21, 1994.

hitherto neglected Jewish experience has not only been seized by political circles such as the National Front, but it has also become a point of scholarly criticism. Students of French memory Eric Conan and Henry Rousso have warned against the "temptation of 'judeocentrism,' which seeks to reread the entire history of the occupation through the prism of anti-Semitism."[143] Against this view, political scientist Pierre Birnbaum maintained that the only way to overcome the obsession was "to leave the book of The History of France open to this page just a bit longer."[144] Similarly, historian Olivier Wieviorka resisted the notion of a debilitating obsession: rather, demands for apology only showed that "many French people want to know more."[145] Public opinion did not seem to perceive the forceful emergence of Jewish memories as problematic. When polled in October 1998, 58 percent of French people (and a higher percentage among 18- to 24-year-olds) replied that discussion of the extermination of Jews during World War Two "was not excessive."[146]

The French case provides a unique way to understand the impact of apology on a society struggling with its history. If strictly used as a process of *judgment*, public apology can appear as a limited, mechanistic condemnation of the past without any far-reaching pedagogical dimension. In fact, many in France objected to this perfunctory *devoir de mémoire* (memory duty) performed through public atonement. A well-known historian of the postwar period found only formalism in repentance: "Making apologies does not connect history to our lives and hardly returns the French community to a place of self-confidence. Memorial piety and judicial interpellations seem to be neither consoling nor prophylactic.... If it is accepted that the more we confess, the better we will become, it is because we lack the force to reformulate an identity enlightened by experience."[147] This may be a valid critique of the ritualism and political correctness of the apology trend. Yet this criticism focuses solely on apology as condemnation and contrition and remains blind to the important hermeneutical potential embedded in this practice: a process of *critical inquiry*, which can "raise the moral threshold of a society," as Roy Brooks, a scholar of reconciliation, claimed.[148]

---

143 *Vichy: An Ever-Present Past*, 198.
144 Pierre Birnbaum, "Sur un lapsus présidentiel," *Le Monde*, October 21, 1994.
145 Quoted in H.R., "Procès Papon; 'Une fonction pédagogique,'" *Impact médecin hebdo*, October 10, 1997.
146 Nicolas Weill, "Les Français face à la mémoire de Vichy et de la Shoah," *Le Monde*, November 27, 1998. This nonetheless represented a decrease from 79 percent who expressed the same opinion in July 1995. Maurice Szafran, "Vichy et les juifs: Chirac a raison," *L'Evénement du jeudi*, July 27, 1995.
147 Jean-Pierre Rioux, "Devoir de mémoire, devoir d'intelligence," *Vingtième siècle* 73 (January–March 2002), 161.
148 Roy L. Brooks, "The Age of Apology," in Brooks, ed., *When Sorry Isn't Enough*, 3.

Despite its limits, civil society's embrace of apology can ultimately be seen as introspective and demystifying, allowing French society to "move on" in a cleansed way. Compared with only ten or fifteen years earlier, court trials, historical commissions, monetary and symbolic reparations, the inauguration of commemorative days, and the revision of textbooks in the 1990s all testify that the apology trend coincided with a profound and manifold reexamination of the past in France. As such, apologies for Vichy were most effective when they combined both critical inquiry and judgment, thereby engendering a healthier relationship between past and present, between the duty of memory and the necessary travail of forgetting.

7

Limited Rehabilitation?

Historical Observations on the Legal Rehabilitation of Foreign Citizens in Today's Russia

ANDREAS HILGER

On June 22, 1941, the German Reich launched an unprecedented attack on the Soviet Union. This new stage of warfare was planned as a war of conquest and annihilation, and it prompted the creation of an international coalition against Germany and its allies. After fierce fighting, Germany surrendered unconditionally in the spring of 1945. The Soviet Union, meanwhile, was able to extend its sphere of influence into Central Europe. At the same time, Stalin seized the opportunities presented by the war in the Pacific: on August 8, 1945, the USSR declared war on Japan. The Red Army marched into Korea and Manchuria, and it occupied the Kurile Islands.[1]

World War II created the framework for Stalin's security forces to expand their activities beyond the border of the USSR.[2] As a rule, prior to World

---

1 For a comprehensive account of the events of the war, see Gerhard L. Weinberg, *A World at Arms: A Global History of World War II* (New York, 1994). For the German-Soviet front: Rolf-Dieter Müller et al., eds., *Hitler's War in the East 1941–1945: A Critical Assessment* (London, 1997). On Japan, see Issa A. Pliev, *Das Ende der Kwantung-Armee* (Berlin, 1984); George Alexander Lensen, *The Strange Neutrality: Soviet-Japanese Relations During the Second World War, 1941–1945* (Tallahassee, Fla., 1972); Tsuyoshi Hasegawa, *Racing the Enemy: Stalin, Truman, and the Surrender of Japan* (Cambridge, 2005). The Soviet perspective on postwar developments is discussed by Vojtech Mastny, *The Cold War and Soviet Insecurity: The Stalin Years* (New York, 1996); Caroline Kennedy-Pipe, *Stalin's Cold War: Soviet Strategies in Europe, 1943–1956* (Manchester, 1995); Vladislav Zubok and Constantine Pleshakov, *Inside the Kremlin's Cold War: From Stalin to Khrushchev* (Cambridge, Mass., 1996).

2 In contrast to these developments, the history of Soviet intelligence operations is a long-established field of historical research. For an introduction, see Christopher Andrew and Vasili Mitrokhin, *The Mitrokhin Archive: The KGB in Europe and the West* (London, 2000); Aleksandr I. Kolpakidi and Dmitri P. Prochorov, *Imperiya GRU. Ocherki istorii rossijskoj voennoj razvedki*, 2 vols. (Moscow, 2000); Andreas Hilger, "Counter-Intelligence Soviet Style: The Activities of Soviet Security Services in East Germany, 1945–1955," *Journal of Intelligence History* 3 (2003): 83–105; A. F. Noskova, ed., *NKVD i polskoe podpole 1944–1945. (Po "Osobym papkam" I. V. Stalina)* (Moscow, 1994). On the internal development of the Soviet apparatus of oppression, see Michael Parrish, *The Lesser Terror: Soviet State Security, 1939–1953* (London, 1996); Amy Knight, *Beria, Stalin's First Lieutenant* (Princeton, 1993);

War II, Stalinist oppression affected only foreign communists. It is estimated that in the 1930s several thousand exiles and immigrants living in the USSR were "purged."[3] The "Great Purge" of the 1930s was followed by the forcible Stalinization of the Baltic states and eastern Poland. The murder of more than 20,000 Polish citizens by the Soviet People's Commissariat of the Interior (NKVD) at Katyn stands as a symbol of Stalin's ruthlessness and violence toward his western neighbor.[4] In 1944–5, the Soviet security forces widened their focus: broad sections of the populations in areas that were not slated for incorporation in the Soviet states became new target groups. In the aftermath of the war, hundreds of thousands of non-Soviet citizens were jailed or deported by Soviet officials in connection with Soviet liberation and occupation policies. Most had been condemned on charges of war crimes or "counterrevolutionary" acts. Such charges were leveled against Nazis and collaborators as well as against resistance fighters, socialists, members of the bourgeoisie, and many nonpolitical individuals, men and women, young and old alike. The following account focuses on this new level of war and postwar oppression of non-Soviet citizens.[5] The unfamiliar and even disturbing grouping of Germans and Poles together, for example, or attackers and attacked under the label "victims of political persecution" is due to the nature of Stalinist security policy – its ideological underpinnings, its simplistic "us-versus-them" mindset, and its indiscriminate, arbitrary use of force and violence against the inhabitants of nonsocialist countries.

I

The Soviet government partly justified the deportation of foreigners to the USSR by arguing that its former enemies should have to contribute

---

Nikita Petrov, "Les transformations du personnel des organes de Sécurité Soviétiques, 1922–1953," *Cahiers du Monde russe*, 42 (2001): 375–96.

3 Kevin McDermott and Jeremy Agnew, *Komintern. Istoriya mezhdunarodnogo kommunizma ot Lenina do Stalina* (Moscow, 2000), 165 f. (engl. original: *The Comintern: A History of International Communism from Lenin to Stalin*, Basingstoke, 1996); Barry McLoughlin, Hans Schafranek, and Walter Szevera, *Aufbruch, Hoffnung, Endstation. Österreicherinnen und Österreicher in der Sowjetunion 1925–1945* (Wien, 1996), 344, 505–6. In addition to foreign communists, a few foreign specialists fell victim to Stalinist campaigns against (bourgeois) "saboteurs" during the 1920s and 1930s. The most prominent example was the Shachty trial in 1928. See, for example, Julie A. Cassiday, *The Enemy on Trial: Early Soviet Courts on Stage and Screen* (DeKalb, Ill., 2000), 110–33.

4 Authoritative documentation can be found in O. V. Yasnov et al., eds., *Katynskaya drama. Kozelsk, Starobelsk, Ostaskov. Sudba internirovannykh polskikh voennosluzhashchikh* (Moscow, 1991); V. P. Kozlov et al., eds., *Katyn. Mart 1940 g. – sentyabr 2000 g. Rasstrel. Sudby zhivych. Ekho Katyni. Dokumenty* (Moscow, 2001).

5 The oppression of foreigners before the war and after Stalin's death was less extensive and less severe than during the war and the last years of Stalin's rule, and for that reason it is of only minor interest in discussion of contemporary policy on rehabilitation. See, e.g., Wilhelm Mensing, ed., *Willi Harzheim 1904–1937. Arbeiterschriftsteller aus Horst* (Essen, 2001), 27; Helmut Damerius, *Unter falscher Anschuldigung. 18 Jahre in Taiga und Steppe* (Berlin, 1990), 316–20.

to the immense task of postwar reconstruction. The major justification for its persecution of foreigners was that it had to take action to punish the crimes and atrocities committed against the Soviet Union, to prevent another war, and to protect its occupation forces. The other Allies did not challenge that claim. In practice, however, Soviet judicial and security officials were guided above all by an unsophisticated concept of the capitalist enemy and an obsession with security that knew neither compromise nor limits. Consequently, the tension between Soviet antifascism, soon to be rechristened anti-imperialism, and Stalinism was quickly resolved in favor of the latter. The repressive Soviet policies of the early postwar period were shaped above all by the peculiarities of Stalinist ideology and methods, thus watering down legitimate war aims and ignoring the Western Allies' planning.

The Soviet Union's claim that it sought to eradicate fascism proved to be a means for establishing new political realities in occupied countries and reconfiguring the international political order. Although Soviet acts of repression against foreign citizens had their origins in the international struggle against Nazism, Stalin's ideology and the methods of Soviet officials developed a purpose of their own in the Soviet-dominated part of the word. Large-scale suppression of political opponents, alleged underground opposition movements, and potential enemies at home and abroad was an important component of Stalin's understanding of politics and ruling.[6] The combination of a simple reliance on brute force as a political instrument and black-and-white ideological preconceptions help to explain the Soviet Union's indiscriminate use of repressive measures against hostile, neutral, and even friendly countries.[7] Moreover, Soviet occupation officials proved to be incapable of countering actual anti-Soviet activities, nor were they able to prosecute genuine war criminals in legally fair or morally convincing

---

6 Nicolas Werth, "Ein Staat gegen sein Volk. Gewalt, Unterdrückung und Terror in der Sowjetunion," in Stéphane Courtois et al., eds., *Das Schwarzbuch des Kommunismus. Unterdrückung, Verbrechen und Terror,* 5th ed. (Munich, 1998), 45–295; Pavel Polian, *Ne po svoei vole . . . Istoriya i geografiya prinuditel-nykh migracii v SSSR* (Moscow, 2001).

7 Comparative accounts of the Sovietization of the countries of Central and Eastern Europe are rare. Moreover, a detailed comparison of Soviet occupation policy in North Korea and, for instance, Poland would be valuable. For an overview, see Norman Naimark et al., eds., *The Establishment of Communist Regimes in Eastern Europe, 1944–1949* (Boulder, 1997); Stefan Creuzberger et al., eds., *Gleichschaltung unter Stalin? Die Entwicklung der Parteien im östlichen Europa 1944–1949* (Paderborn, 2002); Tatyana Volokitina et al., eds., *Sovetskii faktor v vostochnoi Evrope 1944–1953,* 2 vols. (Moscow, 1999); Tatyana Volokitina, Galina Murashko, Albina Noskova, and Tatyana Pokivailova, *Moskva i vostochnaya Evropa. Stanovlenie politicheskikh rezhimov sovetskogo tipa (1949–1953). Ocherki istorii* (Moscow, 2002); Charles K. Armstrong, *The North Korean Revolution, 1945–1950* (London, 2003), 38–70; Eric van Ree, *Socialism in One Zone: Stalin's Policy in Korea, 1945–1947* (Oxford, 1989). Detailed studies of Soviet repression in Germany include Sergei Mironenko et al., eds., *Sowjetische Speziallager in Deutschland 1945 bis 1955,* 2 vols. (Berlin, 1998); Andreas Hilger et al., eds., *Sowjetische Militärtribunale, vol. 2: Die Verurteilung deutscher Zivilisten 1945 bis 1955* (Cologne, 2003).

proceedings. That holds true not only in the cases of Poland and Japan but of Germany as well.

The following figures and examples suggest the nature and extent of Soviet acts of repression against foreign citizens after 1944–5. Unfortunately, reliable figures are still not available and much research remains to be done.

- The USSR made every effort to expose "guilty persons" among the more than 4 million prisoners of war captured by the Red Army beginning in 1939. By 1954, roughly 39,000 POWs had been tried by the NKVD or, as it was renamed in 1946, the Ministry of the Interior (MVD). In addition to 34,000 German and as many as 2,000 Japanese POWs, soldiers from Hungary, Romania, Austria, Denmark, and Italy stood trial as war criminals, "counterrevolutionary spies," or "bandits." Before the forced Sovietization of eastern Poland in 1939–40 and the Katyn massacre, more than 20,000 Polish citizens were held captive by the NKVD's Administration for Prisoners of War and Internees.[8]
- Civilians in territories the Red Army liberated from German occupation fell briefly under the jurisdiction of Soviet military tribunals and so-called special boards of the NKVD and Ministry for State Security (MGB);[9] similar tribunals were established in the Far East.[10] Unsurprisingly, Germans again appear to have made up the largest share of non-Soviet citizens condemned. In the Soviet occupation zone in Germany and, between 1949 and 1955, in the German Democratic Republic, 35,000 civilians were charged with war crimes, counterrevolutionary offenses, or crimes against Soviet occupation forces. The breakdown of the indictments sheds light on Soviet political and ideological priorities: of the 25,000 documented cases, no more than 4,500 involved war crimes or crimes against humanity. The vast majority – some 70 percent – concerned alleged counterrevolutionary crimes, including 7,100 cases of espionage and

---

8 Michail M. Zagorulko, ed., *Voennoplennye v SSSR 1939–1956. Dokumenty i materialy* (Moscow, 2000); Andreas Hilger et al., eds., *Sowjetische Militärtribunale*, 2 vols., Cologne 2001–2003; Stefan Karner, *Im Archipel GUPVI. Kriegsgefangenschaft und Internierung in der Sowjetunion 1941–1956* (Munich, 1994); Keith Sword, *Deportation and Exile: Poles in the Soviet Union, 1939–1948*, repr. (London, 1994); *Represje sowieckie wobec Polaków i obywateli polskich* (Warsaw, 2000); Viktor Karpov, *Plenniki Stalina. Sibirskoe internirovanie yaponskoi Armii. 1945–1956 gg.* (Kiev, 1997); E. L. Katasonova, *Yaponskie voennoplennye v SSSR* (Moskau 2003); Edda Engelke, "Zum Thema Spionage gegen die Sowjetunion," in Erwin A. Schmidl, ed., *Österreich im frühen Kalten Krieg 1945–1958* (Vienna, 2000), 119–36.

9 Agreement between the Polish Liberation Committee and the USSR, July 27, 1944, in *Documents on Polish-Soviet Relations 1939–1945, Volume II: 1943–1945* (London, 1967), 652–3; Resolution of the State Committee for Defence (GOKO) 7558ss, February 20, 1945, in Volokitina et al., eds., *Sovetskii faktor*, vol. 1, 153–5; Report Beria to Stalin, July 9, 1945, in Volokitina et al., eds., *Sovetskii faktor*, vol. 1, 218.

10 Report Molotov et al. to CK KPSS No. 893/i, June 8, 1955, Russian State Archive, Moscow (hereafter GARF), 9401, 2, 466, 10–66. In studies on Soviet occupation policy on northern Korea, this aspect remains somewhat undeveloped: Van Ree, *Socialism*, 120, 152–3, 164–5; Armstrong, *The North Korean Revolution*, 38–70; Bruce Cumings, *The Origins of the Korean War*, 2 vols. (Princeton, 1981–90).

4,000 cases of sabotage.[11] It is estimated that about 1,100 Austrians were also tried before Soviet tribunals, and the proportion of convictions of political offenses is similar to that in East Germany.[12] In Hungary, a number of alleged "werewolves" were prosecuted.[13] Some Czechoslovak citizens were also tried by Soviet tribunals in violation of the treaty signed by the Czechoslovak government and the Soviet commander in chief in the spring of 1945.[14] Soviet justice in Poland was aimed primarily at members of the Armia Kraiowa (People's Army), who stood in the way of Polish communist and Soviet projects. In early 1945, Deputy People's Commissar of the Interior Ivan Serov lured the commanding generals of the Armia and leading representatives of the Polish anti-German underground to Moscow, where they were put on trial as "terrorists," "spies," and "subversive elements" who had operated behind Red Army lines.[15] As late as 1949, 6,252 Poles were counted in gulag camps.[16]

- In 1944–5, formal trials were overshadowed by administrative deportations. At least 270,000 Germans – both ethnic Germans without German citizenship (e.g., from Hungary and Romania) and German citizens – were deported to the Soviet Union for forced labor service.[17] It is known in the cases of Hungary and Czechoslovakia that several thousand non-Germans fell victim to these so-called mobilizations as well.[18] In the Pacific theater of the war, the Red Army and NKVD deported a small number of Japanese civilians as well as POWs.[19]
- In Central Europe, deportations were accompanied by mass internments. In Poland, suppression of the Armia Kraiowa was, again, the main priority of Soviet

---

11 These data come from the Hannah-Arendt-Institut für Totalitarismusforschung, Dresden.
12 Harald Knoll and Barbara Stelzl-Marx, "Österreichische Zivilverurteilte in der Sowjetunion. Ein Überblick," in Hilger et al., Sowjetische Militärtribunale, vol. 2, 571–605.
13 Tamàs Stark, "Hungarian Prisoners in the Soviet Union (1941–1955)," Bulletin du Comité international d'histoire de la Deuxième Guerre mondiale, 27–8 (1995): 203–13; Tamàs Stark, "Ungarische Kriegsgefangene in der Sowjetunion" in Günter Bischof et al., eds., Kriegsgefangenschaft im Zweiten Weltkrieg. Eine vergleichende Perspektive (Ternitz-Pottschach, 1999), 407–16.
14 Milada Polishenska, "The Deportation of Czechoslovak Citizens to the Soviet Internment and Prison Camps, and the Struggle for Their Repatriation, 1945–1950," Bohemia 39 (1998): 371.
15 Report Beria and Vsevolod Merkulov to Stalin and Vyacheslav Molotov, May 31, 1945, in Noskova, ed., NKVD and polskoe podpole, 191–2. See the corresponding interrogations and reports, Noskova, ed., NKVD and polskoe podpole, 123–90; Harald Moldenhauer, "Der sowjetische NKVD und die Heimatarmee im 'Lubliner Polen' 1944/45," in Bernhard Chiari, ed., Die polnische Heimatarmee. Geschichte und Mythos der Armia Krajowa seit dem Zweiten Weltkrieg (Munich, 2003), 275, 296–8; Piotr Kolakowski, "Die Unterwanderung des polnischen Untergrunds durch den Nachrichtendienst und Sicherheitsapparat der UdSSR 1939 bis 1945," in Chiari, ed., Die Polnische Heimatarmee, 212–17.
16 Sword, Deportation and Exile, 143–73; Report Serov et al. to Stalin and Molotov, April 15, 1949, in Noskova, ed., NKVD i polskoe poldpole, 296–8. On Soviet interpretations and conceptions, see Moldenhauer, "Der sowjetische NKVD," 275.
17 Polian, Ne po svoei vole, 191–217; Ute Schmidt, "Strafjustiz einer Siegermacht oder stalinistisches Repressionsinstrument? Zur Tätigkeit und Rolle der sowjetischen Militärtribunale in Deutschland (1945–1955)," in Andreas Hilger et al., eds., Diktaturdurchsetzung. Instrumente und Methoden der kommunistischen Machtsicherung in der SBZ/DDR 1945–1955 (Dresden, 2001), 91–8.
18 Stark, "Hungarian Prisoners"; Polishenska, "The Deportation of Czechoslovak Citizens," 371–81.
19 Vladimir P. Galicki, "Yaponskie zhenshchiny v lageryach dlya voennoplennych," in Problemy voennogo plena, vol. 2 (Vologda, 1997), 256–62.

officials.[20] In the Soviet occupation zone in Germany and, to a lesser extent, in Austria and Hungary, the focus was on eliminating anticipated resistance. While about 130,000 Germans were interned for up to five years in camps on German soil, the vast majority of Poles (and Austrians and Hungarians) were deported to the USSR or handed over to Polish (alternatively, Austrian or Hungarian) security authorities.[21] These transfers were one form that the close cooperation between Soviet forces and their counterparts in the liberated and occupied countries took, and they were also one of several means the Soviets employed in carrying out purges in the wake of World War II.[22]

The more or less unrestrained extension of Stalinist security obsessions and repressive measures was an essential element of Stalin's foreign policy. Consequently, the persecution of non-Soviet citizens and their rehabilitation in the post-Soviet era are embedded in the history of Stalinism and de-Stalinization. Since the rehabilitation of victims can be regarded as a minimum condition of coming to terms with the past,[23] the subject at hand can serve as a case study of Russia's efforts to confront the legacy of Stalinism.

The rehabilitation of foreigners who fell victim to Soviet persecution during and after World War II demands that Russians come to a new understanding of Stalinism and the war. That has been a complicated process for all Russians, the political elite and the public at large alike. Russians' rather schizophrenic views on this complex of issues are illustrated by a December 1999 opinion poll, which found that "66 percent of Russians considered Stalin's rule more good than bad or equally good and bad."[24] According to surveys the Russian Center for Public Opinion conducted on the fiftieth anniversary of Stalin's death in 2003, the figure had risen slightly, to 70 percent, with the share of those who thought Stalin's rule more good than bad reaching 36 percent. Moreover, leaving aside the question

---

20 Report Beria to Stalin, June 17, 1945, in Noskova, ed., *NKVD i polskoe podpole*, 199–201; Information Beria to Molotov, November 24, 1945, Noskova, ed., *NKVD i polskoe podpole*, 238–9; Beria to Stalin, October 21, 1945, in Moldenhauer, "Der sowjetische NKVD," 275; Andrzej Paczkowski, "Polen, der 'Erbfeind,'" in Courtois et al., *Das Schwarzbuch*, 408–10.
21 Mironenko et al., *Sowjetische Speziallager in Deutschland*; Sword, *Deportation and Exile*, 164–5.
22 The indirect control and guiding of newly created national security services is documented, for instance, in the context of preparation and organization of trials against leading national communists since the late 1940s. George Hermann Hodos, *Schauprozesse. Stalinistische Säuberungen in Osteuropa 1948–1954*, new ed. (Berlin, 2001); Hermann Weber et al, eds., *Terror. Stalinistische Parteisäuberungen 1936–1953* (Paderborn, 1998).
23 Elke Fein, *Geschichtspolitik in Russland. Chancen und Schwierigkeiten einer demokratisierenden Aufarbeitung der sowjetischen Vergangenheit am Beispiel der Tätigkeit der Gesellschaft MEMORIAL* (Münster, 2000), 200.
24 Cited in Vadim J. Birstein, *The Perversion of Knowledge: The True Story of Soviet Science* (Cambridge, Mass., 2001), 300. See also Jurii Aksyutin, "Popular Responses to Khrushchev," in William Taubman et al., eds., *Nikita Khrushchev* (New Haven, 2000), 176–208.

of the merits of Stalin's rule, 53 percent of those surveyed considered Stalin a great historical figure.[25] Other surveys have consistently found that Stalin is a historical figure whom Russians especially esteem. One, for example, found him to be highly regarded by 40 percent of Russians – only Lenin and Peter the Great were more widely admired – and considered the second most successful leader, behind Vladimir Putin, since 1917.[26] The qualified nature of contemporary memory of Stalin is also evident in the plans announced sixty years after World War II to build new monuments to honor him in his capacity as the leader in the war against Hitler.[27]

Since the end of the Cold War, after years of concealment (in the East) or lack of interest (in the West),[28] Soviet oppression during and after World War II has become a topic of national discourse in the countries where it occurred. The ongoing shaping and reshaping of collective memories[29] and efforts to rectify redefined or rediscovered wrongs of the past have been taking place simultaneously in several countries, and their national efforts have influenced one another. Consequently, Russia's efforts toward international reconciliation, together with its efforts at reexamining its past, have also contributed to the reassessment abroad of Soviet coercive actions against foreign citizens.

To understand current Russian approaches to the rehabilitation of victims of repression – its vocabulary, its peculiarities, and its shortcomings – the history of Soviet rehabilitation policy after Stalin must be taken into consideration.[30] The term rehabilitation – *reabilitatsiya* – itself is a product of the Soviet system: it means restoration of the "good name" and reputation of innocent victims. In practice, rehabilitation could include release from

---

25 David Satter, "Stalin's Legacy," *National Review Online*, March 14, 2003; Gregory Feifer, "Russia: With Hindsight People See Stalin as Positive Leader," Radio Free Europe, March 4, 2003 (http://www.rferl.org/nca/features/2003/03/04032003180319.asp.).
26 Jeremy Bransten, "Russia: Rights Groups Want to Renew Public Discussion of Stalin's Purges," Radio Free Europe, March 25, 2004 (http://www.rferl.org/featuresarticle/2004/03/12944220–6120–4374-be64.html); Johannes Voswinkel, "Väterchen Putin," *Die Zeit*, March 11, 2004.
27 Corresponding plans are reported for Belgorod, the Krimea, and Moscow. *The Scotsman,* January 20, 2005 (http://news.Scotsman.com/international.cfm?id=69292005); MosNews, January 19, 2005 (http://www.mosnews.com/news./2005/01/19/notstalin.shtml).
28 The fate of POWs and expellees figured prominently in German public debates in the first decade after the war, but interest then waned.
29 See, e.g., Robert G. Moeller, *War Stories: The Search for a Usable Past in the Federal Republic of Germany* (Berkeley, 2001); Yoshikuni Igarashi, *Bodies of Memory: Narratives of War in Postwar Japanese Culture, 1945–1970* (Princeton, 2001). For comparative studies, see Manfred Kittel, *Nach Nürnberg und Tokio. "Vergangenheitsbewältigung" in Japan und Westdeutschland 1945 bis 1968* (Munich, 2004) and Christoph Cornelißen, ed., *Erinnerungskulturen: Deutschland, Italien und Japan seit 1945* (Frankfurt am Main, 2003).
30 Alexander N. Yakovlev et al., eds., *Reabilitatsiya: kak eto bylo*, 3 vols. (Moscow, 2000–4); Alexander N. Yakovlev, ed., *Reabilitatsiya. Politicheskie protsessy 30–50-kh godov* (Moscow, 1991).

prison, the overturning of convictions, the return of confiscated property, and/or compensation.[31]

II

The first rehabilitations of the post-Stalin period came with de-Stalinization under Nikita Khrushchev. In 1953, Lavrentii Beria put a stop to impending new purges and downgraded the gulag system as Communist leaders jockeyed for power.[32] The later thaw under Khrushchev aimed at stabilizing the Communist Party's position of power and, at the same time, served Khruschev's own political ambitions. Consequently, the suppression of his political opponents as well as of dissidents, "deviationists," and "enemies of the state" did not cease completely even after Khruschev's "Secret Speech" of 1956 denouncing Stalin's repressive policies.[33] To avoid any discussion of legality and the legitimation of Lenin's late heirs or of the socialist structure of the brutally collectivized and industrialized state, rehabilitation under Khrushchev was restricted to cases from the second half of the 1930s, which meant it was largely confined to Stalin's Bolshevist victims.[34] In the broader context of de-Stalinization, efforts to reestablish "socialist legality" also led to some convictions being redesignated or revised and to the commutation of sentences. Soviet courts and public prosecutors were entrusted with the reexamination of political cases.[35] In 1988, the

---

31 A. N. Artizov and Ju. V. Sigachev, "Vvedenie," in Alexander N. Yakovlev et al., eds., *Reabilitatsiya: Kak eto bylo. Dokumenty Prezidiuma CK KPSS i drugie materialy. Mart 1953 – fevral 1956* (Moscow, 2000), 7.
32 A. I. Kokurin et al., eds., "Novyj kurs L. P. Berii," *Istoricheskii arkhiv* (1996), No. 4, 132–64. On the doctors' plot, the construction of hostile groups, and preparations for unleashing terror, see Jonathan Brent and Vladimir P. Naumov, *Stalin's Last Crime: The Plot Against the Jewish Doctors, 1948–1953* (New York, 2003).
33 In 1958, e.g., 1,416 Soviet citizens were convicted of "anti-Soviet agitation." Moreover, political persecution took on new forms, including the use of psychiatric institutions. See Nanci Adler, *Victims of Soviet Terror: The Story of the Memorial Movement* (London, 1993), 137, and Vladimir Naumov, "Repression and Rehabilitation," in Taubman et al., *Nikita Khrushchev*, 96.
34 Stephan Merl, "Entstalinisierung, Reformen und Wettlauf der Systeme 1953–1964,"in Stefan Plaggenborg, ed., *Handbuch der Geschichte Russlands, Vol. 5: 1945–1991. Vom Ende des Zweiten Weltkriegs bis zum Zusammenbruch der Sowjetunion* (Stuttgart, 2002), 182–98; Marc Junge, *Bucharins Rehabilitierung. Historisches Gedächtnis in der Sowjetunion 1953–1991* (Berlin, 1999), 18, 39–45; William Taubman, *Khrushchev: The Man and His Era* (New York, 2003), 236–89; Alexander Pyzhikov, *Khrushchevskaya 'ottepel' 1953–1964* (Moscow, 2002), 15–115; A. P. van Goudoever, *The Limits of Destalinisation in the Soviet Union: Rehabilitations in the Soviet Union since Stalin* (London, 1989); Naumov, "Repression and Rehabiliation," 85–112; Jane P. Shapiro, "Rehabilitation Policy under the Post-Khrushchev Leadership," *Soviet Studies* 20 (1968–9): 490–5; Yu. S. Borisov and A. V. Golubev, "Politicheskaya reabilitatsiya v SSSR (1950–1960-e gg.) v osveshchenii zapadnoi istoriografii," *Otechestvennaya istoriya* (1992), No. 5, 205–9.
35 Andreas Hilger and Jörg Morré, "SMT-Verurteilte als Problem der Entstalinisierung. Die Entlassungen Tribunalverurteilter aus sowjetischer und deutscher Haft," in Hilger et al., *Sowjetische Militärtribunale*, vol. 2, 685–756.

KGB reported that 1.2 million individuals convicted of political offenses had been rehabilitated by 1962 and another 157,000 between 1962 and 1983.[36] According to later Russian sources, as many as 800,000 Soviet citizens were rehabilitated between 1954 and 1961.[37] For the period between 1962 and 1987, the Russian Chief Military Prosecutor's office recorded only 35,000 rehabilitations.[38]

On account of the motivations behind and limited aims of the post-Stalin thaw, the foreigners who were rehabilitated were mainly communist exiles who had become enmeshed in the wheels of Stalin's justice system in the late 1930s.[39] In addition, as a result of efforts at improving socialist legality, a few POWs and civilians were rehabilitated. One, for example, was the former POW Herbert Karl J. He had been condemned as a war criminal on December 24, 1949, and sentenced to 25 years' imprisonment. On July 30, 1956, a military court ruled that the 1949 investigation and trial that resulted in J.'s conviction "did not present any evidence" that he had, as charged, been incriminated in the mass murder of Soviet civilians; J.'s conviction was thereupon overturned.[40]

De-Stalinization in the 1950s stopped short of a reconsideration of Stalin's foreign policy and the "sphere of influence" he won for the Soviet Union.[41] Nevertheless, Stalin's successors realized they needed to take a different approach to the inherited problem of foreign prisoners if they wanted to ease Cold War tensions and improve the Soviet Union's international image.

36 Notice Head of KGB, V. M. Chebrikov, as published in Yakovlev et al., eds., *Reabilitatsiya. Kak eto bylo*, vol. 3, 77–8.
37 Vesnovskaya, "Statistika," 409; N. Michailov, "Vo imya zakonnosti, spravedlivosti i pravdy," in Yakovlev, ed., *Politicheskie protsessy*, 7; Fein, *Geschichtspolitik in Russland*, 66.
38 According to the Chairman of the Supreme Court of the USSR, between 1964 and 1987 240 (!) Soviet citizens were rehabilitated. Historians see a total stop of rehabilitations after 1962–4. See Leonid Kopalin, "Zur Rehabilitierung ausländischer Opfer der sowjetischen Militärjustiz," *Deutschlandarchiv* 27 (1994): 884; Naumov, "Repression and Rehabilitation," 34. Kathleen E. Smith, *Remembering Stalin's Victims: Popular Memory and the End of the USSR* (Ithaca, 1996), 140–1. On public nonjudicial rehabilitations, see Shapiro, "Rehabilitation Policy," 495–8; Junge, *Bucharins Rehabilitierung*.
39 Meinard Stark, "'Traten keine Probleme auf...'. Zur Rückkehr deutscher politischer Exilantinnen aus der UdSSR," in Annette Kaminsky, ed., *Heimkehr 1948* (Munich, 1998), 282–98; Peter Erler, "'Mich haben die persönlichen Erlebnisse nicht zum nörgelnden Kleinbürger gemacht'. Deutsche GULag-Häftlinge in der DDR," in Annette Leo, ed., *Vielstimmiges Schweigen. Neue Studien zum DDR-Antifaschismus* (Berlin, 2001), 173–96; McLoughlin, Schafranek, Szevera, *Aufbruch*, 505–6; Report Rudenko and Serov, January 31, 1955, in Yakovlev et al., eds., *Reabilitatsiya. Kak eto bylo*, vol. 1, 188–90.
40 Resolution of August 3, 1956, Federal Archive Germany, Berlin, DO1, 32.0, 39708+39708a. These files also contain several similar decisions from the same period.
41 See Mark Kramer, "The Early Post-Stalin Succession Struggle and Upheavals in East-Central Europe: Internal-External Linkages in Soviet Policy Making," *Journal of Cold War Studies* 1 (1999): no. 1, 3–55, no. 2, 3–38, no. 3, 3–66; János Rainer, *The New Course in Hungary in 1953* (Washington, 2002); Jan Foitzik, ed., *Entstalinisierungskrise in Ostmitteleuropa 1953–1956. Vom 17. Juni zum ungarischen Volksaufstand. Politische, militärische, soziale und nationale Dimensionen* (Paderborn, 2001). See also the works cited in note 1 to this chapter.

The presence of more than 30,000 non-Soviet citizens in the gulag – above all Germans, Hungarians, Japanese, Romanians, Czechs, Chinese, and Austrians[42] – was an obstacle to limited détente with the West. The new leadership in Moscow therefore resorted to mass amnesties to mitigate earlier judicial excesses. It took two and a half years of internal debate, complicated by both the power struggle in the Kremlin and disturbances in the Eastern bloc, for the leaders of the Communist Party to decide what to do about imprisoned foreigners.[43] Convicted Austrian POWs and civilians, for example, were released and repatriated under the terms of the Austrian State Treaty (May 1955).[44] Their German counterparts were released several months later, when the Soviet Union and West Germany established diplomatic relations.[45] Japanese prisoners were released in 1956, after the Soviet Union and Japan issued a joint declaration formally ending the state of war between them.[46] These measures did not, however, constitute a serious engagement with the legacy of Stalinism. The mass repatriation of foreign prisoners was not accompanied by a reexamination of the convictions and sentences handed down by Stalinist courts, nor was the process complemented by the rehabilitation of individual prisoners.

Foreigners were thus part of the ambiguous de-Stalinization of the 1950s. They were released or rehabilitated when it served the interests of the Soviet leadership. Especially as it pertained to foreigners, de-Stalinization did not call into question the foundations of the Soviet state or the fundamental premises of the Soviet order. Moreover, Soviet authorities continued to insist that the country had acted legitimately in seeking to protect itself and in prosecuting suspected war criminals.

---

42 Kruglov et al. to Beria, April 10, 1953: "Peresmotreny prigovory v otnoshenii inostrantsev," Istochnik (1994): no. 4, 108–10.
43 "Peresmotreny prigovory"; Vladimir A. Kozlov et al., eds., '*Osobaya papka*' *N. S. Khrushcheva (1954–1956 gg.). Perepiska MVD SSSR s TsK KPSS (1957–1959 gg.). Iz materialov Sekretariata MVD SSSR 1954–1959 gg. Katalog dokumentov* (Moscow, 1995) and the corresponding documents in GARF, 9401, 2.
44 Gerald Stourzh, *Um Einheit und Freiheit. Staatsvertrag, Neutralität und das Ende der Ost-West-Besetzung Österreichs 1945–1955*, 4 ed. (Wien, 1998), 420–1, 440–7, and corresponding documents, Gerald Stourzh, *Um Einheit und Freiheit. Staatsvertrag, Neutralität und das Ende der Ost-West-Besetzung Österreichs 1945–1955*, 4 ed., 615–66; Article 18 of the Austrian State Treaty, in Gerald Stourzh, *Kleine Geschichte des österreichischen Staatsvertrages. Mit Dokumententeil* (Graz, 1975), 199.
45 Andreas Hilger, "Faustpfand im Kalten Krieg? Die Massenverurteilungen deutscher Kriegsgefangener 1949/50 und die Repatriierung Verurteilter 1950 bis 1956," in Hilger et al., *Sowjetische Militärtribunale*, vol. 1, 262–72; Hilger and Morré, "SMT-Verurteilte."
46 A. M. Petrov, "Poslednye plenniki vtoroi mirovoi voiny. Dokumenty iz fondov TsK KPSS o yaponskich voennoplennykh," *Istoricheskij archiv* (1993), No. 1, 68–78; Sergei I. Kuznetsov, *Yaponcy v sibirskom plenu (1945–1956)* (Irkutsk, 1997), 151–159; Karpov, Plenniki Stalina, 278–83. On repatriations to the People's Democracies see GARF, 9401, 2, files 465–7; Sword, *Deportation and Exile*, 196–8.

The approach to victims of oppression remained unchanged from the 1950s until the final years of the Soviet Union. Rehabilitation was carried out on a restricted basis and instrumentalized for political ends, and long periods of the past were excluded from discussion or reexamination. With the gradual rejection of Khrushchev's concept of de-Stalinization, the curtailment of public criticism of Stalin, and the declining political usefulness of rehabilitation to the Kremlin, Khrushchev's immediate successors had "no particular reason to maintain the rehabilitation policy."[47] The policy was revived only under Mikhail Gorbachev. In keeping with Gorbachev's sharp distinction between the Leninist foundations of the USSR and the subsequent Stalinist "distortions" of Leninism and the period of stagnation under Brezhnev, the entire period of Stalin's dictatorship was opened to investigation.[48] Approximately 1 million Soviet citizens were rehabilitated during Gorbachev's final years in office.[49]

Gorbachev nonetheless found it impossible to make founding father Lenin or the entire sweep of Soviet history the subjects of critical reassessment. The decree "On Ceasing Outrages Against Monuments Connected with the History of the State and Against Symbols of the State" that Gorbachev felt compelled to declare in October 1990 illustrates the inconsistencies in Soviet policy.[50] Only after the dissolution of the Soviet Union and after the ban of the Communist Party was legislation addressing political repression throughout the entire Soviet era enacted.[51] The Law on Rehabilitation (1991) was deeply influenced by the human rights movements in Russia. At the same time, it also reflected Boris Yeltsin's self-confident and purposeful policy of opposition to the Soviet Union, Gorbachev, and the Communist Party, and it thus played a role in Yeltsin's bid for power.[52] That

---

47 Shapiro, "Rehabilitation Policy," 495. See the telling discussion in the politburo in 1984 about the readmission of Molotov into the ranks of the Communist Party. Taubman, *Khrushchev*, 647–50.
48 On September 28, 1987, the politburo decided to establish a commission for the investigation of repressions of the Stalinist years: "Vo imya zakonnosti, spravedlivosti i pravdy," *Izvestiya TsK KPSS* 5 (1989): 107–10. Its minutes are partially published in Yakovlev et al., *Reabilitatsiya. Kak eto bylo*, vol. 3. For a detailed study of additional steps up to 1991, see R. W. Davies, *Soviet History in the Yeltsin Era* (London, 1997), 16–30.
49 Davies, *Soviet History*, 17; Yakovlev et al., *Reabilitatsiya. Kak eto bylo*, vol. 3, 509–10 (Report Commission for Party Control, July 1990).
50 Davies, *Soviet History*, 29.
51 The corresponding project was rejected in 1990 by the Supreme Soviet of the Soviet-Russian Socialist Federal Republic, home page: http://www.memo.ru.
52 Davies, *Soviet History*, 33–75; Fein, *Geschichtspolitik in Russland*, 208–22. The political changes and maneuvers are covered by Michael McFaul, *Russia's Unfinished Revolution: Political Change from Gorbachev to Putin* (Ithaca, 2001), and Gordon M. Hahn, *Russia's Revolution from Above: Reform, Transition, and Revolution in the Fall of the Soviet Communist Regime, 1985–2000* (New Brunswick, 2002).

tactical motivation notwithstanding, the law rejected arbitrary and politically driven justice as an instrument of governmental policy, and in principle it opened the way for a comprehensive critical reevaluation of the Soviet past.[53] As of October 30, 2004, more than 600,000 people had been cleared of wrongdoing under the Law on Rehabilitation,[54] which brought the total number of rehabilitations since Stalin's death to roughly 4.5 million.[55]

As noted earlier, Russia's desire to improve its international standing meant it had to address other nations' interest in the fate of their citizens who had been held prisoner in the Soviet Union. The Law on Rehabilitation was, accordingly, amended in 1992 to cover foreign citizens who had been convicted by Soviet courts and tribunals for political reasons.[56] Today, individuals can petition to have their convictions repealed. In practice, however, only a very limited number of non-Russian citizens are eligible for compensation, and the compensation itself is meager, amounting to no more than U.S. $300. Other provisions for former victims of political persecution are reserved for Russian or former Soviet citizens.

Under the Law on Rehabilitation, the Chief Military Prosecutor is responsible for the rehabilitation of foreigners. In the first decade, the prosecutor's office received, in round figures, 1,000 petitions from Japan, 600 from Austria, and 400 from Hungary. By the spring of 2004, the prosecutor's office had received about twenty thousand requests from Germany. Only 13 Japanese and 50 Hungarian petitions were rejected; by contrast, 25 percent of the Austrian and 10 percent of the German petitions were rejected.[57] In some instances, the prosecutor's office turned down petitions

---

53 The human rights–movement memorial kept demanding, among other improvements, more general and more transparent regulations, clearer proceedings, and an unambigious political condemnation of the Soviet system. Fein, *Geschichtspolitik in Russland*, 204, 216–17.
54 "Russia Marks 12th Anniversary of Law on Rehabilitation of Repression Victims," http://www.hri.org/news/balkans/rferl/2004/04–11–01.rferl.html#14.
55 Sharon LaFraniere, "Russia Keeps Stalin Locked in Its Past," *Washington Post,* September 24, 2002.
56 Published with amendments of December 17, 1992, in Neil J. Kritz, ed., *Transitional Justice: How Emerging Democracies Reckon with Former Regimes*, vol. 3, *Laws, Rulings, and Reports* (Washington, D.C., 1995), 797–805. See the Russian collection of documents related to the whole process of rehabilitation: *Sbornik zakonodatelnykh i normativnykh aktov o repressiyach i reabilitatsii zhertv politicheskikh repressii*, 2 vols. (Kursk, 1999).
57 Leonid Kopalin, "Die Rechtsgrundlagen der Rehabilitierung widerrechtlich repressierter deutscher Staatsangehöriger," in Hilger et al., *Sowjetische Militärtribunale*, vol. 1, 367–8, 384; Klaus-Dieter Müller, "Aus der Geschichte gelernt. Gemeinsame Aufarbeitung von Kriegsgefangenen- und Zivilistenschicksalen," in *Verfolgung unterm Sowjetstern. Stalins Lager in der SBZ/DDR. XV. Bautzen-Forum der Friedrich-Ebert-Stiftung* (Leipzig, 2004), 49; Harald Knoll and Barbara Stelzl-Marx, "'Wir mussten hinter eine sehr lange Liste von Namen einfach das Wort verschwunden' schreiben': Sowjetsiche Strafjustiz in Österreich 1945 bis 1955," in: Andreas Hilger et al., eds., *Sowjetisierung oder Neutralität? Optionen sowjetischer Besatzungspolitik in Deutschland und Österreich, 1945–1952* (Göttingen, 2006). According to press reports, Poland waited until at least 2002 for special Russian regulations concerning Polish victims. We do not have any material at our disposal that give detailed reasons that

on the grounds that it did not have the jurisdiction to consider the cases in question. It also sometimes cited the lack of pertinent documentation in declining to overturn convictions. More often than not, however, the Chief Military Prosecutor has upheld convictions. In those instances, the previously presented evidence is deemed sufficient to support the conviction.

III

Russian rehabilitation policy reflects a widespread reluctance to fully come to terms with the Stalinist past. By generally failing to take into account three related aspects of the justice system under Stalin, current policy fails to do justice to the victims of political persecution. The first is its procedural arbitrariness and sheer brutality. Torture, for example, was common before it was officially banned in April 1953.[58] Soviet military tribunals tried defendants in secret sessions without counsel; foreign defendants were not provided with translators. The OSO ("Special Boards") in Moscow passed judgment solely on the basis of MGB and NKVD reports: defendants were not present during the proceedings. The sentences imposed by both regular tribunals and quasi-legal administrative institutions were marked by a dramatic disproportion between the offense and the punishment, and the harshness of sentences was magnified by the infamous living conditions in the gulag.[59]

This disproportion was in large measure the result of the second major feature of the Stalinist legal system, the normative role of ideology. Every deviation from official socialist values was interpreted, both in the law and by the officials responsible for administering it, as a serious crime against the party, the people, and, above all, the Soviet state.

The Soviet judiciary was, thirdly, used time and again by the state to perform very concrete tasks as the situation required. It operated in parallel with the extensive security bureaucracies. As noted earlier, for example, the prosecution of Nazis, collaborators, and war criminals in countries under Russian occupation after the war went hand-in-hand with the imposition of Stalinist rule.

---

led Poland and Russia to the conclusion that the current legislation is inappropriate for these cases. Vitaly Cherkasov, "Vladimir Putin on Rehabilitation on Polish Victims of Stalin Reprisals," *Pravda*, English edition, January 16, 2002 (english.pravda.ru/society/2002/01/1625726.html).

58 Order Beria No. 0068, April 4, 1953, in Kokurin et al., "Novyj kurs," 151.

59 The latest account is Anne Applebaum, *Gulag: A History* (New York, 2003). For a bibliographical overview, see Hélène Kaplan, "The Bibliography of the Gulag Today," in Elena Dundovic et al., eds., *Reflections on the GULAG. With a Documentary Appendix of the Italian Victims of Repression in the USSR* (Milan, 2003), 225–46.

IV

Rehabilitation decisions today rest on the reexamination of the records of Soviet-era investigations and court proceedings, and Russian officials face a number of challenges in assessing those records. They must, for example, often evaluate confessions that had been obtained under torture. In many cases, conviction rested solely on the defendant's confession. Confession might also be used to confirm otherwise scanty evidence. Given the security services' notorious ability to see almost anything as evidence of wrongdoing or conspiracy, it is clear that procedural flaws could have wide-reaching consequences. In addition, the old files reveal Stalinist tendencies to judge events from the viewpoint of the highest possible "Bolshevist vigilance" against political opposition and social deviation. Relying on Stalinst-era records thus carries the danger of perpetuating the arbitrariness of the original judicial proceedings. Moreover, reviews of earlier judicial proceedings do not address the open perversion of legal standards or the shocking departures from legal procedure (e.g., torture and denial of counsel). Such abuses generally do not figure in rehabilitation decisions. And although the Rehabilitation Law of October 1991 holds open the possibility that individuals guilty of such abuses can be prosecuted, neither the Chief Military Prosecutor nor any other state agency has yet launched proceedings against anyone suspected of complicity in judicial persecution.[60] The possibility that the review of Stalinist-era convictions might perpetuate injustice is compounded by the many practical impediments to appealing negative rehabilitation decisions. Petitioners, for instance, are given access to their files only after rehabilitation.

The failure to fully come to terms with Stalinist justice plays an even more important role in the case of so-called nonpolitical convictions. The Rehabilitation Law of October 1991 distinguishes political and nonpolitical prosecution in accordance with Soviet legal norms. In holding to that distinction, current rehabilitation policy ignores both the ideologically motivated tightening of Soviet criminal law and the ideologically motivated criminalization of deviant behavior.[61] Both led to a radicalization of legal

---

60 Fein, *Geschichtspolitik in Russland*, 183–4.
61 About this Stalinist characteristic, see Paul M. Hagenloh, "'Socially Harmful Elements' and the Great Terror," in Sheila Fitzpatrick, ed., *Stalinism: New Directions* (London, 2000), 286–308; Louise I. Shelley, *Policing Soviet Society: The Evolution of State Control* (London, 1996), 14–37; Cordula Wohlmuther, "Lageralltag und Strafjustiz," in Hilger et al., *Sowjetische Militärtribunale*, vol. 1, 145–76; Peter H. Solomon, *Soviet Criminal Justice under Stalin* (New York, 1996), 408–53; Donald Filtzer, *Soviet Workers and Late Stalinism: Labour and the Restoration of the Stalinist System after World War II* (Cambridge, 2002), 27–9, 159–65.

policy.⁶² Under two special *ukaz* (decrees) of June 1947 issued by Stalin, even minor instances of theft of state (or private) property could be punished by twenty years' imprisonment.⁶³ Exhausted, half-dead POWs who failed to fulfill labor quotas were liable to prosecution for deliberate "counterrevolutionary sabotage" aimed against the USSR, as were the individuals held responsible for deficient reparations shipments from the Soviet occupation zone in Germany.⁶⁴ The outlook embodied in these decrees survived Stalin and was widely embraced. "Today," an unknown Soviet citizen wrote in a private letter in the late 1950s, "in our society there are some people – thieves, swindlers, murderers, hooligans, speculators, to say it in a few brief words: parasites, filth that does not want to work and lives at the expense of others. These people are enemies of our socialist order."⁶⁵

By ignoring the ideological undertone in many putatively nonpolitical judicial proceedings and in reverting to the "law-and-order" attitude of an earlier era, contemporary rehabilitation policy excludes the problem of the politically motivated disproportion between alleged offense and punishment in nonpolitical trials from its agenda. Likewise, as noted earlier, it fails to take into account the extraordinarily harsh conditions prisoners endured in the penal system.

With regard to foreign citizens, the deficiencies of contemporary rehabilitation policy are aggravated by additional Stalinist-era legal aberrations. According to the penal code in effect at the time, crimes committed by aliens outside of the USSR did not come under Soviet law.⁶⁶ Foreigners living under Soviet occupation were nonetheless prosecuted under repressive Soviet laws and procedures, but those who were convicted of nonpolitical offenses are effectively denied the possibility of rehabilitation. The Main Military Procuracy routinely rejects reexamination of such cases on the

---

62 Filtzer, *Soviet Workers*, 29.   63 Wohlmuther, "Lageralltag," 148–56.
64 Wohlmuther, "Lageralltag," 160–74. Relevant trials in the context of Soviet reparation policy in East Germany are documented in a report of the Chief of the Soviet Administration of Commandant's Headquarters in Dresden, October 18, 1945, GARF, 7212, 1, 58, 90–91; petition of January 1953 in Federal Archive Berlin, Party and Mass Organizations, NY 4036, 736b, 337; Report of the Chief of the Administration of Commandant's Headquarters in Thuringia, October 11, 1948, GARF, 7184, 1, 188, 171; Orders No. 212, 252, 278, and 279 of the Soviet Military Administration of Thuringia, dated May 3 and 20 and June 15, 1946, Federal Archive Berlin, DX1, SMA orders.
65 Pyzhikov, *Khrushchevskaya ottepel*, 238; in general, see pages 235–40; Elena Zubkova, *Russia After the War: Hopes, Illusions, and Disappointments, 1945–1957* (London, 1998), 164–70, 181–7. For pro-Stalin movements after March 1953, see Vladimir A. Kozlov, *Mass Uprisings in the USSR: Protest and Rebellion in the Post-Stalin Years* (Armonk, N.Y., 2002).
66 Articles 2–4 of the Penal Code of the Russian Socialist Federative Soviet Union from 1926. Friedrich-Christian Schroeder, "Rechtsgrundlagen der Verfolgung deutscher Zivilisten durch Sowjetische Militärtribunale," in Hilger et al., *Sowjetische Militärtribunale*, vol. 2, 37–58.

grounds that they are not covered by the Law on Rehabilitation. Alternatively, it redefines the charges and applies other – equally invalid – sections of the penal code after the fact.[67] Many cases of illegal possession of weapons by a civilian, for instance, that had been prosecuted as the political offenses of banditry (section 58.2 banditry) or sabotage (section 58.14) have been redefined as the ordinary criminal offense of illegal possession of weapons (section 182).[68]

By focusing on political charges, contemporary rehabilitation policy does not make amends for the Stalinist tendency to criminalize many aspects of social life. It overlooks the penetration of ideology into law-making as well as the behind-the-scenes political control of show trials and secret trials.

The Rehabilitation Law of October 1991 prohibits rehabilitation of individuals whose convictions for "high treason in the form of espionage, betrayal of military or state secrets and desertion to the enemy; espionage, terror or subversion; acts of violence against the civilian population and prisoners of war, crimes against peace, humanity, and justice" were "wellfounded."[69] In light of the special standing that Russia's secret services continue to enjoy and the persistence of the "Soviet ethos of secrecy,"[70] this enumeration does not only summarize former legal regulations but seems to perpetuate several Soviet-era legal ideas. This passage of the Rehabilitation Law attests to the continuing significance of the Great Patriotic War in the official political culture of today's Russia. It also illustrates the problem of dealing with the Stalinist understanding of "reasons of state" at a time when the idea of the strong state still holds sway in Russia.[71]

Petitions from foreigners for rehabilitation in connection with convictions for war crimes, Nazi crimes, or collaboration with the Nazis are routinely denied.[72] Whereas the International Military Tribunal in Nuremberg and the follow-up trials in the West have provided considerable information

---

67 The formal reason of not being competent for reexamination according to the wording of the law does not address the core of the problem, since the Russian legal system – in the tradition of the USSR – offers the possibility to correct wrong decisions of courts and tribunals by so-called protest in the way of the procuracy's competence of general supervision.
68 Files Günther P. und Wolfgang S. (HAIT Archive, Dresden).
69 Kritz, ed., *Transitional Justice*, vol. III, 797–805.
70 Davies, *Soviet History*, 108; J. Michael Waller, *Secret Empire: The KGB in Russia Today* (Boulder, Colo., 1994), esp. 183–246; Ian Traynor, "KGB's Rehabilitation Becomes an Issue," May 1, 2002, www.guardian.co.uk; Jack, *Inside Putin's Russia*, 311–14.
71 A telling example from the inner-Soviet context is a decision of the Russian Supreme Court in 1999. The famous murder of Pavel Morozov remained qualified as "terror" "because of class hatred." See decision of April, 27, 1999, and report of Procuracy (February 25, 1999) in D. A. Shibaev, ed., "Obzhite, shchenjata-kommunisty, popadetes mne gde-nibud. Iz sledstvennogo dela po obvineniju v ubijstve Pavla I Fedora Morozovych. 1932–1999 gg.," in *Istoricheskij archive* (2004), No. 2, 97–101.
72 The formal argumentation of not being competent is discussed in footnote 67.

about the vast scale of war crimes and crimes against humanity committed by German soldiers and civilians on Soviet soil against Soviet citizens, there was little interest in Stalinist-era Soviet trials in establishing individual guilt for such offenses in fair, procedurally correct trials. Investigations were initiated by the Soviet State Security or the Communist Party and planned, prepared, and supervised by party and NKVD-MGB officials, and by Stalin himself. These authorities set out in great detail the course and outcome of all trials, determining who would be tried, what evidence would be presented, the reasons for conviction, and the sentences that would be handed down.

In 1949–50, the politburo had several thousand German POWs tried as war criminals on account of their allegedly "reactionary" beliefs and the part they might play in Western rearmament. It was simply "unsuitable," Soviet officials argued, to repatriate "revanchist" and "reactionary" officers and generals who could be used in the planned West German military forces and intelligence service. The sentences they received were to be backed up with vague official reports about German war crimes.[73] Show trials conducted in the years 1943–7 had followed similar political scripts.[74] Even in proceedings against defendants such as concentration camp personnel charged with mass murder, the evidence of individual guilt presented at Soviet trials was incomplete, and the course and outcome of such trials were determined by political considerations.[75] The sentences often followed a 1943 decree of the Presidium of the Supreme Court, the so-called Ukaz 43, which prescribed capital punishment for foreign war criminals and Soviet "traitors" and "spies." Stalin was behind this decree, and it reflected the ideologically rooted fears of connections between the Soviet Union's internal and external enemies. The decree was retroactive and was even invoked against Japanese POWs who had not had the opportunity to commit the "required" crimes against the Soviet Union.[76]

The authorities responsible for deciding on rehabilitation petitions today tend to ignore the prodigious evidence of the political nature of Stalinist-era trials and to disregard the political instrumentalization of justice under Stalin.

---

73 Instruction No. 746/364/213 of MVD, MGB, Procuracy, November 29, 1949, GARF, 9421, 1, 44, 46; Sergei Kruglov et al. to Molotov, February 2, 1950, GARF, 9401, 2, 270, 35–53.
74 Twelve protocols of a high-ranking political and security commission in 1947: GARF, 9492, 1a, 510; Andreas Hilger, Nikita Petrov, and Günther Wagenlehner, "Der 'Ukaz 43'. Entstehung und Problematik des Dekrets des Präsidiums des Obersten Sowjets vom 19. April 1943," in Hilger et al., *Sowjetische Militärtribunale*, vol. 1, 199–209.
75 Winfried Meyer, "Stalinistischer Schauprozeß gegen KZ-Verbrecher? Der Berliner Sachsenhausen-Prozeß vom Oktober 1947," *Dachauer Hefte* 13 (1997), No. 13, 153–80.
76 On the Chabarovsk trial of December 1949, see Sheldon H. Harris, *Factories of Death: Japanese Biological Warfare, 1932–45, and the American Cover-Up* (London, 1994), 92–3, 128–9, esp. 226–30.

That, in turn, impedes discussion of the Stalinist instrumentalization of Soviet suffering. In distinguishing between legitimate and unfounded convictions, Russian authorities today posit an implausible separation between Stalin's regime and its justice system and try to distinguish between two inseparable pasts. Contemporary rehabilitation policy rests on the view that there was an independent state sphere even under Stalin and, consequently, that those who actively opposed the Soviet state do not deserve rehabilitation.[77] This line of argument has become the official position of the government in recent years, and the weak independent judiciary has not been in a position to challenge it. Rehabilitation decisions thus reflect the problematic attitudes toward law prevalent in today's Russia.

The importance of World War II in Russian historical memory[78] and the idiosyncrasies in the application of the rule of law create an additional peculiarity concerning the rehabilitation of foreigners. The Rehabilitation Law of October 1991 covers all the various repressive measures against Soviet and foreign citizens carried out on Soviet soil. It does not make provision, however, for foreigners who suffered persecution at Soviet hands by so-called administrative means outside of Soviet territory. Accordingly, individuals in Soviet-occupied areas who were deported or interned without having been properly tried are excluded from the rehabilitation process even though they were subject to the same accusations as those unjustly convicted in the Soviet Union. Indeed, the accusations leveled against them were often less serious. There was, moreover, little practical difference in the consequences of internment and formal conviction: the chances of survival in internment and deportation camps were not much better than in the gulag.[79]

Until 1994–5, Russian authorities applied the general principles of the Rehabilitation Law to foreigners who had been interned outside of Soviet territory. Since 1995, however, they have systematically rejected rehabilitation petitions from members of that group on the grounds that there is no legal basis for reexamining their cases. In 1999, the President's Commission on Rehabilitation attempted to bring the different interpretations into line with each other, but its draft amendment was stalled by the Duma, which

---

77 Oesten Baller, "Die juristische Bewältigung des kommunistischen Unrechts in der Russischen Föderation," in Georg Brunner, ed., *Juristische Bewältigung des kommunistischen Unrechts in Osteuropa und Deutschland* (Berlin, 1995), 163–4.

78 Sabine Rosemarie Arnold, *Stalingrad im sowjetischen Gedächtnis. Kriegserinnerung und Geschichtsbild im totalitären Staat* (Bochum, 1998), 396–400.

79 Alexander von Plato, "Zur Geschichte des sowjetischen Speziallagersystems in Deutschland. Einführung," in Mironenko et al., *Sowjetische Speziallager*, vol. 1, 44; Ivan Chukhin, *Internirovannaya yunost. Istoriya 517-go lagerya internirovannykh nemok NKVD SSSR* (Moscow, 1995).

obviously feared the financial burdens that enacting the amendment would carry. The rather artificial distinction between convicts and nonconvicts is in line with the general fear on fiscal grounds of possible compensation claims.[80] More importantly, officials in Moscow continue to emphasize that the postwar internments were part of Allied denazification policy. They overlook fundamental differences between Western and Soviet practices during the occupation of Germany. In the Western zones, suspected war criminals were interned while their cases were under investigation: they were then either brought to trial or released. In the Soviet zone, there was never serious investigation of internees' wartime actions. As a result of vaguely worded orders the NKVD issued in the spring of 1945, numerous low-level functionaries and opponents of the political order that was taking shape in the Soviet zone were interned for five years.[81]

The current discussion of repression during the occupation is hindered by a decision Soviet officials made at that time for practical reasons: some internees were held in Nazi concentration camps, including Buchenwald and Sachsenhausen. Russian authorities now often shift attention away from the repressive Soviet practices during the occupation by pointing to the dangers inherent in drawing superficial comparisons between Hitler and Stalin. Justified as that warning may be, it should not be allowed to impede serious examination of the Soviet internment camps.[82]

Extending the Law on Rehabilitation to cover foreigners is not on anyone's political agenda in Russia. There has been no discussion in Russia of the foreigners deported to the Soviet Union for forced labor. Russian officials obviously think there is no reason to reconsider the Soviet justification of the deportations as "reparations through work." They prefer to avoid discussion of compensation to former forced laborers or of similarities between Stalinist and Nazi "political" practices.

V

Its deficiencies notwithstanding, the Rehabilitation Law of October 1991 did create new opportunities for the victims of political persecution. The shortcomings outlined herein stem in part from the general problem of trying to address the legacy of Stalinist political persecution and miscarriages of

---

80 See Günther Wagenlehner, *Die russischen Bemühungen um die Rehabilitierung der 1941–1956 verfolgten deutschen Staatsbürger. Dokumentation und Wegweiser* (Bonn, 1999), 150–1.
81 Lutz Niethammer, "Alliierte Internierungslager in Deutschland nach 1945. Vergleich und offene Fragen," in Mironenko et al., *Sowjetische Speziallager*, vol. 1, 97–116.
82 Wagenlehner, *Die russischen Bemühungen*, 134–46, 150–3; Ian Traynor, "Atrocity Museum Angers Russians," *The Observer*, December 23, 2001.

justice by exclusively legal means. Since political persecution of foreigners during and after World War II was rooted in Nazi misdeeds and in Stalinist objectives and exaggerations, the task of making appropriate decisions appears to be like the choice between the Scylla of whitewashing Nazi culprits and the Charybdis of upholding unfounded Stalinist repression. The almost unavoidable shortcomings of the legal approach make clear that it is necessary to understand rehabilitation as a complex process that must be implemented on several levels. The rehabilitation of victims of political persecution has to be complemented by action in the political, judicial, and social spheres. Equally compelling arguments can be made for and against prosecuting former Soviet officials.[83] It is clear, though, that there are two indispensable "technical" preconditions for a satisfactory response to the Stalinist miscarriage of justice: lustration of former functionaries and compensation – financial and social – for individuals who served long prison terms in inhuman conditions. Past injustices should also be acknowledged in nonmaterial form through official and social commemoration. Finally, the search for comprehensive and critical historical knowledge is an essential part of this process and presents the only possibility of defining the wrongs of the past.[84]

Russian attempts to come to terms with the past have been marked, however, by a lack of interest and effort. By and large, Russian officials and Russian citizens alike want either to separate inseparable aspects of the past or to simply suppress memory of Stalinist crimes and abuses. Russians today accept that Russians were both victims and victors in the era of Stalin and Hitler but not that they were also perpetrators. The results of many opinion polls suggest that Russian society's response to the past is shaped by a complex combination of factors: self-exculpation, exhaustion after the struggles and hardships of Soviet and post-Soviet times, nostalgia for the Soviet Union, revived nationalism, and deep-seated "Soviet" habits and mindsets.[85] Moreover, younger Russians have shown a remarkable lack of

---

83 The pros and cons are discussed at length in Kritz, *Transitional Justice*.
84 On the subject of history after dictatorship, see the special issue "Redesigning the Past," *Journal of Contemporary History* 38, no. 1 (2003).
85 Among newer accounts, see Donald D. Barry, *Russian Politics: The Post-Soviet Phase* (New York, 2002); Lilia Shevtsova, *Putin's Russia* (Washington, 2003); Alexander N. Domrin, "Ten Years Later: Society, 'Civil Society,' and the Russian State," *The Russian Review* 62 (April 2003): 193–211; Rudra Sil and Cheng Chen, "State Legitimacy and the (In)Significance of Democracy in Post-Communist Russia," *Europe-Asia Studies* 56, 3 (2004): 347–68; Stephen White and Ian McAllister, "Dimensions of Disengagement in Post-Commuist Russia," *Journal of Communist Studies and Transitions Politics* 20, 1 (2004): 81–97; Russian Institute for Social and National Problems, "10 Jahre russische Reformen – aus dem Blickwinkel der Bevölkerung," in Gabriele Gorzka et al., eds., *Russlands Perspektive: Ein starker Staat als Garant von Stabilität und offener Gesellschaft?* (Bremen, 2002), 313–18, 330–50.

interest in the Soviet past.[86] The country's political and bureaucratic caste has shown its "understanding" of the public's attitude by shying away from compensation commitments to victims of Stalinist persecution,[87] by trying to rebuild a strong state, and by not questioning either the state's legitimacy or its imperial claims.[88]

Waning interest in the rehabilitation of victims of political repression thus goes hand in hand with the limits on compensation to victims, with the strong position of the communists, and with the refusal to remove former perpetrators from office or to bring them to justice. Official accounts of the past have begun to concentrate on the putatively positive and heroic aspects of the Soviet era. The government has also revived Soviet symbols and has imposed new restrictions on access to archival materials;[89] creating a positive history for Russia means having to brush over much of the past. Public indifference to Stalinist political persecution has contributed to a line of continuity between Soviet and contemporary Russian political priorities – and those priorities do not include building a strong civil society or promoting the rule of law:[90] "What in the west is seen as a divide between democracy and authoritarianism is in Russia considered the problem of a weak state versus a strong one."[91] Putin's so-called efficient state[92] clearly corresponds to deep-seated ideas and desires.[93]

---

86 Adler, *Victims of Soviet Terror*; Adam Hochschild, *The Unquiet Ghost: Russians Remember Stalin* (New York, 1994); Smith, *Remembering Stalin's Victims*; Hahn, *Russia's Revolution from Above*, 497–549; Davies, *Soviet History*, 71–82; Catherine Merridale, "Redesigning History in Contemporary Russia," *Journal of Contemporary History* 38 (2003): 13–28; Fein, *Geschichtspolitik in Russland*, 254–7; Matthew Wyman, *Public Opinion in Postcommunist Russia* (London, 1997); Bransten, "Russia."
87 Julius Strauss, "2 Pound-a-Month Sop to Stalin's Russian Victims," *Telegraph*, February 7, 2003 (www.telegraph.co.uk).
88 This is discussed with regard to Chechnya by Barbara Spinelli, *Der Gebrauch der Erinnerung. Europa und das Erbe des Totalitarimus* (Munich, 2002), 282–97. See the general observations of Andrew Jack, *Inside Putin's Russia* (Oxford, 2004), xiii–xv, 8–22; Margareta Mommsen, *Wer herrscht in Rußland? Der Kreml und die Schatten der Macht*, 2nd ed. (Munich, 2004), 161–92.
89 Nikita Petrov, "Zehn Jahre Archivreform in Russland," in Harald Knoll et al., eds., *Konflikte und Kriege im 20. Jahrhundert. Aspekte ihrer Folgen* (Graz, 2002), 143–59; Davies, *Soviet History*, 90–110; Fein, *Geschichtspolitik in Russland*, 196–200. See www.rusarchives.ru/lows/fz.shtml for texts of old and new Russian laws on archives.
90 This is underlined by McFaul, *Russia's Unfinished Revolution*, 326–8; Wyman, *Public Opinion*, 120–3, 138–9, 231–5. On the late Soviet Union, see Peter H. Solomon, "Legality in Soviet Political Culture: A Perspective on Gorbachev's Reforms," in Nick Lampert et al., eds., *Stalinism: Its Nature and Aftermath. Essays in Honor of Moshe Lewin* (Armonk, N.Y., 1992), 260–87; Peter H. Solomon et al., eds., *Courts and Transition in Russia: The Challenge of Judicial Reform* (Boulder, Colo., 2000).
91 Kseniya Yudaeva, Moscow Carnegie Center, as cited by Jack, *Inside Putin's Russia*, 346. Similarly, Wyman, *Public Opinion*, 131.
92 Mommsen, *Wer herrscht in Rußland*, 235.
93 See his "Open Letter to Russian Voters," February 25, 2000, as cited in Jeffrey Kahn, *Federalism, Democratization, and the Rule of Law in Russia* (Oxford, 2002), 238–9: "In a non-law-governed (i.e. weak), state the individual is defenceless and not free. *The stronger the state, the freer the individual*. . . . I know there are many now that are afraid of order. But order is nothing more than rules. And let

The half-heartedness of rehabilitation legislation reflects ambiguities in post-Soviet policy and society. The inherent shortcomings of the Law on Rehabilitation and the way the rehabilitation process has been implemented seem to be integral components of the postcommunist transition that has followed the implosion of Soviet power and Russia's "revolution from above."[94] If the comprehensive and successful rehabilitation of victims of persecution is taken as a prerequisite for the establishment of democracy in former dictatorships, the Russian experience demonstrates the bitter truth that "we know the 'point of departure'... but there is no way of knowing a priori the 'point of arrival'" of posttotalitarian societies.[95] The relationship between the new and the old has not yet been defined, and perhaps only a future generation will see an incentive in undertaking a truly comprehensive and compelling rehabilitation policy.[96]

those who are currently engaged in substituting concepts for one another, trying to pass off the absence of order for genuine democracy – let them, I say, stop looking for hidden dirty tricks and trying to scare us with the past. 'Our land is rich, but there is no order in it', they used to say in Russia. Nobody will ever say such things about us in future" (emphasis in original).

94 This analytical approach is introduced and discussed by Hahn, *Russia's Revolution from Above*; McFaul, *Russia's Unfinished Revolution*.

95 Vladimir Gelman, *Regime Transition, Uncertainty and Prospects for Democratization: The Politics of Russia's Regions in a Comparative Perspective* (Berlin, 1999), 11; cf. Spinelli, *Der Gebrauch der Erinnerung*, 322–30; Sil and Chen, "State Legitimacy," esp. 358–63. In general, the twisted development with its last shifts toward "more state" is reflected in changing labels for constitutional and political appearance – from "unfinished revolution" and "incomplete democracy" via "delegative democracy" to "managed," "manipulated," "virtual democracy," or "superpresidentialism" and "civilised tsarism." Donald D. Barry, *Russian Politics*, 169; Shevtsova, *Putin's Russia*, 62, 273. Mommsen, *Wer herrscht in Rußland*, 115, 227–8; McFaul, *Russia's Unfinished Revolution*, 21–2; Gadis Gadhiev, "Power Imbalance and Institutional Interests in Russian Constitutional Engineering," in Jan Zielonka, ed., *Democratic Consolidation in Eastern Europe*, vol. 1: *Institutional Engineering* (Oxford, 2001), 269–70; Hahn, *Russia's Revolution from Above*, 505–13; Jack, *Inside Putin's Russia*, 320–1; Kahn, *Federalism*, 238–9. More optimistic views stress the numerous and indeed far-reaching achievements of the last fifteen years, but have the danger of underestimating strong indicators for a not only less-Western-styled, but at the same time more bureaucratic and authoritarian, development in Russia: Tatyana Karaman, "Political Efficacy and Its Antecedents in Contemporary Russia," *Journal of Communist Studies and Transition Politics* 20, 2 (2004): 30–49; Andrei Shleifer and Daniel Treisman, "A Normal Country," *Foreign Affairs* 82, 3 (2004): 20–38; Timothy J. Colton and Michael McFaul, "Putin and Democratization," in Dale R. Herspring, ed., *Putin's Russia: Past Imperfect, Future Uncertain* (Lanham, Md., 2003), 13–38.

96 Merridale, "Redesigning History," 27–8.

8

Politics, Diplomacy, and Accountability in Cambodia

Severely Limiting Personal Jurisdiction in Prosecution of Perpetrators of Crimes Against Humanity

STEVE HEDER

This chapter critically examines the negotiations from 1997 to 2004 between the Royal Government of Cambodia (RGC) and the United Nations over the establishment of a court to achieve accountability for genocide and other crimes against humanity committed in Cambodia when it was ruled by the Communist Party of Kampuchea (CPK, or the "Khmer Rouge"), from April 17, 1975, to January 7, 1979. It questions the historical, legal, and moral adequacy of the resulting agreement between the RGC and the UN to establish UN-assisted Extraordinary Chambers in the Courts of Cambodia, focusing in particular on the courts' personal jurisdiction clauses, which were evidently intended to limit prosecutions of those responsible exclusively to CPK senior leaders and one other CPK official. It argues that this limitation – presented by its original proponents as reproducing the Nuremberg model of trials of senior authors of the Nazi genocide – aimed to preclude scrutiny of the possible culpability of former

In addition to the participants at the March 2003 German Historical Institute conference, "Historical Justice in International Perspective" who provided many comments on the paper that was the original basis for this chapter, others who read it and made comments include Brad Adams, Audrey Ardema, David Ashley, Touch Bora, David P. Chandler, George Cooper, Craig Etcheson, Julia Fromholtz, David Hawk, Michael Hayes, Bruce Laskey, Ian Martin, Richard Rogers, William Schabas, Demelza Stubbings, Heleyn Unac, Eric Weitz, and Scott Worden, as well as a number of Cambodian government and UN officials who wish to remain anonymous. Not all of them agree with the conclusions I reach, for which I am of course fully responsible. Funding and facilities for the research that went into this chapter were provided by the British Academy, the Arts and Humanities Research Board of the United Kingdom, the Leverhume Trust of the United Kingdom, the Center for Advanced Holocaust Studies at the U.S. Holocaust Memorial Museum, the British government, and the Documentation Center of Cambodia. I express my gratitude to them all for their generous assistance. The research for this study was ended in 2005.

CPK cadres who are members, protégés, or associates of the RGC and the Cambodian People's Party (CPP), which dominates the government. As of 2005, these ex-CPK figures included the RGC prime minister, Hun Sen, and the chairman and honorary chairman of the CPP, Chea Sim and Heng Samrin, respectively. Much Cambodian and international interest was naturally – if not openly – fixed on the pasts of such powerful or prominent Cambodian politicians. The highly restrictive personal jurisdiction of the extraordinary chambers appeared, however, to be intended to preclude investigation and possible prosecution of many other onetime CPK personnel, some in other positions of authority, mostly at the local level, and some ordinary Cambodian citizens. Trials in the extraordinary chambers, as envisioned by the negotiators of the agreement, thus seemed destined to leave largely or entirely unresolved the extent of individual involvement of the overwhelming majority of past CPK members, regardless of current political status, in CPK crimes against humanity. Not only would the guilty be protected, but the innocent might be left under clouds of suspicion that would not be legally cleared. At best, therefore, the RGC-UN agreement could be part of a wider, deeper, and more sustained effort at accountability for CPK crimes, an arguably necessary but nevertheless incomplete step in the right direction. Even this may not be achieved in the absence of concerted and focused international and domestic scrutiny and pressure for the trials to go as far as the letter of the law allows and to be as fair and in accord with international standards as possible.

I have argued elsewhere that the extraordinary chambers' almost exclusive focus on the culpability of senior CPK leaders reflected and reinforced an overly simplified historical understanding of how genocide, crimes against humanity, and similar mass killings took place in Hitler's Third Reich, in Stalin's Soviet Union, and in what CPK Central Committee Secretary Pol Pot called Democratic Kampuchea (DK).[1] While not denying the ultimate culpability of these regimes' dictators for such enormous atrocities, I stressed how recent scholarship on the Holocaust and Stalinism has questioned the adequacy of totalitarian, intentionalist, top-down conspiracy models as complete explanations for killings. I argued that it is necessary to look at the extent of local initiative and responsibility in precipitating and expanding murderous policies and practices, as well as to examine variations in individual responsibility among the dictators' chief lieutenants.

---

1 Steve Heder, "Reassessing the Role of Senior Leaders and Local Officials in Democratic Kampuchea Crimes: Cambodian Accountability in Comparative Perspective," in Jason Abrams, Raya Jami, and Beth Van Schaak, eds., *Awaiting Justice: Essays on Khmer Rouge Accountability* (Lewiston, 2005).

With regard to DK, I adduced testimony and archival evidence that CPK killings – half a million or more according to the best available estimates – must be analyzed as a similar complex of multilayered phenomena. Some were centrally premeditated and planned mass and other murders ordered by Pol Pot, CPK Central Committee Deputy Secretary Nuon Chea, and certain other members of the party's formal top leadership organs: the Central Committee and its even more elite Standing Committee. These murders were committed via a clear chain of command through which explicit and specific instructions were passed to subordinates tasked to carry them out. These subordinates included Kang Kech Iev (alias Duch), a middle-ranking CPK cadre who headed S21 (or Tuol Sleng), a secret interrogation/execution center that answered to Pol Pot and Nuon Chea, either directly or through the chairman of the armed forces general staff, Son Sen. However, only a fraction – perhaps 20,000 – of the total killings took place there; most of the victims were members of the CPK or its armed forces who were purged and accused of betraying Pol Pot's and Nuon Chea's vision of revolution.

Beyond S21, other subordinates were part of the general CPK administrative hierarchy that divided DK into zones, sectors, districts, and, finally, agricultural production cooperatives, to which most of Cambodia's population was confined. Orders to kill were passed down through this hierarchy, sometimes directly from Pol Pot and Nuon Chea to local authorities, such as district chiefs, sometimes via CPK zone and sector party bosses, who in turn passed the instructions further down the chain. The victims of these centrally organized executions included hundreds of thousands of members of whole categories of people, whom top leaders aimed to wipe out. These comprised, most notably, officers and officials of the Khmer Republic regime that the CPK had defeated militarily in April 1975 and members of Cambodia's resident Vietnamese community who remained in the country despite CPK efforts to expel them.

However, hundreds of thousands of other killings – perhaps the majority of them – were committed by regional and local authorities acting not as part of such a tight chain of command. Rather, these CPK officials functioned as part of a looser and more diffuse hierarchical structure of delegated and discretionary authority, in which the top provided only vague, general guidelines that gave wide latitude to subordinates – all the way to the bottom – to decide who should be killed. Formally speaking, these discretionary executions were supposed to be approved at the zone level, but in practice, district party authorities seem to have made most of the decisions, although many killings were also committed arbitrarily at the behest of the heads of agricultural cooperatives. In perpetrating these murders, lower-level CPK authorities were thus certainly not "just following orders," and in many instances, they seem to have killed more indiscriminately than the party senior leadership envisaged. I have suggested that although this tendency on the part of local authorities was in some ways an inevitable result of the general policies pursued by the top leadership, above all their demands for an immediate and total communization of Cambodia and their empowering of local structures to kill real and imagined enemies of this project, the magnitude of these executions was beyond what the top leadership intended or was aware of. Indeed, the victims included large numbers of people who, as a matter of central policy, were supposed to be "reeducated" and transformed into proletarianized peasant supporters of the CPK regime, but whom some local authorities simply massacred. Among these victims were many so-called new people, urban residents who were forcibly deported to the countryside and "deposited" in agricultural cooperatives in 1975, and members of Cambodia's Chinese and Islamic Cham ethnic minorities. There is some evidence that by 1978, the leadership may have decided to eliminate all Cham.[2]

This chapter shows that in agreeing to a senior-leaders-only formula as the main basis for the trials of CPK perpetrators in the extraordinary chambers, the UN was aware of such problems but acted contrary to the advice of a UN-appointed group of experts and other current and former UN officials familiar with the evidence of CPK crimes. It indicates that the United States played a key role in pushing the UN to accept this approach, which the United States asserted was the best one possible given the political realities in contemporary Cambodia. This was part of a larger pattern of pressure on the UN by the United States and other governments

---

2 Some of my main conclusions about CPK crimes have received corroboration in the recent work of others. The foreign lawyer most familiar with the evidence has affirmed that "centralized abuses represent only a fraction of the overall injustice inflicted on Cambodians" under CPK rule, noting that their experience of atrocities "was intensely local." John D. Ciorciari, "Political Transition and Justice in Cambodia," *Searching for the Truth* 51 (March 2004; translated from the Khmer edition by the Documentation Center of Cambodia). A researcher who has spent years studying CPK prisons has written that the district party secretary was often "the man who really officially made the decisions about . . . life and death" in the detention system. Henri Locard, "The Khmer Rouge Prison System in the Provinces of Kompong Thom & Siemreap (1970–1979)," paper presented at the European Association for South-East Asian Studies Conference, Paris, September 2004, 8. Meng-Try Ea's *The Chain of Terror: The Khmer Rouge Southwest Zone Security System* (Phnom Penh, 2005) concurs with the growing consensus that most of the killings took place at district security offices, although he adduces evidence that they were approved at the next level up in the CPK structure, the sector (*dambon*, also known as region). Further investigation is needed to resolve this point, but it would of course not exonerate CPK district authorities, even if they were following orders from superiors, immediate or higher. In any case, Meng-Try agrees that because some district and sector security centers probably executed more people than S21, those responsible for them should stand trial as "most responsible" for local killings. "Author Investigates Imprisonment and Execution Under the Khmer Rouge," *Cambodia Daily*, November 5–6, 2005.

with diplomatic interests to pursue vis-à-vis the RGC. Most importantly, after obtaining UN acquiescence to a severely limited personal jurisdiction, they also forced it to agree to involve itself in assisting with what the UN was certain would be much less than fair trials, as the CPP's control over the Cambodian court system via its domination of the RGC was sufficient to ensure that the extraordinary chambers would not adhere to international standards of judicial independence and impartiality. They have further limited the court's prosecutorial reach by insisting that the budget for investigations, trials, and defense be kept low.

Finally, this chapter suggests that to a certain extent, this outcome replicates a pattern originally institutionalized in late 1978 by the Vietnamese communists, whose military intervention in Cambodia precipitated the collapse of the DK regime. In overthrowing the CPK, the Vietnamese decided, despite knowing better, to focus all blame for DK-era crimes on two top CPK leaders. They also pursued Vietnamese interests in Cambodia by working politically with other former CPK members, regardless of their pasts, including by organizing a trial with international participation of the two CPK leaders the Vietnamese thought it expedient to target.

Although the motivations of the UN and the Vietnamese were completely different – the UN hoping against hope to inject additional elements of fairness into the proceedings while the Vietnamese were only making political propaganda – the parallel is striking. It is to the earlier Vietnamese effort that I now turn, as a prelude to my account of the negotiations between the UN and the RGC and their results.

The Vietnamese Solution

Even before their army crossed en masse into Cambodia in late 1978, the Vietnamese communists had a very good idea of what was happening in DK. First, they knew from their own past experiences with revolutionary violence that a combination of central direction and local autonomy would lead to the kinds of killings and the pattern of differential responsibility for them that had characterized the CPK. This mix had led to a similar dynamic of massacres in Vietnam, albeit on a smaller scale, first during a radical land-reform campaign in North Vietnam in the 1950s[3] and then again during the communists' insurgency in South Vietnam in the

---

3 For an authoritative inside view, see "DRV Land Reform Program – 1954–56 (Report Based on an Interview Conducted by the Reporting Officer with a Former Communist Cadre Who Rallied to the GVN in the Summer of 1973)," Douglas Pike Collection, Texas Tech University Vietnam Archive, Lubbock. For the best assessment from an anticommunist perspective, see Hoang Van Chi, *From Colonialism to Communism* (New York, 1964), 209–11, 223.

1960s.⁴ Second, because they had played a foundational role in the construction of local CPK authority structures, including security organs with the power to carry out executions, in 1970–1, they were well aware of the autonomy these bodies enjoyed in the CPK hierarchy.⁵ Third, they had extensive knowledge of realities under CPK rule from 1975 through 1978, compiled from the testimony of Cambodian refugees who had fled to Vietnam,⁶ the interrogation of CPK defectors and prisoners of war,⁷ and examination of large caches of CPK internal documents captured prior to their all-out assault.⁸

Nevertheless, the Vietnamese adopted a policy of co-opting former CPK elements who were willing to cooperate with them in the foundation in January 1979 of the People's Republic of Kampuchea (PRK), a modified communist regime that the Vietnamese would dominate for the next decade. They appointed recent CPK defectors to staff some of the highest positions in their client regime, starting notably with the trio Heng Samrin, Chea Sim, and Hun Sen. All three were originally cadres of the CPK East Zone, which bordered on Vietnam, but had fled DK in 1977 and 1978 to avoid purge and execution in the East Zone itself or at S21. Heng Samrin, the former commander of a division of East Zone troops, headed the PRK front apparatus; Chea Sim, the former secretary of Ponhea Kraek district in East Zone Sector 20, was its minister of interior; and Hun Sen, a former junior military cadre in the East Zone Sector 21 regional armed forces, was its minister of foreign affairs.

During the remainder of 1979 and into 1980, the three were joined in the cabinet and at the top levels of the central government by various former CPK members. As interior minister, Chea Sim was adept at bringing additional DK-era cadres into the administration nationwide, and he helped the Vietnamese select them for postings as province chiefs. They in turn favored other pre-1979 party members in their own recruitment of cadres. Chea Sim also oversaw the integration of former CPK security personnel into the PRK police. Inside the PRK, it was an open secret that its former CPK authorities included – as one internal report put it – "some who

---

4 Michael Charles Conley, *The Communist Insurgent Infrastructure in South Vietnam: A Study of Organization and Strategy* (Washington, D.C., 1967), 53, 74, 67–8, 84.
5 See U.S. Embassy, Phnom Penh, Khmer Republic, "Documents Illustrating Vietnamese Subversion in Cambodia" (1970).
6 Vu Can, "Refugees from the Phnom Penh Regime Bear Witness," *Kampuchea Dossier I* (Hanoi, 1978), 31.
7 Chey Saphon, Director of the History Section, Revolutionary People's Party of Kampuchea, interview by author, Phnom Penh, August 4, 1990.
8 For a partial list of Vietnamese holdings, see *Ban Tạp Hop Cac Tai Lieu Ve Campuchia* (An Index of All the Research Materials on Cambodia), in the author's possession.

have blood debts, who have killed with their own hands or issued direct orders to kill . . . or who made lists of cadres, Party members and the masses and reported them to the higher level to be killed." Their culpability was, however, argued away: "examining and considering [the issue of their blood debts] is extremely complicated because under Pol Pot there were some people who acted directly and some who acted from a distance, some people with a lot of blood debts and some with a few, some people who were compelled to do things and some who did them of their own accord." Moreover, it was asserted, some ex-CPK members who truly had blood debts had not been "moved by malice" when they killed. Anyway, for those who had been threatened with purge by Pol Pot and turned against him, there should generally be no talk of blood debts. The best solution was simply to post those notoriously responsible for killings away from places where they would be immediately recognized by the population.[9]

While overseeing this institutionalization of impunity for those cooperating with them, the Vietnamese had arranged for the staging of a show trial of Pol Pot and his brother-in-law Ieng Sary, a member of the party Standing Committee who had been DK foreign minister, in August 1979. In fact, this sham proceeding – which the PRK proclaimed was based on Nuremberg principles – followed the script of earlier Vietnamese propaganda for an imaginary trial of U.S. "senior leaders" for their allegedly Hitler-like war crimes in Vietnam. Its exclusive focus on Pol Pot and Ieng Sary reflected the Vietnamese belief that other CPK senior leaders, such as Party Deputy Secretary Nuon Chea and armed forces General Staff Chairman Son Sen, were historically friendlier to them than Pol Pot and Ieng Sary. It also left open the door to additional CPK members who might still be willing to collaborate with them. The PRK Revolutionary People's Tribunal they guided from behind the scenes duly sentenced Pol Pot and Ieng Sary to death in absentia for genocide, despite the fact that no evidence linking the two directly to crimes was presented. The verdict simply argued that they should be "held responsible for ordering and planning the perpetration of the crime of genocide" and were personally responsible for it because "Pol Pot . . . held the highest office" and Ieng Sary "shared leadership with Pol Pot."[10]

Among those whose pasts were therefore left unexamined was, of course, Chea Sim, who escaped scrutiny for his possible role as district party

---

9 Evan Gottesman, *Cambodia After the Khmer Rouge: Inside the Politics of Nation Building* (New Haven, 2003), 33, 46, 54, 60, 67–8, 75.
10 Steve Heder, "Hun Sen and Genocide Trials in Cambodia: International Impacts, Impunity, and Justice," in Judy Ledgerwood, ed., *Cambodia Emerges from the Past: Eight Essays* (De Kalb, Ill., 2002), 184–93.

secretary of Ponhea Kraek. According to testimony by some local residents, he allegedly oversaw the execution of thousands of people there. Heng Samrin also escaped scrutiny, despite evidence implicating his troops in serious war crimes – massacres of civilians – committed during cross-border raids into Vietnam when he was their commander. As for Hun Sen, against whom some allegations have been made, they have proved spurious. No hard evidence linking him directly to crimes has come to light, and a growing body of evidence indicates he would not be liable to prosecution even by a court with an expansive personal jurisdiction.[11]

The 1980s and the 1991 Paris Agreements

During the 1980s, Heng Samrin rose to be PRK chief of state, Chea Sim became chairman of its National Assembly, and Hun Sen its prime minister. Meanwhile, Pol Pot and Nuon Chea were holed up along the Thai-Cambodian border, along with the rest of the surviving members of the CPK top leadership, including Ta Mok, a onetime zone secretary who had become number three in the party; former armed forces staff chief Son Sen, ex–foreign minister Ieng Sary, and Khieu Samphan, who had been DK chief of state. From there, they led a guerrilla war against the PRK – with Chinese military aid and UN recognition as the representative of Cambodian sovereignty – until 1991, when they signed the internationally sponsored Paris Agreements with the successor to the PRK, the State of Cambodia. However, they balked at participating in elections organized by the UN under the terms of this peace accord, returning to guerrilla warfare and remaining in insurgency after these elections – held in 1993 – resulted in the transformation of the State of Cambodia into the Kingdom of Cambodia, in the Royal Government of which Hun Sen was one of two co-premiers. It was during this time that Heng Samrin and Chea Sim became the honorary and actual chairmen, respectively, of the Cambodian People's Party, the reinvention of the PRK's erstwhile communist Revolutionary People's Party.

The DK remnants continued to fight the RGC until the old CPK leadership collapsed into open conflict in its bases straddling the Thai-Cambodian border in 1996–7. In August 1996, former DK foreign minister Ieng Sary defected to the RGC and was granted an amnesty for his 1979 genocide conviction – a decision reflecting Hun Sen's insistence on extending the

---

11 Heder, "Reassessing the Role," supplemented by field research conducted in Cambodia during 2005. On Vietnamese knowledge of the crimes of Heng Samrin's troops, see Dang Vu Hiep, ed., *Su Doan 10: Binh Doan Tay Nguyen* (10th Division: Central Highland Corps) (Hanoi, 1987), 164–6.

original Vietnamese policy of co-opting anyone prepared to defect. In June 1997, several top cadres, including former General Staff Chairman Son Sen, were murdered on Pol Pot's orders. Thereafter, other top cadres led by CPK number three Ta Mok deposed Pol Pot and detained him until his death under possibly suspicious circumstances in 1998. The leadership further unraveled with more defections, like that of former Central Committee member Kae Pok, who was literally embraced by Hun Sen. It had disintegrated completely by early 1999, after the defection of former Party Deputy Secretary Nuon Chea and Central Committee member Khieu Samphan, whom Hun Sen publicly welcomed at a ceremony in his home in Phnom Penh. This left Ta Mok the only former member of the Standing Committee of the Central Committee at large, until Hun Sen decided to refuse his offer of surrender and instead arrested him in March 1999.[12]

The United States, the UN, and the Senior Leaders Formula

The international and domestic furor provoked by the amnesty of Ieng Sary prompted Thomas Hammarberg, the independent special representative of the UN secretary-general for human rights in Cambodia,[13] to push for UN involvement in a process of judicial accountability for DK-era crimes. As a result of Hammarberg's determined personal efforts, an April 1997 resolution by the intergovernmental UN Commission on Human Rights called on the UN secretary-general to examine any request from Cambodia for help prosecuting those responsible for past international crimes, using a formulation suggesting no particular theory of how they were committed or by whom.[14] In discussions with Hun Sen and his then–Co–Prime Minister Prince Norodom Ranariddh in June 1997, Hammarberg remained diplomatically agnostic about this, committing himself only to helping the RGC find "appropriate means... to establish the truth about the atrocities" and "to bring to justice those found guilty" of committing them.[15] This prompted a letter to UN Secretary-General Kofi Annan from Hun Sen and Ranariddh – drafted for them by officials of the UN Secretariat's

12 Heder, "Hun Sen and Genocide," 194–200.
13 I say "independent" because the holders of such positions are not regular employees of the UN Secretariat or any UN agency, but rather are external experts not on UN salary who advise its secretary-general. Hammarberg was a Swedish ambassador-at-large and former secretary-general of Amnesty International.
14 UN Commission on Human Rights, "Situation of Human Rights in Cambodia" (E/CN.4/1997/49), April 11, 1997. The commission is intergovernmental in that it comprises representatives of the governments of selected UN member-states.
15 UN General Assembly, "Report of the Secretary-General, Situation of Human Rights in Cambodia" (A/52/489), October 17, 1997.

specialist Center for Human Rights in Cambodia – asking for UN assistance in bringing to justice "those persons responsible for the genocide and crimes against humanity during the rule of the Khmer Rouge," possibly in an international criminal tribunal like those established for Yugoslavia and Rwanda under the authority of the UN Secretary Council.[16] Hun Sen apparently signed the letter because he hoped to use the threat of international jurisdiction to pressure Thailand to stop giving sanctuary to any remnants of Pol Pot's imploding insurgency.

However, UN human rights officials in Cambodia were well aware that how far the scope of individual accountability for DK atrocities should go was going to be a highly contentious political issue inside the CPP and the RGC.[17] They knew it would run up against the problem that any truly international prosecution would become an open-ended process because an independent prosecuting body such as an international tribunal would not engage in a politically selective prosecution, as to do so would be "morally repugnant and legally unprecedented." In particular, no truly independent prosecutor would agree to focus solely on the top leadership of the CPK.[18] Still, a generalized presumption that an investigation of the party's central political leaders was the most logical place to start prompted UN human rights officials to seek information about who they were before looking at other potential suspects.[19]

Political concerns did indeed begin to crop up. The upshot of the Hun Sen–Ranariddh letter was a December 1997 resolution by the General Assembly of UN member-states. On the one hand, this gathering of all the world body's governmental representatives recommended that Kofi Annan appoint an independent group of experts[20] to evaluate existing evidence and propose further measures to address the issue of individual accountability

---

16 Letter from RGC Co-Premiers Prince Norodom Ranariddh and Hun Sen to UN Secretary-General Kofi Annan, June 21, 1997. The UN Center for Human Rights, headquartered in Geneva, comprised, like other specialist bodies of the UN Secretariat, UN professional staff servicing the UN secretary-general.
17 Memorandum by David Hawk, UN Center for Human Rights, Cambodia Office, "UN Consideration of 21 June Request by RGC for Assistance re Khmer Rouge Violations and Leaders," June 26, 1997.
18 Memorandum by Balakrishnan Rajagopal, UN Center for Human Rights, Cambodia Office, "Pragmatics of Prosecuting the Khmer Rouge," June 1997.
19 This was certainly in line with my own instincts at the time, and in a note to them at their request, I recommended that the UN focus first on those who had been members of the CPK Standing Committee when it was in power, second on other members of the Party Central Committee when it was in power, and third on leading cadres of S21. Steve Heder, "Collating Evidence on Those Responsible for CPK Crimes," July 3, 1997. The memorandum named sixteen individuals in these three categories.
20 Again, I say "independent" because the members of such groups are chosen from outside the UN system.

for CPK crimes, thus seeming to make the scope of prosecutions a question of evidence. On the other hand, it also expressed specific "concern that no Khmer Rouge leader has been brought to account for his crimes," suggesting that the focus of the experts' evaluation should be the amnestied Ieng Sary and the then–still-living anti–Hun Sen CPK supremos along the Cambodian border with Thailand, including Pol Pot, Nuon Chea, Ta Mok, Khieu Samphan, and Kae Pok.[21] Hammarberg soon seemed to endorse something like this dual approach. He was careful, however, to stress that the extent of the CPK leaders' responsibility must be judicially clarified to ascertain whether they were among those responsible for widespread abuses, but he added that investigations should also identify other alleged "most serious violators of human rights" for prosecution.[22]

This evenhanded position was challenged by the United States in April 1998. Apparently concerned with coming up with a proposal for a trial that was acceptable to Hun Sen,[23] the United States informally circulated a draft Security Council resolution to establish an International Tribunal for Cambodia for the sole purpose of prosecuting "senior members of the Khmer Rouge leadership who planned or directed serious violations of international and humanitarian law" committed in Cambodia between April 1975 and January 1979. Admitting this would mean that only "certain persons" among those responsible would be tried,[24] the draft attached a statute for the proposed tribunal, reiterating these politically defined, very limited powers of prosecution.[25] This was in contrast to steadfast U.S. demands in other contexts for adherence to general legal principles requiring prosecutors to investigate wherever the evidence led.[26] It provoked protests from nongovernmental human rights groups, including the U.S.-based Lawyers' Committee for Human Rights, which pointed out that there was no foundation in international law or practice for limiting prosecution in this fashion, precluding in advance trials of "individuals who were not in senior leadership positions, but whose crimes might have been just

---

21 UN General Assembly, "Situation of Human Rights in Cambodia" (A/RES/52/135), December 12, 1997.
22 UN Commission on Human Rights, "Report of the Special Representative of the Secretary-General on the Situation of Human Rights in Cambodia" (E/CN.4/1998/95), February 20, 1998.
23 See David J. Scheffer, "Justice for Cambodia," *New York Times*, December 21, 2002.
24 U.S. Permanent Mission to the UN, "Resolution to Establish an International Tribunal for the Prosecution of Certain Persons Responsible for Serious Violations of International Humanitarian Law in the Territory of Cambodia During the Period 15 April [sic] 1975–7 January 1979," April 28, 1998.
25 "Annex: Statute of the International Tribunal for Cambodia."
26 Ambassador-at-Large for War Crimes Issues David J. Scheffer, Fifth Hauser Lecture on International Humanitarian Law, "Perspectives on the Enforcement of International Humanitarian Law," February 3, 1999.

as abhorrent."[27] However, the rising influence of political considerations was evident in July 1998, when Kofi Annan mandated the creation of the independent group of experts envisaged by the General Assembly.[28] He instructed that their evaluation of the evidence should aim at "bringing to justice Khmer Rouge leaders," adding that in principle this could be done in either an international or a national venue.[29]

Because one of the three appointed experts, Steven Ratner, was already familiar with some of the evidence the trio was to consult, he knew that the U.S. proposal and the direction in which Kofi Annan was moving were potentially flawed. In a memorandum to Hammarberg in August 1998, he pointed out that the evidence indicated that "atrocities were committed by very large numbers of people with varying levels of governmental authority." He also backed up Hammarberg's position that the culpability of leaders could not be assumed: it would have to be proven.[30] Ratner's position was based on general legal principles set out in a 1997 book in which he emphasized that "definitive findings concerning the guilt of individuals ... require an examination of detailed evidence regarding precise events and the role of individual actors in them."[31]

After Ratner and the other experts visited Cambodia in late 1998 to look closely at the available evidence, they reached similar conclusions. Speaking before Hun Sen accepted the defections of Nuon Chea and Khieu Samphan, they said that the evidence was inconclusive as regards the culpability of individual senior leaders, but they suggested that many thousands of persons might be implicated in crimes. Sorting out who was most culpable would require a trial "impeccable in its independence and its thoroughness and its honesty," relying on "a wholly independent investigator team reporting to an independent prosecutor," with "judges ... equally independent of any pressures."[32]

Such expert legal opinion did not faze the United States, which in December reiterated its basically political position that it was only

---

27 Letter from Stephanie Grant, Lawyers Committee for Human Rights, to all permanent representatives to the UN, May 6, 1998.
28 The three experts chosen to comprise the group were Sir Ninian Stephen, an Australian judge; Rajsoomer Lallah, a Sri Lankan judge; and Steven Ratner, an American legal scholar.
29 UN General Assembly, "Human Rights Situation in Cambodia" (A/RES/52/135), December 12, 1997.
30 Steven Ratner, "Summary of Laws Applicable to Individual Responsibility of Members of the Khmer Rouge Regime," August 5, 1998.
31 Steven R. Ratner and Jason S. Abrams, *Accountability for Human Rights Atrocities in International Law* (Oxford, 1997), 243–4.
32 UN Center for Human Rights, Cambodia Office, "Press Conference by the United Nations Group of Experts, 17 November 1998, 11am–12.30pm, Hotel Le Royal, Phnom Penh."

interested in a process that would lead to accountability for "most senior" CPK leaders,[33] a policy that it continued assiduously to promote.[34] This provoked further vigorous ripostes from human rights lawyers. One warned that limiting personal jurisdiction in this manner was a risky and unprincipled approach that would allow numerous actual murderers to escape prosecution – no matter how many people they had killed – and encourage any subordinate who was accused of mass executions to promote the idea that everything was decided by Pol Pot, a claim that would be left legally unchallenged because prosecutors would be denied standard professional discretion to investigate subordinates.[35]

The experts' report – completed and transmitted to Hun Sen's government in February 1999 – was made public in March 1999, shortly after Hun Sen ordered the detention of Ta Mok. The experts pointed out that "international law has long recognized that persons are responsible for acts even if they did not directly commit them" and that criminal responsibility should thus cover not only "military commanders and civilian leaders" who ordered atrocities, but also those who "knew or should have known that atrocities were being or about to be committed by their subordinates and... failed to prevent, stop or punish them." This meant there was a "need to investigate the roles of those... officials in responsible governmental positions with actual or constructive knowledge of the atrocities."[36] However, they stressed that except for certain cadres at S21 (an allusion to S21 Chairman Kang Kech Iev and some of his staff, all still at large at the time), the available documentary evidence did not directly implicate "individuals, whether at the senior governmental level or the regional or local level."[37] They cautioned that the formal

list of top governmental and party officials may not correspond with the list of persons most responsible for serious violations of human rights in that certain top governmental leaders may have been removed from knowledge and decision-making; and others not in the chart of senior leaders may have played a significant role in the atrocities.

33 U.S. Department of State, "Statement by M. Lee McClenny, Acting Spokesman: Surrender of Top Khmer Rouge Leaders Nuon Chea and Khieu Samphan," December 27, 1998.
34 For examples in 1999–2000, see State Department official Ralph Boyce's "Testimony Before the Senate Foreign Relations Committee, Subcommittee on East Asian and Pacific Affairs," March 9, 1999; and U.S. Ambassador-at-Large for War Crimes Issues Scheffer's insistence that all concerned should "keep their eye on the big picture" by focusing on bringing "senior Khmer Rouge leaders to justice." "UN Pressured over Cambodia Tribunal," Associated Press, UN, March 14, 2000.
35 Brad Adams, "Snatching Defeat from the Jaws of Victory?" *Phnom Penh Post*, January 25, 1999.
36 UN General Assembly, "Report of the Group of Experts for Cambodia Established Pursuant to General Assembly Resolution 52/135" (A/53/850/S/213/Annex), February 1999, paragraphs 80–1.
37 Ibid., paragraphs 49–55.

In other words, while notorious leading officials should certainly be investigated, they should not be the exclusive targets of investigation. Instead, prosecutors should be free to charge anyone alleged to be among those most responsible for the most serious violations of human rights during CPK rule, including not only senior leaders with responsibility over the abuses, but also those at lower levels who were directly implicated in the most serious atrocities. They suggested this might result in the trial of some 20 to 30 persons.[38]

Human rights lawyers welcomed the experts' rebuttal of the politicized position of the United States,[39] but Kofi Annan – who had commissioned the report – was not to be budged. Transmitting it to the Security Council and General Assembly, the UN secretary-general pointedly recalled that the experts had been mandated to look at the evidence "with a view to determining the nature of the crimes committed by Khmer Rouge leaders." Contradicting the carefully qualified text of the experts' report, he claimed they had concluded there was sufficient evidence to justify legal proceedings against CPK senior figures, omitting mention of any other potential suspects. He added that Hun Sen was concerned that even a trial of top CPK cadres would only "create a panic among other former Khmer Rouge officers and rank and file" if it was "improperly conducted" from the RGC's point of view.[40]

Hammarberg, Annan's representative, initially straddled the experts' and the secretary-general's stances, endorsing the experts' recommendation that prosecutors should have the discretion to investigate both senior leaders and those at lower levels who were directly implicated in the most serious atrocities while repeating Annan's unfounded assertion that they already had enough evidence to commence prosecution of the leaders.[41] By early July 1999, however, Hammarberg seemed to have gravitated toward Annan's

---

38 Ibid., paragraphs 109–10. A subsequent review by its legal counsel of the documentary evidence held at the Documentation Center of Cambodia, the prime source of such material, remarked that in addition to data relevant to CPK senior leaders, this repository contained "ample materials to provide evidence against many local" CPK officials, adding that the number of potential suspects was "staggering." John D. Ciorciari, "Evidentiary Value of the Holdings of the Documentation Center of Cambodia (DC-Cam) in the Prospective Trials of Former Khmer Rouge Leaders and Other Perpetrators of the Most Serious Offences" (Phnom Penh: DC-Cam, November 1999), 7, footnote 2.
39 Memorandum by Brad Adams, "Some Ideas to Salvage a Legitimate KR Tribunal," May 1999.
40 UN General Assembly and Security Council, "Identical Letters Dated 15 March 1999 from the Secretary-General to the President of the General Assembly and the President of the Security Council" (A/53/850/S/1999/231), March 16, 1999.
41 UN Commission on Human Rights, "Presentation to the UN Commission on Human Rights by Thomas Hammarberg, the Special Representative of the UN Secretary-General on Human Rights in Cambodia, Geneva, 22 April 1999."

position, speaking of a "trial against the responsible Khmer Rouge leaders," without reference to other potential suspects.[42]

Pursuant to Annan's position, the UN Secretariat's Office of Legal Affairs (OLA) drafted a proposal for a "Nuremberg-type trial" of DK leaders, although – as it later stated in another context – international standards of justice and fairness require that in trials for crimes against humanity, "the process itself not be selective, and that the principle of accountability be given comprehensive interpretation."[43] The OLA proposal echoed the experts' report by alluding to the possibility that – in addition to senior leaders – others "most responsible for the most serious violations of human rights" be tried, but it presumed the main objective would and should be prosecution of the major political and military leaders of the DK regime. Ignoring the specifics of the report, it assumed that all DK leaders must be tried because "their responsibility for the crimes committed flows from their positions as leaders and the principle of 'command responsibility.'" They therefore were – ipso facto – "part of a conspiracy to commit genocide and other crimes against humanity" and could be prosecuted – Nuremberg style – in a joint trial of the whole leadership, "a well-defined group of probably less than a dozen."[44]

The UN human rights officials most familiar with the evidence were unhappy with the direction of developments since the experts produced their report, complaining that "for not entirely dissimilar reasons, the OLA, the US and Hun Sen wanted the same thing": a "politically-defined and limited jurisdiction."[45] They noted that "to explicitly state that senior leaders... shall be brought to trial appears to ignore the concept of presumption of innocence."[46] In a private critique, a former UN official knowledgeable about the evidence becoming available by this time wrote that the OLA proposal flew in the face of what UN human rights programs had been trying to achieve in the field of justice in Cambodia, namely, due process of law for individuals. Commenting that the Nuremberg approach

---

42 Memorandum by Special Representative of the UN Secretary-General for Human Rights in Cambodia Thomas Hammarberg, "UN Position on the 'Mixed' Tribunal," July 8, 1999.
43 UN Office of Legal Affairs, "Non-Paper on Khmer Rouge Trial," January 5, 2000, initialed "HC," presumably for Hans Corell.
44 UN Office of Legal Affairs, "Note to the Secretary-General: A Mixed Tribunal for Cambodia," July 19, 1999.
45 Letter from a former UN official to the author, December 27, 2000.
46 UNOHCHRC [UN Office of the High Commissioner for Human Rights, Cambodia] memorandum, "Draft Comments on the KR Draft Law," January 5, 2000. The Office of the High Commissioner for Human Rights was the successor to the earlier UN Center for Human Rights, being still a specialist UN agency, not an intergovernmental body like the UN Commission for Human Rights, with which it should not be confused.

was widely discredited historically as an example of victor's justice, the critique insisted that the purpose of UN involvement should be to prevent just such an a priori determination of the theory of the case. No independent, objective prosecution could operate with such an ad hominem approach, which would create pressures to overcharge those "against whom the evidence is thin but who 'must' be indicted for political reasons." It was also wrong as a matter of law for the UN to back a presumption that all leaders were involved in a conspiracy, which was likely to prejudice their rights as defendants and would encourage prosecutors to invoke conspiracy when evidence against a senior leader was weak and to try to prejudice judges against all leaders, even though some might not be guilty. Noting that there was no evidentiary basis for such a prepackaged case against the leadership, the critique characterized the Nuremberg approach as "amoral" because it was political rather than legal, clearly aiming to target CPK leaders while letting lower-level mass murderers off the hook. This approach ignored existing evidence, suggesting that local officials did most of the actual killing, often based on "voluntary choices about how evil they would act (as the differences in conditions from village to village and district to district attest to)." It glossed over the possibility that district chiefs, for example, had committed mass murder on their "own initiative and without consulting...superiors." The comment concluded that a trial set up to focus on senior leaders while ignoring those who were "'only' local leaders" would be a grave injustice. Instead, the UN should aim to achieve "a different kind of process by highlighting individual (and not collective) responsibility in a setting offering full procedural safeguards in order to produce a just result and a learning experience for Cambodians" by ensuring that the prosecution followed evidence, not people.[47]

Stung by such criticisms, the UN insisted that it had no predetermined list of suspects and that it would be up to the prosecutor to connect crimes to individuals, but it held to the position that the focus of the trial should be on "leaders of the KR who were most responsible for the most serious crimes which had been committed."[48] Thus, although OLA was persuaded to drop explicit reference to a Nuremberg-type trial, the main point of the critique fell on deaf ears. In August, with Hun Sen making it clear he wanted a trial that did not go beyond CPK leaders,[49] OLA presented the Cambodian government with the draft of a law for the establishment of a

---

47 Anonymous memorandum, "Comments on the OLA Proposal for the KR Tribunal" [2000].
48 UNOCHCHRC, "Unofficial Transcript of the Press Conference Given by the United Nations Legal Experts, Sunway Hotel, 31 August 1999."
49 German Press Agency (DPA), "Partial Transcript of Hun Sen Remarks in Interview on Aug. 17, 1999."

tribunal to prosecute only "Khmer Rouge leaders responsible for the most serious violations of human rights."⁵⁰

Other Dilemmas: UN Participation, Judicial Fairness, and the Duch Problem

The basic die of at most a trial of CPK "senior leaders" was thus cast, as was confirmed in various authoritative official Cambodian and UN documents during the first half of 2000.⁵¹ One must say "at most" because even while endorsing the basic principle of not going beyond the prosecution of senior leaders, Hun Sen tried in practice to stick to his long-standing policy of offering either exemption from prosecution or the prospect of a pardon to all DK suspects, regardless of how senior or how potentially implicated in crimes, as long as they gave up opposition to his government and accepted his political domination and patronage. With regard to the amnestied Ieng Sary, Hun Sen repeatedly suggested that he should not be retried, although the prime minister sometimes sent the opposite signal. Nuon Chea, Kae Pok, and Khieu Samphan were never formally amnestied (having never been convicted of any crime), but Hun Sen gave them assurances of nondiscrimination and allowed them to live freely in retirement in the provinces, even though he also gave mixed messages about whether he would allow them to be tried. This meant he originally put into custody for intended trial only Ta Mok, whom he had refused to let surrender like the others. However, a hitch developed when former S21 chief Duch, whom Hun Sen had permitted to live in quiet obscurity and who had become a born-again Christian, emerged publicly and began talking repentantly and openly to journalists and others about the inner workings of the CPK regime. Apparently to keep him quiet, Duch was detained on Hun Sen's orders in April 1999 and placed, like Ta Mok, in incommunicado detention. Duch and Ta Mok were the only two persons about whose trials Hun Sen spoke unequivocally.⁵²

---

50 UN Office of Legal Affairs, "Law on the Establishment of a Tribunal for the Prosecution of Khmer Rouge Leaders Responsible for the Most Serious Violations of Human Rights," August 1999.
51 On the Cambodian side, see Cambodian People's Party, "Communiqué of the 26th Plenum of the Cambodian People's Party Central Committee," February 8, 2000, and "Communiqué of the 27th Plenum of the Cambodian People's Party Central Committee," July 4, 2000. On the UN side, see an April 2000 UN draft memorandum of understanding on UN-Cambodian cooperation; UN Office of Legal Affairs "[Articles of Cooperation] [Memorandum of Understanding] Between the UN and the RGC [in/Concerning] the Prosecution under Cambodian Law of Crimes Committed During the Period of Democratic Kampuchea" (square brackets in original), April 18, 2000; and UN Commission on Human Rights, "Situation of Human Rights in Cambodia" (E/CN.4/RES./2000/79), April 29, 2000.
52 Heder, "Hun Sen and Genocide Trials," 205–12.

This created problems for defining the personal jurisdiction of those who could be prosecuted, because Duch, as a mid-ranking CPK cadre, did not fit into the category of a senior leader. Following discussions with the RGC, OLA proposed revising its position on personal jurisdiction to cover him by including others "most responsible for the most serious violations of human rights" among those to be tried.[53] After Hammarberg reassured the RGC in October 1999 that the UN wanted to find a legal formulation that would strictly limit prosecutions but include Duch,[54] and the UN General Assembly indicated in a resolution the following month that it would be satisfied if the RGC only brought "to justice the Khmer Rouge leaders most responsible for the most serious violations of human rights,"[55] the OLA proposal for making possible prosecution of Duch was incorporated by the RGC into a draft trial law of December 1999. It spoke of the prosecution of "high-level Democratic Kampuchea leaders and others responsible for serious violations."[56]

However, Hun Sen's continuing prevarications about whether all senior leaders were eligible for trial were exacerbating conflicts with OLA on two other fundamental – and related – fronts: the extent of UN involvement in a court and whether it would meet international standards for fairness. The experts' report had recommended the establishment of a politically independent court similar to the International Criminal Tribunals for the former Yugoslavia and Rwanda, in line with the original June 1997 RGC letter to Kofi Annan and the U.S. proposal of April 1998. This had since become a nonstarter because, having already achieved his objective of bringing about a collapse of the remnant CPK insurgency, Hun Sen rejected an international court and insisted that any trial must instead be in the extraordinary chambers of the domestic courts – that is, in a judicial system over which the CPP maintained tight political supervision. He declared a willingness to allow international assistance in a domestic trial, as in 1979, but rejected a compromise proposal from OLA for a "mixed tribunal" under

---

53 Ralph Zacklin, UN Office of Legal Affairs, "Comments on the Draft Law Concerning the Punishment of the Crime of Genocide and Crimes Against Humanity," August 27, 1999.
54 He suggested introducing a specific focus on members of the Standing Committee of the CPK Central Committee, plus others "responsible for the most egregious crimes," which was his attempt to specify Duch without explicitly naming him. Report by Thomas Hammarberg, "Efforts to Bring the Khmer Rouge Leaders to Justice: Discussions Between the Cambodian Government and the UN," 1999, 22, 27–8.
55 UN General Assembly, "Situation of Human Rights in Cambodia" (A/RES/54/171), December 17, 1999.
56 Royal Government of Cambodia, "Law on the Establishment of Extraordinary Chambers in the Courts of Cambodia to Prosecute Crimes Committed During the Democratic Kampuchea Period," December 1999 (government translation).

predominantly international control, with majority participation by UN-nominated personnel as well as a single, UN-nominated prosecutor. OLA's concern was to ensure that UN participation would be sufficient to both give international court officers the prosecutorial and judicial independence to pursue accountability for all senior leaders, even if Hun Sen objected, and to ensure they were fairly tried, regardless of Hun Sen's momentary preferences that they be condemned or exonerated. The United States intervened in late 1999 and repeatedly in 2000 in an attempt to broker a complex compromise on the court's composition. According to the U.S.-backed formula, a minority of UN-nominated judges and a majority of Cambodian judges effectively appointed by Hun Sen would have to agree to decisions on the basis of a "supermajority" procedure that would give the international jurists more influence over the trials than implied by their minority status, and that a similar procedure would resolve disputes between two co-prosecutors, one international and one Cambodian. However, the UN was never convinced that Hun Sen was negotiating in good faith or that the U.S. formula could square the circle: it remained skeptical whether all senior leaders against whom there was evidence would be charged and whether trials would be fair. Particularly galling for the UN – but only symbolic of the larger issues – was Hun Sen's refusal to explicitly abrogate Ieng Sary's amnesty in the draft legislation passed into law under CPP sponsorship in January 2001. The law provided for the establishment of the extraordinary chambers according to the compromise formula suggested by the United States, pending UN agreement.[57] Kofi Annan finally vented the UN's frustration at all this by formally ending negotiations in early 2002, citing continuing skepticism that the extraordinary chambers could function independently, impartially, and objectively.[58]

Meanwhile, the senior-leaders-plus-Duch approach had been finalized in the otherwise fruitless negotiations between OLA and Hun Sen representatives.[59] The UN stressed it wanted to find a definition of the court's personal jurisdiction that was fully in line with the limitations "intended by the government," ceding that the formulation adopted would be the RGC's political decision. OLA proposed several wordings that might be appended

---

57 Stephen R. Heder, "Dealing with Crimes Against Humanity: Progress or Illusion?" *Southeast Asian Affairs 2001* (Singapore: Institute of Southeast Asian Studies, 2001), 129–40.
58 UN Secretariat, "Highlights of the Noon Briefing by Fred Eckard, Spokesman for the Secretary-General of the United Nations, UN Headquarters, New York, February 8, 2002: UN Drops Talks with Cambodia Over Khmer Rouge Trial."
59 In announcing the negotiations, the UN explained that it aimed at the establishment of a court to try DK "senior leaders." UN Secretariat, "Daily Press Briefing of Office of Spokesman for Secretary-General," June 19, 2000.

to the basic focus on senior leaders to cover Duch, including its earlier suggestion: those "most responsible for crimes and serious violations."[60] In communications with UN member-states, OLA now talked in terms of a trial of "senior leaders of the Khmer Rouge et al.,"[61] while Hun Sen reminded Special Representative Hammarberg that the "et al." must not include anyone who – like Chea Sim, Heng Samrin, and Hun Sen himself – could be credited with having "helped to overthrow the genocide" after defecting from the CPK.[62]

RGC-UN unity on this front rendered futile pleas by Cambodian human rights organizations to hold legally accountable all those most responsible for atrocities and internal concern among UN human rights officials that the UN position seemed to reduce everything – including investigations – to a very limited number of people.[63]

In the end, the RGC settled on defining the extraordinary chambers' personal jurisdiction in the January 2001 law passed under its direction as "senior leaders of DK and those who were most responsible for crimes and serious violations."[64] Although it seemed that this might in practice leave significant prosecutorial scope to charge "most responsible" lower downs who did not enjoy CPP political protection, it was based on the understanding that the text would be most narrowly construed, precluding even such a partial pursuit of the letter of the law. That this was the RGC intention was made obvious during December 2000 parliamentary discussions of the government draft of the law. Speaking to the assembly, RGC senior minister and influential CPP figure Sok An – who was in charge of negotiations with the UN – stressed that the law aimed "to try a small targeted group," a "group that is not widespread," that was defined "distinctly and obviously to the smallest number," and that excluded "all

---

60 UN Office of Legal Affairs, "Draft 5 July 2000: [Articles of Cooperation] [Memorandum of Understanding] Between the UN and the RGC [in/Concerning] the Prosecution under Cambodian Law of Crimes Committed During the Period of Democratic Kampuchea" (square brackets in original); "Phnom Penh, 5 July 2000 at 6:00 PM: Law on the Establishment of Extraordinary Chambers in the Courts of Cambodia for the Prosecution of Crimes Committed During the Period of Democratic Kampuchea" and "5 July 2000: Law on the Establishment of Extraordinary Chambers in the Courts of Cambodia for the Prosecution of Crimes Committed During the Period of Democratic Kampuchea."
61 Hans Corell, UN Office of Legal Affairs, "Note to Interested Member States: Establishment of a National Court in Cambodia to Try Senior Leaders of Khmer Rouge et al.," July 12, 2000.
62 "Khmer Rouge Leaders Will Not Escape the Law: Hun Sen," Agence France-Presse, New York, September 11, 2000.
63 COHCHR [Cambodia Office of the High Commissioner for Human Rights], "Note for the File," July 2000.
64 Royal Government of Cambodia, "Law on the Establishment of Extraordinary Chambers in the Courts of Cambodia for the Prosecution of Crimes Committed During the Period of Democratic Kampuchea," Article 1 (government translation).

the lower ranks and the rank-and-file" from prosecution. Other members of Hun Sen's CPP in the assembly declared that except for senior leaders, everyone else "who used to serve in the Democratic Kampuchea regime," including political and military cadres and combatants, need "not worry at all" about being prosecuted.[65]

A Forced UN–RGC Draft Agreement

The United States and a number of other governments were determined to see a trial go forward on this basis, demanding that the UN set aside what they said were obstructive and unrealistic concerns about fairness.[66] After U.S.-backed demarches by France, Japan, and Australia,[67] Kofi Annan agreed in August 2002 that OLA would resume negotiations only if he were given a mandate by the Security Council or the General Assembly ordering him back into talks. The secretary-general continued, however, to express concerns that the envisaged trial would not meet international legal standards.[68] In November 2002, the Third Committee of the General Assembly – which is responsible for preliminary discussion of human rights issues – adopted a draft resolution instructing Annan to revive the dialogue. The text welcomed the January 2001 Cambodian legislation that Annan considered inadequate to guarantee fair trials and called for a quick agreement with the RGC for UN participation based on that law. While emphasizing "the importance of ensuring the impartiality, independence and credibility" of a trial and appealing to the Cambodian government to guarantee this, it provided only vague reference to international standards.[69] Put forward by Japan and France, the draft was passed by the

---

65 Documentation Center of Cambodia, "Minute on the Session of the National Assembly of the Kingdom of Cambodia," December 29, 2000; UNCOHCHR, "The NA Session Starts the Debate on Draw Law on KR Trial," December 29, 2000. During discussions of the law in the Cambodian Senate in January 2001, Sok An reiterated that the number prosecuted should be small, or it would "create problems." Anonymous translation of discussions at the Senate, on January 12, 2001.
66 See Royal Government of Cambodia, "Statement from the Royal Government of Cambodia in Response to the Announcement of UN Pullout from Negotiations on Khmer Rouge Trial," Phnom Penh, February 2002.
67 "Govt Optimistic on KR Trial," *Cambodia Daily*, July 4, 2002; "Reported UN Snub on KR Shocks Govt," *Cambodia Daily*, July 5, 2002; "UN Wants Mandate Before Resuming Talks on Khmer Rouge Trial," Kyodo News Service, Bandar Seri Begawan, July 29, 2002; "Japan Appeals for Support for Khmer Rouge Tribunal," Kyodo News Service, Bandar Seri Begawan, August 1, 2002.
68 UN Secretariat, "Daily Press Briefing by the Office of the Spokesman for the Secretary-General," August 20, 2002; UN News Center, "Mandate from Key UN Bodies Needed to Restart Talks on Khmer Rouge Trials," August 20, 2002.
69 UN General Assembly, Third Committee, "Khmer Rouge Trials" (A/C.3/57/L.70), November 13, 2002.

Assembly's Third Committee with abstentions by several northern European states with strong records of human rights promotion, whose representatives complained it did not call strongly enough for a fair trial.[70] In undertaking to carry out the Third Committee mandate, Annan vowed that OLA would conduct negotiations "in such a way as to ensure that prosecutions and trials . . . comply with established international standards regarding the independence and impartiality of the judiciary, the effectiveness, impartiality and fairness of prosecutors and the integrity and credibility of the legal process."[71] In this context, the full General Assembly, under pressure from the United States and other interested governments, endorsed the text of the Third Committee's draft in December 2002.[72]

Talks between the UN and the RGC duly resumed in January 2003. The UN made it clear that its objective was still to try DK leaders,[73] thus meeting in advance an RGC demand that there should be no reformulation of the court's personal jurisdiction.[74] Indeed, the government took this opportunity to reiterate the original 1979 Vietnamese-PRK policy of focusing on ringleaders but practicing leniency toward other political and military cadres or combatants who were "sincerely repentant."[75] The architect of the original U.S. policy of restricting prosecution to senior leaders pleaded for other issues to be resolved so that those who he asserted must have "masterminded the deaths" of those who died under CPK rule could be tried according to such a formula.[76]

The RGC also tried to assert that the Cambodian judiciary had overcome many of its previous weaknesses.[77] However, a contemporaneous review by the UN's specialist human rights machinery of progress toward

---

70 UN General Assembly, Press Release, "Third Committee Recommends Continuation of Office of High Commissioner for Refugees Through End of 2008" (GA/SHC/3728), November 19, 2002; Youk Chhang, "Ease Doubts About the KR Trial," *Cambodia Daily*, November 28, 2002.
71 Letter of UN Secretary-General Kofi Annan to Mr. Jan Kavan, President of the General Assembly, November 22, 2002.
72 UN General Assembly, "Khmer Rouge Trials" (A/RES/57/228A), December 18, 2002.
73 UN News Service, "Cambodia Accepts Annan's Invitation to Start Talks on Khmer Rouge Court," December 26, 2002.
74 Royal Cambodian Permanent Mission to the UN, "Statement by the Cambodian Delegation to the UN Regarding the Establishment of Extraordinary Chambers Within the Courts of Cambodia," January 13, 2002.
75 Royal Government of Cambodia, "Presentation by His Excellency Sok An, Senior Minister, Minister in Charge of the Office of the Council of Ministers, Kingdom of Cambodia, and President of the Task Force for Cooperation with Foreign Legal Experts and Preparation of the Proceedings for the Trial of Senior Khmer Rouge Leaders," at the Conference on The Rule of Law and the Legacy of Conflict, Gaborone, Botswana, January 16–19, 2003.
76 Scheffer, *New York Times*, December 21, 2002.
77 Royal Cambodian Permanent Mission to the United Nations Regarding the Establishment of Extraordinary Chambers Within the Courts of Cambodia," January 13, 2003.

judicial reform in the country suggested otherwise,[78] as had a recent General Assembly resolution, which expressed concern about interference by the executive in the independence of the judiciary.[79] In this light, OLA reintroduced the UN's original proposal for a UN-dominated mixed tribunal. The RGC, on the other hand, insisted on the formula contained in the January 2001 legislation, with majorities of Cambodian judges in all chambers and two co-prosecutors, operating under supermajority procedures.[80] Japan, France, Australia, and other governments, with U.S. support, responded to this impasse by demanding that the UN focus on those parts of the resolution requiring it to conclude an agreement based on the 2001 law.[81] With such backing, Hun Sen's representatives were not to be moved.[82]

In March 2003, UN representatives went to Phnom Penh for a second round of talks, with an agreement between OLA and Hun Sen's negotiators still seeming distant, given the latter's continuing deep skepticism about the possibility of a fair trial,[83] but with the United States, Japan, and Australia, among others, publicly urging compromise.[84] This governmental pressure was decisive. The UN and the RGC therefore initialed a draft agreement for UN participation along the lines of the 2001 law, with a few amendments.[85]

The March 2003 memorandum of understating provided:

- For prosecution of "senior leaders of Democratic Kampuchea and those who were most responsible for" DK-era atrocities (including genocide, crimes against humanity, and certain other international crimes);
- For two extraordinary chambers within the Cambodian court system: a trial chamber with three Cambodian judges and two international judges and a supreme court chamber with four Cambodian judges and three international judges;
- For two "co-prosecutors," one Cambodian, one international;
- That if the judges were unable to make decisions unanimously, the supermajority formula would require an affirmative vote of four judges in the trial chamber and of five judges in the supreme court chamber;

---

78 Cambodia Office of the High Commissioner for Human Rights, "Note on Legal and Judicial Reform for the Mid-Term Consultative Group of Donors Meeting, January 2003."
79 UN General Assembly, "Resolution Adopted by the General Assembly: Situation of Human Rights in Cambodia" (A/RES/57/225), December 18, 2002.
80 UN General Assembly, "Report of the Secretary-General on Khmer Rouge Trials" (A/57/769), March 31, 2003.
81 "Khmer Rouge: 'Last Chance' for Justice," *Asia Times Online*, February 19, 2003.
82 *Le Monde*, January 24, 2003.
83 "Differences Remain High Between Cambodia and UN over Trial," Kyodo News Service, Phnom Penh, March 3, 2003.
84 "UN Arriving Today for KR Trial Talks," *Cambodia Daily*, March 13, 2003.
85 "Draft Agreement Between the United Nations and the Royal Government of Cambodia Concerning the Prosecution Under Cambodian Law of Crimes Committed During the Period of Democratic Kampuchea," March 17, 2003, initialed by Hans Corell and Sok An.

- That if the co-prosecutors disagreed about whether to proceed with a prosecution, one of them could request a decision from a pretrial chamber composed of three Cambodian and two international judges, with a vote-blocking prosecution requiring a supermajority of at least four judges;
- That the contentious issue of the amnesty granted to Ieng Sary in 1996 should be decided by the extraordinary chambers themselves, invoking a supermajority procedure, if necessary;
- That the extraordinary chambers' operations would be in accordance with Cambodian law and international fair-trial standards.

When announcing the accord, OLA called attention to a provision in it allowing the UN to withdraw its cooperation if the extraordinary chambers failed to function properly.[86] Reporting to the General Assembly on the pact, Annan restated his belief that greater international participation to ensure trial fairness would have been preferable and alluded to ongoing doubts about the judicial credibility of the extraordinary chambers.[87]

Reservations surfaced again when the General Assembly's Third Committee tabled a draft resolution,[88] adopted by consensus in early May 2003, endorsing the draft agreement,[89] which was followed by a similar resolution adopted by the General Assembly itself in mid-May[90] and set the scene for the agreement's approval by the Cambodian legislature and parliamentary amendment of the 2001 law to bring it into conformity with the agreement.[91] Although the Third Committee's resolution passed without a formal vote,[92] some countries' representatives voiced "serious concerns" about whether international standards would be upheld by the extraordinary chambers, therefore calling for their functioning to be closely monitored by the international community.[93]

---

86 UN Office of Legal Affairs, "Statement by Under-Secretary-General Hans Corell upon Leaving Phnom Penh on 17 March 2003."
87 UN General Assembly, "Report of the Secretary-General on Khmer Rouge Trials" (A/57/769), March 31, 2003.
88 UN General Assembly, Third Committee, "Khmer Rouge Trials" (A/C.3/57/L.90), April 29, 2003.
89 UN General Assembly, Third Committee, "Third Committee Approves Draft Resolution on Khmer Rouge Trials" (GA/SHC/3734), May 2, 2003.
90 UN General Assembly, Press Release, "General Assembly Approves Draft Agreement Between UN, Cambodia on Khmer Rouge Trials" (GA/10135), May 13, 2003; UN General Assembly, "Khmer Rouge Trials" (A/RES/57/228B), May 13, 2003.
91 Royal Cambodian Permanent Mission to the UN, "Statement by H.E. Mr. Ouch Borith, Ambassador, Permanent Representative of the Kingdom of Cambodia to the United Nations," May 1, 2003.
92 "UN Committee OKs Creation of Khmer Rouge Tribunal," Kyodo News Service, New York, May 2, 2003.
93 "Netherlands Statement on the Khmer Rouge Trials, UN General Assembly, 2 May 2003."

Conclusion

The Cambodian National Assembly did not meet to discuss the agreement and amending the law until October 2004, after a general election and prolonged governmental crisis ended in the collapse of efforts to effect political reform and instead led to further consolidation of Hun Sen's and CPP's domination.[94] Members of parliament from other parties questioned the court's personal jurisdiction, complaining that it would let former CPK local authorities, from the zone down to the cooperative level, responsible for serious atrocities get away with murders committed on the basis of their own arbitrary decisions. In rejecting their concerns on behalf of the CPP, Deputy Prime Minister Sok An stressed the court's personal jurisdiction was a done deal with the international community, saying that further discussion was pointless. He reiterated that senior leaders were "the most important targets" of the tribunal, noting that "no more than ten" of these were in the prosecution frame. He said that a few lower-ranking ex-CPK members suspected of having committed crimes "much more serious" than their comrades might be prosecuted, if evidence could be adduced that their acts could be so characterized.[95] The CPP also used the done-deal argument to shrug off suggestions from other parties, Cambodian civil society,[96] international criminal law experts,[97] and UN officials that the 2001 legislation be modified to explicitly empower the court to adopt international precedents on procedure and evidence,[98] dismissing their contentions that this was necessary to ensure justice. Cambodian human rights activists remained convinced that Cambodian judges for the tribunal would be selected for

---

94 Steve Heder, "Hun Sen's Consolidation: Death or Beginning of Reform?" *Southeast Asian Affairs 2005* (Singapore, 2005).
95 Documentation Center of Cambodia, "Transcript: The First Session of the Third Term of the Cambodian National Assembly, October 4–5, 2004," supplemented by the author's notes on the debate at the assembly, at which he was present. An unofficial translation of the final text of the amended law is posted on www.cambodia.gov.kh/krt/, under the title "The Law on the Establishment of the Extraordinary Chambers as Amended 27 Oct 2004."
96 Cambodian Human Rights Action Committee, "Recommendations on Revised Draft Law on the Law on the Establishment of the Extraordinary Chambers in the Courts of Cambodia for Prosecution of Crimes Committed During the Period of Democratic Kampuchea," August 27, 2004.
97 Open Society Justice Initiative, "Informal Meeting Minutes: Organizational NGO Group on KR Tribunal (EC) Legal Issues," February 19, 2004; and "Technical Advisor Visit: Summary Report," July 5–14, 2004. The lawyers suggested other ways in which rules of procedure and evidence could be adopted, such as passage by the assembly itself, but CPP also rejected this possibility. For a discussion of procedural issues, see Scott Worden, "An Anatomy of the Extraordinary Chambers," in Abrams et al., *Awaiting Justice*.
98 In the mid-2004 draft of what became Kofi Annan's October 2004 report on the tribunal (see note 103), he said "some important procedural issues will have to be decided internally by the Extraordinary Chambers," but this was dropped in the final version, after the government rejected the notion. Text in author's possession.

their political pliability rather than their professional qualifications.[99] Privately, government officials also believed that Hun Sen was still determined to exert political control over the trials, achieve outcomes according to scripts written by him, and – above all – protect ex-CPK members in CPP ranks from being prosecuted for or implicated in crimes as he saw fit,[100] thus denying the tribunal the first prerequisite for ultimate success: a strong domestic political commitment to criminal accountability.[101] Pressures from the chief foreign backers of the tribunal, notably Japan, France, and Australia, to keep trial costs down was a further factor favoring a narrow and politicized interpretation of the court's personal jurisdiction, minimizing the number prosecuted to stay within budget and reducing the number of expensive international staff in favor of cheaper government appointees.[102] This prompted UN Secretary-General Annan to affirm that the number prosecuted was likely to be even fewer than indicated by Sok An. While restating the principle that it was the prerogative of the co-prosecutors and co-investigating judges to decide "who exactly is to be investigated and prosecuted," he said that for planning and budgeting purposes a total of five to ten indictees was being assumed.[103]

The assembly's approval of the treaty with the UN and amendment of the 2001 law to conform with it excited little public interest,[104] which was not a surprise given that one opinion poll found that almost half those surveyed felt that substandard trials would be worse than none at all.[105] Cambodian human rights organizations expressed the hope that they might be "one way to begin to . . . learn some truth" about what happened under CPK rule,[106] while voicing concern that domestic and international pressures were likely to severely hamper their ability to do more.[107] The tribunal promised to

---

99 Letter to H. E. Kofi Annan, Secretary-General of the United Nations, dated October 9, 2004, and signed by representatives of forty-seven Cambodian nongovernmental organizations.
100 Anonymous senior CPP and other government officials, including two deputy prime ministers, interviews by author, Phnom Penh, April–November 2004.
101 International Center for Transitional Justice, "Basic Considerations on Domestic and Hybrid Prosecution Initiatives" (paper presented at the United Nations Office of the High Commissioner for Human Rights Transitional Justice Workshop, Geneva, Switzerland, September 2004), 3.
102 "Donors Want KR Tribunal Budget Cut," *Cambodia Daily* June 4, 2004; "Price of Justice for Khmer Rouge Up $10m," *Phnom Penh Post*, June 4–17, 2004.
103 UN General Assembly, "Report of the Secretary-General on Khmer Rouge Trials" (A/59/432), October 12, 2004.
104 "Cambodia's Legislature Bars Government from Pardoning Khmer Rouge," Associated Press, Phnom Penh, October 5, 2004.
105 Khmer Institute of Democracy, *Survey on the Khmer Rouge Regime and the Khmer Rouge Tribunal 2004* (Phnom Penh: 2004), 9.
106 Cambodian Human Rights Action Committee, "Funding of the Proposed Extraordinary Chambers in the Courts of Cambodia for the Prosecution of Crimes Committed by the Khmer Rouge," November 11, 2004.
107 NGO letter to Kofi Annan.

perform the great service of demolishing the ongoing denials by senior CPK leaders like Nuon Chea, Ieng Sary, and Khieu Samphan of responsibility for or even knowledge of massive executions, as well as their efforts to shift all blame to the late Pol Pot and Son Sen, overzealous subordinates, or each other.[108] However, it seemed much less likely to confront the fact – noted by many Cambodians who experienced the CPK regime – that the killings were "complicated" because they went "from the ground to the top" and involved at least some current government officials.[109] In the countryside, people complained that former junior CPK cadres continued to be appointed by the CPP as local government authorities and that the truth about their background would remain obscure because the tribunal focused on former senior leaders.[110] The legislation left very uncertain the extent to which trials would deal with claims by menial cadres who admitted involvement in executions in which they were only following orders and acted under threat of death, portraying themselves as victims of the regime and placing all blame on the top leadership, although witnesses of the lower downs' actions bitterly ridiculed such self-justifications.[111]

The expectations of former CPK members, such as ex–district secretary Chea Sim, were clear and publicly expressed at the twenty-fifth and twenty-sixth anniversaries of the DK's 1979 collapse in the face of the Vietnamese invasion. These occasions were marked in government media by broadcasts of fictionalized accounts of the regime (such as the film *The Killing Fields*) and speeches by Chea Sim. He condemned CPK "genocide," took credit for overthrowing DK, and declared that the government and the UN would be "able to completely close down this dark chapter" of Cambodian history by "successful implementation of the law to form an extraordinary tribunal."[112] He himself promulgated both the agreement with the UN and the tribunal law, signing them as Cambodia's acting chief of state.[113] It was incredible

---

108 "Khmer Rouge VIP Says He Will Face Genocide Tribunal," Associated Press, January 18, 2004; "Former Khmer Rouge Leaders Set the Record Straight," *Cambodia Daily*, February 28–9, 2004; "Pol Pot's Cronies Smug in a Garden of Bone and Ashes," *Cambodia Daily*, April 22, 2004. For Khieu Samphan's full denial, see his *L'histoire récente de Cambodge et mes prises de position* (Paris, 2004).
109 "Ordinary Cambodians Losing Faith in Tribunal," *Cambodia Daily*, January 2, 2004.
110 "People Criticize Appointment of Former Khmer Rouge Leader as District Deputy Governor," *Kampuchea Thmei*, October 17, 2003.
111 "Khmer Rouge Jailers Claim to Be Victims," Associated Press, Phnom Penh, January 4, 2004; "Chhouk Rin Set to Face Final Appeal," *Cambodia Daily*, January 20, 2004.
112 United Nations Foundation, UN Wire, "Cambodian Party Chief Vows Justice for Khmer Rouge Victims," January 6, 2004; "In Cambodia, an Anniversary Renews Calls for Genocide Trials," *New York Times*, January 7, 2004; "25 Years On, Khmer Rouge Atrocities Torment Cambodia's Youth," Agence France-Presse, January 6, 2004; "Cambodia Urges U.N. to Find Money for Genocide Trial Before Time Runs Out," Associated Press, Phnom Penh, January 7, 2005.
113 "Chea Sim Passes Legislation for KR Tribunal," *Cambodia Daily*, November 6–7, 2004.

enough that these came into force in the name of an official who elsewhere would have been a possible target of prosecution for the crimes the laws were designed to punish. It was even more extraordinary that this fact passed without public protest, or even comment, an indicator of the political and diplomatic unchallengeability of the much broader impunity it symbolized, and of resigned domestic and international acceptance of it. Certainly, given the political and diplomatic circumstances, it seemed impossible that the court would dare to attempt to ascertain whether the likes of Chea Sim or Heng Samrin were among those "most responsible" for CPK crimes. A slim hope remained that the prosecution might touch a few of the many other, politically less well protected, lower-level perpetrators whose crimes put them within the court's mandate. However, realizing even this prospect was going to require successfully fighting enormously uphill political and diplomatic battles, and the likelihood was that the only accountability for these criminals would come in the extrajudicial judgment of history, during or after the trials.

PART IV

Reconciliation

9

Settling Histories, Unsettling Pasts

Reconciliation and Historical Justice in a Settler Society

BAIN ATTWOOD

Over the last thirty to forty years, settler societies such as Australia have been forced to confront the nature of their colonial pasts as new political movements and new histories have provoked controversy over historical injustices. Much contemporary discussion has come to resemble the ongoing debates in countries such as Germany about forgetting, responsibility, guilt, atonement, and compensation.[1] This has proven enormously unsettling. Modern states are forged largely through historical narratives. These can provide nations with a sense of being a moral community, which arguably is what "gives nationalisms their greater or lesser appeal and staying power."[2] Consequently, a nation's loss of certainty regarding its moral worth can threaten both national identity and identification with the nation. This is especially so in settler societies, it can be argued. Most states have problematic origins and have had to undergo a transition from de facto coercive power to de jure authority, but this is perhaps more evidently the case for settler states because their origins are considered to be more recent.[3]

In Australia and other settler societies in recent times, the foundational historical narratives that settler communities previously took for granted have been discredited by new national histories. This confrontation with

---

1 Mark McKenna, "Metaphors of Light and Darkness: The Politics of 'Black Armband History,'" *Melbourne Journal of Politics* 25 (1998): 70.
2 Gyanendra Pandey, *Remembering Partition: Violence, Nationalism and History in India* (Cambridge, 2001), 152.
3 It might also be argued that the problem of historical injustice is much greater in settler societies dealing with the legacy of colonialism than in the case of societies dealing with the legacy of short-lived totalitarian regimes (such as Nazi Germany), because this is more entrenched and thus more intractable as a consequence of having occurred over a much longer period of time, affecting generations of colonized peoples, and because it is embedded in the political and cultural structures of those societies. As a result we should question the universal applicability of notions such as "transitional justice."

the colonial past has been especially shocking in the Australian case, largely because settler Australians "are not used to thinking of [their] history as contentious, morally compromised or volatile, as dangerous as, say, Japanese or South African history."[4] Coming to terms with this past has been difficult in Australia, then, not just because of the nature of its past but because of the nature of its history-making across a good deal of the twentieth century – a form of historical amnesia that has been called "the great Australian silence."[5]

In this chapter I consider the nature of the history-making in Australia in the closing decades of the twentieth century, and I critically analyze its implications for historical justice in the Australian nation-state. In Australia, as in many other countries during this period, I suggest that at least two fundamentally different kinds of history-making have been at work. The first is history of a more or less conventional academic kind, which was often complicit with the liberal democratic state of the nineteenth and twentieth centuries and its goal of developing a "modern," unitary nation. The second, closely related to a series of memorializing practices, might be given the name "subaltern pasts" or "Aboriginal histories." I am adopting and adapting here a term formulated by Dipesh Chakrabarty. He has argued:

Some constructions and experiences of the past stay "minor" in the sense that their very incorporation into historical narratives converts them into pasts "of lesser importance" vis-à-vis dominant understandings of what constitutes fact and evidence (and hence vis-à-vis the underlying principle of rationality) in the practices of professional history. Such "minor" pasts are those experiences of the past that always have to be assigned an "inferior" or "marginal" position as they are translated into the academic historian's language. These are pasts that are treated . . . as instances of human "immaturity," pasts that do not prepare us for either democracy or citizenry practices because they are not based on the deployment of reason in public life. . . . Let me call these subordinated relations to the past "subaltern" pasts. They are marginalised not because of any conscious intentions but because they represent moments or points at which the archive that the historian mines develops a degree of intractability with respect to the aims of professional history. In other words, these are pasts that resist historicisation.[6]

---

4 David Carter, "Working on the Past, Working on the Future," in Richard Nile and Michael Peterson, eds., *Becoming Australian* (St. Lucia, 1998), 12.
5 W. E. H. Stanner, *The 1968 Boyer Lectures: After the Dreaming* (Sydney, 1969), 7, 24–5, 53. It should be noted that historical and other discourses are very important in the Australian context because the vast majority of its non-Aboriginal peoples only "know" Aborigines through these, since they seldom encounter them in everyday life.
6 Dipesh Chakrabarty, *Provincialising Europe: Postcolonial Thought and Historical Difference* (Princeton, 2000), 100–1.

In recent years in Australia, Aboriginal histories have contested the legitimacy of the nation-state and exposed the fact that the discipline of history is not the only way of relating the past. Consequently, it can be argued that the symbolic and material rectification of historical injustices requires the recognition not only of the different rights of indigenous peoples but also of peoples' different histories – and the futures they imagine. This can be seen through a consideration of reconciliation in Australia and two historical narratives I have called "native title" and "the stolen generations."

Aboriginality, History, and Reconciliation

In the 1960s, Aboriginal and non-Aboriginal political campaigners in Australia began demanding rectification of historical injustices in new ways. Most importantly, they claimed rights on the grounds of Aborigines' status as the indigenous peoples, especially to land (land rights) but also to shape their own destinies (self-determination). These demands both called up and necessitated histories of difference of one kind or another, since indigenous rights are inherently based on historical claims. These histories challenged the triumphialist and historicist logic of conventional settler history.[7]

At the same time that these political campaigns to redress historical injustices grew in strength, non-Aboriginal academic historians turned their attention to studying colonialism in Australia, producing histories of colonialism that emphasized racism, the dispossession of Aboriginal peoples, the degradation of their culture, the denial of their rights, and Aboriginal survival and Aboriginality. Beginning in the 1970s, this new history began to circulate in a growing number and range of cultural forms in Australian public life – monographs, essays, novels, plays, poetry, feature films, documentaries, exhibitions, and so forth. Indeed, there was a veritable explosion in representations of the Aboriginal past. Yet, as we shall see, there was much that remained conventional in this particular history-making.

Across much the same period, Aboriginal people themselves increasingly took an interest in history and represented themselves and their own pasts and cultures in the form of life story, family history, dance, painting, photography, song, and so on. In this process, historians as well as anthropologists and linguists played an important role, in particular by collaborating with Aborigines in the production of oral histories of one kind or another.[8] In important respects, these Aboriginal pasts or histories departed radically

---

[7] See Bain Attwood, *Rights for Aborigines* (Sydney, 2003), part V.
[8] See Bain Attwood and Fiona Magowan, eds., *Telling Stories: Indigenous History and Memory in Australia and New Zealand* (Sydney, 2001).

from those of conventional history, but for some time the implications of these differences were not readily apparent.

By the 1990s, all this history-making had produced enormous unsettlement among many settler Australians. Because history is commonly understood as an account of the past that is completed and so unalterable, it provides, especially in the context of rapid change, a sense of order, so that any challenge to it can be unsettling, making what has long seemed familiar unfamiliar.[9] As several commentators have remarked, Australians have experienced "the most profound renegotiations of their histories,"[10] and "[d]ebates concerning who rightfully belongs and the conditions of that belonging now haunt contemporary Australia."[11] Consequently, there has been a growing conviction among many Australians that the Aboriginal past is integral to any sense of Australia's future even though Aboriginal people constitute a small minority – little more than 2 percent – of the Australian population. Concern about the implications of the new Australian history has been particularly intense among conservatives and new conservatives. They responded by launching a "history war."[12] In this war, they reacted particularly violently to any suggestions that the concept of genocide might be applied to any aspect of government policy toward Aboriginal people in the nineteenth and twentieth centuries.[13]

The heightened significance of Aboriginal matters owes much to the Australian nation-state's appropriation of Aboriginality since the 1950s. Because Australia, like many nation-states, found it increasingly difficult to produce a distinct nationality, it turned to Aboriginality as a way of addressing this problem. Drawing on representations of Aboriginal culture that are inherently historical in nature, it articulated Aboriginality in terms of its apparent antiquity, primordiality, and primitivism.[14] Somewhat later, in the early 1970s, radical Aboriginal demands for rights and sovereignty – and the resulting crisis of legitimacy for the nation-state – forced governments at the federal level to adapt established methods of governing Aboriginal people. They ostensibly abandoned the postwar policy of assimilation and adopted a policy of self-determination. This required the

---

9 See Ken Gelder and Jane Jacobs, *Uncanny Australia: Sacredness and Identity in a Postcolonial Nation* (Melbourne, 1998), 17, 22.
10 Paula Hamilton and Paul Ashton, "Blood Money? Race and Nation in Australian Public History," *Radical History Review* 76 (2000): 189.
11 Haydie Gooder, "Review of Peter Read, *Belonging*," *Australian Historical Studies* 32 (2001): 356.
12 For a discussion of this, see Stuart Macintyre and Anna Clark, *The History Wars* (Melbourne, 2003), and Bain Attwood, *Telling the Truth about Aboriginal History* (Sydney, 2005).
13 For a consideration of this, see Attwood, *Telling the Truth about Aboriginal History*, chapter 4.
14 See Bain Attwood, "Introduction: The Past as Future: Aborigines, Australia and the (Dis)Course of History," in Bain Attwood, ed., *In the Age of Mabo: History, Aborigines and Australia* (Sydney, 1996), vii–xxxviii.

Australian state to nurture Aboriginality through new cultural and political forms in order to justify different rights for Aborigines.[15]

This strategy was only partially successful, however. The Australian state was unable to detach Aborigines and Aboriginality from the other dimension the past bestows on them, that of precedence, or to defuse the postcolonial struggle based on this. During the 1970s and 1980s, Aboriginal spokespersons continued to express political demands for indigenous rights and sovereignty, and they increasingly did so in international forums where they had some power to embarrass Australia by bringing its reputation as a liberal democracy into disrepute. In the late 1980s, relations between Aborigines and the Commonwealth government entered a state of crisis. The government had reneged on its commitment to introduce national land rights legislation and drawn back from consideration of a treaty or a compact. In this context, it proposed a formal process of reconciliation between Aborigines and settler Australians, headed by the oddly named Council for Aboriginal Reconciliation, which was accepted by all parties represented in the Commonwealth parliament.

Shared History

The term "reconciliation" was never really defined, but the emphases of the Council were relatively clear. Arguably it was primarily an exercise in nation-building. It sought to unify Aboriginal and non-Aboriginal peoples within the Australian nation and refused to countenance any Aboriginal political demands that could not be accommodated readily by the unitary nation-state, such as those requiring recognition of Aboriginal sovereignty. The secondary goal of reconciliation – social justice or self-determination – was contained by the Council's nationalist project. Its "vision statement" read: "A united Australia which respects this land of ours, values the Aboriginal and Torres Strait Islander heritage, and provides justice and equity for all."[16]

The differences and tension between the two projects informing reconciliation – Australian nationalism and Aboriginal self-determination – were reflected in its history work. Reconciliation and historical truth, it must be

---

15 See Jeremy Beckett, "Aboriginality, Citizenship and Nation State," *Social Analysis* 24 (1988): 3–18.
16 Council for Aboriginal Reconciliation (henceforth CAR), *Walking Together: The First Steps* (www.austlii.edu.au/other/IndigLRes/car/1994/1/2). Reconciliation has been the subject of several critiques. See, for example, Haydie Gooder and Jane Jacobs, "Belonging and Non-Belonging: The Apology in a Reconciling Nation," in A. Blunt and C. McEwan, eds., *Postcolonial Geographies* (New York, 2002), 200–13. For a contrary view, see John Morton, "Abortive Redemption? Apology and Indigenous Tradition in Australian Reconciliation," *Journal of the Polynesian Society* 112 (2003): 238–59.

emphasized, were believed to go hand in hand. The Council made "sharing histories" one of its "key issues." This was defined as "a sense of all Australians of a shared ownership of their history." Most often this was figured as a goal of "shared history." "Disharmony and discord can be overcome," the Council claimed in 1993, "when Australians . . . come together to better understand and learn about the history of division and oppression."[17]

The Council's ideal of shared history was cast in the traditional terms of the discipline. History was largely conceived as an objective body of historical knowledge that would include all the empirically testable facts, especially the ones previously excluded, which would be added together and assembled as an accurate and hence truthful account of the past. This would be taught to all Australian citizens, particularly settler Australians. It was a history lesson. This pedagogical project was informed by a set of assumptions that had influenced two or more generations of historians working on the history of Aboriginal-settler relations in Australia, beginning with Charles Rowley, a historian charged with overseeing a large social science research program on Aboriginal people in the mid-1960s.[18] As Henry Reynolds, a leading scholar in the field that has come to be called "Aboriginal history,"[19] has observed: "Much critical, revisionist history springs from a belief that Australia should do better and is capable of doing so. It is written in hope and expectation of reform, crafted in the confidence that carefully marshaled, clearly expressed arguments can persuade significant numbers of Australians to change their minds and redirect their sympathies. Beyond that confidence in individuals is a firm belief in the capacity of Australian democracy to respond to new ideas which in time can reshape politics and recast institutions, laws and customs."[20]

Reconciliation, therefore, articulated what was a new history content-wise, but it was quite conventional in its form. It was deemed to be a single factual account of the nation's history, compiled by objective historical research, that would constitute a common or unified collective understanding of its past and so serve as the basis for national reconciliation.[21] So it

---

17 CAR, *Walking Together*; CAR, *Addressing the Key Issues for Reconciliation* (www.austlii.edu.au/other/IndigLRes/car/1993/9/2).
18 See C. D. Rowley, *The Destruction of Aboriginal Society* (Canberra, 1970), 5, 8–9; Ramola Yardi and Geoffrey Stokes, "Foundations for Reconciliation in Social Science: The Political Thought of C. D. Rowley," *Melbourne Journal of Politics* 25 (1998): 47, 51, 55, 61.
19 For a consideration of the ways in which "Aboriginal history" can be defined, see Bain Attwood, "The Paradox of Australian Aboriginal History," *Thesis Eleven* 38 (1994): 118–37.
20 Henry Reynolds, *Why Weren't We Told: A Personal Search for the Truth About Our History* (Melbourne, 1999), 245.
21 See Heather Goodall, "Too Early or Not Soon Enough? Reflections on Sharing Histories as Process," *Australian Historical Studies* 33 (2002): 7–9.

is that we find Reynolds, a convert to the cause, asserting: "Without some reconciliation of stories, some *convergence* of stories, it is hard to see how the broader agenda of reconciliation can be advanced. Is reconciliation possible between two peoples who fundamentally disagree about their shared past, who differ widely in their explanation of the reason why things are as they now are?"[22] The answer was clear. Another leading historian in the field, Peter Read, contended: "national reconciliation demands reconciled historical narratives." In other words, reconciliationists hold that Australia can only develop into a reconciled nation if both Aborigines and settler Australians embrace more or less the same historical narrative, that is, if they acquire a shared history.[23]

In this political project, both peoples, as Dipesh Chakrabarty has observed, "have to transcend the pulls of their respective identitarian affiliations in order to agree on the facts of an injustice committed in the past" and thus "meet as equal citizens of some future Australia."[24] The Council's discussion paper *Sharing Histories*, which historians such as Reynolds played a role in formulating, asserted that there was to be "a shared sense of history" among Australians, one that recognized that "[we] have, or can develop, a common sense of time and place through the created historical record."[25]

What was this shared history to comprise? Informed by what the Council called "the newer [academic] histories," reconciliationist history emphasized the grim truth about the colonization of Australia, that is, the refusal to recognize Aborigines as the original owners; the dispossession, destruction, and displacement of Aboriginal people; the formal racial discrimination that followed; and the marginalization of Aborigines. Thus, the Council's "brief look at a long history" (in its final report to the Commonwealth parliament) pointed out that the British colonies had been established "without consent and without negotiating a fair deal with the original inhabitants.... Many Aboriginal people were dispossessed and displaced from their lands, forced into reserves, and killed in battles for their land.... As numbers declined and traditional lifestyles and cultures were disrupted, Aboriginal ... peoples became marginalized."[26]

22 Reynolds, *Why Weren't We Told*, 171, my emphasis.
23 Peter Read, *Belonging: Australians, Place and Aboriginal Ownership* (Melbourne, 2000), 186.
24 Dipesh Chakrabarty, "Reconciliation and Its Historiography: Some Preliminary Thoughts," *UTS Review* 7, 1 (2001): 11.
25 CAR, *Sharing History*.
26 CAR, *Reconciliation: Australia's Challenge: Final Report of the Council for Aboriginal Reconciliation to the Prime Minister and the Commonwealth Parliament* (www.www.austlii.edu.au/other/IndigLRes/car/2000/16).

In addition to encouraging settler Australians to "share" or "own" this history of the colonial past, however, the Council exhorted non-Aboriginal Australians to share Aboriginal peoples' *precolonial* history, often represented as Aboriginal "cultures and histories" or as "heritage" (which is a more commodifed form of the past than history). By doing this, the authors of *Sharing Histories* asserted that "non-indigenous Australians are able to lengthen and strengthen their association with this land." They stated:

> The reconciliation process seeks to encourage non-indigenous Australians to deepen and enrich their association with this country by identifying with the ancient Aboriginal and Torres Strait Islander presence in Australia.... It is only through indigenous Australians that non-indigenous Australians can claim a long-standing relationship with and deeper understanding of Australia's land and seas... inherit[ing] a tradition and a set of knowledge and understanding which extends the history of Australia beyond the last 206 years, to the thousands of years of Aboriginal... settlement in this land. Thus a sense of identity and pride can be gained from the length of time indigenous Australians are known to have lived here.[27]

Just as the Council called on Australians to acquire or own a shared historical narrative, it also tried to point up the ways in which Aboriginal and settler Australians had a shared colonial past. However, given both the nature of the past and the new academic historiography, this was a very minor theme. More commonly, the Council sought to redeem the history of settler peoples in Australia, mostly by drawing on histories of white humanitarianism that were ready-made for creating a sense of precedence and tradition among present-day supporters of reconciliation.[28] "In the wider society, ever since the early days of colonisation and settlement," it argued, "dissenting voices have been raised, arguing against the harsh treatment of Aboriginal... peoples and calling for recognition of their rights, including for just agreements for land." In its final report the Council presented this past in terms of a "gradual awakening," propounding a history of progress in which non-Aboriginal Australians had repudiated the past by redressing its wrongs.[29]

In this, as in many other respects, the Council's history-making was historicist in that it treated history in the manner the discipline has usually done, as a matter of the past. By insisting on the very temporal categories – past, present, and future – that lie at the heart of its operations, history, it has been argued, creates a sense of distance between the past and the present that

---

27 CAR, *Sharing History*.
28 For an example of such a history, see Henry Reynolds, *This Whispering in Our Hearts* (Sydney, 1998).
29 CAR, *Sharing History*; CAR, *Reconciliation*.

tends to deny the past its presence. That is, it denies the ways in which the past might be present.[30] Thus, the Council tended to cast historical wrongs as "past wrongs" or "the injustices of the past," and so these were somehow figured as though they are no longer present. At most, it represented the plight of Aborigines today as "the consequence of that history" or as "a legacy of history" but not as some kind of continuation of it.[31]

This is also true of much of the new academic historiography informing the Council's work. Too few settler histories show satisfactorily how the colonial past is still present. On the contrary, as Patrick Wolfe has contended, they have "an insulating effect," representing colonization as "a past event" rather than as a process that is ongoing.[32] In particular, Gillian Cowlishaw argues, historians "have filled a textual gap about our racial past, but they conceive of racism in such a way that it is not seen to be an organic and ongoing part of colonialism"; they have "created a new silence regarding ... this racism" by presenting "a view of the past that fills [Australians] ... with horror at the same time as it distances [them] from it."[33]

Sharing Histories

Shared history can be contrasted with another, subordinate theme in the Council's history work, that of sharing histories. The assumptions informing

---

30 See Mark Salber Phillips, "Distance and Historical Representation," *History Workshop Journal* 57 (2004): 123–41. Anthropologist Deborah Bird Rose has argued that European culture has long conceived of time in such a way that we focus on the future rather than the present. The present tends to become a place from which we turn away, causing "a massive elision of agency, in the sense of [accepting] our responsibility for outcomes." Historicism, she suggests, "enable[s] us to understand ourselves in an imaginary state of future achievement, and to turn our backs on current social facts of pain, damage, destruction and despair which exist in the present by our agency, but which we will only acknowledge as our past." In this way "the past is not so much that which has already happened, as it is a label to be applied to that which we wish to ... forget, or from which we wish to differentiate ourselves and thus to absolve ourselves from responsibility" ("Dark Times and Excluded Bodies in the Colonisation of Australia," in Geoffrey Gray and Christine Winter, eds., *The Resurgence of Racism: Howard, Hanson and the Race Debate* (Melbourne, 1997), 100–1).
31 CAR, *Addressing the Key Issues*; CAR, *Walking Together*; CAR, *Australian Declaration Towards Reconciliation* (www.austlii.edu.au/au/other/IndigLRes/car/2000/12). Perhaps it is not altogether surprising, therefore, that most settler Australians, even those who acknowledge that Aboriginal people are disadvantaged, do not understand the historical causes of this. Public opinion polls suggest that they "do not believe that there is a link between current disadvantage and the past" even though there is "a widespread feeling throughout Australia that Aborigines have been badly treated in the past" (Saulwick and Muller, "Public Opinion on Reconciliation," in Michelle Grattan, ed., *Reconciliation: Essays on Australian Reconciliation* (Melbourne, 2000), 36).
32 Patrick Wolfe, "Nation and MiscegeNation: Discursive Continuity in the Post-Mabo Era," *Social Analysis* 36 (1994): 96. See also Klaus Neumann, "Remembering Victims and Perpetrators," *UTS Review* 4, 1 (1998): 8–12.
33 Gillian Cowlishaw, "Studying Aborigines: Changing Canons in Anthropology and History," in Bain Attwood and John Arnold, eds., *Power, Knowledge and Aborigines* (Melbourne, 1992), 26–7.

sharing histories differ in significant ways from those underpinning the concept of shared history. As its name suggests, sharing histories, like shared history, called for the sharing of history through telling and listening to historical narratives. However, in such an exchange it mostly had in mind Aboriginal people's tellings of their pasts, whereas shared history tended to emphasize the teachings of settler academic history. More importantly, sharing histories conceived of history as a matter of perspective, of interpretive narratives, rather than as a singular and consensual body of facts whose compilation by historical narrators tended to be occluded.[34]

In keeping with this, many Aboriginal people, at least, seem to have seen reconciliation as a forum in which differently positioned peoples told their histories, heard those of others, and respected their differences rather than rushing toward a future state of "togetherness." This conception of history, unlike shared history, explicitly realizes and confirms the conjunction between past and present. As Heather Goodall has remarked in this context, histories are not so much collections of facts that naturally belong together as they are processes in which interpretive narratives are formulated and mobilized, and so they are "always contingent on the teller, their purpose, the context and the audience to whom they speak." By recognizing this, it can be argued, we are better able to acknowledge the connectedness between past and present, and thus people's current predicaments, and so understand why people's histories are relevant to the present.[35]

In turn, sharing histories acknowledges the simple fact that not only are there different historical perspectives of the colonial past but that these will continue to be articulated. It thus assumes that the future of any reconciliation process will depend on a recognition and acceptance of ongoing difference – and so a good measure of contradiction and conflict – rather than involving an attempt to effect closure on a divided past. In keeping with the politics of difference underpinning this approach, sharing histories is clearly informed by an ideal of democracy that departs from that which inflects shared history. Whereas the latter emphasizes development toward a final goal of a unitary nation, the former stresses diversity and a state of ongoing pluralism, thus allowing for self-determination in some form or another.

The different conceptions of history associated with shared history and sharing histories, and their implications for historical justice, can be considered further by reference to the historical narratives I have called native title and the stolen generations, both of which were made central to the discourse of reconciliation in Australia.

---

34 CAR, *Addressing the Key Issues*.   35 Goodall, "Too Early Yet": 12.

Native Title

In 1992, the Australian High Court recognized native title in Australia in its *Mabo* decision, thus vanquishing the previous legal understanding that Aborigines were not the original owners of the country. *Mabo* was hailed as a historic decision by liberals, embraced by the Labor federal government and the popular reconciliation movement as the basis for reconciliation, and portrayed as a means of making a series of radical changes in Aboriginal affairs. Closer examination of both the High Court's ruling and the government's implementation of it, however, reveals that native title was burdened by many of the same weaknesses as "shared history," principally because it sought to contain a disturbing Aboriginal past or history.

On the face of it, the High Court's decision both confirms and evidences the virtues of conventional historical work proclaimed and undertaken by Charles Rowley's social science project in the 1960s and extended by a bevy of historians in the 1970s and 1980s. It seems that historical scholarship, rationally argued, carefully researched, and well evidenced by empirical facts, had delineated the injustices of the past and persuaded the highest court in the land of the need to redress these, thus effecting a turn away from the bad past and toward a good future. For example, in their judgment, William Deane and Mary Gaudron contended that a "conflagration of oppression and conflict... [had] spread across the continent to dispossess, degrade and devastate the Aboriginal peoples." These events, they argued further, "constitute[d] the darkest aspects of the history of this nation" and had left "a national legacy of unutterable shame." As such, they declared, "the nation as a whole must remain diminished unless and until there is an acknowledgment of, and retreat from, those past injustices."[36] There is, indeed, something to be said for this history of progress: the High Court's decision is inconceivable without the change that has taken place in Australian intellectual and cultural life since the 1960s, and the new Australian history did play a role in this.[37]

More especially, it has been claimed that Henry Reynolds's 1987 study *The Law of the Land* swayed the majority of the High Court judges by questioning the previous legal orthodoxy regarding British acquisition of the land in Australia. Reynolds's history was, it has been remarked, "the kind of history that the law can take notice of" since it presents "a sustained, carefully documented and compelling argument." That is, a historian, using

---

36 "Mabo v Queensland No. 2," *Australian Law Journal Reports* 66 (1992): 449, 451.
37 See Richard Broome, "Historians, Aborigines and Australia: Writing the National Past," in Attwood, ed., *In the Age of Mabo*, 71–2.

scientific methods, showed the past as it really was and so produced an objective historical truth – the kind of history the law respects.[38]

However, there are many aspects of both Reynolds's history and the High Court's decision that limited their radical potential.[39] At the same time as Reynolds made a historical case for the recognition of native title and the Court recognized this right to land, both upheld the sovereignty of the Australian nation vis-à-vis that of Aboriginal peoples. This, they more or less asserted, was a matter of history, a matter that had been determined by the past and so was no longer available to be challenged.[40] Both Reynolds and the High Court were similarly colonial in upholding the law of the colonizers inasmuch as they attributed the earlier denial of Aboriginal rights to land to bad law-making by the colonial state rather than to the law itself.[41] In other words, they claimed that the long period in which Aboriginal rights to land were not recognized was merely the result of some mistaken lapse in legal practice – the application of a legal doctrine *res nullius* or *terra nullius* – rather than something fundamental to Anglo-Australian law, let alone the nature of colonialism (in Australia) more generally. Consequently, as Elizabeth Povinelli has observed, the High Court could represent its decision as "the fulfillment of the promise of the common law and the national civilization for which it stands."[42] In this regard, both Reynolds's history and the High Court's judgment can be regarded as revamped forms of Whig history, "a narrative form deeply familiar to Anglo-settler culture," that emphasizes normative principles and is devoted to the notion of a benevolent state.[43]

---

38 Rosemary Hunter, "Aboriginal Histories, Australian Histories, and the Law," in Attwood, ed., *In the Age of Mabo*, 5. For a consideration of Reynolds's *The Law of the Land* and this matter, see my "*The Law of the Land* or the Law of the Land? History, Law and Narrative in a Settler Society," *History Compass* 2 (2004): 1–27.

39 It should be noted that the High Court's ruling was very limited. While it acknowledged native title, it upheld Australian sovereignty and determined that native title had been legitimately extinguished in much of Australia, that compensation was not payable for this expropriation, and that Aboriginal claimants have to demonstrate they have maintained a continuing relationship to their "traditional" land (which few have been able to do).

40 In a later book, Reynolds challenged the sovereignty of the Australian nation-state: *Aboriginal Sovereignty: Reflections on Race, State and Nation* (Sydney, 1996).

41 It can be argued, as more than one legal historian has done, that the judges were "primarily concerned with correcting legal history" and so their ruling was an exercise in the legitimation of the rule of law. In other words, it makes more sense to conclude that the Court was eventually forced by "the crisis of [historical] truth" to "bring [the] law into line with the now-acknowledged 'facts' of history," not so much to redress historical injustice but "in order to restore the law's legitimacy" (Hunter, "Aboriginal Histories," 1, 16; David Ritter, "The 'Rejection of Terra Nullius' in Mabo: A Critical Analysis," *Sydney Law Review* 18 (1996): 7).

42 Elizabeth Povinelli, "The State of Shame: Australian Multiculturalism and the Crisis of Indigenous Citizenship," *Critical Inquiry* 24 (1998): 579.

43 Paul McHugh, "Law, History and the Treaty of Waitangi," *New Zealand Journal of History* 31, 1 (1997): 40, 46, 54, 56.

At the same time, both Reynolds and the Court distanced themselves from the colonial past in keeping with the historicism embedded in historical practice. While Reynolds joined past and present together in many respects, arguing, for example, that settler Australians had not "escaped . . . the same problems which exercised the minds and troubled the consciences of their forebears six or so generations ago,"[44] he distanced them from colonial racism by failing to figure this as "organic and ongoing" (to quote Cowlishaw's words again), as a structure in which they had much invested. For his part, Justice Gerard Brennan, whose ruling is generally regarded as the lead judgment in *Mabo*, asserted: "it is imperative in today's world that the common law should neither be nor seen to be frozen in an age of racial discrimination. The fiction [of *terra nullius*] was justified by a policy which has no place in the contemporary law of this country."[45] By presenting its decision in this way, as though it was passing judgment on the practices of some *ancien régime*, the High Court created the pretence that it was constituting a new order. "In their eyes," Povinelli observes, "*Mabo* rejected past (pre)judicial racial and cultural intolerance and now recognised native title to be a legitimate part of a newly reconstituted nation." It thus achieved, she points out, "a commonsense (post)racist separation" from the colonial past, "entrench[ing] an understanding of the nation as confronting its own discriminatory practices and facing up and eliminating the dark stain on its own history." Yet, as Povinelli points out, this amounted to a mere "rewriting of history" rather than an actual "recognition of and accounting for that history."[46]

The approach of the Keating Labor government was more or less the same as that of the High Court. Prime Minister Paul Keating talked *Mabo* up as "an historic decision." He did so because he hoped the Court's ruling could serve as a new (post)colonial historical narrative for the Australian nation. Keating told Australians in a televised address: "The Court's decision rejected a lie and acknowledged a truth. The lie was *terra nullius* – the convenient fiction that Australia had been a land of no one. The truth was native title." This provided the possibility for a new foundation for Australia, he claimed, "because after 200 years, we will at last be building on the truth." Yet Keating, like the High Court, saw *Mabo* as an opportunity "to transcend the history of dispossession" rather than work through the consequences of this past. Furthermore, Keating celebrated the deep Aboriginal past as "the oldest culture in the world" and claimed it as "a wellspring of our national culture" but insisted that native title only existed insofar as Australian law had

---

44 Henry Reynolds, *The Law of the Land* (Melbourne, 1987), 157.
45 "Mabo": 422.   46 Povinelli, "State of Shame": 579, 588–9, 592.

or would recognize it. "Native title land," he assured the Commonwealth parliament, "is . . . kept fully within the reach of Australian law." In this way, he explained, "Aboriginal Australians [will be given] justice but . . . in a way that [not only] keeps the country cohesive" but actually moves us "closer to a united Australia." Thus the radical potential of the difference of an Aboriginal past or history was contained by the Australian nation.[47]

The Stolen Generations

These historical narratives regarding native title might be contrasted with the stolen generations narrative. In 1995, the Keating government directed Australia's Human Rights and Equal Opportunity Commission to undertake a national inquiry into the removal of indigenous children: the stolen generations. The Commission was determined to use the inquiry "to reveal [the] history [of removals] and the devastating impact it continues to have on the lives of the stolen generations." It urged Aboriginal people to participate by sharing their histories in the form of written submissions and oral testimony and went to considerable lengths to help the stolen generations tell their histories as the inquiry moved around Australia conducting public and private hearings.[48]

The Commission played a major role in shaping the histories presented to it. Its publicity for the hearings emphasized narratives of a particular kind of experience, that of loss and suffering, which it called trauma and which we might call, following Homi Bhabha, "affective histories."[49] For example, it used moving historical documentation like the following plea to a government official in 1903: "I am afraid that my wife will cimmit sueside if the boy is not back soon for she is good for nothing only cry day and night . . . I have as much love for my dear wife and churldines as you have for yours . . . so if you have any feeling atole pleas send the boy back as quick as you can. It did not take long for him to go, but it takes a long time for him to come back."[50] At the hearings themselves, the Commission

---

47 Paul Keating, "The Redfern Park Speech" (1992), in Grattan, ed., *Reconciliation*, 62; Keating, *Address to the Nation: 15 November 1993* (Canberra, 1993) 5; Commonwealth of Australia, House of Representatives, *Parliamentary Debates*, First Session, 1993, 2877, 2880, 2882–3; *Age*, April 29, 1993, June 14, 1993.
48 Human Rights and Equal Opportunity Commission (henceforth HREOC), *Information Paper on the National Inquiry into the Separation of Aboriginal and Torres Strait Islander Children from their Families*, 1, cited in Link Up and Jan Tikka Wilson, *In the Best Interests of the Child? Stolen Children: Aboriginal Pain/White Shame* (Canberra, 1997), 9.
49 Homi Bhabha, cited in Chakrabarty, *Provincialising Europe*, 19.
50 HREOC, *Longing to Return Home* (Sydney, 1995), 12.

encouraged Aboriginal people to "tell their experience" and to do so "in their own way."[51]

In fact, the Commission called forth a distinctive kind of history-telling, that of individual testimony. "Testimony," Shoshana Felman has claimed, "has become the crucial mode of our relation to events of the times."[52] Certainly in much contemporary culture, as Jay Winter has pointed out, "the notion of the 'witness' [has] received [a] kind of validation": "The person who suffered knows about a mystery – the mystery of evil and the miracle of survival – and we who listen may thereby enter the mystery and share the miracle."[53] Testimony, in other words, privileges witnesses who "tell it how it was" and so bear "the truth about history." This made the inquiry's public hearings extraordinarily powerful affective events, resembling to some degree those of the South African Truth and Reconciliation Commission. (The Australian inquiry was, in all likelihood, influenced by the South African commission as well as other models for the public expiation of historical wrongs.)[54] The "predominant themes" of the inquiry, the Human Rights and Equal Opportunity Commission emphasized in its report later, were "[g]rief and loss."[55]

The narrative style of the Commission's report, *Bringing Them Home*, continued this emphasis on personal testimony by including short accounts of forced removal, such as this one:

> I was at the post office with my Mum and Auntie [and cousin]. They put us in the police ute and said they were taking us to Broome. They put the mums in there as well. But when we'd gone [about ten miles] they stopped, and threw the mothers out of the car. We jumped on our mothers' backs, crying.... But the policemen pulled us off and threw us back in the car. They pushed the mothers away and drove off, while the mothers were chasing the car, running and crying after us. We were screaming in the back of the car.[56]

By highlighting such testimony, the Commission's report "made a claim on the nation," shocking it into listening.[57]

---

51 HREOC, *Information Paper on the National Inquiry*, 9; www.hreoc.gov.au/social_justice/stolen_children.
52 Shoshana Felman, "Education and Crisis, or the Vicissitudes of Teaching," in Cathy Caruth, ed., *Trauma: Explorations in Memory* (Baltimore, 1995), 16.
53 Jay Winter, "The Memory Boom in Contemporary Historical Studies," *Raritan* 21 (2001): 56.
54 Paula Hamilton, "Sale of the Century? Memory and Historical Consciousness in Australia," in Katharine Hodgkin and Susannah Radstone, eds., *Contested Pasts: The Politics of Memory* (London, 2003), 143.
55 HREOC, *Bringing Them Home: Report of the National Inquiry into the Separation of Aboriginal and Torres Strait Islander Children from their Families* (Sydney, 1997), 3.
56 HREOC, *Bringing Them Home*, 6.
57 Haydie Gooder and Jane Jacobs, "'On the Border of the Unsayable': The Apology in Postcolonising Australia," *Interventions* 2 (2000): 238.

The report had a dramatic impact. Officially released during the Council's National Reconciliation Convention in May 1997, it immediately became a lead story in the media and won a large and sympathetic nationwide audience. Its account of the history of the stolen generations became widely available in the form of *Bringing Them Home*, a near-700-page tome that sold astonishingly well, a Web version, a smaller booklet, and a video. Its findings were debated in the national and state parliaments, featured in editorials and commentaries on radio and television and newspapers, considered in letters to the editor columns, and depicted in cartoons. In short, the Human Rights Commission's report reached a public that had not previously encountered this history and that had been relatively unmoved by the academic histories of colonialism produced in the previous two or more decades. "No inquiry in recent Australian history," one political commentator claimed, "had a more overwhelming reception nor, at least in the short term, a more culturally transforming impact."[58] This history disturbed many Australians, confronting them with "the terrible realisation that even in their life times Aborigines were the victims of brutal racism."[59]

The impact of the Commission's inquiry and its report clearly owed much to both the form and content of the history it was sharing. In this respect, it had much in common with the Aboriginal histories that had been produced in Australia in the preceding two decades or so. The pasts these represent differ radically from those of academic history in some respects, and so a consideration of their nature helps us understand the difficulty of trying to reconcile histories and, therefore, peoples.

Memory and History

How do these subaltern pasts or Aboriginal histories differ from those of conventional history?[60] The defining characteristic of Aboriginal histories, as for other indigenous histories, is their form, predominantly that of oral history.[61] When historians began to work with oral history in the 1970s, they assumed it would supplement the sources they traditionally used and so assist in their democratic project of recovering those peoples "hidden from history." As such, oral history seemed to pose no great threat to the

---

58 Robert Manne, *In Denial: The Stolen Generations and the Right* (Melbourne, 2001), 5.
59 Raimond Gaita, *A Common Humanity: Thinking About Love & Truth & Justice* (Melbourne, 1999), 110.
60 For the sake of making my argument clear in this section I have overstated the differences between history and memory and between historical and memorial work.
61 Although many are published, most begin as oral histories and are only later transcribed and edited for publication.

discipline's practice. However, as historians soon discovered, any serious engagement with oral history involves an encounter with memory. This causes a realization, in Dipesh Chakrabarty's words, that "[f]ar from being simply complementary to each other, memory and history tell of very different relationships to the past than we can or do possess" and that, although history and memory are related and the ground between them has shifted so that they have become increasingly entangled with one another, "they are not the same."[62] In short, as Paula Hamilton has pointed out, doing oral history with Aboriginal people "changed the relationship between past and present in historical research."[63]

How do memory and history have very different relationships to the past? Even though one always reaches the past in conventional historical work "by starting out from the present" and one is "always concerned with the meanings of historical reality for us, now,"[64] the historian, deemed to be an outsider, strives to represent the past as it happened and to realize the past's alterity, its difference from the present. This procedure usually rests on an assumption that the past is past, and this encourages the historian to regard present and past as disjunctive or at the very least to attend to discontinuities as much as or more than continuities between past and present. The historian's focus on explanation of events – on causes or origins – more than on outcomes or effects also distances the historian from the past as it directs him or her to concentrate on what leads up to the past rather than on the past itself. Likewise, distance is created by the tendency of conventional history to subordinate experience or the lived to the conceptual and the analytical. Furthermore, by assuming that time comprises clearly differentiated categories of past, present, and future – and that the relationship between them is linear or evolutionary – the historian treats the present and future as though they move inexorably away from the past, propelled for the most part by autonomous human agents. Finally, in the task of understanding, the historian assumes that the past can be comprehended and apprehended. Thus mastered, it can be put to rest, made to pass away. This distancing of the past has diminished over the last forty years as social history or "history from below" has paid attention to the historical *experience* of people, but it still remains.

62 Chakrabarty, "Reconciliation and Its Historiography": 9–10.
63 Hamilton, "Sale of the Century": 145. This was all the more so, as Hamilton has argued, because most of these historians found it "impossible, or undesirable, to separate their historical practice from their role as public advocates and activists."
64 Allan Megill, "Recounting the Past: 'Description,' Explanation, and Narrative in Historiography," *American Historical Review* 94, 3 (1989): 647; Jacques Le Goff, *History and Memory*, trans. Steven Rendall and Elizabeth Claman (New York, 1992), xx.

In memory work, it can be argued, the past is not so much represented or re-presented as it is presented or presenced by a personal narrator, an insider who tends to make the past familiar as he or she tries to make sense of it in the present. Thus, in memory work, narrating the past is incontrovertibly a matter of perspective. Indeed, this, and not some purportedly independent or objective account, mostly comprises its raison d'être. In re-membering the past to compose him- or herself in the present, the narrator mostly seeks continuities between past and present and tends to deny discontinuities, let alone admit any sense of alterity. Present and past are brought into greater proximity; "then" and "now" get entangled with one another. This can challenge history's notion of linear or evolutionary development and thus of progress. This is especially so, it has been argued (most famously in the case of the Nazi Holocaust), with "traumatic memory."[65] Here, the past resists historicization and assumes such presence that it lacks and denies any sense of its "pastness," thereby obliterating any differentiation or disjunction between past and present.[66] In memory, especially traumatic memory, moreover, the agency or autonomy of the subject is severely diminished, just as any sense of a narrator's mastery of the past is replaced by a sense of the incomprehensibility and therefore irreducibility of the past. Here the past can readily seem to be (the) present and something that will not pass away.

In memory work, it might also be argued, there can be a greater variety of pasts because perspective predominates. Narrators try to create accounts that are truthful to their past and so one gets many pasts, whereas the goal of the omniscient academic historian has been to produce one past, winnowing its records in order to discover that which he or she deems to be the most accurate.[67] At the same time, it has been argued, memory tends to particularize and individualize, in Gyanendra Pandey's words, "specifying sites and bodies that carry the marks of particular events, making [things] real in everyday, physical, nameable terms," whereas the historian largely seeks to generalize, thus tending to render the past relatively abstract.[68]

---

65 See, for example, Lawrence L. Langer, *Holocaust Testimonies: The Ruins of Memory* (New Haven, 1991).
66 Too much can be made of the past's presence in memory work. In other words, we should not lose sight of memory's discursivity, by which I mean the degree to which so much memory is shaped and thus re-presented by contemporary discourses, including history, most of which are closely connected to the politics of difference. As Luisa Passerini has observed, "memory is above all a form of representation" ("Memories between Silence and Oblivion," in Hodgkin and Radstone, eds., *Contested Pasts*, 238).
67 "*Collective* memory," however, tends to lessen the range of perspectives, as Peter Novick and others have pointed out. See Novick, *The Holocaust in American Life* (Boston, 1999), 3–4.
68 Pandey, *Remembering Partition*, 67, 88.

Memory work's tendency to multiply the number of historical accounts is all the greater because so much of it is bound up with a form of identity politics other than that of one of its earlier forms, that of the nation. It thus tends to favor a different direction in democratic politics from the one history has traditionally supported, toward diversity rather than a unitary nation-state.[69]

Divided Histories

The impact of *Bringing Them Home*, as I have indicated already, owed much to the fact that its historical narrative was predominantly formed by memory work rather than history work, especially memory work that took the form of testimony or witnessing.[70] It was this that gave the past of the stolen generations a presence that no conventional historical work had been able to bestow on the colonial past. Consequently, *Bringing Them Home* caused considerable unsettlement in various quarters. On the one hand, conservatives were troubled, indeed outraged, by its historical interpretation of a recent Australian past. They were vexed, though, not only by the different past this history presented but also by the different relationship *to* the past that it presenced. As such, they and the recently elected federal conservative government, which had already launched an attack on so-called politically correct history that allegedly casts Australia's history in overly "critical" rather than "monumental" terms (to apply Nietzsche's typology of history),[71] worked hard to try and distance the present from this intractable past. On the other hand, the inquiry's call for an apology became the cause célèbre for the reconciliation movement, all the more so because of the conservative Commonwealth government's refusal to give one.

Of particular interest here, though, is the fact that the Commission's history-making, like that of the South African Truth and Reconciliation Commission, attracted considerable criticism across the political spectrum. The Human Rights and Equal Opportunity Commission had, as noted earlier, encouraged a historical approach that emphasized testimony and

---

69 Some of my argument in this and the two preceding paragraphs is informed by Pandey, *Remembering Partition*, 189, and Chakrabarty, "Museums in Late Democracies," *Humanities Research* 9, 1 (2002): 7–8, 10.
70 As I discuss in "'Learning About the Truth': The Stolen Generations Narrative," in Attwood and Magowan, eds., *Telling Stories*, the stolen generations narrative that had emerged in the 1980s was the product of a collaboration between memory and history work but in the 1990s it was increasingly determined by memory and discourses other than history.
71 This assault can be regarded as merely the most recent new conservative attack on the new Australian history, for which see Attwood, *Telling the Truth*, chapters 1 and 3.

thus a notion of historical knowledge that construes truth as a matter of subjectivity and so perspective, but at the same time the overview it presented in *Bringing Them Home* was done in the name of traditional notions of historical truth and so presented as objective, impartial, and authoritative. Academic historians (such as myself) claimed that there were serious weaknesses in the Commission's historical work,[72] just as historians have alleged in reference to the Truth and Reconciliation Commission's history-making.[73] It was objected that memory and history are similar in many respects but also quite different and that the distinction between historical truth and falsehood would be endangered if one lost sight of this.[74] We had a point: conventional historical work is, generally speaking, more reliable than memorial work in establishing what happened in the past.[75]

Such criticism, however, tended to overlook or ignore the point already noted: that the historical truths of *Bringing Them Home* were rather different from those produced by conventional history, referring more to the past's residue in the present than to the pastness of the past.[76] This, then, raised

---

72 See Attwood, "The Stolen Generations and Genocide: Robert Manne's *In Denial*," *Aboriginal History* 25 (2001): 163–72; Attwood, "Learning About the Truth": 208–11.

73 See Colin Bundy, "The Beast of the Past: History and the TRC," in Wilmot James and Linda van de Vijwer, eds., *After the TRC: Reflections on Truth and Reconciliation in South Africa* (Athens, 2000), 14–15, 17–19.

74 This anxiety is apparent elsewhere. Notable examples include Peter Novick, Charles Maier, and Kerwin Lee Klein. Maier and Klein have referred pejoratively to "the memory industry," expressing their fears that it is a discourse that threatens to displace history and arguing that its rise marks "a retreat from transformative politics" (Maier, "A Surfeit of Memory: Reflections on History, Melancholy and Denial," *History and Memory* 5 (1993): 150; Klein, "On the Emergence of Memory in Historical Discourse," *Representations* 69 (2000): 127; Novick, *The Holocaust in American Life*, 1–15). Klein undoubtedly has a point, though, when he notes that excessive claims are now made on behalf of memory: "Memory thus differentiates itself from 'traditional' and 'formal historical discourse' that has been 'sanctioned or valorised by institutional frameworks.'... [H]istory and memory break apart into an unstable chain of antinomies: History is modernism, the state, science, imperialism, andocentrism, a tool of oppression; memory is postmodernism, the 'symbolically excluded', 'the body', 'a healing device and a tool for redemption'. A series of inversions provide drama: slave defeats master, female topples male, and the local resists the universal. The language enlists 'postmodernism' in the service of transcendence, emplotted as a narrative process of 'trauma', 'catharsis' and 'redemption'" ("Emergence of Memory": 138). Nevertheless, it is evident that Klein's remarks are themselves quite excessive.

75 Accounts drawing on memory often suffer from serious omissions, inaccuracies, and distortions since they "tell us not just what people did, but what they wanted to do, what they believed they were doing, what they now think they did" (Alessandro Portelli, "The Peculiarities of Oral History," *History Workshop Journal* 12 (1981): 99–100).

76 This is also true of the South African Truth and Reconciliation Commission. It claimed several kinds of truth – which it called "factual or forensic truth; personal or narrative truth; social or 'dialogue truth'... and healing or restorative truth" – were operating in its hearings (Truth and Reconciliation Commission, *Truth and Reconciliation of South Africa Report* (Cape Town, 1998), vol. 1, chapter 5, para. 29). For a critical discussion of this, see Deborah Posel, "The TRC Report: What Kind of History? What Kind of Truth?" in Posel and Graeme Simpson, eds., *Commissioning the Past: Understanding South Africa's Truth and Reconciliation Commission* (Witwatersrand, 2002), 147–72.

the thorny question of how one negotiates different historical narratives in a pluralist liberal democracy.

"Reconciling" Histories

This clash of historical truths illustrates the phenomenon this chapter has been exploring: the fact that at least two radically different forms of history-making were and are at work in many democratic nation-states today. They cannot be reconciled without considerable epistemic violence being done to one or the other. The problem with shared history, I have argued, is that the state insists that everyone should have the same kind of history. It forecloses on reconciliation by insisting that all parties should adopt the conflicted past that actually divides them. In other words, it demands a shared future in which different histories and different historical identities dissolve into one another.

This is a badly flawed conception of reconciliation. As long as any society contains at least two cultural traditions, one that identifies with the colonizers and another with the colonized, it is inevitable that there will be conflicting attitudes, opinions, and feelings about the colonial past.[77] It also rests on a questionable assumption that the most important truths are factual, empirically proven ones instead of moral and interpretive ones. Rather than bemoan these realities, it makes more sense to acknowledge that the liberal ideal of a unified nation-state, like the old academic historian's ideal of objectivity, is but a noble dream and to recognize that different histories are maintained because "[historical] truth is tied to . . . collective identity."[78] As Michael Ignatieff has commented: "The idea that reconciliation depends on shared truth about the past is possible. But truth is related to identity. What you believe is true depends, in some measure, on who you believe yourself to be. . . . People do not easily or readily surrender the premises upon which their lives are based. . . . Resistance to historical truth is a function of group identity."[79]

This means, as Richard Mulgan has argued, that any reconciliation between Aboriginal and non-Aboriginal people "cannot be expected to [involve agreement on] all aspects of the past." A more sensible path, he

---

77 Richard Mulgan, "Citizenship and Legitimacy in Postcolonial Australia," in Nicolas Peterson and Will Sanders, eds., *Citizenship and Indigenous Australians: Changing Conceptions and Possibilities* (Melbourne, 1998), 193.
78 Heribert Adam and Kanya Adam, "The Politics of Memory in Divided Societies," in James and van de Vijwer, eds., *After the TRC*, 44.
79 Michael Ignatieff, *The Warrior's Honor: Ethnic War and the Modern Conscience* (London, 1999), 173–4, 185.

suggests, "is to admit the continuing existence of some conflicting cultural perspectives but to moderate and accommodate them through shared commitment to certain political values, such as democratic principles and human rights, including Aboriginal rights." In this context, he concludes, "the key terms should not be words like 'reconciliation' and 'consensus', which imply the transcending of disagreement, so much as 'accommodation' and 'compromise', terms that recognise, and legitimate, the existence of conflicting values and interests, though within a framework of peaceful mutual adjustment."[80]

What does this mean for historical work? First, historians (and other social scientists) need to recognize the limits of their own discipline(s), accepting that history is, in Dipesh Chakrabarty's words, "only one among [many] ways of remembering the past" and that it is a "limited good." Second, historians must curb their discipline's imperial tendencies toward other ways of relating (to) the past. By acknowledging these matters, Chakrabarty suggests, we will be better able to allow "a certain measure of equality between [our] histories and other constructions of the past."[81] For their part, the producers of subaltern or Aboriginal pasts might recognize the limited good of their narratives, acknowledging that if history has a tendency to impede understanding of the ongoing influence of the past and its contemporary meanings for people, memory has a tendency to cloud understanding of that past as it was. Most importantly, we will have to consider *how* different historical narratives can talk to one another and *what* they are going to be talking about so that there can be a basis for ongoing dialogue – for mutually unsettling exchanges of diverse pasts and histories – rather than the development of a final settlement, some final (re)solution of the past for the present.

---

80 Mulgan, "Citizenship and Legitimacy," 193. Mulgan, as Morton would argue, tends to play down the fact that "peaceful mutual adjustment" cannot readily be achieved without conceptual violence and social antagonism ("Abortive Redemption": 240).
81 Chakrabarty, *Provincialising Europe*, 106, 112. Arguably, historical practitioners also need to allow for the unsettlement that an encounter with traumatic pasts can cause. Dominick LaCapra has emphasized "[t]he role of empathy and empathic unsettlement" in historical research, writing: "Opening oneself to empathic unsettlement is...a desirable affective dimension of inquiry that complements and supplements empirical analysis. Empathy is important in attempting to understand traumatic events and victims.... It places in jeopardy...totalising narratives that deny the trauma that called them into existence by prematurely...harmonising events, and often recuperating the past in terms of uplifting messages or optimistic, self-serving scenarios.... Without discounting all forms of critical distance (even numbing 'objectivity') that may be necessary for research, judgment, and self-preservation, one may also appeal to the role of empathy in raising doubts about positivistic or formalistic accounts that both deny one's transferential implication in the problems one treats and attempt to create maximal distance from them – and those involved in them" ("Trauma, Absence, Loss," *Critical Inquiry* 25 (1999): 722–3).

10

Fitting Aotearoa into New Zealand

Politico-Cultural Change in a Modern Bicultural Nation

RICHARD S. HILL AND BRIGITTE BÖNISCH-BREDNICH

Reparations and *Rangatiratanga*

At the burial in 2001 of a leading Maori tribal negotiator, his successor looked straight at the New Zealand government representatives and issued a statement resonant of challenge: "Just because we have gained some compensation for past injustices, don't think we are going to go away."[1] His people, Waikato-Tainui, had reached a major settlement with the New Zealand state/Crown in recompense for past injustices perpetrated on them. This had been a pioneering breakthrough in processes developed to address demands for historical justice, which had been escalating in Maoridom since a vibrant politico-cultural "Maori Renaissance" from the early 1970s.[2] The spokesperson was, however, highlighting a common tribal perspective: that a compensation package could constitute only the *beginning* of a process of "transitional justice" for Maori.[3]

---

1 Field notes of personal observation by the authors, Hopuhopu, Waikato, 2001.
2 See Douglas Graham, *Trick or Treaty?* (Wellington, 1997), 73–9, for a summary from the perspective of the minister in charge of Treaty of Waitangi negotiations at the time of the settlement, and David McCan, *Whatiwhatihoe: The Waikato Raupatu Claim* (Wellington, 2001), for a tribally approved version.
3 "Transitional justice" is in one sense an anachronistic term for the New Zealand situation, insofar as it is applied primarily (in the words of the International Center for Transitional Justice) to "societies emerging from [relatively recent] repressive rule or armed conflict" or to recent directional change from "evil" toward liberalization and democracy: Ruti G. Teitel, *Transitional Justice* (Oxford, 2000), vii, 3–5. However, the Center includes in its terms of reference "established democracies where historical injustices or systemic abuse remain unresolved" (Mission Statement, *Annual Report 2003/4*), and this is applicable to New Zealand and similar jurisdictions. For an introduction to some relevant comparative literature, see Vincent O'Malley, *Indigenous Land Rights in an International Context: A Survey of the Literature Relating to Australia, New Zealand and North America* (Wellington, 2000). Both the ideology and methods of Maori struggles over the last several decades have been informed by, and have informed, the actions and aspirations of indigenous peoples elsewhere. They have also been characterized by the same imperatives as those seeking transitional justice: the "moral reconstruction of political relationships through truth telling, reparations and forgiveness" (Mark R. Amstutz, *The*

His assertion referred particularly to his tribal confederation's ongoing quest for *rangatiratanga*, or autonomy. It was a statement of intent reflecting the continuing Maori search for the full and integral reinsertion of Aotearoa (the principal indigenous name for New Zealand) into the politico-cultural life of the nation. Through such words, and in similar sentiments expressed by countless other Maori, the tribes were saying that the achievement of substantial reparations, while necessary, was not sufficient to fully reconcile Maori and non-Maori and heal the wounds of the past.

In the modern nation-building project that New Zealand has been in effect engaged in for more than two decades, a country formerly regarded as the most loyal and homogeneously "British" of the colonies/postcolonies of the Empire and Commonwealth has *officially* become bicultural. This reflects profound changes in social attitudes among the dominant white (*pakeha*) population, including its response to the Maori Renaissance. Historians have been involved in the evolution of such changes and in official actions that have flowed from them, especially those touching on race relations.[4] Since the late 1980s, the Crown's responses to pressure from Maori and their *pakeha* supporters have focused largely on the question of compensation for its historical breaches of the Treaty of Waitangi, the 1840 founding document of the nation.[5]

The reparations exercise has produced some degree of backlash from within the *pakeha* population and is far from complete; the most realistic predictions see finality as being at least two decades away. It has been and remains a fraught and difficult process. That said, the role of Treaty-based compensation settlements in the emergence of Aotearoa/New Zealand, a combined name frequently used to describe an increasingly bicultural

---

Healing of Nations: The Promise and Limits of Political Forgiveness [Lanham, Md., 2005], 16); the search for a political process that combines achieving justice with "social stability and reconciliation" (Neil J. Kritz, ed., *Transitional Justice: How Emerging Societies Reckon with Former Regimes: Volume 1, General Considerations* (Washington, D.C., 1995), xiii); and ways to close "open accounts from the past" (Jon Elster, *Closing the Books: Transitional Justice in Historical Perspective* [Cambridge, 2004], ix). Resonances with transitional justice issues around the globe can be seen in the many references to "healing" in recent New Zealand official and unofficial sources: see Robert Consedine and Joanna Consedine, *Healing Our History: The Challenge of the Treaty of Waitangi* (Auckland, 2001), and Office of Treaty Settlements, *Healing the Past, Building a Future: A Guide to Treaty of Waitangi Claims and Negotiations with the Crown* (Wellington, 2002), and cf. for example, chapter 9, "Healing from the Past," in Priscilla B. Hayner, *Unspeakable Truths: Facing the Challenge of Truth Commissions* (New York, 2001).

4 Historical revisionists on race relations matters, such as the late Michael King, became well-known national figures. The highest profiled of these is James Belich, whose televised version of his *The New Zealand Wars and the Victorian Interpretation of Racial Conflict* (Auckland, 1986) brought new ways of looking at race relations history to sizable audiences of New Zealanders.

5 Claudia Orange, *The Treaty of Waitangi* (Wellington, 1987) and her updated account *An Illustrated History of the Treaty of Waitangi* (Wellington, 2004); for a brief overview of Crown-Maori Treaty relations, see Bryan Gilling and Vincent O'Malley, *The Treaty of Waitangi in New Zealand History* (Wellington, 2000).

country, has been and can be only a contributory one. Finding a viable form of accommodating Maori aspirations for autonomy needs to be the fundamental quest. While historians of Crown-Maori relations will no doubt be required to remain focused on the processes of proving the case for reparations, there is considerable potential for them to more fully engage in the complex discourses relating to attaining *rangatiratanga* and thereby contribute to the emergence of a truly biculturalist sociopolitical mode of life in a reconstituted, postcolonial nation of Aotearoa/New Zealand.

Maori and *Pakeha*

One of the most iconic beliefs of *pakeha* until the last quarter of the twentieth century was that New Zealand had experienced excellent, even perfect, race relations for most of the time since 1840 and that this happy state of affairs constituted "the best race relations in the world."[6] As an American academic commented in 1960, the "tourist is reminded time and again that the Maori enjoys complete equality with the European; that there is no colour bar and no racial prejudice or discrimination in New Zealand."[7] This national myth helped disguise the fact that New Zealand's indigenous people had been overwhelmed and marginalized by the political economy and culture of the West. From the beginning of the colony, official policy decreed that Maori should and would fully assimilate to the "superior" culture and eventually disappear as a people. The "excellent race relations" discourse presupposed that this was what was actually happening. With Maori perceived (after they had been militarily defeated) to be on an inevitable and ultimately terminal retreat before Anglo-Saxon civilization and progress, the institutions and people of the dominant culture could formally be magnanimous and relatively nondiscriminatory. Indeed, official and quasi-official statements in the century after the Anglo-Maori Wars (which finished in the early 1870s) would depict New Zealand as 98.5 percent British, counting Maori in that figure.[8]

---

6 See, for random examples, J. B. Condliffe, *A Short History of New Zealand* (Christchurch, 1927), 1; I. L. G. Sutherland, "Maori and Pakeha," in Horace Belshaw, ed., *New Zealand* (Berkeley, 1947), 48, 72; F. L. W. Wood, *This New Zealand* (Hamilton, 1946), 166; Keith Sinclair, "Why Are Race Relations in New Zealand Better Than in South Africa, South Australia, or South Dakota?" *New Zealand Journal of History* 5, 2 (October 1971): 121–7.

7 David P. Ausubel, *The Fern and the Tiki: An American View of New Zealand National Character, Social Attitudes, and Race Relations* (New York, 1965), 150; see also Harry A. Kersey Jr., "Opening a Discourse on Race Relations in New Zealand: *The Fern and the Tiki* Revisited," *Journal of New Zealand Studies* (October 2002): 1–18.

8 For this and other key race relations discussions, see James Belich, *Paradise Reforged: A History of the New Zealanders from the 1880s to the Year 2000* (Auckland, 2001), the second part of Belich's revisionist general history of New Zealand (the first volume was published in 1996: *Making Peoples: A History of the New Zealanders from Polynesian Settlement to the End of the Nineteenth Century*); for the 98.5 percent

Pakeha in general, and many academics and officials in particular, had failed to notice that Maori, generally out of sight in their isolated rural villages, had not disappeared beneath "Britishness." Demographic changes, especially "race recovery" after the devastation of the nineteenth century and then a massive urban migration following World War II, began to bring Maori back into the public spotlight. This was even more the case following the beginnings of the Maori Renaissance, assisted by the fact that it reflected international as well as internal indigenous developments. Under pressure from both Maori radicalism and a liberalizing *pakeha* electorate, the Crown gradually and grudgingly came to abandon its assimilationist policy. The retreat was definitive by 1990, when official attitudes toward the commemoration of "150 years of nationhood" generally reflected a "Two People, One Nation" paradigm. This was an enormous change from the previous "One People" rhetoric, which had been based on the words of the founding lieutenant-governor of the colony at Waitangi in 1840: *He iwi tahi tatou* – "We are now one people."[9]

By 1990, then, the country had been officially deemed bicultural.[10] Insofar as this reflected a Crown response to the pressure of the Maori Renaissance, it was narrowly politically driven. But, more broadly, it reflected a context of major alterations in *pakeha* culture and worldview. Such paradigmatic changes were themselves in part a response to Maori politico-cultural reassertion, backed up by dissemination of revisionist historical findings. Citizens of European origin had increasingly been discovering that New Zealand's past had not just a Eurocentric international heritage, but also a significant antipodean/South Pacific dimension. While the first nationalist history was published in 1959,[11] it took the aftermath of Britain's 1973 decision to "join Europe" (and thereby accelerate the weakening of colonial ties to the "Mother Country"[12]) for New Zealand–focused history to thrive.

It took even longer for Maori to gain a prominent and continuous position in the historiography and stories of the nation.[13] For decades,

---

reference, 232. For other significant modern general histories, see Geoffrey Rice, ed., *The Oxford History of New Zealand* (Auckland, 1992), an updated version of a 1981 publication edited by W. H. Oliver and B. R. Williams; and Michael King, *The Penguin History of New Zealand* (Auckland, 2003).

9 William Renwick, ed., *Sovereignty and Indigenous Rights: The Treaty of Waitangi in International Contexts* (Wellington, 1991), 199; Alan Ward, *A Show of Justice: Racial "Amalgamation" in Nineteenth Century New Zealand* (Auckland, 1995), 42.

10 Brigitte Bönisch-Brednich and Richard Hill, "From Monoculturalism to Biculturalism in Twentieth-Century New Zealand/Aotearoa," *Cultures of the Commonwealth* (Spring 2002): 29–47.

11 Keith Sinclair, *A History of New Zealand* (Harmondsworth, 1959).

12 Belich, *Paradise Reforged*, part 5.

13 For early examples of revisionist history aimed at a popular audience, see Dick Scott, *Ask That Mountain: The Story of Parihaka* (Auckland, 1975); Tony Simpson, *Te Riri Pakeha* (Martinborough, 1979); and Angela Ballara, *Proud to Be White? A Survey of Pakeha Prejudice in New Zealand* (Auckland, 1986). For an interpretation of a "race relations historiographical revolution," see

scholars had generally accepted the interrelated myths of the assimilated Maori and excellent race relations. But demographic change and then the Maori Renaissance made it increasingly difficult to ignore the fact that Maori continued to exist as a collective identity; as a tribal-based people, albeit with many and varied organizational modes; and as independent agents determined to resist powerful official and dominant culture forces attempting to suppress their sociopolitical organization and culture. Not only had they never abandoned their identification as Maori, they had never forgotten their history of colonial subjugation and were determined that the Crown should acknowledge and address its past actions and omissions. They had orally passed on tribal stories from generation to generation, many stressing dispossession of indigenous resources by the Crown and settlers. From the time of the Maori Renaissance, these fed into an increasing *pakeha* awareness that New Zealand's past and present were far from that of near-perfect race relations, that New Zealand in fact shared the subjugation/resistance rhythms of other colonial and postcolonial nations.[14]

Maori and Crown

It was the Treaty of Waitangi, signed by Maori chiefs with Crown representatives, which had long been the hegemonic symbol of excellence in ethnic interaction. Academic and popular history had focused on its first article, which (in the English version)[15] transferred sovereignty to Britain, and on its third (and final) article, which gave Maori the same rights as *pakeha*. For the indigenous people, however, Article II was the key clause. It asserted, inter alia, their full rights to possession of all material and other resources so long as they wished to retain them. The Maori protest movement that

---

Lorenzo Veracini, *Negotiating a Bicultural Past: An Historiographical "Revolution" in 1980s Aotearoa/New Zealand* (Wellington, 2001).

14 For recent Australasian discussions of such processes, see Klaus Neumann, Nicholas Thomas, and Hilary Eriksen, eds., *Quicksands: Foundational Histories in Australia and Aotearoa New Zealand* (Sydney, 1999); Bain Attwood and Fiona Magowan, eds., *Telling Stories: Indigenous History and Memory in Australia and New Zealand* (Wellington, 2001); Augie Fleras and Paul Spoonley, *Recalling Aotearoa: Indigenous Politics and Ethnic Relations in New Zealand* (Auckland, 1999); and Andrew Sharp and Paul McHugh, eds., *Histories, Power and Loss: Uses of the Past – A New Zealand Commentary* (Wellington, 2001). For an example of revisionist history utilizing Maori oral as well as written sources, see Judith Binney, *Redemption Songs: A Life of Te Kooti Arikirangi Te Turuki* (Auckland, 1995).

15 The English and Maori versions were neither straight translations nor fully compatible. For a sampling of literature on this problematic issue, see Bruce Biggs, "Humpty Dumpty and the Treaty of Waitangi," in I. H. Kawharu, ed., *Waitangi: Maori and Pakeha Perspectives of the Treaty of Waitangi* (Auckland, 1989); Paul Moon, *Te Ara Ki Te Tiriti; The Path to the Treaty of Waitangi* (Auckland, 2002); Richard Dawson, *The Treaty of Waitangi and the Control of Language* (Wellington, 2001); and D. F. McKenzie, *Oral Culture, Literacy and Print in Early New Zealand: The Treaty of Waitangi* (Wellington, 1985).

burgeoned in the 1970s–1980s came to center its demands on the Crown's breaches of this clause.

These violations had come about in essentially three broad ways in the nineteenth century (though they continued through the twentieth), the net result being general socioeconomic marginalization of Maori:

1. large-scale, and often pressured, purchase of land from the 1840s through the 1860s by the Crown, without the state fulfilling its contractual agreements, such as setting aside an adequate amount of land for Maori to participate in the new capitalist economy;
2. invasion of regions whose tribes refused to sell their land in the 1860s, with extensive land confiscations following bloodshed; and
3. the establishment and operations, from 1865, of the Native Land Court, which was created to individualize the customary, collective land tenure of Maori, thereby paving the way for further extensive land alienation.[16]

By 1900, Maori had lost most of their land, and their population had fallen to a postcontact low of some 40,000.

But the tribes devised fight-back strategies that were ultimately successful. In the 2006 census, those identifying themselves primarily as Maori numbered 565,329 out of a total national population of 4,143,282.[17] Maori comprise not only a numerically significant proportion of the populace but also a powerful force in society and politics. It is this strength that has resulted in even conservative governments accepting that a reparations policy is essential for a peaceful and progressive future for the nation. In the 1990s, the Crown negotiated with Maori to transfer more than half a billion dollars in land, money, and other resources to several claimant groups, and further settlements followed or are to come. Just as significantly as material reparations, cultural redress has been included in the compensation processes: protection of sacred sites, comanagement of natural resources, renaming of geographical features, and the like.[18] Moreover, for many Maori, the most important breakthrough has been the willingness of the Crown to apologize for its past breaches of the Treaty of Waitangi.

From the very beginning of the Treaty settlements processes, Maori have, however, seen material compensation, cultural redress, and apology

---

16 For a general discussion of Treaty violations and their long-term ramifications, see Alan Ward, *An Unsettled History: Treaty Claims in New Zealand Today* (Wellington, 1999).
17 Statistics New Zealand, *2006 Census of Population and Dwellings* (Wellington, 2007). While a Maori-*pakeha* binarism is useful for analytical and self-identification purposes, there are many complexities in New Zealand's cultural and ethnic dynamics; see, for example, Alan Webster, *Spiral of Values* (Hawera, 2001), or (for a typical "popular" article) Margot Butcher, "What Is Maori? Who Is Pakeha?" *North & South* (August 2003): 37–47. In the 2006 national census, a total of 643,977 people declared themselves to be of Maori descent.
18 Office of Treaty Settlements, 96–144.

as only part of their goal. Article II of the Treaty, which indigenes have always regarded as the most significant, promised *te tino rangatiratanga* – "full chieftainship" in the English version. Maori interpreted this broadly as a promise of politico-cultural partnership with the Crown. Tribal struggles with the Crown in the nineteenth century reflected a determination to force it to respect *rangatiratanga*. Through such means Maori sought to gain some form of autonomy as a people, to continue "Aotearoa" as well as to adjust to "New Zealand."

Throughout the first three-quarters of the twentieth century, although both *pakeha* society and scholars did not generally notice, Maori continued to assert the right for their social organization and culture to survive and thrive independently and on its own terms. They sought collective autonomous power over their own destinies, in fact, even during the difficult times of the great urban migration. Their methods and goals were necessarily located within the broad parameters of New Zealand's Western economy, political system, and culture, but Maori were nevertheless distinctively self-determinationist.[19]

From colonial times, the Crown had responded to intense Maori pressure with settlements that provided small amounts of compensation. Early in the twentieth century, for example, "landless natives" from the South Island were given some reserves; in the 1920s, central North Island "lakes tribes" were provided with revenue-based settlements; in the 1940s–1950s, "full and final" monetary compensation was negotiated with some tribal groups.[20] A key early response to the Maori Renaissance was the 1975 establishment of a standing commission of enquiry, the Waitangi Tribunal, to make recommendations to the Crown on contemporary grievances. In 1985, under pressure from *pakeha* and the Tribunal as well as from Maori, parliament empowered it to hear claims dating back to 1840. From 1989, processes of direct negotiations that bypassed the tribunal were also pioneered. The Crown all the while considered – and continues to consider – that a reparations approach was the key way by which Maori could move from "grievance mode to development mode."[21]

---

19 For a sampling of Maori versions of the long search for *rangatiratanga*, see Ranginui Walker, *Ka Whawhai Tonu Matou: Struggle Without End* (Auckland, 1990); Mason Durie, *Te Mana, Te Kawanatanga: The Politics of Maori Self-Determination* (Auckland, 1998); and Ani Mikaere, *Maori and Self-Determination in Aotearoa/New Zealand* (Hamilton, 2000).

20 Richard S. Hill, *State Authority, Indigenous Autonomy: Crown-Maori Relations in New Zealand/Aotearoa 1900–1950* (Wellington, 2004), and *Settlements of Major Maori Claims in the 1940s: A Preliminary Historical Investigation* (Wellington, 1989).

21 These were the words used by Tamihana Tupoutahi Te Winitana, adviser to the minister in charge of Treaty of Waitangi negotiations in the 1990s, Rt. Hon Sir Douglas Graham, and they became part of the official vocabulary of the times.

Amid a great deal of tough bargaining, progress on settlements was rapid during the 1990s. At the beginning of the decade, for example, the Waikato-Tainui confederation, headed by Sir Robert Mahuta (with whose *tangi*/funeral this chapter commenced), was offered a $20 million package in "full and final" compensation for nineteenth-century invasion, conquest, and confiscation of great tracts of fertile land. Within four years, it had pushed the Crown up to a final offer worth a total of $170 million and settled for that sum in 1995. This and other settlements were effected in the context of protracted hearings and negotiations as well as continuous publicity on Treaty of Waitangi issues.

As a result of compensation-based processes and publicity, popular discourse has accommodated a continuing process of demystification about aspects of the country's past and present. No longer are "excellent race relations" endemic to the received wisdom about the past, for example. Although there can be significant backlashes against Treaty claims and settlements, and even a "Treaty fatigue" among generally sympathetic *pakeha*,[22] there seems to be an emergent societal consensus that the wrongs of the past need to be righted. Most Maori leaders and activists, in turn, have both retreated from the confrontational slogans and tactics of earlier protest-orientated movements and adjusted their demands to the potentially attainable. Along with *pakeha* liberals, Maori tribal and other leaders now tend to employ the language of healing, reconciliation, and mutual respect between the two peoples and their cultures.[23] The Crown's willingness to address the issue of reparations – although its motivations are mainly expedient responses to sociopolitical problems – has, in short, been a relatively successful initiative from the perspective of social peace and relative justice.

The compensation approach has also dovetailed with government policies aimed at "closing the [socioeconomic] gaps" or "reducing inequalities" between Maori and *pakeha*. The myth of excellent race relations had become entrenched partly because before the urban migration Maori were seldom encountered in everyday life by *pakeha*. As individuals and families uprooted from tribal social control structures flocked to population centers, massive

---

22 For a typical newspaper article on this, see *New Zealand Herald*, February 5, 2003 ("Survey Shows New Zealanders Suffering Treaty Fatigue"). References to Treaty weariness are endemic in media and political coverage; for example, in the Radio New Zealand program *Insight*, February 2, 2003, or the speech of a Maori minister of the Crown, Hon. John Tamihere, in parliament on August 27, 2003.

23 Themes of healing wounds have been used at the governmental level, sometimes controversially: for example, Tariana Turia, "Trauma and Colonisation: Speech to the 9th Annual Australasian Society for Traumatic Stress Studies" (typescript, March 9, 2002), which received great publicity.

societal adjustment problems arose. There was little government assistance for a collectively organized people to adapt to the individualized social order of the cities, and crime and disorder among Maori escalated. When the national economy eventually ran into difficulties, especially after New Zealand ceased to be London's key supplier of meat and dairy products, urban Maori, who constituted much of the poorest paid and "most dispensable" of the proletariat, suffered disproportionately. Maori came even more to dominate the adverse social indicators relating to such key matters as health, crime, incarceration rates, income, welfarism, housing conditions, and unemployment. The rubric of splendid race relations was even further exposed as a national myth.

Eventually, governments began to respond to Maori assertions and demands, to adverse statistics relating to Maoridom, and to *pakeha* backlash against Maori crime and disorder. Among these responses, increasing efforts to close the gaps featured prominently. By the late 1980s, the Crown's efforts to address the socioeconomic differentials between Maori and *pakeha* came to incorporate the idea of assisting the reestablishment of tribal resource bases. The provision of compensation to tribes that had proven their historical claims would, it was argued, be a useful component of such restoration. In this way the quest for historical justice became entangled with the Crown's aims to effect greater equality, at least equality of opportunity, between the two principal peoples of New Zealand.[24]

The Maori Quest for Autonomy

Both compensation and socioeconomic approaches represented a huge change from the state's previous policy of complacent assimilationism. Whatever the state's motivation might have been, neither of the new approaches was posited on the ultimate disappearance of Maoridom. But they both missed what most *pakeha* had also missed: the central importance to Maori of attaining autonomy/*rangatiratanga*. In short, they registered neither the voices of Maoridom nor some key findings of the new historiography. The latter had, at least implicitly, endorsed the perspective of Maori spokespersons that collective control over their own destiny was of greater significance than policies of compensation and/or moving toward socioeconomic parity. Even if such policies were to be totally successful – and

---

24 In Treaty discourse "equality" is generally seen to be a Crown duty under Article III; it can alternatively be interpreted as a prerequisite for improving "order and regularity" in society.

they remain far from this, actually or potentially – reparations and socio-economic parity could never form more than a subset of the overarching Maori aspiration for self-determination.[25]

To its considerable surprise, the Crown has been finding out that, at the same time as it needs to defend its indigenous policies vigorously against *pakeha* backlash both inside and outside parliament, compensation and greater equality, although significant, are far from sufficient. It has responded only slowly and reluctantly to that discovery, and its view of Maori has remained trapped within past paradigms exemplified by earlier generations of historians who never understood the imperatives of Maoridom. When revisionist history, including autonomist interpretations, penetrated the Treaty settlement processes, it was able to do so partly because its findings tended to resonate with the record of indigenous oral testimony.[26]

Indeed, in 1996, the Waitangi Tribunal became briefly more revisionist on the question of autonomy than most modern historians. With regard to the Maori claims in a significant region, it stated that

> through war, protest, and petition, the single thread that most illuminates the historical fabric of Maori and Pakeha contact has been the Maori determination to maintain Maori autonomy and the Government's desire to destroy it. Despite the vicissitudes of war and the damage caused by expropriation and tenure reform, [the Taranaki Maori] stand on autonomy has not changed. Nor can it, for it is that which all peoples in their native territories naturally possess.[27]

The Crown has remained skeptical of the validity of any such arguments, even when they are expressed more moderately and with much evidential backing. It brands assertions of autonomy as ideologically motivated, and this underpins its continued espousal of the official view, first expressed at the founding of the colony, that its sovereignty is indivisible. Yet the evidence is clear that Maori have always sought to operate Aotearoa within

---

25 See the Treaty process report by Richard S. Hill, "Autonomy and Authority: Rangatiratanga and the Crown in Twentieth Century New Zealand" (Wellington, 2000), for the period after midcentury. For much greater elaboration of this argument with regard to the first half of the twentieth century, refer to Hill, *State Authority*. For a brief summary of such an approach, see Richard S. Hill and Vincent O'Malley, "Das Streben der Maori nach Rangatiratanga (Autonomie)," in Hartmut Jäksch, ed., *Maori und Gesellschaft: Wissenschaftliche und literarische Essays* (Berlin, 2000) (also available as *The Maori Quest for Rangatiratanga/Autonomy, 1840–2000* [Wellington, 2000]).

26 The autonomy interpretation is not uncontested. Anthropologist Lyndsay Head, for example, has argued that while "autonomy is [now] the organising principle of the analysis of nineteenth-century Maori experience," this ignores Maori who were neutral or assisted the Crown and removes the concept of "rebellion" from the literature: "The Pursuit of Modernity in Maori Society: The Conceptual Bases of Citizenship in the Early Colonial Period," in Sharp and McHugh, eds., *Histories*, 97. Suffice to say here that the present authors' definitions of and writings relevant to autonomy address both issues identified by Head as being absent from the general literature.

27 Waitangi Tribunal, *The Taranaki Report: Kaupapa Tuatahi* (Wellington, 1996), 6.

New Zealand, to share power in some form with the state. A key Court of Appeal decision in 1987, related to protecting potential reparations resources from irretrievable alienation, gave Maori hope that *rangatiratanga* would soon be placed on the Crown's agenda; compensation could be used to assist tribes or other groups to establish autonomous control over their own affairs.

There was a brief period in 1990–1 when devolved governance was offered to tribes, but a change in government led to a rescinding of the measure. In any case, many Maori had questioned the motives behind the arrangement and the degree of autonomy it actually offered. History provided some guidance here. The limited degree of devolution proffered seemed to be replicating previous circumstances where the Crown had appropriated tribal organizational energies for its own purposes: officialized *Runanga* (councils) in the 1860s, Maori Councils from 1900, Maori war effort organizations in the two world wars, a Labour Party electoral alliance with (and absorption of) a mass pan-tribal movement from the 1930s, and various officially endorsed post-1945 organizations that were supposedly independent but were in fact far from it.[28]

More broadly, a number of Maori leaders have queried whether devolution of specific powers can be an adequate expression of Maori aspirations, given that the process necessarily operates within the parameters of the Crown's claim to indivisible sovereignty. Yet while the main political result arising from the 1987 judgment, the devolution experiment, fell far short of autonomy, its general results were not insignificant. Under Maori and judicial pressure, the government had become considerably more serious about addressing the need for reparations; potentially, greater pressure could force major concessions to *rangatiratanga*.

But this was the period when New Zealand was undergoing a right-wing political turn that trumpeted the state's withdrawal from as many aspects of public ownership and regulation as possible. There was a widespread (and justified) suspicion that the architects and operators of the country's neo-liberal policies were not interested in Maori aspirations at all. Their intentions were to hand the problems of Maoridom to Maori themselves to address, at the very time when their own policies were causing indigenes to suffer disproportionately in terms of unemployment and various other types of social distress. The minimal-state ideologues who had gained political

---

28 For some nineteenth-century appropriations, see Richard S. Hill, *Policing the Colonial Frontier: The Theory and Practice of Coercive Social and Racial Control in New Zealand, 1767–1867*, 2 vols. (Wellington, 1986), and Vincent O'Malley, *Agents of Autonomy: Maori Committees in the Nineteenth Century* (Wellington 1998). For an overview of twentieth-century Maori assertions and Crown appropriations, see Hill, "Autonomy and Authority," and for a brief summary of these from 1840 to 2000, see Hill and O'Malley, "Das Streben."

office were seen to be divesting themselves of problems they had exacerbated in the first place. They were "unburdening the welfare state" partly in the guise of addressing Maori aspirations.[29]

Whatever the motivations of the political decision makers, Maori quickly assessed that official devolution (in its 1990–1 and later, watered-down, versions) did not offer anything near self-determination for tribes or other groups. Some had already noted that while 1989's five *Principles for Crown Action on the Treaty of Waitangi* had a welcome "Principle of Redress," the "Rangatiratanga Principle" merely acknowledged the right of "self-management" for a tribe.[30] This meant little more than that Maori, collectively organized, had the right to run their own affairs within the existing law – just like any other group of citizens. There was some comfort that the Crown conceded that its overarching principle, *kawanatanga*/governance, needed to be "qualified" by *rangatiratanga*. But this seemed to do no more than endorse the Court of Appeal's guidelines that, in matters of interest to them, Maori should be consulted, and that this should be done in good faith and with an element of active protection of Treaty of Waitangi interests.

The *Principles for Crown Action* remain generally operative today – as guiding instruments of the political executive – complementing but effectively outweighing other principles emerging from the judiciary and the Waitangi Tribunal.[31] Maori demand much more. Principally, in effect, they seek a constitutional (or equivalent) change that represents the forging of a *meaningful* partnership. But the government has consistently and adamantly stated, as confirmed in 2003 by Prime Minister Helen Clark, that it will neither consider nor debate any such thing.[32] Over the past two decades, then, there has been a significant impasse between the Crown and tribal or other indigenous leaderships. Maori increasingly demand some significant form of autonomy, but the state remains unmoved. However, there does remain considerable hope in many quarters, both Maori and *pakeha*, that Maori aspirations can be addressed in a meaningful way.

---

29 Jane Kelsey has most cogently encapsulated Maori and leftist perspectives on this subject: see her *A Question of Honour? Labour and the Treaty, 1984–1989* (Wellington, 1990), and *The New Zealand Experiment: A World Model for Structural Adjustment?* (Auckland, 1995).
30 Department of Justice, *Principles for Crown Action on the Treaty of Waitangi* (Wellington, 1989).
31 Te Puni Kokiri, *He Tirohanga o Kawa ki te Tiriti o Waitangi: A Guide to the Principles of the Treaty of Waitangi as Expressed by the Courts and the Waitangi Tribunal* (Wellington, 2002). The *Principles for Crown Action* are often referred to by government ministers when they are asked in parliament to specify the principles of the Treaty, and they remain a guideline in many circumstances; for example, they have been adopted by Victoria University of Wellington.
32 For some suggestions regarding constitutional change, see Colin James, ed., *Building the Constitution* (Wellington, 2000); for prime ministerial comment, *Dominion Post*, February 6, 2003.

Embracing Biculturalism

Such an optimistic assessment rests largely on the huge changes that have taken place within *pakeha* culture over the last third of a century and their intersection with post-Renaissance Maoridom. As a result of profound intellectual, ideological, and cultural challenges to orthodox mores beginning in the 1960s, most New Zealanders have considerably altered their worldviews – and politicians have followed. A society that once virtually celebrated its conservatism and its colonial status has since 1980, to select just a few examples, banned all things nuclear, legalized homosexuality and abortion, greatly liberalized drinking laws, refused entry to racially selected sporting teams, removed the stigma attaching to such things as divorce and single parenthood, established civil unions as an alternative to traditional marriage, and, not least of all, embraced a working form of biculturalism.

The Crown's endorsement of biculturalism in the 1990 commemoration was one of many reflections of a gradual *pakeha* acceptance of a number of the arguments of the Maori Renaissance of the 1970s–1980s. Certainly, biculturalism remains a far from unproblematic concept, in both its official and unofficial manifestations. In their interactions with the indigenous people, for example, governments prefer to deal with tribes/*iwi* rather than with newer collectivities, such as pan-tribal Maori urban authorities, or with the subtribal entities (*hapu*) that generally form the organizational powerhouses of Maoridom.[33] This is one of many issues that foster tension in Crown–Maori relations.

Further difficulties are experienced between the state and many of its non-Maori constituents because of the Crown's relationship with Maori, however inadequate Maori might perceive this to be. There are many problems, for example, over official forms of biculturalism, with New Zealanders of European origin often deploring a bureaucratic political correctness that has created its own esoteric lexicon of euphemisms and acronyms. Pacific Island and "new immigrant" groups (especially those from Asia) are often bewildered by what they see as special treatment for a single ethnicity.

But that said, generally, and crucially, the great majority of the population has seemingly accepted bicultural modes of seeing and doing. On the available evidence, most New Zealanders have adopted the concept of "Two Peoples in One Nation." The two major peoples are doing more than

---

33 The *hapu* was the traditional social unit; larger groups gained greater coherence partly because of post-1840 exigencies (and in some cases the *whanau*/extended family formed the major operative unit of Maoridom): Angela Ballara, *Iwi: The Dynamics of Maori Tribal Organisation from c. 1769 to c. 1945* (Wellington, 1998).

just coexisting with a degree of respect for each other's culture. They are also mixing, melding, and intermarrying. Their cultures are envisaged as simultaneously operating both together and apart within the one nation.[34] General acceptance of biculturalist daily living has greatly contributed to societal acceptance of the need for reparations and for reducing racially based adverse social indicators in areas such as health, welfare, and education. *Pakeha*, then, have gone some way along with the Maori project of fitting Aotearoa back into New Zealand. This seems to hold out some hope of an ultimately successful adaptation of *rangatiratanga* within the political economy – of a successful reinsertion of Aotearoa within New Zealand.

Indeed, from an anthropological perspective, Maori cultural revival and the politics of reconciliation have shaped New Zealand's identity so much in the last third of a century that it is now legitimate to refer to the entity of New Zealand/Aotearoa.[35] This aspect of modern nation-building has helped the country adjust to the identity trauma of "abandonment" by the United Kingdom. New Zealand's loss of both its major (and guaranteed) market and its principal source of cultural sustenance for *pakeha* should not be underestimated.[36] This has sparked a prolonged and public debate. In the nation-building discourse, the various elements of a postcolonial nation are seeking, among other things, to redefine the country culturally, and reference to the former "Mother Country" is increasingly marginal. For example, discussion of what defines *pakeha* is prevalent – how Europeans, as whites were labeled for most of the country's history, became *pakeha* and to what extent that transformation reflects awareness of a "Maori otherness."[37]

Even if a number of non-Maori are uneasy about Maori culture and politics intruding publicly into their everyday lives, and even if many do not share the official enthusiasm for some forms of biculturalism, they have learned to live with Maori and their culture as part of a daily reality without resiling from or even reflecting on it to any great degree. Many would

---

34 This was symbolized in September 2003 when the Toi Whakaari/New Zealand Drama School presented *Troilus and Cressida*, setting it during the nineteenth-century New Zealand Wars and interspersing Maori language, song, and dance throughout the Shakespearean script; the production crew, and cast were multiethnic, mostly Maori and *pakeha*.
35 This and following paragraphs are based partly on the authors' fieldwork observations and discussions with colleagues at the Stout Research Centre for New Zealand Studies, Wellington. It might be noted that in our formulation of New Zealand/Aotearoa, New Zealand comes first, a reflection of the power relationship between state/*pakeha* and Maori, reserving Aotearoa/New Zealand as a description for a racially harmonious ideal. It might also be noted that Aotearoa is a contested term, even within Maoridom.
36 For the most sophisticated debate on this issue, see Belich, *Paradise Reforged*, Part 5.
37 Michael King, *Being Pakeha: An Encounter with New Zealand and the Maori Renaissance* (Auckland, 1988); Michael King, *Being Pakeha Now: Reflections and Recollections of a White Native* (Auckland, 1999).

be surprised, for example, to know the number of Maori words they use in everyday conversation. In the *Dictionary of New Zealand English*, some 12 percent of the main headword entries are of Maori origin, while the *New Zealand Oxford Dictionary* contains significant numbers of Maori words among its 12 percent of "New Zealandisms."[38] Words such as *iwi*, *hapu*, *whanau* (extended family), *powhiri* (welcome), *hui* (meeting), *utu* and *tapu* (customary laws), *mana* (status, standing), *whakapapa* (genealogy), *kaumatua* and *kuia* (male and female elders), *marae* (tribal meeting place), *taonga* (treasure), *wahi tapu* (sacred places), *koha* (donation), and *pa* and *kainga* (Maori settlements) are found in everyday conversation, newspapers, signposts, radio broadcasts, television shows, and so on.

One of the authors of this chapter recently observed considerable puzzlement on the faces of foreign tourists as the *pakeha* guide used words such as *kaitiaki* (guardian) as if they were unproblematic for his audience. *Pakeha*, in fact, routinely use Maori words to interpret their own lives and concerns to themselves and others. *Whanau*, for example, is often used to refer to a group of friends or work colleagues in addition to its more literal kinship reference to an extended family. Most official (and many unofficial) speeches routinely begin and end with Maori phrases. *Pakeha*, once widely considered a derogatory term, is now used by most New Zealanders of European descent to describe their own identity. Since 1990, it has been used as a self-descriptive term in censuses and other official documentation.

Kia ora, a flexible concept for "hello," "goodbye," "I agree," "all is well," and general affirmation, is ubiquitous in official and social life, whereas twenty-five years ago a telephone operator was officially and publicly censured for using it in the course of her official duties.[39] The relatively recent *pakeha* acceptance of an integral Maori role in sociopolitical life might be but a small phenomenon compared to the massive adaptation of Maoridom to the West. But the overt embodiment of Maoriness in everyday speech and conceptualizing is a reflection of an increasingly deeper integration of *tikanga Maori* (Maori customs) into *pakeha* society. Aotearoa has penetrated, to a greater or lesser extent, the mental and physical spaces, the functions and ceremonies, and the private and public arenas of New Zealand.

Along the way, white New Zealanders are becoming more familiar with and appreciative of the Maori world and *matauranga Maori* (indigenous

---

38 H. W. Orsman, ed., *The Dictionary of New Zealand English* (Auckland, 1997), vii; Tony Deverson and Graeme Kennedy, eds., *The New Zealand Oxford Dictionary* (South Melbourne, 2004). For an example of numerous works on the relatively recent impact of Maori on the English language in New Zealand, see John Macalister, "Trends in New Zealand English: Some Observations on the Presence of Maori Words in the Lexicon," *New Zealand English Journal* 13 (1999): 38–49.
39 In 1987 Maori became an official language of the country: Orange, *Illustrated History*, 161.

worldviews). Many *pakeha* have experience of *marae* and their associated complexes, especially the *wharenui*, or meetinghouse. This occurs in many different contexts: private functions, official ceremonies, cultural learning situations, hostings of visiting sports or cultural clubs, welcomes for visiting dignitaries, and so forth. Such familiarity has become all the more possible as Maori adapt their customs to a predominantly nonrural life, with *marae* and other institutions becoming established in the urban spaces. *Marae* are, indeed, increasingly being set up in government departments, hospitals, universities, and other institutions. On them, symbols and rituals of reconciliation and intercultural exchange are proclaimed and enacted. They are, in fact, in some ways major beachheads for the assertion of *rangatiratanga*; for example, *manuhiri* (visitors) need to follow *marae* protocols. In learning to respond appropriately to symbolic challenges, speeches of welcome, rules of debate, and so on, more and more *pakeha* are taking into account *matauranga* and *tikanga Maori. Marae*, in short, have become powerful sites of bicultural interaction and learning, complementing their traditional role as tribal headquarters of *rangatiratanga*.

Away from the intense focus of the *marae*, there are many other reflections of the reinsertion of Aotearoa into New Zealand, quite apart from obvious situations such as increasing attention to and respect for Maori culture in schooling and other training circumstances. The mapped landscape is changing, for example, partly as a result of reparations packages. Compensation in the form of cultural redress frequently includes, for instance, the renaming of sacred *maunga* (mountains) or other geographical features. This goes to the heart of the Maori worldview: incorporating Taranaki and Aoraki into the names, respectively, of Mounts Egmont and Cook, epitomizes much more than remapping the landscape. The mountains are integral to the cosmology and genealogy of surrounding tribes, which regard themselves as *kaitiaki* of the peaks. Many tribes, indeed, regard "their" mountains as constituting part of their ancestry, one facet of their integral and reciprocal relationship with the land. This latter point is increasingly appreciated by non-Maori, and the Maori self-descriptive term *tangata whenua*, "people of the land," is now widely used by *pakeha*.[40]

In the urban space of the capital, Wellington, the massive modern national museum looms large. It is biculturally conceived, executed, and operated.[41] It has new and old *marae* and *wharenui,* and Maori exhibitions, performances,

---

40 Many difficulties remain, especially over reaching an accommodation between conservationist and *rangatiratanga* principles: see, for example, Ward, *Unsettled History*, 58.
41 Brigitte Bönisch-Brednich, "Die Konzeption von Te Papa – Our Place: Neuseelands Nationalmuseum," *Werkstatt Geschichte* (2001): 98–102.

functions, and ceremonies play a prominent role in its daily life. Exhibits in the Maori spaces are controlled by Maori, who apply their own protocols. For example, a brief account of the Chatham Islands/Rekohu/Wharekauri – the multiple names indicates past contestation – does not mention a pre-Treaty invasion and massacre by mainland New Zealand tribes that resulted in the enslavement and near genocide of the Moriori people. The descendants of both the invaded and the invaders decided on the presentation in accord with their own practices of recording and disseminating the past, in which present concerns – in this case, reconciliatory – are given a high priority. In the face of some academic controversy, the *iwi* involved have remained adamant that they will relate their past in their own way.[42]

There is some considerable public concern among *pakeha* that the museum has moved beyond biculturalism to embrace a political correctness that elevates Maori culture and mores above those of *pakeha*. While such complaints do not seem to be justified in terms of the balance of the exhibitions, the fact is that the official name of the museum, Te Papa Tongarewa/Museum of New Zealand, is seldom used, even by the museum itself. It is known to the whole country, and internationally, simply as Te Papa, or Our Place. Te Papa is immensely popular, with visitor numbers far exceeding all expectations. In many ways it symbolizes, physically and conceptually, modern New Zealand/Aotearoa.

Shaping Reconciliation

If the processes and experiences that have led to everyday biculturalism were to be generally replicated with regard to the Maori aspiration for *rangatiratanga*, this might provide sufficient electoral backing for the government and Maori to negotiate a form of autonomy acceptable to the majority of Maori and non-Maori alike. It is far too early to say which, if any, of the many ideas debated within Maoridom about the most appropriate form(s) of autonomy will prove viable for cementing in place a durable living relationship between the Crown/*pakeha* and Maori.[43] One proposed key step toward *rangatiratanga* that has a long track record is some form of Maori tribal or political unity. Maori members of parliament, for example, have

---

42 For a detailed discussion about differences of historical interpretation between cultures, see Michael Herzfeld, *Anthropology: Theoretical Practice in Culture and Society* (Oxford, 2001), 55–69. A sizable file at Te Papa records the Chathams controversy, including the dismay of some prominent Western historians at the joint Maori/Moriori agreement on how to present their past.
43 Ken S. Coates and P. G. McHugh, *Living Relationships/Kokiri Ngatahi: The Treaty of Waitangi in the New Millennium* (Wellington, 1998).

historically formed caucuses whose operations are able to transcend party boundaries. Since New Zealand gained a proportional representation electoral system in 1996, there have been a number of calls to institutionalize such loose caucusing by the formation of an overarching Maori party. The strategy was initially an attempt to gain sufficient balance-of-power strength to make significant gains for *rangatiratanga*. In 2004, the Maori Party was founded, and it has established a broad base of support throughout the country.[44]

In addition to debate on the means to autonomous ends, the desired forms that those ends might assume are themselves under intensive consideration. Proposals centered on a national political solution to the quest for *rangatiratanga* include a reconstitution of the parliamentary system itself. This often involves proposals for an upper chamber to supplement New Zealand's House of Representatives, one that will scrutinize all legislation from a Treaty of Waitangi perspective, and for the establishment of a Maori House of Representatives that is separate from but at least coequal with the existing "*pakeha* House." There are also many tribal-based and other proposals for effecting autonomy at the regional and local levels. As New Zealand moves slowly, but seemingly inexorably, toward becoming a republic, the accompanying debate might well prove to be an opportunity for Maori leverage to advance the quest for *rangatiratanga* – especially since tribal leadership has generally opposed breaking the nation's link to the monarchy, given that Queen Victoria's representatives signed on her behalf the Treaty on which so many of their hopes are symbolically or otherwise pinned.[45]

Any notion of constitutional or other concession to Maori autonomy will no doubt be met with great resistance, for there is considerable public opposition to any increase in special provisions for Maori in law and society – let alone to any change that implies even a degree of self-determination. National Party leader Bill English, in declaring that the Treaty of Waitangi is one of the two "burning issues" of the decade, accused the Labour-led government of promoting "segregation between Maori and the rest of New Zealand" in such matters as legislation to provide for special Maori seats in

---

44 Lindsay Cox, *Kotahitanga: The Search for Maori Political Unity* (Auckland, 1993). For typical "Maori party" media coverage before the emergence in 2004 of the Maori Party, see Malcolm Aitken, "A Pan-Maori Party: An Exciting New Vision or a Pipe Dream?," an interview with Mana Motuhake party leader Willie Jackson, at http://www.scoop.co.nz/mason/stories/HL0309/S00038.htm, dated September 4, 2003. For the Maori Party's formation, see *Sunday Star-Times*, July 11, 2004; *New Zealand Herald*, July 12, 2004; *Dominion Post*, July 13, 2004.

45 For some discussion on constitutional matters, see F. M. Brookfield, *Waitangi and Indigenous Rights: Revolution, Law and Legitimation* (Auckland, 1999); also see James, ed., *Building the Constitution*, and Andrew Sharp, *Justice and the Maori: The Philosophy and Practice of Maori Claims in New Zealand since the 1970s* (Auckland, 1990, 2d ed., 1997).

local government.[46] His successor, Don Brash, went considerably further, reverting fully to the populist "One People" stance in a speech at Orewa in January 2004 and thereby gaining a surge of (white) support in the polls.[47] Clearly, such sentiments – fueled by media highlighting of specific cases of over-the-top official political correctness – do reflect a significant degree of *pakeha* opinion, especially at times of publicity about Maori stances and claims deemed to be on the lunatic fringe or threatening to the social fabric.[48] But it is noticeable that governmental change has seldom altered the broad thrust of official policies toward Maori, which remain focused on repairing the damage of the past – on healing, reconciliation, and removing socioeconomic inequality. Ongoing policies of negotiating reparations and reducing inequalities, in particular, reflect a general electoral acceptance that Maori needs and claims require addressing.

While historians have had some role in this bicultural discourse, their performance to date has been mixed. In the reparations arena, some have been seemingly "captured" by their Crown or Maori clients, or by the Waitangi Tribunal, which has, for example, attempted to link current socioeconomic deprivation of tribes directly with past acts and omissions of the Crown. Some historians who have begun to question aspects of Treaty settlement processes and scholarship have fed public distrust over the veracity of the historiography of Treaty revisionism. So too has the Tribunal itself, which, for example, (in)famously used the word "holocaust" to describe events in colonial Taranaki. Moreover, it remains to be seen how many historians working on reparations-based history will eventually be willing and able to turn their skills to understanding and interpreting to the *pakeha* public the collective Maori quest (and that of other indigenes) to determine their own future.[49]

---

46 *Dominion Post*, January 23, 2003. Also see "Treaty Needs Redefining," *New Zealand Herald*, February 10, 2003.

47 *Dominion Post*, January 28, 29, 2004; *New Zealand Herald*, January 29, 2004. It is likely that Brash had been influenced by the intense, confused, and often "redneck"' public debate over Maori claims to foreshore and seabed areas, and a favorable public response to government attempts in 2003 to mollify *pakeha* opinion by announcing (without initial consultation with Maori) that it would curtail tribal capacity to pursue such claims through legal processes: see, for example, *Dominion Post*, August 19, 2003. These government policies were themselves in part a response to Bill English's predecessor's strong "antiseparatist" stance on the foreshore and seabed controversy: see, for example, "The National Party Supports One Standard of Citizenship," New Zealand National Party Press Release, August 27, 2003.

48 For a recent headline and cover page that may well have alarmed many *pakeha* Aucklanders, see "Utu: The Treaty Claim over $75 Billion Worth of Prime Auckland Real Estate," *Metro* (Feburary 2003): 30–41.

49 W. H. Oliver, *Looking for the Phoenix: A Memoir* (Wellington, 2002), has provoked debate with his chapter 11 ("Histories and Politics"), as has Giselle Byrnes, *The Waitangi Tribunal and New Zealand History* (South Melbourne, 2004). For a New Zealand–United States comparative perspective, see

One inherent difficulty in progress toward indigenous autonomy in New Zealand is that Maori generally take the position that their methods and worldviews need to be incorporated into the official and unofficial, intellectual and popular discourses of the nation. This exercise has not advanced very far, even in Waitangi Tribunal and Crown interactions with Maori. Such institutions do attempt to take some account of *tikanga Maori* and indigenous approaches to knowledge. But because, for example, Maori history is oral-based, official and judicial recognition of indigenous versions of the past is marginal compared to that of a Western history posited on sources written during or soon after the period under scrutiny. And although Treaty compensation is mostly based on ethical rather than legal transgressions, lawyers are highly involved in the resolution processes, to the chagrin of Maori claimants – and indeed of *pakeha* historians and other scholars subjected to cross-examinations alien to their own disciplines.[50]

Scholars face potentially much greater difficulties, however, with regard to the ongoing working out of a new relationship between Crown and Maori. Little of the necessary historical and other research and analysis with regard to Maori aspirations has been undertaken, and there tends to be considerable *pakeha* resistance to that which has. But *pakeha* scholars could play a significant role by, for example, working with Maori counterparts to help interpret to the *pakeha* public the factors underlying a number of issues that have gained high profile in the media. These have puzzled or enraged great numbers of Europeans, helped poison hopes of a more rapid development of biculturalism, and hampered progress toward Crown recognition of *rangatiratanga*.

Misunderstandings have arisen, in particular, as a result of a palpable tension between the need for economic and technological progress in a country still feeling the effects of the devastating social consequences of being opened up to the international free market, and official commitment to consult with Maori and respect their culture. In late 2002–early 2003, there was, for example, considerable media-led public frustration at Maori tribes delaying a much-needed highway development in order to protect the swampy habitat of a one-eyed *taniwha*, a river monster that is mythical in *pakeha* eyes but prominent in the Maori worldview.[51] At the same time, another *taniwha* was helping impede the building of a prison; *wahi tapu* sites

---

Harry A. Kersey Jr., *Indigenous Sovereignty in Two Cultures: Maori and American Indians Compared* (Wellington, 2000).
50 Richard S. Hill and Brigitte Bönisch-Brednich, "Politicizing the Past: Indigenous Scholarship and Crown-Maori Reparations Processes in New Zealand," *Social and Legal Studies* 16:2 (2007): 163–81.
51 See, for example, *Dominion Post*, January 10, 2003; and Colin James, "Labour's Cultural Challenge – The Taniwha Term," *New Zealand Herald*, January 7, 2003.

were allegedly preventing some Bay of Plenty *pakeha* from developing their properties (television viewers were forewarned: "Wait till you hear about this one: prepare to go ballistic!"); and Maori concerned about, among other things, the filming of a sacred mountain were causing difficulties for the makers of the Tom Cruise film *The Last Samurai*. Many *pakeha* fear that the prolonged negotiations with tribes or other groups in which government and private developers and enterprises often need to engage will impede the nation's economy – jeopardizing, for example, an international film industry that has been boosted by the success of Peter Jackson's *Lord of the Rings* trilogy.[52]

White New Zealanders are often, too, concerned about aspects of Maori cultural norms that conflict with or sit uneasily alongside Western beliefs. *Pakeha* are, for example, generally a secular people in daily life and cherish firm separation between church and state. In the colonial period, Maori easily melded a belief in multiple gods and other indigenous spiritual phenomena with conversion to Christianity. As a result of a recently developed respect for Maori culture on the part of the Crown and other institutions, *karakia* (prayers) are now frequently incorporated into many official and other meetings and ceremonies. *Pakeha*, then, are routinely expected to take part in religio-cultural events, and a refusal to do so can be interpreted as cultural insensitivity. This can lead to interracial tension and resistance to biculturalism even among generally empathetic *pakeha*.

Already, however, most people of European background acquiesce in such ceremonies, including sitting through long speeches in Maori that they cannot understand. They do so out of both a general respect for biculturalism and an appreciation that it is up to Maori to select the cultural tools and circumstances they deem appropriate to their reassertion as a discrete people. Such relative tolerance holds out hope for *pakeha* reconciliation to *rangatiratanga*. Meanwhile, however, more interpretation between the two cultures is needed, and this is an area in which scholars, including anthropologists, can play a greater role. There is a definite need, in particular, to analyze the various problems arising from both Maori and *pakeha* strategically essentializing aspects of Maori culture for their own purposes.

Such matters as *taniwha* delaying construction projects and the perceived hampering of the work of international moviemakers create bewilderment among new immigrants as well as dismay for many *pakeha*. Recent arrivals

---

52 For a sampling of tension within the period of a fortnight, see *New Zealand Herald*, January 13, 2003; *Dominion Post*, January 14, 2003; *The Daily News*, January 16, 2003; Jeremy Hansen, "The Hollywood Hill," *The Listener*, January 25, 2003. For the Bay of Plenty incident, see *Sunday Star-Times*, October 5, 2003.

quickly come to question the sincerity of the official commitment to celebrating diversity. While citizens and state do tend increasingly to acknowledge, if not celebrate, differences, in the final analysis there are limitations placed on the capacity to manifest diversity.[53] This is partly a reflection of the fact that the official culture is bicultural rather than multicultural. Thus a government department will typically note that the "Crown does not have the same obligation actively to support [nonindigenous minority cultures or ethnicities] in New Zealand that it has in respect of the survival of Maori culture. Unlike those other cultures, New Zealand . . . is the only place where Maori culture is at 'home'; they were the first human beings in the islands."[54]

In short, it is now generally agreed in state and many civic circles that, under the Treaty of Waitangi, Maori have special "Treaty partnership" rights in addition to those of general citizenship. These rights have not yet been identified with any degree of clarity. But only when they have been negotiated and ascertained, Maori argue (and the Crown tends to agree), can attention be fully paid to the aspirations of new immigrants to negotiate their own multicultural position inside an officially bicultural country. This might seem to many new and aspiring citizens to be divisive, but even on such a fundamental issue Maori are increasingly talking a language of conciliation and negotiation. Some Maori scholars stress everyday social mingling, especially intermarriage: "The differences from our colonial past are being settled in the bedrooms of the nation."[55] Another has suggested that the very concept of biculturalism needs to be reconsidered. Instead, it might be replaced by an "interculturalism" that accommodates a "plurality of differences and visions" that includes all ethnicities of modern New Zealand. Such a "relational approach will demand negotiation, collaboration, compromise and much sacrifice."[56]

It will also require, however, as a bottom line, a place for the expression of *rangatiratanga* by the *tangata whenua* that no other culture or ethnicity can occupy. But the fact that approaches to the bicultural discourse, and proffered solutions to its problems, are becoming more innovative and sophisticated in some quarters is an encouraging sign of potential for multicultural harmony inside a nation comprised substantively of two peoples, one of which continues to struggle to seek an appropriate status within postcolonial paradigms.

53 See, for example, Brigitte Bönisch-Brednich, *Keeping a Low Profile: An Oral History of German Immigration to New Zealand* (Wellington, 2002), 223–8.
54 Ministry of Justice, "Healthy Constitutional Relationships in a Culturally Diverse Society," Discussion Document (Wellington, 2001).
55 Ranginui Walker, "Hostages of History," *Metro* (February 2001): 82–6.
56 Paul Meredith, "Revisioning New Zealandness: A Framework for Discussion," draft paper, n.d.

Summary

The country that once held itself up as having excellent race relations has come to realize that its historical and (to a lesser extent) contemporary ethnic interactions are far from unproblematic. The challenge to complete New Zealand's reparations processes, to reduce socioeconomic disparities between the peoples within the country, to *really* "celebrate cultural diversity" in New Zealand/Aotearoa, and ultimately to find a way of empowering *tangata whenua* in terms of an autonomous sociopolitical positioning is a huge one. But New Zealand has a nation-building discourse that is beginning to address, actually or potentially, all of these. The Maori quest for *rangatiratanga* seems at least partly attainable, insofar as it is backed by a living, relational biculturalism within society. As a result of huge changes in public and political consciousness, New Zealand is now arguably in the international vanguard of finding practical ways for indigenous peoples and descendants of colonizers to interrelate positively with each other, on a daily basis, politically, culturally, and organizationally – so that two peoples do indeed happily inhabit one nation, as the official slogan implied in 1990.

The chief judge of the Maori Land Court, a Maori jurist who also heads the Waitangi Tribunal, maintains that New Zealand is "more efficient probably than just about anywhere in the world" on the negotiation of reparations.[57] The major practical and conceptual challenge for the country is now to begin to turn any such efficiency in the direction of effecting *rangatiratanga*, of reinserting Aotearoa more firmly and permanently into New Zealand. This is not to denigrate the importance of other challenges, including those of finding a place for minority ethnicities[58] and tackling the overarching problems of inequality that are inherent in a class-based social system, but to note that this problem, on the Maori agenda for some seventeen decades, is one for which a solution is increasingly urgent.

Despite state refusal to date to contemplate anything resonant of constitutional change in the direction of autonomy, there is emerging evidence of official and *pakeha* realization that something needs to be done to seriously address, at least in part, Maori claims and aspirations on this issue. In the Speech from the Throne at the opening of the new parliamentary term in 2002, for example, the governor-general, on behalf of the New Zealand Crown, stated that "this government values and remains

---

57 Chief Judge Joe Williams, *Insight*, Radio New Zealand, February 2, 2003.
58 Michael King, Anthony Haas, and Richard S. Hill, "Reconciling Biculturalism and Multiculturalism in Aotearoa/New Zealand," *e-Future Times* (June 2004), http://www.futurestrust.org.nz/e-FutureTimes/e-FTVol12.html.

committed to strengthening its relationship with tangata whenua. That means fulfilling its obligations as a Treaty partner to support self determination for whanau, hapu and iwi."[59] This and similar political statements, added to (and reflecting) the country's increasingly bicultural lifestyle, comprise but one indication that New Zealand may be able to pioneer practical ways of peoples living and working together, in particular, of making "Two Peoples, One Nation" a reality as well as a slogan.

The difficulties involved cannot be underestimated, as both *pakeha* enthusiasm for Brash's attack at Orewa on alleged governmental privileging of Maori separateness and the response of the government revealed. This response, in its various manifestations, attempted to distance the Labour-led government from its Maori followers. Race-based policies were to be eliminated in favor of needs-based policies; and the government forged ahead to negate, by legislative fiat, judicial-based progress in long-standing tribal claims to foreshore and seabed areas. Maori resisted the legislation vigorously and unitedly, deeming it to be a new confiscation. But despite the severe strains in Crown-Maori relations throughout 2004, by the end of the year the opposition's polling gains from the Orewa speech had disappeared, despite its attempts to depict even the foreshore and seabed legislation as pandering to Maori because of some minimal concessions embodied in it. In early 2005, a polling company's "Mood of the Nation" report, while characterizing race relations as "the most important problem facing this country today," also found that the majority of the population felt that the situation was improving and would continue to improve.[60] The government, moreover, had already conceded that there should be "a stocktake" of the country's constitutional arrangements, with a view ultimately to considering any necessary changes that might emerge, and few believed that the role of the Treaty of Waitangi could, whatever the wishes of the two major political parties, be omitted from such deliberations.[61]

At the beginning of 2005, the Labour-led government faced a Maori Party that looked poised to cut significantly into Labour's support among Maori (and was to do so). There was little evidence of the *pakeha* backlash of a year before, and negotiations to address historical injustice were continuing. A settlement had been reached with Te Arawa (returning lakebeds and

---

59 Governor-General of New Zealand, "Speech from the Throne," http://www.beehive.govt.nz/throne.cfm.
60 *The Listener*, December 25, 2004; *Sunday Star-Times*, December 20, 2004, and January 16, 2005; *Dominion Post*, December 20, 2004, and January 4, 17, 2005.
61 Colin James, "Stirring National Pride Brings Constitution into Focus," *New Zealand Herald*, January 11, 2005; John Tamihere, MP, "Speech to Waitakere Rotary Club," January 19, 2005, http://www.scoop.co.nz/mason/stories/PA0501/S00153.htm.

offering cultural and financial redress and an apology) in December 2004 and another with Te Roroa the following month.[62] Commentators generally agreed that "there can be no turning back the page" over Maori assertion of their distinct identity within the New Zealand polity; indeed, they agreed that the troubles of 2004 had strengthened Maori resolve and assisted rather than hindered the long-term Maori struggle to assert *rangatiratanga*. The Maori Party reportedly struck "fear into Labour's heart,"[63] and would continue to do so. In 2008, with an election looming toward the end of the year, a sizable number of Treaty settlements were being negotiated and signed, and all significant political parties were showing public respect (though not generally full support) for Maori positions. No one outside of an extremist anti-Treaty fringe believed that the old policies of assimilation could or should be reverted to.[64] The only question concerned how, socially and officially, Aotearoa's role in a "Two People, One Nation" New Zealand should and would be configured.

62 *New Zealand Herald*, December 20, 2004; *Dargaville and Districts News*, January 10, 2005.
63 John Armstrong, "Tariana Turia Is Politician of the Year," *New Zealand Herald*, December 18, 2004.
64 For examples of populist white backlash, see Richard S. Hill, *Anti-Treatyism and Anti-Scholarship: An Analysis of Anti-Treatyist Writings* (Wellington, 2002). For assimilation in the nineteenth and twentieth centuries, see, respectively, Ward, *Show of Justice*, and Hill, *State Authority*.

11

The Politics of Judging the Past

South Africa's Truth and Reconciliation Commission

BRONWYN LEEBAW

Jeffrey Benzien received a medal for his work with Cape Town's Terrorist Detection Unit, where he perfected a form of torture known as the "wet bag" method. He received a very different sort of recognition in 1996 when the story of his appearance before South Africa's Truth and Reconciliation Commission (TRC) was widely circulated in the international press. Several of Benzien's former victims attended his hearing, including Tony Yengeni, who was then a member of South Africa's first postapartheid parliament. Yengeni confronted his former torturer. "What kind of man," he asked, "uses a method like this one . . . to other human beings . . . listening to those moans and cries and groans . . . what kind of human being can do that Mr. Benzien? . . . I'm talking now about the man behind the wet bag."[1] At Yengeni's insistence, Benzien then proceeded to demonstrate the wet bag method before the audience at the TRC. Speaking on his behalf, Benzien's commander, Johannes Lodiwikus Griebenauw, remarked, "it was accepted by all in the police force that the end justified the means."[2] In 1997, the

---

This chapter is based on an earlier article, "Legitimation or Judgment? South Africa's Restorative Approach to Transitional Justice," *Polity* (October 2003). I would like to thank the late Michael Rogin for his support throughout the research and writing of an earlier draft of this chapter. For valuable comments and suggestions on this research, I am also grateful to John Cioffi, Wendy Brown, Hanna Pitkin, Robert Post, Robert Kagan, Harvey Weinstein, Eric Stover, Victor Peskin, Brad Roth, Malcolm Oliver, and participants in the conference "Historical Justice in International Perspective," organized by the German Historical Institute. The Institute for the Study of World Politics, the Department of Political Science at the University of California, Berkeley, and the Institute for International Studies at Berkeley provided financial support that made this research possible. I am also grateful to the Centre for the Study of Violence and Reconciliation in Johannesburg for hospitality and extensive use of their excellent archives and to the many leaders and activists in South Africa who took the time to meet with me.

1 Antjie Krog, *Country of My Skull* (Johannesburg, 1998), 73.
2 *Application in Terms of Section 18 of the Promotion of National Unity and Reconciliation Act No. 34 of 1995* (1997).

TRC announced a decision to grant amnesty to Benzien, stating: "[T]he offences for which the applicant seeks amnesty were committed during and arose out of the conflicts of the past between the State and Liberation Movement."[3] Benzien returned to the police force, where he continued to work alongside another of his former victims, Gary Kruser.[4]

Confrontations between victim and perpetrator at the TRC captured the imagination of leaders and scholars around the world. Yet aside from its role in conveying some of the drama of South Africa's transition, the TRC contributed a unique combination of institutional and theoretical innovations to the emerging field of transitional justice. This chapter traces the interplay of political compromise and historical judgment throughout several phases in the life of South Africa's Truth and Reconciliation Commission in order to identify a set of problems as well as potential contributions of truth commissions to the broader goal of democratic change.

The TRC is one of numerous national and international institutions that have emerged in recent decades to advance "transitional justice" as part of a process of democratic change.[5] Successor regimes have long dealt with the political violence committed under prior rulers through trials, administrative purges, or reparations. More recently, truth commissions, which investigate historical patterns of violence, have become prominent tools for responding to past abuses.[6] Transitional justice efforts, whether in Rwanda, Guatemala, or South Africa, confront a common set of problems associated with criminalizing massive, systematic violence that was once a part of the very fabric of social and political life under a prior regime. Political violence typically requires the complicity or active participation of a large proportion of the population and results in great suffering for another large proportion of the population. In addition to addressing demands for justice, transitional justice institutions confront the divisions, hatreds, fears, and instability that are the legacies of institutionalized violence and repression.

South Africa's Truth and Reconciliation Commission began to take shape in 1993, when, after more than four decades of institutionalized racial

---

3 *Application in Terms of Section 18.*
4 Ivan Powell, "Where Have All the Apartheid Bastards Gone?" *Daily Mail and Guardian,* June 21, 2000.
5 See Neil J. Kritz, ed., *Transitional Justice: How Emerging Democracies Reckon with Former Regimes* (Washington, D.C., 1995); A. James McAdams, ed., *Transitional Justice and the Rule of Law in New Democracies* (Notre Dame, Ind., 1997); Ruti Teitel, *Transitional Justice* (Oxford, 2000); Alexandra Barahona de Brito, Carmen González-Enríquez, and Paloma Aguilar, eds., *The Politics of Memory: Transitional Justice in Democratizing Societies* (Oxford, 2001); and Jon Elster, *Closing the Books: Transitional Justice in Historical Perspective* (Cambridge, 2004).
6 Priscilla Hayner, *Unspeakable Truths: Confronting State Terror and Atrocity* (New York, 2001), 14.

segregation and a longer history of brutal dispossession, South Africa's liberation movements reached an agreement with state representatives to end apartheid and hold democratic elections. The interim constitution outlined the principles that were to guide the process of dealing with the past: "[T]here is a need for understanding but not for vengeance, a need for reparation but not for retaliation, a need for *ubuntu* but not victimization."[7] The call for understanding and *ubuntu* (roughly "humaneness") summarized an agreement to forego broadly punitive measures, including lustration and prosecution. The TRC would grant amnesty to individual applicants, but only on the condition that they provide full disclosure of their involvement in human rights violations and demonstrate a "political objective" for their actions.[8] The threat of prosecution would remain for those who did not cooperate with the TRC, while the offer of amnesty would serve as a gesture of reconciliation as well as an incentive to disclose information. Members of liberation movements and former state officials were required to submit amnesty applications.

Despite the commission's origins in political compromise, South African leaders also argued that it advanced a "different kind of justice," restorative justice that might better address the unique tensions of the transitional context than prosecution.[9] In lieu of punishment, restorative justice relies on tools of mediation and dialogue to generate spaces for expressions of approbation, remorse, and pardon in order to address the underlying causes of conflict. The broader movement for restorative justice encompasses a wide array of alternative dispute-resolution practices, juvenile justice, indigenous justice, and various forms of mediation. Restorative justice is associated with John Braithwaite's theory of deterrence based on "reintegrative" shaming, which ideally demonstrates respect for individuals while condemning their deeds.[10] Restorative justice programs have typically been implemented in small or homogenous communities, and Braithwaite argues that the theory will fail in places where criminal law does not reflect a majoritarian

---

7 *Constitution of the Republic of South Africa Act no 200*, 1993.
8 *Promotion of National Unity and Reconciliation Act no 34. South Africa*, July 26, 1995.
9 See Charles Villa-Vicencio, "Restorative Justice: Dealing with the Past Differently," and Johnny de Lange, "The Historical Context, Legal Origins and Philosophical Foundation of the South African Truth and Reconciliation Commission," in Charles Villa-Vicencio and Wilhelm Verwoerd, eds., *Looking Back, Reaching Forward: Reflections on the Truth and Reconciliation Commission of South Africa* (Cape Town, 2000); Desmond Mpilo Tutu, *No Future Without Forgiveness* (London, 2000), 54–5; 155–7; Alex Boraine, *A Country Unmasked: Inside South Africa's Truth and Reconciliation Commission* (Oxford, 2000), 278–99; 387–400.
10 John Braithwaite, *Crime, Shame and Reintegration* (Cambridge, 1989), 54–65.

morality.[11] In contrast, the TRC pursued restorative justice in a context characterized by gross inequality and long-standing conflicts as part of a process of fundamental political change.

Although South Africa's TRC was not the first truth commission, it has probably become the most famous. It has influenced the design of more recent truth commissions, as well as broader debates over the role of truth commissions as forms of transitional justice. Many scholars have voiced support for the TRC's claim that truth commissions advance important goals associated with democratic change. It is widely argued that truth commissions address the needs of victims in a manner that prosecutions cannot, by providing them with the opportunity to share their stories or with new information about past abuses.[12] Priscilla Hayner, of the International Center for Transitional Justice, argues that truth commissions fill a unique niche: "They paint a larger picture, looking at many thousands of victims, whereas trials (which are critically important as well) must, by definition, focus on specific events of wrongdoing."[13] Hayner adds that truth commissions should also be valued for the ways that they have made "creative use of local customs to promote healing and reconciliation." Amy Gutman and Dennis Thompson are skeptical regarding the healing powers of truth commissions but argue that the TRC promoted the principle of reciprocity, which requires a search for moral agreement or, where that is impossible, for mutual respect and an "economy of moral disagreement" that will enable participants to minimize their rejection of positions they oppose.[14] James Gibson draws on extensive survey research to argue that the TRC succeeded in promoting interracial reconciliation.[15]

Critics have been troubled by the common claim that truth commissions aid victims of political violence in a therapeutic process of recovery. Brandon Hamber, of South Africa's Centre for the Study of Violence and Reconciliation, observes that "many victims have described feelings of initial relief following the hearings and then, weeks or months later, feelings of despondency and re-emergence of trauma."[16] Others charge that the TRC's adoption of restorative principles confuses justice with therapy and

---

11 Braithwaite, *Crime, Shame*, 96–7.
12 Martha Minow, *Between Vengeance and Forgiveness*, 62–4; Teresa Godwin Phelps, *Shattered Voices: Language, Violence, and the Work of Truth Commissions* (Philadelphia, 2004).
13 Priscilla Hayner, "More Than Just the Truth," *UNESCO Courier*, available at http://www.unesco.org/courier/2001_05/uk/droits.htm (accessed May 4, 2004).
14 "The Moral Foundations of Truth Commissions," in *Truth v. Justice*, 22.
15 James L. Gibson, *Overcoming Apartheid: Can Truth Reconcile a Divided Nation?* (New York, 2004).
16 Brandon Hamber, "The Burdens of Truth," *American Imago* 55 (1998): 19.

so undermines any effort to assign responsibility for past abuses.[17] Based on ethnographic research in South Africa's townships, Robert Wilson argues that restorative justice failed to resonate with most South Africans because it clashed with the dominant perception of justice as "proportional punishment for wrongdoing."[18] Robert Meister suggests that the logic of "healing" associated with restorative justice abandons radical change in favor of a talking cure.[19]

This chapter addresses ongoing debates on the significance of South Africa's TRC by examining the ways that conflict and compromise shaped changing approaches to remembrance and judgment through several stages in the life of the commission. The next section charts the influence of four historical episodes on the development of ideas associated with the TRC. It argues that South Africa's restorative approach was not only adopted as a way to conceptualize national "healing" and compromise but also as a way to advance social change. In restorative justice theory, social change and the "restoration" of relationships may be mutually reinforcing goals when guided by the shared norms of a community. The TRC, however, aimed to "restore" something that never was, a South African political community with shared values and goals.[20] The paradoxical quality of this aspiration was reflected in a tension between two goals associated with the TRC investigations. African National Congress (ANC) officials initially hoped the commission would articulate an official break with the previous order by condemning apartheid as a deeply unjust and racist political system. Yet over time, the TRC would strive to depoliticize its condemnation of past violence by transforming competing political positions into a shared rejection of human rights violations committed by all parties and a common interest in "healing."

The third section of the chapter argues that attention to the tensions between these goals helps to shed light on problems as well as potential contributions of the South African model. Truth commissions may serve to obfuscate transitional compromises in a manner that legitimates denials and justifications of past atrocities or the closing off of avenues for further social and political change. Yet they may also play a critical role in exposing the limitations of justice, reconciliation, and democratic reform in a transitional

---

17 Kenneth Roth and Alison Des Forges, "Justice or Therapy?" *Boston Review* (2002), available at http://bostonreview.net/BR27.3/rothdesforges.html.
18 Richard A. Wilson, *The Politics of Truth and Reconciliation in South Africa: Legitimizing the Post-Apartheid State* (Cambridge, 2001), 229.
19 Robert Meister, "Human Rights and the Politics of Victimhood," *Ethics and International Affairs* 1602 (2002): 118–23.
20 Bronwyn Leebaw, "Restorative Justice for Political Transitions: Lessons from the South African Truth and Reconciliation Commission," *Contemporary Justice Review* 43 (2001).

context. By investigating and remembering past injustices for which a remedy is not politically available or possible, truth commissions may provide a basis for critically reexamining both the prior regime and the compromises that frame a political transition. The tensions between these goals reflect the complexity of the political role of contemporary transitional justice institutions, which seek to legitimate the political compromises that facilitate democratic transitions without foreclosing an ongoing struggle for further change – to "close the book" on the past while insisting on the critical role of remembering past brutalities.

Four Influential Episodes

Informal Justice and Opposition to the Apartheid State

Informal justice was not new to South Africa, which had a long history of traditional "chief's justice" in the villages and "people's courts" in the townships. These courts did not develop in isolation but were at different junctures supported and promoted by the state.[21] As early as the 1970s, a variety of tribunals appeared in urban areas.[22] They were not generally designed to confront the apartheid system, and many were officially recognized by the minister of justice.[23] This changed in the mid-1980s, when informal justice was adopted as part of the radicalization of antiapartheid activism. By 1985, the black townships were in a situation of virtual civil war as residents fought to drive the state out of their communities. That year, the ANC-in-exile called for the populace to make the townships "ungovernable," which gave rise to new forms of governance, known as "people's power."[24] In this context, people's courts were a prominent feature of the South African political scene, championed as an attempt to create adjudicative structures that would reflect popular notions of justice for a postapartheid society.[25] In this era, people's courts utilized informal justice to implement punitive forms of redress in the service of radical social and political change.

---

21 Wilson, *The Politics of Truth and Reconciliation*, 190.
22 T. W. Bennet, *A Sourcebook on African Customary Law* (Cape Town, 1991), 90.
23 Wilson, *The Politics of Truth and Reconciliation*, 192.
24 Robert Price, *The Apartheid State in Crisis: Political Transformation in South Africa 1975–1990* (New York, 1991), 192–202.
25 Wilfried Schärf and Baba Ngcokoto, "Images of Punishment in the People's Courts of Cape Town 1985–1987: From Prefigurative Justice to Populist Violence," in N. Chubani Manganyi and Andre du Toit, eds., *Political Violence and the Struggle in South Africa* (Johannesburg, 1990), 342.

A somewhat different conception of informal justice was also associated with radical social change in certain theological circles of the 1980s. "Contextual theology" developed in South Africa in an effort to mobilize the churches to confront apartheid.[26] In 1985, members of the movement published the *Kairos Document*, which accused South African theologians of appealing to reconciliation to quell the demand for social and political change and called for social analysis and political strategy to supplant this uncritical application of formal theological principles.[27] *Kairos* distinguishes between "genuine reconciliation" and "false reconciliation" by arguing that justice must accompany genuine reconciliation. Justice, according to the document, should not be reduced to questions of individual guilt but rather should entail a radical change in social structure. Charles Villa-Vicencio, an original signatory of *Kairos*, became director of the *TRC Report*. Frank Chikane, who addressed public debates on the framing of the TRC legislation, and Bongani Finca, who served as a TRC commissioner, were also original signatories of the *Kairos Document*.

In these very different contexts, informal justice was embraced as a vehicle to radical change, while formal justice and formalism more generally were identified with efforts to legitimate the status quo. During the transition, African National Congress leaders would voice a similar critique of formal justice. Yet whereas informal practices had once been associated with the opposition to state-led justice, the TRC would be identified as a tool to legitimate the formal justice apparatus of the new South Africa. Thus, while TRC officials, such as Villa-Vicencio, cite earlier examples of informal justice as the basis for restorative justice, the *TRC Report* notably calls for an end to people's courts.[28]

Negotiations to End Apartheid

In 1990, President F. W. de Klerk announced the "unbanning" of the ANC, the South African Communist Party (SACP), and the Pan African Congress (PAC). Negotiations soon intensified, and the fate of exiles and political prisoners became a central question. The process of releasing prisoners began in 1990 in accordance with the Norgaard principles, which had been developed for use in the UN settlement of the Namibian

---

26 Tristan Anne Borer, *Challenging the State: Churches as Political Actors in South Africa* (Notre Dame, Ind., 1998), 85–91.
27 *The Kairos Document: Challenge to the Church: A Theological Comment on the Political Crisis in South Africa* (Grand Rapids, Mich., 1985).
28 Villa-Vicencio, "A Different Kind of Justice: The South African Truth and Reconciliation Commission," *Contemporary Justice Review* 1 (1998): 407–28.

conflict.[29] The Norgaard principles, which became the basis for the TRC's "political objective" requirement for amnesty, provided amnesty for those charged with political crimes and specified terms for evaluating the relationship between the political objective and action taken.[30] Meanwhile, the South African security forces began to pressure de Klerk to provide unconditional amnesty for every policeman and soldier. After the first round of multiparty Convention for a Democratic South Africa (CODESA) negotiations broke down, Joe Slovo, secretary general of the South African Communist Party whose wife, Ruth First, had been assassinated by state officials, voiced support for an "amnesty in which those seeking to benefit will disclose in full those activities for which they require an amnesty," as a compromise in exchange for democratic change.[31] Other key figures, including Boutros Boutros Ghali and Archbishop Desmond Tutu, echoed his support for this selective form of amnesty.[32] The National Party continued to lobby for an unconditional amnesty but eventually agreed to the requirement of "full disclosure" on the condition that it would also apply to members of the liberation movements.[33]

At the same time, several leaders associated with the ANC also expressed skepticism regarding the moral value of transitional prosecution. Albie Sachs, now a justice on South Africa's Constitutional Court, was involved in the negotiations and conferences that developed the initial framework of the TRC. George Bizos helped to draft the amnesty provisions and then to present them to parliament. Willie Hofmyer became an ANC representative of the Justice Portfolio Committee in parliament, which drafted the TRC legislation, and Kader Asmal was the minister of justice when the legislation was passed. These were human rights advocates involved in prosecuting human rights violations committed under the former state, yet in contrast to international human rights advocacy organizations, they did not necessarily view prosecution as the best means to attain those goals in the transitional context.

According to Bizos, ANC leaders voiced doubts regarding the value of the Nuremberg model for the South African transition as early as 1988.[34]

---

29 ANC Department of Political Education, *The Road to Peace: Resource Material on Negotiations* (1990), 52–3. On the history of the amnesty provisions, see Erik Doxtader, "Easy to Forget or Never (Again) Hard to Remember? History, Memory, and the 'Publicity' of Amnesty," in Charles Villa-Vicencio and Erik Doxtader, eds., *The Provocations of Amnesty: Memory, Justice, and Impunity* (Cape Town, 2003), 121–55.
30 *TRC Report,* vol. 1, 51.
31 Joe Slovo, "Negotiations: What Room for Compromise?" *African Communist* (1992): 36–40.
32 Lynn Berat and Yossi Shain, "Retribution of Truth-Telling in South Africa? Legacies of the Transitional Phase," *Law and Social Inquiry* 20 (1995): 177.
33 George Bizos, interview by author, Johannesburg, March 30, 1999.
34 Bizos, *No One to Blame?* 229–30.

To begin, they argued that the country lacked the institutional and social foundations to support a program of retroactive prosecution. Given the scale of the crimes, the refusal of the majority of whites to recognize apartheid-era repression as criminal, the unreformed judicial system, and the fragility of the new regime, transitional criminal prosecutions would be socially divisive and would threaten the stability of the new regime.[35] Thus, South African leaders rejected the argument made by prominent human rights advocates that a "duty to prosecute" under international law would aid transitional countries in deterring future human rights abuses by removing legal decisions from the scene of domestic political struggle.[36] "Reconciliation" in this view could not be generated by prosecutions but would rather be necessary as a foundation for a just order.

The idea of a truth commission that would address the needs of victims was also informed by ANC lawyers who had experienced formal prosecutions as unfair to victims and, more generally, to the poor. As a human rights lawyer, Hofmyer rarely saw a successful criminal prosecution and observed that victims were often disoriented in the courtroom, which made it easier for skilled defense lawyers to manipulate their testimony.[37] Bizos made similar comments regarding his own experience as a lawyer, adding that *transitional* prosecutions would do even less for victims given the limited number of prosecutions possible for massive, systematic crimes.[38]

ANC leaders also began to suggest that the historical records generated in trials were inadequate as a basis for condemning systematic injustice. Kader Asmal, widely viewed as influential in the origination of the TRC, argued that because criminal investigations are confined to the individual guilt or innocence of a few leaders, they potentially distort questions of guilt and responsibility for systematic crimes. The rigorous burden of proof in a judicial proceeding may mean that many of those responsible for atrocities are deemed "not guilty."[39] The narrow scope of judicial fact-finding is compounded by the high costs of trials, which limit the number that can be held.[40] Because prosecutions are designed to investigate the accused, they may not provide a space for victims to tell their side of the story. The formal setting of judicial proceedings and the pressures of cross-examination

---

35 "They said, just use a criminal justice model. This would put us at each other's throats forever" (Johnny de Lange interview, Cape Town, March 4, 1999). See also Robert Asmal, Louise Asmal, and Suresh Roberts, *Reconciliation Through Truth: A Reckoning of Apartheid's Criminal Governance* (Cape Town, 1996), 18.
36 Diane Orentlicher, "Settling Accounts: The Duty to Prosecute Human Rights Violations of a Prior Regime," *Yale Law Journal* 100 (1991): 2537–2615.
37 Interview by author, Cape Town, March 6, 1999.
38 Interview by author, Johannesburg, March 30, 1999.
39 Asmal et al., *Reconciliation Through Truth*, 19.
40 The costly Malan trial had resulted in an acquittal (*TRC Report*, 1, 123).

may prevent victims from coming forward.[41] ANC leaders expressed the hope that their alternative framework would establish a clearer case for the importance of social and political change beyond the rule of law. As Johnny de Lange put it, "[w]e had to broaden our perception of justice beyond punishment. We had to look at the fate of victims and the whole political and social framework in which the violations took place."[42]

These statements explicitly reject the idea that the moral claims of transitional justice could be divorced from the political context of the transition. The arguments contain the suspicion of formalism that animated some activist circles of the 1980s. At the same time, ANC leaders suggested that the historical records developed in the process would stand in tension with transitional compromises. By condemning apartheid as a system, the historical judgment of the proposed commission would underscore the limitations of bargains that were made with apartheid leaders. As Asmal argued, this would provide a basis for future leaders to continue the work of democratic transition by pursuing social change. This suggests a critical role for remembrance in the refusal to reduce the meaning of justice to formal legal categories or to what is politically possible.

Debating TRC Legislation

In the fall of 1995, the new South African parliament, led by the ANC, passed the National Unity and Reconciliation Act, which outlined a mandate for the truth commission. South Africa's truth commission was the first to be developed through the legislative process. According to members of the Justice Portfolio Committee, two conferences sponsored by the Institute for the Study of Democratic Alternatives (IDASA) influenced the framing of the Act.[43] The conferences, which took place in 1994, were entitled "Dealing with the Past" and "Truth and Reconciliation."[44] At these conferences, the idea of the TRC as a tool for "healing the nation" took shape as an alternative paradigm for transitional justice.

The IDASA conferences provided a forum for the emerging network of human rights advocates and leaders involved in transitional justice around

---

41 Asmal et al., *Reconciliation Through Truth*, 21.
42 "The Historical Context, Legal Origins, and Philosophical Foundations of the South African Truth and Reconciliation Commission," in Villa-Vicencio and Verwoerd, eds., *Looking Back, Reaching Forward*, 24.
43 Johnny de Lange, interview by author, Cape Town, March 4, 1999; Willie Hofmyer, interview by author, Cape Town, March 6, 1999.
44 The papers presented at these conferences were published in two volumes: Alex Boraine, Janet Levy, and Ronel Scheffer, eds., *Dealing with the Past* (Cape Town, 1994), and Alex Boraine and Janet Levy, eds., *The Healing of a Nation?* (Cape Town, 1994).

the world to discuss ideas, share experiences with local leaders, and contribute to the development of a theoretical basis for the TRC. Those present at the IDASA conferences included Juan Mendez and Aryeh Neier, both of Human Rights Watch; leaders from Latin America, such as José Zalaquett, and Eastern Europe, such as Joachim Gauck and Adam Michnik, who had been involved in truth commissions and lustration programs; local South African nongovernmental organizations; representatives from churches and South African intellectuals; members of the South African government, including Kader Asmal and Constitutional Court Justice Albie Sachs; and internationally known media professionals, such as Tina Rosenburg.[45]

Zalaquett's comments at the second IDASA conference stressed the role of truth commissions in addressing the psychological impact of torture, as well as the trauma suffered by survivors who lack information about abuses.[46] For a number of reasons, Zalaquett's arguments regarding the therapeutic value of truth commissions resonated with South African leaders and representatives who attended the conferences.[47] Zalaquett's contextual and political approach to transitional justice resonated with the ANC's rejection of legalism. Like Zalaquett, many of those present were human rights advocates who had moved into positions associated with state power and were now involved in nation-building and the development of rule of law. Finally, Zalaquett's discussion of the therapeutic potential of truth commissions resonated with the perspectives of new South African leaders who were becoming associated with the TRC during this phase and might be loosely grouped together as members of "healing professions," including doctors, therapists, and religious leaders. Mamphele Rampele, a medical doctor and longtime liberation struggle activist, gave a speech at one IDASA conference that compared the violent legacy of South Africa's past to "an abscess" that "cannot heal properly unless it is thoroughly incised and cleaned out."[48]

The idea that the TRC investigations would "heal" political relationships was consistent with the communitarian basis of earlier informal justice practices but differed in its application to a nation-building process, implying an anticipated future community rather than an existing one. The difference in context would also signify a different role for the communitarian orientation of informalism. Whereas earlier it had fostered the politicization of

---

45 Boraine, *A Country Unmasked*, 17.
46 Boraine and Levy, eds., *The Healing of a Nation?* 49–55.
47 On the influence of Zalaquett's arguments in South Africa, see Antjie Krog, *A Country Unmasked*, 43.
48 Boraine and Levy, eds., *The Healing of a Nation?* 34.

community grievances, now healing would signify depoliticization, gesturing toward a body politic with shared wounds, and a therapeutic process that would transcend ongoing political divisions. The focus on psychic trauma and therapy shifts attention away from questions of political responsibility, as medical and psychiatric framings of problem and response cannot articulate relationships of exploitation and systematic group-based oppression. Depoliticizing past injustices in this fashion would provide a way to legitimate the compromises that facilitated the transition, yet this clashed with the earlier ANC goal of a truth commission that would condemn apartheid as a system. These competing aspirations would also influence the articulation of South Africa's restorative approach to transitional justice by leaders involved in the administration of the commission.

Restorative Transitional Justice

The National Unity and Reconciliation Act, which established the TRC, was passed by parliament on July 19, 1995. In December of that year, Nelson Mandela selected seventeen truth commissioners from a list of candidates prepared by a specially appointed committee, which held public, televised hearings to interview nominees.[49] According to Albie Sachs, the potential commissioners were screened for their ability to impartially evaluate the manner in which diverse parties had undermined "respect for human dignity."[50] The list included seven women and ten men who represented a variety of racial and religious groups. In addition to several lawyers and human rights activists, the group included religious leaders, such as the Reverends Khoza Mgojo and Bongani Finca, and would be chaired by Archbishop Desmond Tutu. Two medical doctors, Fazel Randera and Wendy Orr, were chosen as truth commissioners, as was a psychiatric nurse, Glenda Wildschut.

Wilhelm Verwoerd, who helped to write the "Concepts and Principles" chapter of the *TRC Report*, identifies Desmond Tutu as having been very influential in developing the idea to associate the TRC with restorative principles. Tutu argued that the TRC challenged common assumptions about the very meaning of justice.[51] Commissioners and others involved with the TRC began to read about restorative justice and to discuss a recent book by Jim Consedine, entitled *Restorative Justice: Healing the Effects of Crime* (1995). Consedine's analysis connects restorative justice to Christian

49 Boraine, *A Country Unmasked*, 71–5. 50 "Fourth D. T. Lakdawala Memorial Lecture."
51 Interview by author, Stellenbosch, March 10, 1999.

values of forgiveness and mercy, and in his introduction, he identifies the South African transition as "restorative justice practiced on a grand scale."[52] Tutu would similarly associate the TRC with healing and forgiveness, and he identified *ubuntu* as the basis for restorative justice, defining both as involving a concern "with the healing of breaches" and "restoration of imbalances."[53]

According to Verwoerd, the commissioners were also influenced by the landmark Constitutional Court judgment *S. v. Makwanyane and Another* (1995), which ruled the death penalty unconstitutional and incorporated *ubuntu* into South African jurisprudence as a principle of justice. Judge Madala argued that *ubuntu* necessitates the recognition of the humanity of the perpetrator of even the most heinous offenses.[54] The judges further explained *ubuntu* as connoting values of community, interdependence, reciprocity, and, in the words of Judge Madala, a "balancing of the interests of society against those of the individual."[55] This set of ideas was invoked in *Azanian Peoples Organization (AZAPO) and Others v. President of the Republic of South Africa and Others* (1996), in which the court used the principle of *ubuntu* to uphold the state's right to grant amnesty in response to a challenge brought by Steve Biko's widow under South Africa's constitutional provision of an individual's right to have complaints settled by a court of law.[56] These cases helped to develop the theoretical basis of the emerging restorative focus of the TRC commissioners. The *Makwanyane* case used *ubuntu* to divorce justice from retribution. The *AZAPO* case held that the goals of community-building could trump individual rights-based claims.

Throughout the TRC hearings, South Africa's restorative approach to transitional justice was articulated as a process associated with forgiveness and mercy that would "heal" past "wounds." In the *TRC Report*, this healing paradigm is embraced, as in the 1995 legislative debates, as a way to depoliticize past injustices. Desmond Tutu introduces the report by stating that "[o]ur country is soaked in the blood of all of her children, of all races and of all political persuasions."[57] This reflects the hope that the TRC would legitimate an as-yet-unrealized political community and the compromises made to facilitate it. Yet the TRC aspiration to provide a basis for critical judgment and ongoing reform is also reflected in the *TRC Report*, which, quoting Asmal, states, "the issues of structural violence, of unjust and inequitable social arrangements, of balanced development in the future,

---

52 Jim Consedine, *Restorative Justice: Healing the Effects of Crime* (Lyttelton, New Zealand, 1995), 10.
53 Tutu, *No Future,* 55.
54 1995 (6) BCLR 665 (CC), 671–3.
55 1995 (6) BCLR 665 (CC), 751, 756, 759.
56 1996 (8) BCLR 1015 (CC).
57 *TRC Report* 1, 1.

cannot be properly dealt with unless there is a conscious understanding of the past."[58] The report also stresses that reconciliation requires "the redress of gross inequalities . . . wide-ranging structural and institutional transformation."[59] The idea that the healing of political divisions and the condemnation of systematic abuses are both desirable elements of democratic change, however, has often led to a neglect of the tension between them.

Political Compromise and Historical Judgment

By identifying a tension at work in South Africa's restorative approach to transitional justice, I do not mean to imply that it is necessarily destructive or paralyzing. A danger associated with truth commissions is that in the effort to overcome this tension, the historical records that they produce will be *reduced* to a legitimation of transitional compromise that creates an illusion of consensus, naturalizes the legacy of past injustices, and functions to foreclose avenues to further change. Yet truth commission investigations may also play a critical role in revealing the moral and political limitations of transitional compromises and illuminating possibilities for further change. These potential dangers and contributions cannot be measured in relation to abstract standards of justice. In evaluating truth commissions, it is important to pay close attention to the ways that conflict and compromise frame their mandates and investigations. In the following sections, I consider how such an analysis sheds light on the TRC.

Compromise and Legitimation

Although truth commissions do not prosecute or punish individual offenders, they define and investigate specific offenses. During the 1995 parliamentary debates, the National Party condemned the commission as a "witch hunt" and fought the idea of a commission that would criminalize apartheid as a system. National Party representative Danie Schutte told parliament that "[i]f there is any suggestion that a distinction is to be made between persons who fought for or against the previous government, it can only be perceived as being discriminatory."[60] Democratic Party representative Dene Smuts voiced her fear that the TRC would produce a revisionist official history, based on "moral relativism" that justifies atrocities committed by the ANC.[61] General Constand Viljoen suggested that the TRC should analyze

---

58 *TRC Report* 1, 49.   59 *TRC Report* 1, 110.
60 *Hansards, Parliamentary Debate*, May 17, 1995, 1375.
61 *Hansards, Parliamentary Debate*, May 17, 1995, 1386.

"the fight against Communist expansionism" in assessing the philosophy of apartheid.[62]

In response, ANC members reminded their new colleagues that the struggle against apartheid was widely recognized as a just war. The General Assembly of the United Nations had labeled apartheid a "crime against humanity" on numerous occasions, and in 1976, the UN Security Council unanimously stated that "apartheid is a crime against the conscience and dignity of mankind."[63] Kader Asmal told parliament that any truth commission would be obliged to "recognize in the most meaningful way the illegitimacy of the system that preceded the Government of National Unity, because it bears ultimately the entire responsibility for what happened in our country."[64]

Eventually, the parliament agreed to frame investigations in relation to the concept of "gross violations of human rights" committed by all parties to the conflict. This would balance the TRC's condemnation of apartheid as a system with the message that all sides made mistakes. Jon Elster notes that this type of "evenhanded" policy is only seen in negotiated transitions and argues that it is tied to the desire for outgoing elites to "create an appearance that its human rights violations were justified by those of the opposition."[65] Jim Gibson views the message that all sides made mistakes as the main explanation for his finding that the TRC contributed to reconciliation.[66] In any case, the decision to focus on "gross human violations of human rights" was widely perceived as a political concession on the part of the ANC.[67] It meant not only that the liberation movements would be compelled to admit error, but also that they would be scrutinized in accordance with the same criteria as the apartheid state. The primary inquiry, then, would concern guilt and suffering associated with illegalities *within* the apartheid framework, rather than the system of apartheid itself. This marks a striking departure from the 1967 UN Economic and Social Council resolution that established the UN Commission of Human Rights specifically to "examine information relating to gross violations of human rights and fundamental freedoms as exemplified by the *policy of apartheid* in South Africa."[68]

---

62 Brian Stuart, "Truth Probe 'Could Name Ministers,'" *Citizen,* February 25, 1995.
63 GA Res.2189; GA Res 39/72A; GA Res 2074; Security Council Resolution 392 (June 19, 1976); Security Council Resolution 556 (December 13, 1984).
64 *Hansards, Parliamentary Debate*, 17 May 17, 1995, 1381.
65 Elster, *Closing the Books*, 197.
66 Gibson, *Overcoming Apartheid*, 159, 336.
67 "ANC Relents on Truth Commission," *Business Day* (January, 13, 1995).
68 Resolution 1235, 42. UN ESCOR Supp. (no. 1) at 17, UN Doc. E/4393 (1967). My emphasis.

The historical records of the TRC were also framed in relation to the TRC's terms for granting amnesty. South Africa's "political objective" requirement reverses the logic that has animated human rights approaches to accountability. In human rights and humanitarian law, it is the element of organization, the "systematic" quality of atrocities, organized for political purposes, that makes "crimes against humanity" more contemptible than random acts of violence. In contrast, individuals are granted amnesty at the TRC *because* they committed "gross violations of human rights" for a political purpose. The "political objective" requirement would allow architects of crimes against humanity to attain amnesty while leaving abuses that were expressions of individual sadism or hatred subject to punishment.

Some hoped that the TRC's proportionality requirement would raise the threshold for amnesty, but this was complicated by the commission's interpretation of "gross violations." Parliamentarians held conflicting views as to the precise definition of "gross violations of human rights" yet agreed that the term should be reconciled with the distinction between just cause of war (*jus ad bellum*) and justice in war (*jus in bello*).[69] Although the ANC could legitimately claim to have a just cause of war, they could be scrutinized by the TRC for failure to observe justice *in* war, and this could be defined by the category "gross violations of human rights." The idea of "gross violations" was thus defined as an act that was excessive in relation to the objective of armed conflict – the "political objective." The fact that "gross violations" were defined at the outset as lacking proportion apparently curtailed the use of proportionality as a limiting principle.

To the extent that the "healing" focus of the commission implied a process guided by shared values and goals, this would obfuscate the political compromises that framed the TRC investigations. The idea of a therapeutic investigation also conflicted with the ANC's original goal of condemning apartheid as a system. Of the 21,000 victims that gave statements to the TRC, 1,800 would be chosen to appear at public hearings. It was hoped the statement-taking process, as well as the public testimony, would have therapeutic value for victims and their relatives and would provide "unique insight into the pain of South Africa's past."[70] The informal, supportive environment of the TRC was designed to facilitate both goals.[71] Victims were provided with therapeutic assistance in the form of "briefers," who were hired specifically to support victims when the testimony became

---

69 *TRC Report*, 1, 66.
70 *TRC Report*, 1, 112.
71 *TRC Report*, 1, 128.

traumatic, and victims would be free to explain their stories as they chose, in their own languages.[72]

Many of those who had fought with the liberation movements, moreover, did not identify with the victim label, and the *TRC Report* acknowledges that the widespread refusal of ANC supporters to come to the commission was a factor that "severely constrained" its ability to provide a "complete" picture of the past.[73] The clash between the logic of national healing and the logic of the liberation struggle is illustrated by the testimony of Sandra Adonis, who became a student leader at age 15 and left school in the mid-1980s, after two of her friends were shot by the police, to join an armed resistance group. As she told the commission,

We do not need their apologies. Well, I do not need them. . . . I mean, I have lost my education and I have lost my childhood although we have in return received our freedom and our democracy in this country. . . . I do not think we have gained anything because we are still in the same position as we use to be, unemployed, homeless, abandoned and there is nobody who looks back and says, well, these are the people that have fought the struggle, that have been part of the struggle, and have brought us to the point where we are now.[74]

According to the *TRC Report*, three factors influenced the selection of individuals to appear at public hearings: the nature of abuse in the community or area; an effort to represent all sides of the conflict, so as to present a picture of abuse from as many perspectives as possible; and an effort to represent members of various gender, age, and racial groups in the area where the hearings were held.[75] The commission made special appeals for whites to come forward and held several hearings focusing on issues relevant to the white community.[76] One dramatic outcome of the effort to represent victims from all sides of the conflict was that whites were approximately four times as likely to be selected to appear in hearings as blacks.[77] The attempt to showcase the experiences of victims from all sides of the conflict, rather than the disproportionate victimization of the black population, signaled that the TRC would give priority to interracial healing over condemning the role of apartheid policies in the suffering of a majority of the population.

---

72 *TRC Report*, 1, 283–4, 366.
73 *TRC Report*, 5, 199.
74 *TRC Youth Hearings*, CT/01110 (May 1997).
75 *TRC Report*, 1, 148.
76 *TRC Report*, 1, 169.
77 Audrey Chapman and Patrick Ball, "The Truth of Truth Commissions: Comparative Lessons from Haiti, South Africa, and Guatemala," *Human Rights Quarterly* 23 (2001): 39.

The amnesty process and the goal of understanding "the motives and perspectives" of perpetrators would also clash with the goal of condemning apartheid as a system.[78] Questioning at the amnesty hearings differed fundamentally from that at a criminal trial because guilt was not at issue. Establishing the "political objective" often involved open-ended questions to the applicants, who would explain in depth how they became associated with political violence. The questioning also aimed to establish how political leaders had encouraged and supported abuses through propaganda and socialization. Jean Pierre Du Plessis explained that his father "believed that the White race was an exalted race on the earth... all the other races were mud races... sub-races, and didn't really have a right to exist." The commissioners asked if his father was convincing. Du Plessis responded, "[m]y father is probably the most logical person I know." Du Plessis also discussed his experience in the South African Defence Force, where he was instructed that the struggle against apartheid was a fight against the "Communist monster," an enemy that "had to be destroyed at all costs."[79] The TRC's goal of understanding diverse perspectives and fostering a space to deliberate the meaning of past violence sat uncomfortably alongside its goal of censure and seemed to preclude the development of a coherent method for critically assessing the various perspectives that were voiced at the commission.

For example, the chapter of the *TRC Report* dealing with "causes, motives and perspectives of perpetrators" begins by asserting that just as a cough and fever are symptoms of pneumonia, so too can a "syndrome" of a "culture of human rights violations" be identified by symptoms such as "emerging obsessive ideology, hyperarousal, diminished affective reactivity, and group dependent aggression."[80] The chapter analyzes the behavior of the state forces and the liberation groups alike in relation to this psychological profile. It is not until twenty-three pages into the chapter that racism is even mentioned as a factor.[81] The chapter's political analysis uncritically paraphrases the view that the state was bound to fight the ANC to stop the Marxist-Communist threat. It presents the ANC statement that it was fighting a just war against systematic dispossession and racial oppression and the National Party's contention that it was fighting primarily a Cold War struggle, as though these were two equally legitimate perspectives on the conflict. Erik Doxtader observes that amnesty serves as a reminder of the contingency of human judgment "in times when the integrity of the law

---

78 *Promotion of National Unity and Reconciliation Act*, chapter 2, at 3.1a.
79 *TRC Amnesty Hearings* (July 1996).   80 *TRC Report*, 5, 259–60.
81 *TRC Report*, 5, 282.

and politics is suspect."⁸² Yet by retaining the claim to present a moral narrative while shifting to a psychological framework of analysis designed to avoid such judgment, this chapter of the *TRC Report* implicitly condones major justifications for the repression and violence committed by the apartheid state.

When the ANC rejected the *TRC Report* and sought to block its publication in protest of what it viewed as a distorted characterization of the struggle against apartheid, Human Rights Watch roundly condemned the ANC and praised the TRC for withstanding this pressure.⁸³ Regardless of the ANC's motivations, it is striking that Human Rights Watch did not comment on the allegation that the commission distorted the past. Without attention to this dimension of transitional justice, human rights advocates have neglected the danger that truth commissions, in response to political pressure, may construct selective accounts of the past that function to obfuscate the causes and consequences of political violence. Debates on truth commissions and transitional trials often treat the historical findings of these institutions as an incidental residue of the decision to punish or pardon, to pursue justice or reconciliation. Yet the story they tell about past injustices is one of the most politically and morally significant facets of these institutions. To the extent that truth commission reports merely reflect transitional compromises and concessions, they may function to naturalize inequalities that are the legacy of the past, foreclose criticism and attention to the limitations of initial transitional bargains, or, at worst, legitimate the myths that once justified systematic injustices. Yet critics of the TRC's healing narrative have tended to be too sweeping in their dismissals, neglecting the ways that the TRC also demonstrates and expands on the possibility of critical remembrance championed by its earliest proponents.

Critical Potential

Political judgment plays a role in laying out the terms of all transitional justice projects, yet restorative justice explicitly allows political judgment to guide the process. For Sheldon Wolin, the basic dilemma of political judgment is "how to create a common rule in the context of difference."⁸⁴ Hannah Arendt, like Wolin, connects the concept of political judgment to an idea of democratic politics as involving the interplay of incommensurable

---

82 Erik Doxtader, "Easy to Forget," 126.
83 "HRW Welcomes Release of South African Truth Report: Criticizes Attempts to Censure Report," Press Release, October 1998.
84 Sheldon Wolin, *Politics and Vision: Continuity and Innovation in Western Political Thought* (Boston, 1960), 61.

moral perspectives that cannot be reconciled through an appeal to timeless or transcendent norms.[85] While Arendt and Wolin stress the role of contestation in political judgment, Paul Ricoeur focuses on the element of decision, which announces a provisional end to deliberation and its attendant uncertainties.[86]

The work of the TRC was influenced by political judgments made to advance the transition, to condemn apartheid as a system, and to soften and blur that condemnation. Throughout, political judgment involved compromises that aimed to close options for further debate. Yet because they do not lay claim to the status of timeless truth, political judgments may be contested and the practice of remembering past injustices in the truth commission context may provide a unique basis for such contestation. Arendt's discussions of forgiveness and truth are often quoted in transitional justice debates, but perhaps the most important avenue of her thinking for these questions concerns the perplexities of judgment in the absence of community. She begins the volume *Between Past and Future* with a quote from Rene Char: "Our inheritance was left to us by no testament."[87] In the absence of a traditional transmission of values, she argues, a new way of appropriating guidance from the past would be needed. Arendt's introduction to *Illuminations*, a collection of essays by Walter Benjamin, praises what she takes to be his project of rethinking history and tradition by "tearing fragments out of their context and arranging them afresh."[88] She sees this as a way to draw guidance from the past, while simultaneously underscoring the distance between past and present. Arendt refers to this as "pearl diving" and suggested that fragments of the past, removed from context, might shed light on new possibilities for political community, while rejecting the idea that past identities, values, and compromises are simply inherited. South Africa's TRC demonstrates how the interplay of political judgment and remembrance may play a critical role in an ongoing process of democratic change.

The restorative justice focus on context, consequences, and dialogue provided a basis for the *TRC Report* to condemn apartheid as a system, evaluate its legacy, and air a range of critical challenges to the new government. The victim and amnesty hearings focused on gross violations of human rights. However, the TRC also held special hearings to examine the role of South

---

85 See, especially, Hannah Arendt, *Lectures on Kant's Political Philosophy*, Ronald Beiner, ed. (Chicago, 1982), 72–7.
86 Paul Ricoeur, *The Just*, trans. David Pellauer (Chicago and London, 2000), 127–33.
87 "Notre heritage n'est precede d'aucun testament." Hannah Arendt, *Between Past and Future: Eight Exercises in Political Thought* (New York, 1961), 3.
88 Hannah Arendt, "Introduction," in Walter Benjamin, *Illuminations* (New York, 1968), 47.

African institutions in supporting apartheid, including political parties, business and labor, the faith community, the legal system, the health sector, prisons, and compulsory military service. These investigations did not focus on individual acts but rather on how apartheid operated as a system. The entire fourth volume of the *TRC Report* is devoted to these institutional hearings and takes a critical view of justifications and denials. In stark contrast to the chapter addressing motivations of perpetrators, the chapter on the institutional responsibility of the legal community states that the organized legal profession "connived in the legislative and executive pursuit of injustice," by supporting the National Party's bid for legal legitimacy.[89] The volume also censures the media for a policy of appeasing the state and failing to maintain its independence.[90] It cites several faith communities, notably the Dutch Reformed Church, as "agents of oppression" and argues that the military chaplaincy legitimated abuses by suppressing dissent within the military.[91] The volume argues that business in general and the mining industry in particular were instrumental in designing apartheid policies and states that the "brutal suppression of striking workers, racist practices and meager wages is central to understanding the origins and nature of apartheid."[92] This chapter is consistent with the restorative principle of examining the underlying causes of crime and reflects the original idea that the TRC would use an informal process to facilitate a broad investigation of apartheid as a system.

The restorative principle of examining the consequences of past crimes also appears in the *TRC Report* as a critical challenge for broader social change. A chapter addressing the consequences of historical injustices begins by stating that "the apartheid system was maintained through repressive means, depriving the majority of South Africans the most basic human rights.... Its legacy is a society in which vast numbers of people suffer from pervasive poverty and lack of opportunities."[93] In addition to the long-term psychological and physical impact of violence on individuals, the chapter outlines the consequences of human rights violations for communities, focusing on racial and social engineering under apartheid and intracommunity conflict resulting from collusion with the state.[94] Testimony detailing the physical and emotional toll of past abuses may generate a more profound awareness of past injustices and the significance of their legacy in a process that refuses to reduce diverse experiences of suffering and loss to categories amenable to legal remedy.

89 *TRC Report*, 4, 101.
90 *TRC Report*, 4, 188.
91 *TRC Report*, 4, 71.
92 *TRC Report*, 4, 34.
93 *TRC Report*, 5, 125.
94 *TRC Report*, 5, 157–60.

Albie Sachs has argued that the main strength of the TRC was that it was based "essentially on dialogue, on hearing all different viewpoints, on receiving inputs from all sides."[95] The TRC hosted several public discussions throughout the life of the commission, at which numerous critics addressed the multiple shortcomings of the process. The effort to air conflicting views at the TRC mitigated some of the dangers that might otherwise be associated with an official legitimating truth, and the *TRC Report* includes numerous criticisms voiced prior to its publication. For example, Mahmood Mamdani had argued that the TRC focus on gross violations of human rights would distort the history of apartheid and proposed that it would be better to analyze the responsibility of apartheid's *beneficiaries* rather than the "perpetrators" of apartheid's worst excesses. This argument is paraphrased in volume one of the *TRC Report* and is presented as a warning regarding the limitations of the commission.[96] Volume four returns to Mamdani's focus on the beneficiaries of apartheid in critically assessing testimony presented by members of the business community.[97]

The *TRC Report* also contains a chapter on reconciliation, which consists primarily of long narratives. Laurie Nathan's statement to the TRC is quoted at length: "The white community should confront its pervasive racism.... We should acknowledge collective responsibility for our efforts and our acquiescence in constructing and maintaining a wretched system of discrimination, exclusions, and repression."[98] Cynthia Ngewu's testimony is also quoted: "We do not want to return evil by another evil. We simply want to ensure that the perpetrators are returned to humanity."[99] A man who lost his brother to a South African Defense Force raid is quoted describing his path from intense violent hatred of all whites to the idea that his hatred would "negate everything that my brother stood for."[100] These examples gesture toward the possibility of relationships in a future political community that would break from inherited conceptions of community and identity.

By remembering causes and consequences of systematic injustices, truth commissions may underscore the limits of what passes for justice in the

---

95 "Fourth D. T. Lakdawala Memorial Lecture," 12.
96 *TRC Report*, 1, 133.
97 *TRC Report*, 4, 43. The final addition to the *TRC Report*, released in March 2003, recommends that all beneficiaries contribute to a reparation fund for victims (*Truth and Reconciliation Commission of South Africa Report* [Cape Town, 2003], 6, 8).
98 *TRC Report*, 5.
99 *TRC Report*, 5, 366. Ngewu's son was killed by the South African Security Police in a famous incident known as the "Gugulethu 7."
100 *TRC Report*, 5, 375.

context of transition and provide a basis for pursuing ongoing reforms. By remembering gestures of remorse, forgiveness, and reparation, truth commissions may illuminate possibilities for future political relationships that are not readily apparent during the transition. One of the motivations for the TRC in South Africa was to establish a critical historical record as a basis for ongoing social change. Yet truth commissions are created in the context of political conflict and compromise over the very definition of past crimes, where a major aspiration is to legitimate the new regime. Restorative justice also became appealing as a way to connect justice to the goal of community reconstruction on a national scale. The danger is that gestures toward healing will be confused with moral consensus, or that history will be reduced to the legitimation of political compromises. Indeed, truth commissions do seek to legitimate the compromises that led to democratic change. Yet they also set out to condemn past repression and systematic injustice, thereby calling into question bargains made with those responsible. The tension between these two goals stems from the political aspirations of transitional justice projects and has thus been neglected in critical assessments based solely on abstract conceptions of justice. In evaluating the merits of trials versus truth commissions, as well as future efforts to combine them, it will be important to consider how they address this tension and to critically assess the relationship between the political compromises and the historical records of these projects.

PART V

Conclusion

12

"The Issue That Won't Go Away"

A. JAMES MCADAMS

In the beginning of the second book of his *Untimely Meditations*, Friedrich Nietzsche uses the image of a grazing cow to make a point about humanity's complex relationship with its past. The cow projects an image of happiness because it can spend all day and all night doing whatever it wants, eating, sleeping, chewing, and wandering about. It has no consciousness of what has come before each of its movements. It appears contented because it lives "ahistorically" in blissful ignorance of even a momentary event. In contrast, Nietzsche argues that human beings are routinely assaulted by history and the living memory of past wrongs, misdeeds, and injustices. Yet humans do have one distinct advantage over the cow. Unlike the beast, which can never be truly happy because it lacks the ability to reflect on its own condition, humans can aspire to authentic fulfillment. They enjoy the capacity – the "agency" (*plastische Kraft*), Nietzsche calls it – to choose what to forget. Their task is to cultivate those memories that are essential for life and expunge those that will hold it back.[1]

The chapters in this volume provide ample testimony to the abiding challenge of drawing this distinction and acting in conformity with it. As John Torpey observes in his chapter, Western democracies have been beset by an "avalanche of history" since the end of World War II.[2] Germany's military defeat and the revelation of the crimes of the Holocaust touched off a flood of demands for the punishment of wrongdoers, material restitution, truth-telling, and various types of conditional reconciliation. Since then, as we have seen, from Germany to France, South Africa to New Zealand, the advocates of these measures have called for policies of "active remembering" to attend to the wounds of dictatorship and the abuse of power. The authors

---

1 Friedrich Nietzsche, "Unzeitgemässe Betrachtungen," in *Werke in Zwei Bändern*, v. 1 (Munich, 1967), 115–16.
2 John Torpey (Chapter 1) in this volume.

of the South Korean "Report on the Presidential Truth Commission on Suspicious Deaths" (2002), one of the first such documents of the twenty-first century, justified their proceedings in terms that are instantly familiar to both students and practitioners of historical justice. "A genuine transition from an old era," the report states, "requires the clearing away of the contradictions and malpractices of the past order. It has been so, and has to be so; for we know from history that our nation will pay a heavy price, sooner or later, if we do not observe this imperative."[3]

It is not surprising that these historical undertakings have given birth to a robust industry of expert guidance on the art of coming to terms with the past. Since at least the early 1990s, political activists, international lawyers, pastors, and self-proclaimed do-gooders have traveled from one country to another proclaiming the news of their trade. If past crimes cannot be totally overcome, they contend, they can at least be managed, manipulated, massaged, and steered in ways that serve the needs of a fledgling democracy in the present and help it to flourish in the future. Doing something is supposedly always better than doing nothing.

In this cause, these "entrepreneurs of memory" (Torpey) have found their credentials bolstered by a burgeoning scholarly literature on the subject. The academic experts maintain that historical justice is not only a normative good but a science that can be applied in a methodical and differentiated fashion from case to case. For example, many social scientists maintain that those democratic regimes that have resulted from the overthrow of a dictatorship will require different measures from those that have come to power by negotiation. Leaders of the first regime type should be encouraged to confront crimes directly because their predecessors are no longer around to challenge their authority, let alone to return to power. Conversely, the representatives of negotiated transitions must recognize that they are in a much weaker position due to their continuing vulnerability to attack and overthrow. Whatever kinds of deals they have struck with their adversaries, whether honorable or sordid, they should resist the temptation to scrutinize the past too closely, lest it come back to haunt them.

Likewise, many experts seem to assume that the imperative to act on injustice is proportional to the severity of the offenses in question. In the case of egregious rights violations or indisputable crimes against humanity, there will be intense public and international pressure to satisfy the demands of the victims and to mend their fractured society. In contrast, lesser offences – the loss of a home, the destruction of a career, the betrayal

---

3 *A Hard Journey to Justice*, First Term Report of the Presidential Commission on Suspicious Deaths of the Republic of Korea (10/2000 to 10/2002), 11.

of a friendship – are supposedly harder to address. Presumably, there will be far fewer advocates of retributive action. Their cries for justice will be drowned out by the calls of their less interested compatriots to get on with life and to focus on practical tasks like institution-building and economic reconstruction.

I doubt that anyone will deny the importance of these distinctions. It is hardly contestable that South Africa's narrowly defined approach to criminal trials in the mid-1990s was shaped by markedly different conditions (a "negotiated transition") from Greece's aggressive trials of the "colonels" two decades earlier (a "regime of overthrow"). For similar reasons, it is well known that Chile's "truth and reconciliation" commission of 1990 (based on a largely negotiated transition) subscribed to a somewhat different agenda from its Argentine predecessor (a partially collapsed military regime) in 1983. Different histories, different leaders, and different decisions make distinct responses inevitable.

There is, however, another way of thinking about our topic that should help to bring together the diverse causes of historical justice in this volume. Instead of beginning with the self-evident fact that these examples are different, let us pose the opposite question. What factors do all of these cases have in common? Many onlookers will find the question counterintuitive. In geographical terms, few expressions of modern dictatorship or the systematic violation of human rights could be more different from, say, Pol Pot's unfathomable crimes against humanity and the displacement of Greenlanders during the Cold War.[4] One can make the same point about the differences between the Vichy regime's anti-Semitic policies and the persecution of indigenous peoples in Australia.[5] Hence, at first glance, the task of acting on these circumstances would seem radically different from one case to the next. By the same token, if we focus on cases with a broad historical sweep, say Europe in the wake of World War II and again during the postcommunist 1990s, the challenge appears equally daunting.

Nevertheless, if we can identify similarities among these cases – a necessarily more demanding task than pointing to differences – wouldn't this discovery tell us something about our ability to live up to Nietzsche's challenge to choose those memories of injustice that are useful to humanity and to reject those that are not? One possibility is that we will gain a provocative glimpse into the challenges awaiting any country after its departure from dictatorship or, in a broader sense, any people who has suffered grievous harm. Can the past ever be overcome in the manner the entrepreneurs

---

4 Compare Chapter 8 by Steve Heder in this volume with Chapter 5 by Svend Aage Christensen and Kristian Søby Kristensen.
5 Compare Chapter 6 by Julie Fette in this volume with Chapter 9 by Bain Attwood.

of memory desire? If they want to be taken seriously, the experts have no choice but to face up to this question. A second benefit is that we will better understand a fact that this volume demonstrates as well as any other. Throughout the world, scholars show no sign of ceasing to publish books, organize symposia, advise policy makers, and lecture on the subject of coming to terms with the past. Historical justice is an issue that seemingly won't go away.

In this chapter, I propose to explore this issue by focusing on the supposedly incomparable case of postunification Germany. How often have we been told since the day of national unity – October 1, 1990 – that Germany is different? The country is wealthier, more stable politically, and less ethnically diverse than most states facing similar circumstances. In fact, Germany's special responsibility for the crimes of the Holocaust has arguably made its leaders even more attuned to the imperative to combat injustice. But precisely because of these differences, few states are better suited for my comparative exercise. If commonalities can be found between Germany's reputedly exceptional instance of historical justice and other cases, we are well advised to look for them everywhere.

To engage this thought experiment, I begin with a brief description of the Federal Republic of Germany's head-on encounter with the communist legacy. To account for something, we must agree about what we are seeking to explain. Contrary to the common wisdom, this is not easy; I have addressed this point in my *Judging the Past in Unified Germany*.[6] Then I will suggest three ways – one of which is still in gestation – in which Berlin's actions were not significantly different from many other states' in transitional situations. These are: 1) the constraints of precedent, 2) the illusion of resolution, and 3) the "eternal return" of the past. In terms of justice per se, if my reading of these common challenges is correct, this is not a completely uplifting story. But at the end of this chapter, I shall offer some insight into why the attempt to come to terms with injustice, however difficult, should matter to us at all.

Germany: A Special Case of Historical Justice?

Germany has always seemed to be a "special case."[7] In the late nineteenth century and throughout the twentieth century, German officials and

---

6 A. James McAdams, *Judging the Past in Unified Germany* (New York, 2001).
7 For this section of my chapter, I have drawn on material originally included in my article "Transitional Justice after 1989," *Bulletin of the German Historical Institute*, 33 (Fall 2003): 53–64. A German version appeared under the title "Vergangenheitsaufarbeitung nach 1989. Ein Deutscher Sonderweg?" in *Deutschland Archiv* 36, 5 (2003): 851–60.

intellectuals repeatedly appealed to concepts like the *Sonderweg* ("special path") in seeking to bolster their conceptions of a unique national identity. Likewise, after the debacles of two world wars, their European neighbors searched for special solutions – *Sonderlösungen*, if you will – to the recurrent problem of German power. Our temptation is to think that the 1990s were no different. Germany would again be special.

In the months following the opening of the Berlin Wall in late 1989, when the two German states were on the verge of coming together, experts argued that East Germany's fate would be dramatically different from that of any of its Soviet-bloc neighbors. After all, the German Democratic Republic (GDR) alone had a national counterpart in the West. Its weaknesses were matched by the other state's strengths. In contrast to the other new democracies of Eastern Europe, only the GDR faced the prospect of *total* transformation according to the economic and political principles of a liberal capitalist order. Only its leaders faced the certainty of being divested of meaningful political roles in the unified German state. Indeed, as this unequal East-West relationship was played out, it was logical to assume that East Germany would be the one place among all of the formerly communist states where historical justice was fully realized.

In one respect, these predictions have turned out to be accurate. More than in other parts of Eastern Europe, the former GDR experienced virtually the gamut of efforts to act on the crimes and injustices of dictatorship. Throughout the 1990s, criminal courts were the scene of numerous prosecutions for the shooting deaths at the Berlin Wall and along the inter-German border. Hundreds of thousands of civil servants from the old regime were vetted for their "suitability" for continued employment in the new democratic order. Administrative courts reviewed competing claims for thousands of houses, dachas, parcels of land, and other forms of property that had been confiscated under the old dictatorship. And, by decade's end, two parliamentary commissions had completed investigations of a host of wrongs that could not be resolved by statute.

If quantity had the same meaning as quality, the search for common experiences would end here. Nonetheless, despite the fact that Germany's leaders sought to address a greater number and broader spectrum of offenses than any of their peers, these efforts were met with widespread dissatisfaction among those who had suffered the most under the communist dictatorship. Their driving concern was about the *quality* of justice that was ultimately achieved. When we think about the many different cases that are typically considered in scholarly studies of historical justice, including a majority of those described in this book, this point should not be news to any of us.

Disappointment, disillusionment, and disgruntlement are to be expected. Still, why should this shared dilemma matter at all?

The Constraints of Precedent

The first reason for disappointment is that the pursuit of historical justice is not a straightforward exercise in volition. It is not a policy smorgasbord, where one pauses to review a menu of options and then chooses the most attractive course: "I'll take two truth commissions, one short trial, and no property issues." If only the challenges of governance were this straightforward! Rather, the ability of democratic leaders to control the political agenda is always less than they hope for and, for that matter, than outsiders think. A century and a half ago, Karl Marx made this point in *The Eighteenth Brumaire of Louis Bonaparte*. "Men do not make [history] by themselves," he wrote, "but under circumstances directly encountered, given and transmitted from the past."[8]

For example, not long after the demise of the apartheid system, South African rights activists invited a slough of policy makers, practitioners, and intellectuals from fledgling democracies in Latin America and Europe to learn about the various strategies for dealing with our topic. The idea was not merely that the representatives of the postapartheid order would compare and contrast their circumstances with their counterparts' experiences. Rather, many hoped that after reviewing diverse cases, they could make well-informed decisions about the approach that best suited their needs and, if all went well, that had the greatest likelihood of being palatable to their citizens.

A senior Chilean participant in this exercise told me proudly at the time that the South Africans had selected his country as their model because it represented the least confrontational path for the diverse pretenders to political power. Looking back, I am not persuaded that South Africa followed a Chilean model in all respects. For example, the prospect of conducting criminal trials was considered much more seriously in the former case than in the latter. In the postapartheid regime, defendants could be prosecuted for failing to testify truthfully. Still, it is more important to recognize that the government's decision to take action came before much of the public debate. Well before the "retrospective justice shuttles" had touched down in Johannesburg and Cape Town, the leaders of the African National Congress and the National Party had already formalized their decisions in the interim

---

8 Karl Marx and Friedrich Engels, *Selected Works* (New York, 1968), 97.

constitution of 1993. Here and there, rights advocates and experts debated the meaning of ambiguous terms in the document – for example, the loaded concept of "amnesty" – but the legal framework for all subsequent discussions had been set.

At this point, social scientists would undoubtedly contend that this particular outcome was the predictable result of a negotiated transition. Accordingly, they would argue, one could expect a different outcome from a regime of overthrow. In fact, this is what critics confidently predicted about unified Germany's intentions. For many, the country's predominantly western leadership was bent on imposing "victor's justice" on its vanquished counterparts, regardless of the damage it would do to the credibility of German legal traditions and the rule of law. Precisely because West Germany's policies had been validated in the court of history, the Berlin government could and, they were certain, would impose its will as it wished. To use a favored expression of the GDR's longtime party secretary, Erich Honecker, one would have to be "blind as kittens" not to recognize this fact. However, if we look closely at two of the Federal Republic's most prominent efforts to achieve historical justice in the 1990s – the opening of the once-secret files of East Germany's security police (the Stasi) and the return of expropriated property to its original owners – we can see that these assumptions were not quite correct.

Consider the controversy that broke out in 1990 over the millions of Stasi files that suddenly became available after the Berlin Wall's fall.[9] Despite observers' first impressions, the fact that authorities gained access to these documents was not at all an opportunity for self-satisfaction and gloating. Contrary to expectations and against the demands of many East German dissidents, West German officials initially balked at the prospect of giving the Stasi's victims access to the tainted remnants of dictatorship. At a time of turbulence and uncertainty in the East, they feared that the opening of these records would have explosive consequences. Furthermore, outside of a handful of Stasi officials, no one could know for sure what information might be found in the files. Interior Minister Wolfgang Schäuble underscored his conviction that there were more important things to be done than stirring up ugly memories. Chancellor Helmut Kohl noted that it would be best to destroy the files outright.

Yet despite their apprehensions, Germany's leaders quickly discovered that they could do little to prevent these records from entering the public sphere. In many respects, their predicament was a natural outgrowth

9 McAdams, *Judging the Past*, chapter 3.

of decisions that were outside of their control and that had been reached months before unification. Thousands of personal dossiers and surveillance reports had been captured in January 1990 when outraged citizens stormed the Stasi's Berlin-Normannenstraße headquarters. Shortly thereafter, journalists, well-meaning activists, and a variety of opportunists had already begun to circulate large portions of the records for popular consumption. As a result, the GDR parliament, the Volkskammer, rushed to pass legislation on what its representatives considered to be the appropriate uses of the files. Hence, even before West German officials arrived on the scene and regardless of their wishes, the opening of the Stasi's records was well under way.

In much the same fashion, Kohl and his colleagues found their hands similarly tied on the issue of property restitution.[10] The suddenness of the GDR's collapse precipitated a landslide of disputes over the disposition of tens of thousands of properties lost, stolen, or expropriated since World War II. In an ideal world, unified Germany's leaders preferred to pick and choose when they would become involved in the adjudication of these matters. But, here too, their options were shaped by circumstances "encountered, given, and transmitted from the past," that is, a somewhat more remote past.

Months before the signing of the Unification Treaty, the point at which West Germany's legal system was officially transferred to the territory of the GDR, the Volkskammer had taken another step toward redressing the old regime's offenses by returning scores of nationalized firms to their original owners. For the FRG, this fait accompli, too, raised uncomfortable matters of precedent. If these companies could be returned, then why not other forms of property as well? Further complicating matters, this was not the only precedent for addressing open property disputes. West Germany itself had set the stage decades earlier under Konrad Adenauer. In the 1950s, the founders of the new democracy committed their government to compensating the Jewish victims of Nazism for their property losses during Hitler's "aryanization" campaigns. Of course, as long as Germany was divided, this policy could not be applied to the GDR. Unification raised the issue anew.

Each confrontation with history made good sense when considered on its own terms. Nonetheless, the unwieldy conditions of the times made it impossible – in both these and other cases – to compartmentalize policy making. One could hardly confine the government's measures to those cases that seemed the least destabilizing. Once West German authorities moved

---

10 McAdams, *Judging the Past*, chapter 5.

ahead on one controversy, it seemed, they were immediately confronted with other disputes. Among these were the fantastically complex issue of the Soviet Union's postwar expropriation of nearly a third of the landed property of the area that would eventually become the GDR; the destruction of scores of houses and apartment buildings to clear the way for the Berlin Wall's construction; and, in the GDR's waning days, the purchase by hopeful citizens of state-controlled houses and other properties that many had occupied for their entire lives.

In all of these cases, there is much to admire about the Solomonic care with which German administrative courts sought to reach fair and consistent rulings about the disposition of such properties. At least from the perspective of the chancellor's office, this was not an opportunity for victor's justice. Unfortunately, few of the ordinary parties to these disputes found much satisfaction in the courts' decisions. On the contrary, the losers in the restitution and compensation battles could not help but conclude that justice had been denied to them. Ironically, having enjoyed a taste of justice, the beneficiaries felt all too often that they should have received even more.

The Illusion of Resolution

This dilemma brings me to a second feature of transitional justice, the illusion of overcoming the past. We often hear from both rights activists and scholars that the most sensible goal in the face of disappointment is to search for that fine line between doing too much and doing too little. On the one hand, they tell us, governments must provide the victims with the assurance that wrongdoing will be addressed. On the other hand, wise leaders must also look to their country's future by reconciling aggrieved parties to a life together. Can it be any wonder, then, that those who take responsibility for this synthesis are frequently depicted as healers? Their charge is to attack the "ills," "wounds," "festering sores," "traumas," "tumors," and "cancers" of historical injustice while simultaneously preparing a divided society for the return to good health. But if this is healing, tell that to the family of the murdered activist Steve Biko, who sought in vain to have South Africa's amnesty law overturned.[11] Or tell that to the families of Orlando Letelier and Ronnie Moffitt, whose car was blown up by the Chilean intelligence service while visiting Washington, D.C., in 1976.

---

11 For example, see John Dugard, "Retrospective Justice: International Law and the South African Model," in A. James McAdams, ed., *Transitional Justice and the Rule of Law in New Democracies* (Notre Dame, Ind., 1997), 269–90.

The problem with justice, qualitatively speaking, is that it is hard to recognize, and even then, one never knows when one has received enough of it. Hannah Arendt tells us that some crimes – genocide, mass murder, and torture – are so horrific that it is impossible to know how to deal with them in a satisfactory manner, let alone how to understand them.[12] Yet even smaller offenses, like those described earlier, are not so banal that they can be easily forgiven or passed over. Over time, the memory of injustice seeps into the lives of everyone around it. Not only do the victims despair for lack of a resolution, but even the perpetrators can find themselves confined to a legal and moral limbo that can be lifted only through withdrawal from society and death. The latter is exactly what happened to the elderly members of the GDR's former politburo.

If we consider the outcome of the much-publicized trials of the GDR's former communist elite, it is clear that Germany has been no exception to the rule. Unified Germany was not the first state in the latter half of the twentieth century in which democratic leaders sought to achieve justice through criminal prosecutions; Greece, Bolivia, and Argentina did the same.[13] However, Germany's trials were arguably the most thorough. They were perfect examples of Max Weber's "slow boring of hard boards" from the first moment to the last. Beginning in 1990 – once again, as a result of decisions reached before unification – an array of politburo members, military officers, and lowly border guards were indicted on charges of ordering or facilitating the shooting deaths of hundreds of East Germans who had sought to flee their country. In painstaking fashion, local and appellate courts reviewed mountains of evidence and agonized over the appropriate legal principles for assessing culpability. Although fewer than 30 defendants were convicted and only a handful spent time in jail, I personally believe that most of these decisions were rendered fairly and conscientiously.[14]

Still, the disturbing result of the entire endeavor is what did not happen. Instead of provoking introspection and debate, the trials were largely received with disinterest and boredom by the majority of German citizens.

---

12 Hannah Arendt, *The Human Condition* (Chicago, 1958), 241.
13 For analyses of these cases, see McAdams, *Transitional Justice*.
14 One notable exception to this rule, in my opinion, is the trial of former politburo member Herbert Häber. In July 2000, Häber was acquitted of having participated in decisions that led to shooting deaths along the Berlin Wall. The court concluded that he had done everything in his power to minimize tensions between the Germanys, especially along the intra-German border. Yet on November 6, 2002, the Federal Court of Review (Bundesgerichtshof) overturned the acquittal on the grounds that the criminal court had not sufficiently considered the charges against him. Häber was then retried and convicted, although he was immediately paroled.

At the same time, there was precious little evidence of reconciliation – or even dialogue – between the activists who defended these measures as a vital part of Germany's healing process and the wrongdoers who stood to lose the most from convictions. Before the last judgment was rendered, both sides had been thoroughly marginalized. The heroes of 1989 were reduced to pleading their cause to each other while their counterparts were revealed to be little more than lonely old men wasting away in desolate living rooms. To paraphrase another passage from the *Eighteenth Brumaire*, what began as tragedy during four decades of communist rule seemed predestined to return as farce in a new political order.[15] Disillusionment on both sides was inevitable.

The Eternal Return

If this were where the similarities among states' diverse experiences with historical justice came to an end, my story would be interesting but of limited long-term significance. Why then does this topic continue to intrigue us? Indeed, what intellectual forces have brought the contributors to this volume together? A major reason, and the last of my three points, is that the unaddressed or underaddressed issues of the past need not go away. Not only do they defy resolution, but they can return again and again. In fact, one of the most striking features about many scholarly treatments of historical justice is how many of them deal with events that took place before their authors were born. If this is "transitional justice," this has been quite a long transition!

One frequently noted reason for the staying power of these issues has to do with the interests of the victims themselves. As long as these persons are alive or as particularly vocal descendants can be located, demands for justice and rectification will prosper. In their chapter, as we have seen, Richard S. Hill and Brigitte Bönisch-Brednich cite a leading Maori negotiator to this effect: "Just because we have gained some compensation for past injustices, don't think we are going to go away."[16]

In addition, when one aggrieved group steps forward to levy its demands, it is not uncommon for another interest group to follow suit. Consider the following train of events. In 1988, the advocates of Japanese Americans who were deported to internment camps during World War II finally forced the Reagan administration to make compensation payments by arguing that few

---

15 Marx and Engels, *Selected Works*, 97.
16 Richard S. Hill and Brigitte Bönisch-Brednich (Chapter 10) in this volume.

of their clients would be around much longer to benefit from an admission of guilt. In quick succession, the Jewish survivors of Nazi slave-labor camps drew on their own longevity concerns to intensify long-standing demands for compensation from German corporations that had profited from their misery; a final settlement was reached only in 2002. Continuing this cascade, as Manfred Berg outlines in his chapter, African-American descendants of American slaves began demanding reparations for the injustices inflicted on their forefathers.[17] In a typical case in 2003, Ina McGee, the 69-year-old great-granddaughter of a former slave, provided the following rationale for her family's decision (which included support from her 99-year-old mother) to initiate a class-action suit against three Texas corporations: "The Germans got theirs. The Indians got theirs and may get more. Everyone has received reparations except for African-Americans. It's our turn now."[18]

Such interest-based explanations undoubtedly account for the resurgence of many demands for compensatory justice. Nonetheless, they are not necessarily reliable predictors of the salience and vitality of these issues over time. Furthermore, they may not be true to the spirit with which these claims are raised. More than a century after the wrongs took place, Ina McGee can define a *part* of her identity in terms of her descent from persons she never knew because there is much about her demands that transcends biology. Of course, slavery is no longer a tangible reality in the United States. What is tangible, however, is the continuing existence of social and economic conditions – inequality, structural unemployment, endemic poverty – that one can trace back to the institution of slavery.

In this light, it is no accident that African-American demands for reparations have intensified over the past decade as public support for affirmative action, the most visible means of redressing historical injustice in the United States, has waned. The more that preferential hiring and race-based university admissions policies are challenged in the courts, the greater is the likelihood that those persons who have the most to lose from a change in policy will seek new vehicles for expressing their discontent. In this not exactly literal but symbolically significant way, the grievances of a new era can be planted in the fissures and faults of another age.

It is too early to tell how or whether comparable parallels will be drawn in Germany, say, twenty-five or thirty years after the fall of the Berlin Wall. However, if future generations desire, they will have no problem finding reasons for relating their government's actions in the first decade of unification to contested issues in their own age.

---

17 Manfred Berg (Chapter 3) in this volume.   18 *Houston Chronicle*, January 20, 2003.

The groundwork has already been laid. While the debates over the merits of historical justice in the 1990s were clearly heartfelt, they were also part of a more comprehensive dispute over how Germany was to be unified. Thus, one side's nervousness about the applicability of western legal norms and mores to the former GDR and the shadow of "victor's justice" reflected deeper concerns about how quickly the German government should have dismantled the old socialist system. Conversely, the other side's eagerness to push for justice and accountability spoke to a conviction that one could not act quickly enough. The fissures of conflict were manifest.

With the benefit of hindsight, we can understand why the Kohl administration's aggressive implementation of the latter course led to severe economic dislocations in the East, the collapse of the region's social security net, and a tacit feeling among eastern Germans that they had been relegated to a second-class status in their new homeland. But let us imagine that this mood of disenfranchisement were somehow to be sustained over the coming decade. The prospect is not far-fetched. It is true that the region's economic infrastructure has been slowly rebuilt and that most of the GDR's former citizens now enjoy the benefits of the German *Sozialstaat*. Nonetheless, more than a decade and a half after the fact, many easterners feel that they remain less than equal partners in the unification project. There are still few eastern Germans in prominent government positions, and many westerners continue to treat their compatriots with notable condescension. Should these latent tensions be aggravated by other frustrations in the years to come, even unrelated ones, isn't it possible that a disgruntled Dresdener or an alienated Berliner will be tempted to reach for his or her former identity and proclaim in Kennedyesque fashion: "Ich bin ein Ostdeutscher."

If this were to happen, or to the extent that it is already happening in the East, there are some rich opportunities for rekindling old debates about Berlin's reckoning with the GDR's crimes. For example, one hotly contested aspect of the debate over the Stasi files was their use in vetting East German officials for ties to the secret police. Although we will never have the exact figures, approximately 40,000 administrators were fired outright or forced into early retirement as a result of these findings. How might one capitalize on this issue to serve future controversies? Conceivably, someone who wanted the German government to pay greater attention to selecting easterners for high governmental posts could argue that these dismissals confirmed that Berlin was never fully committed to treating all Germans equally. Conversely, those who disputed the idea of affirmative action could just as easily contend that federal authorities had disqualified far fewer officials than they should have. For aggrieved persons on both sides, it would not be hard to come up with complaints about other nagging issues in the post-Wall period, even – or especially – at the cost of misrepresenting the past.

Admittedly, these particular scenarios exist only in the realm of theory. There is no guarantee that any conflicts will take the form I have described. Yet the point is not whether disgruntled citizens use one or another criticism of past policy to call attention to enduring social and political disputes. Rather, I am arguing that wherever they should arise, demands for justice and for the admission of wrongdoing exhibit a stubborn resiliency that will make them difficult to step over lightly. It may seem irrational, but this fact will be self-evident to anyone who has sought to make sense of centuries-old conflicts, like those between the Serbs and the Croats, the Greeks and the Turks, and the English and the Irish. Popular memories often have little to do with the facts. For this reason, one should at least hold open the possibility that memories of the unification of eastern and western Germany will be no different.

The Long-Term Meaning of Historical Justice

Where are we left once we recognize these three similarities among states' efforts to come to terms with their past? Those persons who are optimistically moving down the path of some form of historical justice may be disappointed, even distressed, after reading this account. After all, the three obstacles do not tell us much about what can be done. Instead, they are about what *cannot* be guaranteed. They involve factors one cannot control, issues one cannot resolve, and controversies one cannot escape.

Assuming that my argument is correct, however, this need not mean that there is nothing positive to say to those hopeful individuals who still want to act on injustice. From my perspective, the recognition of one's limitations is actually a source of good news. If the attempt to repair long-standing wrongs is not about using a utilitarian calculus to decide what one should, or should not, aspire to accomplish, then it must be about something more fundamental in life that transcends individual cases. As Hannah Arendt emphasized in her controversial assessment of Adolf Eichmann's "unthinkable" crimes, one does not need to anguish over the difficulty of achieving justice before one acts on the problem.[19] One takes action because it is the right thing to do. I would push Arendt's point one step further. Doing the right thing should not depend on the gravity of the offenses. It should

---

19 Hannah Arendt, *Eichmann in Jerusalem* (1963: Middlesex, 1976), 277–8.

be one's first consideration in dealing with every instance of injustice. In this way, principled decision makers rise above the calculators and opportunists who first test the wind's direction before deciding what to do.

From this standpoint, it is also good news that democratic leaders must contend with a strong element of uncertainty in making their decisions. Because they can never be sure about the consequences of their actions, they will have no reason to wallow in self-satisfaction. If any factor can prevent them from becoming like Nietzsche's cud-chewing cow, it is the extent to which the indeterminacy of their choices forces them to return to their principles again and again.

One cannot overstate the importance of this issue. We are generally accustomed to speaking about historical justice in terms of its retrospective purposes. But as Karl Jaspers argued in a seminal work about the mission of postwar Germany, the attempt to reckon with the past has significant *prospective* functions as well.[20] The spirit and energy that democratic leaders bring to a common problem provide their citizens with important signals about what they can expect from their new institutions. Should the representatives of a successor regime be unresponsive to popular demands or act in ways that are incompatible with their founding ideals, they will never gain the trust of a population that has long been subjected to cynical manipulation. Conversely, these leaders stand a good chance of winning this credibility if, from the first moment, they show their dedication to the principles of fairness and decency that were denied to their citizens in the past. The recognition of universal norms happens to be an essential condition for all democracies because it transcends the idea that states are so unique that they cannot learn from each other. As we have seen throughout this volume, there is no guarantee that the new leaders will gain support just because they take the matter of historical justice seriously. Nonetheless, their chances of meeting with some success will be a lot better than if they fail to address the issue at all.

20 Karl Jaspers, *The Question of German Guilt*, trans. by E. B. Ashton (Westport, Conn., 1978).

Index

Adenauer, Konrad, 51, 99, 298
Adonis, Sandra, 281
African Americans,
   and affirmative action, 33, 37, 78, 82, 302
   racial discrimination and race relations in the U.S., 72–73, 88–91
   see also civil rights movement; slavery and reparations
African National Congress (ANC), *see* South Africa
Algeria
   and a French apology for torture during war, 146, 152, 157–61
   and French colonialism, 157–61
amnesty grants, 160, 299
   in Cambodia, 194, 203
   in South Africa, 267, 272, 280, 282, 299
   in the Soviet Union, 174
Annan, Kofi, 195, 196, 198, 200, 204, 205, 210, 212
Anne Frank (stage production), 100
Aotearoa, *see* New Zealand
apartheid, *see* South Africa
apology, 2, 46, 109, 135–63
   Catholic Church to French Jews, 138, 144–48, 155
   and closure, 142, 162–63
   and comfort women of WWII, 57
   corporations and civil groups issuing apologies, 71, 142–44, 148–55

   Danish government to indigenous Greenlanders, 131
   France and the Algerian War, 157–61
   Holocaust victims, 51, 55
   Jacques Chirac apology for Vichy anti-Semitism, 135–36, 138–42, 145, 154–55, 158, 161
   and Japanese-American WWII internment, 61, 70
   in New Zealand for Treaty breaches, 244, 263
   U.S. slave history, 71, 72, 86
Arendt, Hannah, 33–35, 283–84, 300, 304
Argentina, 293, 300
Arzt von Stalingrad, Der (The Doctor from Stalingrad) (film), 100
Asante, Molefi Kete, 81, 88
Asian Women's Fund (AWF), 57–58
Asmal, Kader, 272–75, 277, 279
Association of Daughters and Sons of Deportees, 140
Atonement and Forgiveness: A New Model for Black Reparations (Brooks), 72
Attali, Jacques, 141
Attwood, Bain, 11, 15
Auschwitz trial (1964), 51, 102
Aussaresses, Paul, 158
Australia and Australian aboriginal people, 5, 11, 13, 15, 217–38
   aboriginal land claims, 219, 228–30
   aboriginal marginalization and oppression, 223, 227, 293

Australia and Australian (*cont.*)
   aboriginal self determination,
     219–21
   Australian Human Rights and Equal
     Opportunity Commission, 230–32,
     235–36
   colonialism, 217–38
   Mabo v. Queensland No. 2, 227–30
   reconciliation as goal, 221–38
   removal of indigenous children, 230–32,
     235–37
Australia:
   and Cambodian justice, 207, 209,
     212
Austria, Austrians, 52, 97, 109, 169–70,
   174, 176
autonomy and self determination:
   Australian aborigines, 219–21
   in Greenland, 119, 127–31
   Maori of New Zealand, 240, 245–50,
     252, 255–63

Badinter, Robert, 140–43
Balkan conflict, 63, 304
Barbie, Klaus, 137
Barkan, Elazar, 3–4, 7, 8, 10, 12, 44, 46,
   49, 69, 93, 110
   The Guilt of Nations, 3–4, 69
Bartolone, Claude, 141
Baumel, Jacques, 141
Beauvoir, Simone de, 63
Benjamin, Walter, 284
Benzien, Jeffrey, 265–66
Berg, Manfred, 302
Beria, Lavrentii, 172
Berlin, Ira, 73
Bhabha, Homi, 230
Biko, Steve, 277, 299
Birnbaum, Pierre, 162
Bittker, Boris, I., 79–80, 81
Bizos, George, 272–73
Black Book of Communism, The
   (Courtois et al), 156
Boer War, 26, 27
Bolivia, 300
Bönisch-Brednich, Brigitte, 15,
   301

Boraine, Alex, 35
Bousquet, René, 137
Boutros Ghali, Bourtros, 272
Bracher, Nathan, 141
Braithwaite, John, 267
Brandt, Willy, 103–04
Brash, Don, 257, 262
Brennan, Gerard, 229
Brezhnev, Leonid, 175
Bringing Them Home (HREOC report),
   231–32, 235–36
Brooks, Roy, 7, 44, 72, 78, 81, 162
   Atonement and Forgiveness, 72
   When Sorry Isn't Enough, 7
Brøsted, Jens, 119, 121
Brown v. Board of Education, 35–36
Buck-Morss, Susan, 28–29
Bundestag, 51, 55, 100, 102, 104
Buruma, Ian, 35, 59
Bush, George H. W., 62
Bush, George W., 37, 127

Cairns, Alan, 23–24, 45
Cambodia, 13, 15, 187–214, 293
   Communist Party of Kampuchea (CPK,
     Khmer Rouge), 15, 187–214
   People's Republic of Kampuchea (PRK),
     192–95
   Royal Government of Cambodia
     (RGC), 187–88, 194–214
   S21 (Tuol Sleng), 189, 199
   United Nations involvement in justice
     process, 187–88, 190, 194–214
   U.S. involvement in justice process, 190,
     197–99, 204–05, 207–09
Canada, 5
   and Chinese immigrant "head tax," 7,
     26–27, 35
Catholic Church:
   apology to French Jews, 138, 144–48,
     155
Central Consistory of France, 147
Chakrabarty, Dipesh, 218, 223, 233, 238
Char, Rene, 284
Chea Sim, 188, 192, 194, 206, 213–14
Chikane, Frank, 271
Chile, 293, 296, 299

Chirac, Jacques:
    1995 apology for Vichy anti-Semitism, 14, 135, 138–42, 145, 154–55, 158, 161
    and Algerian War, 160
Christianen, Svend Aage, 14
civil rights movement (U.S.), 6, 22, 33, 36, 78, 84, 86, 88–89
Claims Conference, see Conference of Jewish Material Claims
Clark, Helen, 250
class action law suits, 23, 31, 35, 107, 109, 120–25
Clinton, William Jefferson (Bill), 86
Cohen, William, 158
Cold War, 98, 103, 105, 111–19, 128, 282, 293
    end of, 23, 30, 106, 294–99
collective guilt, 51, 138, 140–41, 202
colonialism, 23–24, 156
    Algeria, 157–61
    Australia, 15, 217–38
    Greenland, 112, 116–20, 128–31
"comfort women" of WWII, 23, 40, 56–59, 64–65
    financial compensation to, 57–59
    organization of victims, 56–58
Communist Party of Kampuchea (CPK, "Khmer Rouge"), 187–214
Conan, Eric, 162
Conference of Jewish Material Claims, 49–52, 98–99, 109
Conley, Dalton, 37
Consedine, Jim, 276–77
Conseil d'Etat (France), 152–55
Coughlin, Brenda, 46, 136
Council for Aboriginal Reconciliation (Australia), 221–25, 232
counterfactual history, 74–77, 79–80, 85–87
Cowlishaw, Gillian, 225, 229
crimes against humanity charges, 2, 15, 58, 59, 71, 137, 187, 279, 292–93
criminal prosecution, 293, 295
    Auschwitz trial (1964), 51, 102
    of Cambodian senior leaders, 187, 193, 195–214

    demands for, 291, 296
    determining individual vs. collective guilt, 141, 195–203, 271
    Eichmann trial, 102
    of GDR politburo, 300–01
    of Nazi abettors in France, 137, 140–41
    Nuremberg trials, 58, 102, 180–81, 187, 193, 201–02
    SS Einsatzgruppen trials, 102
    in South Arica, 270–74, 277, 293, 296
    in the Soviet Union, 167–69, 177–81
    subordinates acting on orders defense, 2, 189–90, 199, 213
Croix, La, 148, 156

Daniels, Roger, 6
Deane, William, 227
de Berranger, Olivier, 144
Debt: What America Owes to Blacks, The (Robinson), 78
Defarges, Philippe Moreau, 136
de Gaulle, Charles, 140–41
de Klerk, F.W., 271–72
de Lange, Johnny, 274
Delanoë, Bertrand, 159
Delacampagne, Christian, 159
Democratic Kampuchea (DK), see Cambodia
Denmark:
    Danish/US relations, 111–20
    and relocation of Inughuit of Greenland, 111–16, 119–20
    and restitution to Inughuit of Greenland, 111, 120–31
Doxtader, Erik, 282
Du Plessis, Jean Pierre, 282

Eastern Europe, 45
    victims of Nazism, 96, 102–04
Eichmann, Adolf, 102, 304
Eighteenth Brumaire of Louis Bonaparte, The (Marx), 296, 301
Elster, Jon, 279
English, Bill, 256
Enlightenment ideals, 47, 94, 138
Enoksen, Hans, 127

Erhard, Ludwig, 102
European Human Rights Court, 124
Eyerman, Ron, 31

Faces of Injustice, The (Shklar), 6
Fægteborg, Mads, 119, 121
Fagan, Ed, 71
Faulkner, William, 30
Feagin, Joe, 78–79
Federal Law for Compensation of the Victims of National Socialist Persecution (BEG), 50–52, 54
Federal Restitution Law (AKG) (German), 50–52, 54
Felman, Shoshana, 231
Fette, Julie, 8, 14
Finca, Bongani, 271, 276
Finkielkraut, Alain, 140
First, Ruth, 272
Fishkin, James, 74, 87
Ford, Gerald, 61
Ford Foundation, 34
Foucault, Michel, 24
Fouilloux, Etienne, 148
Foweraker, Joe, 43
France, 8, 13, 14, 135–63, 291, 293
  and Algeria, 152, 157–61
  and Cambodian justice, 207, 209, 212
  Chirac apology for Vichy anti-Semitism, 14, 135, 138–42, 145, 154–55, 158, 161
  Conseil d'Etat apology, 152–55
  "Gaullism," 136, 139, 140
  legal profession apologies, 142–44
  Order of Doctors apology, 149–52
  police union apology, 148–49
  public reaction to apology trend, 140–41, 147, 160, 162
Freud, Sigmund, 30
Friedman, Lawrence, 6, 91
Furedi, Frank, 45
Furet, François, 29

Gauck, Joachim, 275
Gaudron, Mary, 227
Gaus, Gerald, 11

gender issues, 41–42, 59, 63
genocide, 25, 35, 40, 220, 300
  in Cambodia, 187, 193–94
  see also Holocaust
Germany: Federal Republic (FRG), 14, 48–56, 93–110, 217, 291, 294, 305
  Bundestag, 51, 55, 100, 102, 104
  see also Holocaust restitution
Germany: German Democratic Republic (GDR), 52, 106, 169, 295, 297–303
  Volkskammer, 298
Germany: postunification, 16, 106–10, 294–304
  integration of former civil servants and officials, 107, 295, 303
  restitution of property in former GDR, 76, 106–07, 297–99
  Stasi files release, 16, 297–98
Germany: Third Reich
  atrocities of, persecution of Jews and others, 48, 52–53, 98, 102, 188
  German POWs in the Soviet Union, 100, 168–70, 174, 176, 181
Gibson, James, 268, 279
Girardet, Raoul, 139, 156
Gist, Richard, 24
Glorion, Bernard, 150, 152
Goethe, Johan Wolfgang von, 29
Goffman, Erving, 32
Goldmann, Nahum, 99–100, 102
Goodall, Heather, 226
Gorbachev, Mikhail, 175
Gordon, Robert, 75, 86
Goschler, Constantin, 14, 49
Greece, 109, 293, 300, 304
Greenland, 14, 111–31
  compensation to Inughuit people, 120–31
  deployment of U.S. nuclear weapons, 117–18,
  Home Rule Government, 119–31
  relocation of Inughuit people of Uummannaq, 5, 111, 114–16, 119–31, 293
  Thule Air Force Base, 111–18, 127–30
Greilsamer, Laurent, 141
Griebenauw, Johannes Lodiwikus, 265

Guilt of Nations: Restitution and Negotiating Historical Injustice (Barkan), 3–4, 69
Gutman, Amy, 268

Häber, Herbert, 300n14
Habermas, Jürgen, 24
Hacking, Ian, 25
Hajdenberg, Henri, 140, 146, 148
Hamber, Brandon, 268
Hamilton, Paula, 233
Hammarberg, Thomas, 195, 197, 198, 200, 204, 206
Hansen, Hans Christian, 117
Harlang, Christian, 124
Harper's Magazine, 71
Hatamiya, Leslie, 61
Hayner, Priscilla, 268
Heder, Steven, 15
Hegel, Georg Wilhelm Friedrich, 28
Heng Samrin, 188, 192, 194, 206, 214
Herero people of Namibia, 25, 27, 35
Hilger, Andreas, 14
Hill, Richard S., 15, 301
Himmler, Heinrich, 52
Hirschfeld, Magnus, 52
historians as expert witnesses, 31, 155
historical justice, historiography of, 27–35, 157–58, 162, 217–38, 292–305
Hitler, Adolf, 53, 183, 184
Hofmyer, Willie, 272, 273
Holocaust
   persecution and atrocities, 40, 136, 145, 162, 291
Holocaust restitution, 7, 23, 25, 40, 43, 48–56, 94–110, 294, 298–99, 302, 305
   Eastern European claims, 96, 103–04
   Federal Indemnification Law (1953), 94, 99, 102, 104
   Federal Law for Compensation of the Victims of National Socialist Persecution (BEG), 50–52, 54
   Federal Restitution Law (AKG), 50–52, 54
   financial restitution, 51, 54, 94–98, 100, 154
   forced laborers, 97, 105, 108
   "forgotten" victims, 54–56, 64, 105–06

German people as victims of Nazism, 51, 94, 95, 99, 104, 109
German public opinion re: restitution and reparations, 51, 98, 104–05
Identifying victims, 95, 101
non-German victims, 48, 49, 94, 96–97
number of victims, 73, 106
as a "template" for subsequent cases, 25–27, 94, 298
return of Jewish art work and property, 49, 97, 100, 106–07, 137
Territorialitätsprinzip, 94–95
U.S. involvement, 49, 96–97, 99, 107
war reparations vs. victim restitution, 49, 94–98, 108
Wiedergutmachung, 3–4, 7, 76, 94–95
See also apology; Conference of Jewish Material Claims; Jews
homosexuals, 42
   as "forgotten victims" by the FRG, 40, 54–56, 64, 105
   persecution by Nazis, 52–54
Honecker, Erich, 297
Horowitz, David, 83–84, 90
   "Ten Reasons Why Reparations for Slavery is a Bad Idea – and Racist Too," 83
   Uncivil Wars: The Controversy over Reparations for Slavery, 83–84
Human Rights Watch, 275, 283
Huntington, Samuel, 40
Hue, Robert, 141
Hungary:
   Hungarian POWs in the Soviet Union, 168–70, 174, 176
Hun Sen, 188, 192–214

Ieng Sary, 193, 197, 203, 213
   amnesty grant, 194–95, 205
Ignatieff, Michael, 237
Illuminations (Benjamin), 284
Inouye, Daniel, 61
Institute for Sexual Science, 52, 56
Institute for the Study of Democratic Alternatives (IDASA), 274–76
intergenerational justice, 32–33, 74–75, 84, 86, 302

International Center for Transitional
    Justice, 5, 34, 268
International Center for Trauma Studies, 35
International Criminal Tribunals, 35
    Rwanda, 35, 196, 204
    Yugoslavia, 35, 196, 204
Inughuit people, *see* Greenland
Israel, 7, 48–51, 64, 99, 103, 108

Japan, 47, 218
    and Cambodian justice, 207, 209, 212
    denial of WWII culpability, 4, 57
    Japanese POWs in the Soviet Union,
        168, 174, 176, 181
    see also comfort women of WWII
Japanese American Citizens League
    (JACL), 60–62
Japanese American internment during
    WWII, 5–6, 23, 26–27, 40, 59–62,
    64, 70, 301
Jaspers, Karl, 34–35, 305
Jewish Agency for Palestine, 96
Jewish Restitution Successor Organization
    (JRSO), 49
Jewish World Congress, 48
Jews:
    exclusion from professions, 48, 136,
        142–43, 149–50
    organized to demand justice and
        restitution, 48–52, 96, 98–100, 107,
        139
    property taken, 48, 97, 106, 137
    response to French apologies, 140,
        146–47, 151
    in Vichy France, 136–38
    see also Holocaust restitution
Johansen, Lars Emil, 128
Johnson, Andrew, 70
Johnson, Lyndon B., 82
Jones, Jacqueline, 90
Jospin, Lionel, 141, 159
Judging the Past in Unified Germany
    (McAdams), 294
Judt, Tony, 161

Kae Pok, 195, 197, 203
Kahn, Jean, 147

Kang Kech Iev, aka Duch, 189, 199,
    203–06
Keating, Paul, 229–30
Khiev Samphan, 194–95, 197, 198, 203,
    213
Killing Fields, The (film), 213
Khmer Rouge, *see* Communist Party of
    Kampuchea
Khrushchev, Nikita, 172
Kiichi, Miyazawa, 58
Klarsfeld, Serge, 140
Kohl, Helmut, 55, 104, 105, 297, 298, 303
Korean comfort women, *see* comfort
    women of WWII
Korean Comfort Women Problem
    Resolution Council, 57
Kouchner, Bernard, 150
Krauthammer, Charles, 82
Kriegel, Blandine, 140
Kristensen, Kristian Søby, 14
Kruser, Gary, 266

Landauer, George, 48
Landman, Todd, 42–43
Lang, Jack, 141
Lanzmann, Claude, 140
Latin America, 40, 45, 296
Law of the Land, The (Reynolds), 227
Law on Rehabilitation (Russia, 1991),
    175–86
Lawyers' Committee for Human Rights,
    197
Leebaw, Bronwyn, 16
Leguay, Jean, 137
Lenin, Vladimir, 171, 175
Le Pen, Jean-Marie, 141
Letelier, Orlando, 299
Levy, Daniel, 25
litigation, *see* class action law suits
Lochak, Danièle, 153
London Debt Agreement (1953), 96–97
Lübke, Heinrich, 103
Luxembourg Treaty (1952), 50, 99

MacKinnon, Catherine, 42
Mahuta, Robert Sir, 246
Maier, Charles, 10, 11, 95

Maki, Mitchell, 60
Mamdani, Mahmood, 286
Mandela, Nelson, 276
Maori people, *see* New Zealand
Marx, Karl, 296
   The Eighteenth Brumaire of Louis Bonaparte, 296, 301
Maspéro, François, 156
Massot, Jean, 153
Matsui, Robert, 61
Matsunaga, Spark, 61
Mazeaud, Pierre, 140
McAdams, A. James, 16
Meister, Robert, 269
Memorial to the Murdered Jews of Europe, 95
memory, 10–11, 13, 25, 73, 232–36, 291
   "entrepreneurs of memory" and the "memory industry," 10, 22, 25, 30–38, 236n74, 292
   studies of, 136–37, 161–62, 234–35
   traumatic memory, 24, 234, 238n81
Mendez, Juan, 275
Mexandeau, Louis, 141
Mgojo, Khoza, 276
Michnik, Adam, 275
Mineta, Norman, 61
Minow, Martha, 46
Mitterand, François, 139, 160
   biography of, 137
Moffitt, Ronnie, 299
Monde, Le, 141
Mörder sind unter uns, Die (The Murders are Among Us) (film), 100
Motzfeldt, Jonathan, 129
Moynihan, Daniel P., 89
Mulgan, Richard, 237
Munford, Clarence, 77, 86
Munz, Ernest, 48

Nathan, Laurie, 286
National Coalition of Blacks for Reparations in America (N'COBRA), 80, 86
National Council for Japanese American Redress, 61

National Union of Uniformed Police (France), 148–49
NATO, 112, 116–17
Neier, Aryeh, 275
Neue Ostpolitik, 103
New Caledonia, 157
New York Times, 37
New York University, 35
New Zealand, 8, 13, 15, 239–63, 291
   apology for Treaty breaches, 244, 263
   autonomy quest/reintroduction of Aotearoa, 240, 245–50, 252, 255–63
   biculturalism, 8, 240–43, 251–63
   colonial subjugation of Maori, 241–43
   cultural redress, 244, 254–55, 262–63
   dispossession of Maori land, 243–45
   Maori reparations, 5, 239–40, 244–47, 257–58, 261–63, 301
   "Maori Renaissance," 239, 242–43, 245, 251
   race relations, 8, 240–43, 259, 261–62
   Treaty of Waitangi, 15, 240, 243–47, 256–58, 260–63
   Waitangi Tribunal, 245–46, 248–50, 257–58, 261
Ngewu, Cynthia, 286
Nietzsche, Friedrich, 36, 235, 291, 293, 305
Untimely Meditations, 291
Norgaard principles, 271–72
Novick, Peter, 9
Nozick, Robert, 87
Nuon Chea, 189, 193, 194–95, 197, 198, 203, 213
Nuremberg trials, 102, 180–81
   and "crimes against humanity: charges, 58, 181
   as a model for subsequent proceedings, 15, 187, 193, 201–02, 272

Obama, Barack, 37
O'Brien, Eileen, 78–79
Ogletree, Charles, 71
Olick, Jeffrey K., 46, 136
opinion polls, *see* public opinion
oral histories, 219, 230–37, 258
   victim testimony, 273, 280–81

Order of Doctors (France), 149–52
Orr, Wendy, 276

Pandey, Gyanendra, 234
Papon, Maurice, 137, 149, 154
   trial of, 141–44, 154, 157
Patterson, Orlando, 90
Péan, Pierre, 137
Peter the Great, 171
Poirot-Delpech, Bertrand, 148
Poland, Poles, 109–10, 168, 170
   and Soviet oppression, 166, 168–70
   WWII restitution, 104
Pol Pot, 188, 189, 193, 194–95, 197, 199, 213, 293
Posel, Deborah, 34
Povinelli, Elizabeth, 228, 229
Poznanski, Renée, 136
Preußische Treuhand GmbH & Co., 109
Pross, Christian, 50
public opinion,
   in France, 140–41, 147, 160, 162
   Germans on Holocaust restitution, 98, 100, 104
   Maori/Crown race relations, 241–43,
   Russians on Stalin and Soviet past, 170–71, 184
   on U.S. slave reparations, 72, 86
Putin, Vladimir, 171, 185

Question of German Guilt, The (Jaspers), 34

Rampele, Mamphele, 275
Randera, Fazel, 276
Rasmussen, Anders Fogh, 130
Rasmussen, Poul Nyrup, 126
Ratner, Steven, 198
Read, Peter, 223
Reagan, Ronald, 61, 104, 120
reconciliation, 13, 31, 34–35, 72, 93, 158, 162–63, 291
   in Australia, 221–38
   in South Africa, 265–87
reintegration of former officials in a new regime,
   in Cambodia, 192–93

   In Germany, 101, 295, 303
"Remembrance, Responsibility, and Future" Foundation (Stiftung "Erinnerung, Verantwortung und Zukunft"), 108
reparations, 13–14, 39, 156
   and the French/Algerian War, 158
   goals of, 34–35
   historical definition and meaning, 4, 21, 44–45, 94
   and the Treaty of Versailles, 21, 44, 94, 98
   World War II, 94, 96, 108
   see also restitution; slavery and reparations
"Report on the Presidential Truth Commission on Suspicious Deaths," (South Korea), 292
Representative Council of Jewish Institutions in France (CRIF), 140
restitution and closure, 10–12, 31, 82, 93, 102–03, 108
restitution: financial compensation and/or return of property, 2, 75, 154, 291, 295, 300–02
   individual vs. collective justice, 2–3, 46, 75–89
   Inughuit of Greenland, 120–31
   Jewish property and art, 97, 100, 107–08, 298
   Maori reparations, 5, 239–40, 244–47, 257–58, 261–63, 301
   Native Americans, 5, 37
   post unification Germany, 297–98
   reabilitatsiya, Russian rehabilitation for victims of Stalin, 171–86
restitution: financial compensation for labor, 2
   forced labor during Nazi regime, 40, 70–71, 96–97, 108, 302
   German civil servants, 101
   U.S. slavery, 75–76; *see also* slave reparations
restitution: financial compensation for suffering,
   comfort women of WWII, 58
   Japanese-American internees, 70, 301

foreign POWs in the Soviet Union, 176, 185
restitution: memorials, museums and educational efforts, 2, 44, 81–82, 95, 103, 149, 159, 160, 244, 254–55, 262–63
  see also apology; Holocaust restitution; reconciliation
Restorative Justice: Healing the Effects of Crime (Consedine), 276–77
Reynolds, Henry, 222, 227–29
Ricoeur, Paul, 284
Rigby, Andrew, 12
Robinson, Randall, 78
  The Debt: What America Owes to Blacks, 78
Rocard, Michel, 141
Roosevelt, Franklin Delano:
  and Japanese-American internment, 60
Rosenburg, Tina, 275
Rousso, Henry, 136, 139, 162
Rowley, Charles, 222, 227
Royal Government of Cambodia, 187–88, 194–214
Russia, 8, 13, 14
  de-Stalinization efforts, 172–86
  Law on Rehabilitation (1991), 175–86
  reabilitatsiya, rehabilitation of Stalinist victims, 170–86
  See also Soviet Union
Russian Center for Public Opinion, 170–71
Rwanda,
  International Criminal Tribunal, 35, 196, 204, 266

Sachs, Albie, 272, 275, 276, 286
Schäuble, Wolfgang, 297
Schwerin, Kurt, 52
Schutte, Danie, 278
Séguin, Philippe, 140
self determination, *see* autonomy and self determination
Serov, Ivan, 169
Sharing Histories (Council for Aboriginal Reconciliation), 223–25
Sherman, William T. General, 69–70

Shklar, Judith, 6, 9
  The Faces of Injustice, 6
Shoah (film), 140
Simpson, Graeme, 4
Sirat, René-Emmanuel, 147
Sitruk, Joseph, 140
slavery and reparations (U.S.), 5, 14, 25, 32–33, 37–38, 69–91
  antireparation arguments, 83–87
  apologies for slavery, 71–72
  beneficiaries and proposed distribution, 33, 37, 79–81, 88
  class action law suits, 35, 71–72
  demands and support for reparations, 37, 70–74, 78–83, 89–91, 302
  education and healthcare as compensation, 81–82
  and race relations in the U.S., 72–73, 88
  redistribution of wealth, 79–81, 87
  Sherman's "forty acres and a mule" order, No. 15, 69–70
  slave trade, 25, 73, 85
  see also African Americans; civil rights movement
Slovo, Joe, 272
Smuts, Dene, 278
Sok An, 206, 211, 212
Son Sen, 189, 193, 194–95, 213
South Africa, 13, 24, 218, 265–87, 291, 293, 296–97, 299
  African National Congress, 269–83, 296
  amnesty grants, 267, 272, 280, 282, 299
  apartheid, collapse of, 23, 45, 266–67, 273, 296
  Centre for the Study of Violence and Reconciliation, 268
  Convention for a Democratic South Africa (CODESA), 272
  National Unity and Reconciliation Act, 274–77
  reparations litigation, 35
  South African Reparations Movement (SARM), 21
  South African Defense Force, 282, 286
  Truth and Reconciliation Commission and the *TRC Report*, 35, 231, 235, 236, 265–87

South Korea, 57–59, 291
South Korean Church Women's Alliance, 57
Soviet Union, 51, 165–86
   forced labor service, 166–67, 169, 179, 183
   German attack of 1941, 165
   German POWs, 100, 168–70, 174, 176, 181
   relations with Denmark, 117–18
   relations with U.S., 111
   Soviet People's Commissariat of the Interior (NKVD), 166, 168, 177, 181, 183
   Soviet zone of occupied Germany, 97, 168–70, 183
   See also Russia
Stalin, Joseph, and Stalinism, 8, 165–72, 177–83
   atrocities committed, 188
   restitution for victims, 8, 176
   Stalinist oppression of foreigners, 165–72, 177–84
Stammers, Neil, 43
Staudte, Wolfgang, 100
statute of limitations issues, 2, 71, 160
Stetz, Margaret, 56
subordinates' culpability, *see* criminal prosecution
Swain, Carol, 73
Switzerland, 2
Sznaider, Natan, 25

Ta Mok, 194–95, 197, 199, 203
"Ten Reasons Why Reparations for Slavery is a Bad Idea – and Racist Too" (Horowitz), 83
Teufel spielte Balalaika, Der (The devil played the balalaika) (film), 100
Thompson, Dennis, 268
Torpey, John, 3–4, 9, 13, 291, 292
Touvier, Paul, 137
transitional governments, 34, 40, 94, 217, 265–87, 292–94
transitional justice, 5–6, 34, 47, 77, 239 n3, 266–70, 274–87

Treaty of Waitangi, *see* New Zealand
truth commissions, 2, 5, 6, 23, 24, 33–35, 265–87, 291–93; *see also* memory
Tutu, Desmond, 35, 272, 276, 277

Uncivil Wars: The Controversy over Reparations for Slavery (Horowitz), 83–84
United Nations, 45
   and Cambodia, 187–88, 190, 194–214
   Commission on Human Rights, 76, 195
   Economic and Social Council, 279
   General Assembly, 196, 198, 200, 204, 207–12, 279
   International Labor Organization, 123
   Security Council and Office of Legal Affairs (OLA), 196, 200–10, 279
   and South Africa, 279
United States
   and Cambodian justice, 190, 197–99, 204–05, 207–09
   and Holocaust restitution, 49, 96–99, 107
   Iraqi War, 94
   Native Americans, 5, 25, 37, 302
   and Japanese American internment of WWII, 5–6, 23, 26–27, 40, 59–62, 64, 70, 301
   racial discrimination in the US, 5, 88
   Thule Air Force Base, Greenland, 111–18, 127–30
   see also slavery and reparations (U.S.)
Untimely Meditations (Nietzsche), 291
Uummannaq, *see* Greenland

Valls, Andrew, 87
Vélodrome d'Hiver tragedy, 138, 140, 149
Verdière, Hubert Colin de, 159
Vereinigung der Verfolgten des Naziregimes (Association of Persecutees of the Nazi Regime), 98
Vergangenheitsbewältigung (coming to terms with the past), 51
Versailles, Treaty of, 4, 21, 44, 94, 98
Verwoerd, Wilhelm, 276, 277

victims, 2, 7, 32–33, 89–90, 292–93
    demands for justice and restitution, 21–24, 31–37, 70–73, 107, 136, 139, 158–59, 221, 301–02
    feelings of shame, 23, 59, 63
    organization of, 43–44, 48–52, 56–59, 62, 96, 98–100, 139
    and reconciliation, 268–69
    reintegration of, 64, 97
    support for, 280–81
    "survivor" status, 26, 36, 93
    "victim competition," 22, 95–96, 99, 156
    See also class action law suits; oral history; truth commissions
"victor's justice," 2, 202, 297, 303
Vietnam:
    Vietnamese in Cambodia, 189, 191–95, 213
Viljoen, Constand General, 278
Villa-Vicencio, Charles, 271
von Wahl, Angelika, 13

Walters, Ronald, 77
Weber, Max, 74, 300
Weizsäcker, Richard von, 55
West, Cornel, 71
When Sorry Isn't Enough: The Controversy over Apologies and Reparations for Human Injustice (Brooks), 7
Wieviorka, Olivier, 162
Wildschut, Glenda, 276
Williams, Joe (Chief Judge Maori Land Court), 261n57
Wilson, Robert, 269
Winter, Jay, 231
Wolfe, Patrick, 225
Wolin, Sheldon, 283–84
women victims, *see* gender issues
World Jewish Congress, 96

Yeltsin, Boris, 175
Yengeni, Tony, 265
Yugoslavia (former):
    assaults on women, 42, 59,
    International Criminal Tribunal, 35, 196, 204
    and World War II restitution, 104
Yun Chong-ok, 57

Zalaquett, José, 275
Zeit, Die, 104